CHINA
RISING
★ ★ ★ ★ ★

CHINA RISING

PEACE, POWER, AND ORDER
★ ★ ★ IN EAST ASIA ★ ★ ★

DAVID C. KANG

COLUMBIA UNIVERSITY PRESS ■ NEW YORK

Columbia University Press
Publishers Since 1893
New York   Chichester, West Sussex
Copyright © 2007 Columbia University Press
Paperback edition, 2010
All rights reserved

A Caravan book. For more information,
visit www.caravanbooks.org

Library of Congress Cataloging-in-Publication Data

Kang, David C. (David Chan-oong), 1965–
China rising : peace, power, and order in East Asia / David C. Kang.
    p.   cm.
Includes bibliographical references and index.
ISBN 978-0-231-14188-8 (cloth : alk. paper) — ISBN 978-0-231-14189-5 (pbk. : alk.
paper) — ISBN 978-0-231-51206-0 (e-book)
1. China—Foreign relations—East Asia. 2. East Asia—Foreign relations—China.
3. China—Foreign relations—1976– 4. East Asia—Politics and government. I. Title.

DS518.15.K36 2008
327.5105—dc22

2007013371

For Michelle

★ ★ ★

CONTENTS

ILLUSTRATIONS

FIGURES

TABLES

ACKNOWLEDGMENTS

I began this book over a decade ago, prompted by Aaron Friedberg's famous 1993 article suggesting that Europe's past might be Asia's future. I wondered why we would use Europe's past—rather than Asia's own past—to explore Asia's future. However, although I was quite well versed in modern Asia, I knew very little about its history. As I researched the historical pattern of East Asian international relations, the more I connected Asian history to its present and future, and the more intrigued I became. This book is a result of that continuing project.

A large number of people have given generously of their time and intellectual energy over the years as I have worked through my ideas. My colleagues at Dartmouth and the Tuck School of Business have formed a uniquely wonderful cohort. They are smart, collegial, and generous with their time, and I fear that the balance of trade has me substantially in debt to their unselfish discussion and feedback about my own work. Bill Wohlforth, Al Stam, Mike Mastanduno, Steve Brooks, Ben Valentino, Darryl Press, Jenny Lind, and Ned Lebow have all been exceptionally generous colleagues with their considerable intellectual firepower. Many of their suggestions appear in this book, for which I thank them profusely and have tried to credit them as directly as possible. As a member of the Center for International Business at Tuck, I have had the opportunity to interact with an extraordinarily wide range of businessmen and scholars throughout East Asia in a working capacity, which provides insights far beyond those that could be gleaned in a short interview. In particular I owe thanks to John Owens and Bob Hansen, who have always supported my research and understood that scholarship is directly in the interests of the Tuck School.

Thanks are also due to numerous colleagues who have read parts (or all!) of the manuscript in various versions. Peter Katzenstein has been an extraordinary intellectual friend and mentor, as well as a careful and thoughtful critic. Victor Cha remains my closest friend in the profession. We have discussed these ideas at length over the years, and while I still haven't managed to change his mind, his friendship has been invaluable and I have learned a tremendous amount from him. Bob Bullock remains an extremely close friend and a careful reader, always pushing me to think more clearly and rigorously.

Others who have provided intellectual guidance for this project, but who should share none of the criticism, include Ang Cheng Guan, Amitav Acharya, Vinod Aggarwal, Muthiah Alagappa, Michael Armacost, Thomas Berger, Paul Chamberlain, Thomas Christensen, Gang Deng, Kent Deng, Leif-Eric Easley, Aaron Friedberg, Ellen Frost, Akiko Fukushima, Evelyn Goh, Peter Gries, Stephan Haggard, Victoria Hui, Min-hua Hwang, John Ikenberry, Iain Johnston, Stuart Kaufman, Byung-kook Kim, Sung-han Kim, Andrew Kydd, David Lake, Deborah Larsen, Tai-Hwan Lee, David Leheny, Richard Little, Evan Medeiros, Alice Miller, Edward Miller, Steven Miller, Derek Mitchell, Kathy Moon, Greg Noble, Robert Ross, Richard Samuels, Len Schoppa, Randall Schweller, Adam Segal, Gi-wook Shin, Dan Sneider, Jack Snyder, Scott Snyder, Yoshihide Soeya, Andrew Stigler, Shiping Tang, Carl Thayer, Ronald Toby, Christopher Twomey, Barbara Walter, Yiwei Wang, Brantly Womack, Xinbo Wu, Yushan Wu, and Young-kwan Yoon.

A large number of businessmen and ministry officials from various Asian countries were also exceptionally generous with their time and insights. Many of them wish to remain anonymous, and I refer to them in the text with simply "personal communication."

Various versions of the argument were presented at Dartmouth College, Ohio State University, Princeton University, Stanford University, the Program on International Security and Politics at the University of Chicago, Columbia University, Cornell University, Georgetown University, the U.S. Air War College, the Institute for Defense and Strategic Studies at Nanyang Technical University in Singapore, Keio University, the Foreign Correspondents Club of Japan, the East Asia Institute in Seoul, Seoul National University, the National Taiwan University, and National Sun-Yat Sen University. For three years I have also presented the ideas in this book as a guest lecturer at the Australian Centre for Defense and Strategic Studies at the Australian Defense College in Canberra, Australia. The Australian CDSS has senior military officers from more than twenty-one countries in the Asia Pacific Region, including twelve from East Asian countries. Other versions of the argument were presented at the annual meetings of the American Political Science Association, the International Studies Association, and the

International Political Science Association. Finally, I have also presented versions of this argument at a number of U.S. government agencies.

The ideas in this book accumulated over years of research and teaching in East Asia. I am particularly grateful to the Korea Foundation, whose exceptional generosity in the form of an Advanced Research Grant allowed me the critical time needed to finish this manuscript. Their support of basic research is central to the continuing growth of Korean studies around the world. The EAI Fellows Program on Peace, Governance, and Development in East Asia, supported by the Henry Luce Foundation, has been generous in its support for travel and research, and allowed me to present versions of my work around East Asia. The Hanoi School of Business in Vietnam hosted monthlong visits in 2000 and 2002; the Asian Institute of Management in the Philippines hosted monthlong visits in 1998, 2001, and 2003; and the Institute for Defense and Strategic Studies at Nanyang Technological University in Singapore hosted me as a visiting scholar in 2004. I supplemented these with numerous shorter visits to Singapore, Indonesia, Taiwan, Hong Kong, Japan, Korea, and China. Finally, Stanford University's APARC Center provided me a sunny and intellectually vibrant venue in which to work for a year in 2005–2006.

I also had very able research assistance from DeAnna Fernandez, Sofia Faruqi, and Ji-young Lee. All of them are superbly organized, very smart, and always pleasant to work with.

Anne Routon at Columbia remains a tremendous editor. I worked with her on my previous book, and was more than happy to return to Columbia with this one. She is a rarity among editors—smart, engaged, and supportive. Her attention and patience have made this book much better than it should be.

CHINA
RISING
★ ★ ★ ★ ★

PART I
THE PUZZLE AND THE ARGUMENT

The temporary hegemony of Western European civilization [over Asia] has distorted our view of the past and made our interest one-sided. Because the world has been dominated by the West for a hundred twenty years—a short span of time yet, in retrospect, an eternity—the West came to consider itself as the focus of world history and the measure of all things.

—W. F. WERTHEIM, "EARLY ASIAN TRADE: AN APPRECIATION OF J. C. VAN LEUR," *FAR EASTERN QUARTERLY*

CHAPTER 1

THE PUZZLE AND CHINA'S AMAZING RISE

THE PUZZLE

In 2006, Chan Heng Chee, Singapore's ambassador to the United States, gave a speech in Houston, Texas, about relations between China and the Association of Southeast Asian Nations (ASEAN). She began her largely positive assessment by discussing the fifteenth-century Ming dynasty's peaceful relations with Southeast Asia, noting, "Dynastic China's relations with Southeast Asia were to a large extent based on 'soft power.' . . . It was China's economic power and cultural superiority that drew these countries into its orbit and was the magnet for their cultivation of relations." She concluded her speech by saying, "there is one message I would like to leave with you today: that there is much optimism in Southeast Asia."[1] Although Singapore is often viewed correctly as one of the closest allies the United States has in East Asia, Ambassador Chan's remarks reveal the complexity and depth of East Asian states' relations with both China and the United States.

Singapore's situation reflects a pattern that has occurred throughout East Asia over the past thirty years. As a region, East Asia since 1979 has been more peaceful and more stable than at any time since the Opium Wars of 1839–1841. Only two states, Taiwan and North Korea, fear for their survival. Furthermore, East Asian states have become increasingly legitimate and stable; they have strengthened regional multilateral institutions; and they have increased their bilateral economic, cultural, and political relations. During that time, China has rapidly emerged as a major regional power, averaging over 9 percent economic growth since the introduction of its market reforms in 1978. Foreign businesses have flocked to invest in China, while Chinese exports have begun to flood world markets. China is modernizing its military, has joined numerous regional and international institutions, and is increasingly visible in international politics. At the same time, East Asian states have moved to increase their economic, diplomatic, and even military relations with China.[2] China appears to have emerged as a regional power without provoking a regional backlash.

Why have East Asian countries accommodated rather than balanced China's rapid economic, diplomatic, and political emergence over three decades? Why has East Asia become increasingly peaceful and stable in that time? This book makes two central arguments. First, East Asian states are not balancing China; they are accommodating it. This contradicts much conventional international relations theory, which says that the rise of a great power is destabilizing. Second, this accommodation of China is due to a specific constellation of interests and beliefs—a particular mix of identities and the absence of fear. Identities are central to explaining the sources both of stability and of potential instability in East Asia, but not to the exclusion of the relative capabilities and interests that traditional realists champion.

Accurately describing East Asia is a critical first step toward explaining how the region came to be as it is. Taiwan is the only East Asian state that fears the Chinese use of force, and no other East Asian state is arming itself against China nor seeking military alliances with which to contain China. Although state alignment strategies are often posed as opposites—military balancing against an adversary, or bandwagoning with the stronger power in hopes of gaining benefits or neutralizing the threat—as a strategy, accommodation lies between these poles. While not balancing China, East Asian states are not bandwagoning with it in all areas, either, and have no intention of kowtowing. East Asian states also vary in their strategies toward China—Japan is far more skeptical of Chinese power than is Vietnam, for example.

The absence of balancing against China is rooted in interests as well as identities. In terms of interests, rising powers present opportunities as well as threats, and the Chinese economic opportunity and military threat for its regional neighbors are both potentially huge. Yet East Asian states see substantially more opportunity than danger in China's rise. Furthermore, the East Asian states prefer China to be strong rather than weak because a strong China stabilizes the region while a weak China tempts other states to try to control the region.

Identity is also central in framing how regional states interpret China's rise. East Asian states view China's reemergence as the gravitational center of East Asia as natural. China has a long history of being the dominant state in East Asia, and although it has not always had warm relations with its neighbors, it has a worldview in which it can be the most powerful country in its region and yet have stable relations with other states in it. Thus to East Asian observers and other states, the likelihood that China will seek territorial expansion or use force against them seems low. Most see China as desiring stability and peaceful relations with its neighbors.

Although those East Asian neighbors share a common lack of fear regarding China, each relationship with China is distinct. Taiwan is a good example. Few claim that China threatens Taiwan as part of an expansionist strategy, or that control of Taiwan would tip the balance of power in the region. Taiwan is not an issue because of power politics; it's an issue because of competing conceptions of whether Taiwan is an independent, sovereign nation state, or whether it is a part of China. For China, the question is nation building, not expansion. Thus Taiwan is not an exception to the general trend in East Asia; it is categorically different from other states. While formally the United States and most other nations agree with China's claim, privately many view Taiwan as "obviously" an independent nation-state, with its own government, currency, economic system, and culture. As a result of this disagreement over Taiwan's identity, Taiwan's status remains an issue in international politics.

Regarding the rest of East Asia, China claims—and East Asian states increasingly believe—that its continued economic growth and domestic stability are predicated on deep integration with, and openness to, the regional and international economies. This grand strategy is often called "peaceful rise."[3] Indeed, the Chinese Communist Party's main claim to legitimacy is its economic record. China realizes explicitly that it would gain very little from starting conflicts with its neighbors but has much to gain from warmer ties.[4] As the best way to advance its interests, "peaceful rise" represents a pragmatic choice. But determining whether this strategy is merely tactical or whether it represents the true nature of China involves an assessment of its identity. In this respect, then, China's concern for sovereignty and nation building is arguably more important to its identity than are nationalistic memories of a "century of shame."

The East Asian states tend to share a view of China that is more benign than conventional international relations theories might predict. South Korea's foreign policy behavior is perhaps the most vivid example of this. Although China could threaten South Korea militarily, and North Korea actually does threaten South Korea, capitalist and democratic South Korea itself seems eager to embrace communist and authoritarian China and North Korea. Furthermore, South Koreans appear to feel more threatened by potential Japanese militarization than they do by actual Chinese military power. This has caused consternation and even anger in Washington because South Korea appears willing to pursue this strategy to the detriment of relations with its longtime democratic ally and protector, the United States.

Much of South Korea's approach to regional relations is based on its interest in avoiding a costly war or a collapse of the North Korean regime, which would directly harm South Korea. However, the key to explaining South Korea's seemingly perplexing foreign policy lies in Korean national identity. For many Koreans, their single most important foreign policy priority is unification of the divided peninsula, and this has led the South to prioritize economic engagement with North Korea and the integration of the peninsula as more important than pressuring the North over its nuclear weapons and missile programs. Indeed, both China and South Korea agree that engagement is the proper strategy to follow with North Korea, in contrast to the United States, which in the early twenty-first century focused on eliminating North Korea's nuclear and missile programs through a strategy of coercion and isolation. Furthermore, Korea has had a long history of close and stable relations with China and, in contrast, has not fully resolved its difficult relationship with Japan. Although South Korea has no intention of returning to the subservient role with China that it played for centuries, it also has little fear of Chinese military aggrandizement. South Koreans view peaceful relations with China as normal, and they are rapidly increasing cultural, economic, and diplomatic ties with China.

Southeast Asia also has a long history of stable relations with China, and in the present era all the states of Southeast Asia are rapidly deepening their economic and political relations with China. Southeast Asians also do not fear Chinese use of force, and their militaries are overwhelmingly focused on border control and internal defense. Even on issues such as the contested ownership of the Spratly Islands, the trend has been toward more cooperation, not less. Indeed, the Chinese, Vietnamese, and Philippine national oil companies are currently engaged in joint exploration in the Spratlys, and all the major claimants have formally agreed not to use force to settle their disputes. While much of this can be explained with reference to economic interdependence, the member states of the ASEAN and China have similar views about respecting sovereignty and about noninterference in national matters. The countries of Southeast Asia also have deep ethnic, cultural, and historical ties with China. This affinity, most notable in the extensive Chinese ethnic minorities in Southeast Asia known as the "bamboo network," is not only responsible for significant investment in China, it is also helping create a regional economy where Chinese growth and East Asian growth are thoroughly intertwined.

Japan's identity crisis lies at the heart of its foreign policy, best exemplified by the decades of speculation about whether or not it could become a "normal" nation. Because postwar Japan did not pursue military or diplomatic policies commensurate with its economic power, observers within and outside of Japan have been unsure about whether this was temporary or permanent, and remain unsure about how Japan views itself and its role in the region. Japan is the one country in the region that has the material capability to challenge China, and Japan remains the most skeptical East Asian country regarding China. Japan will not lightly cede economic dominance to China, and it also remains unsure of Chinese motives. The course of Japan's grand strategy is in flux, and debate within Japan centers on how it should respond to China, on how it can best manage its alliance with the United States, and how it can balance the needs both for military power and economic wealth.

However, the East Asian states do not expect Japanese leadership in the region, and Japan itself is unsure about what its role in Asia should be. There is little in Japanese history, institutions, or worldview that would lead to the conclusion that it will attempt a leadership role today. Even after Japan became the world's second-largest economy, it did not challenge U.S. predominance but rather embraced it through a close security alliance. And Japan failed to translate its economic advantage into regional political leadership or even sustained goodwill with its neighbors. Despite Japan's more assertive foreign policy in the past few years, it remains deeply entwined in its alliance with the United States and is unlikely to directly compete with China by itself.

Finally, U.S. power complicates but does not fundamentally alter these East Asian dynamics. The United States remains the most powerful nation in East Asia, and all states—including China—desire good relations with it. Decisions the United States makes will have an impact on East Asian regional stability, and the United States has been increasingly debating its stance toward China. However, even the United States has not yet chosen an outright balancing strategy, and it is thus unsurprising that East Asian states also have not. Furthermore, East Asian states have generally not been eager for greater U.S. military deployments in the region, precisely because they view such deployments as the beginnings of a containment coalition against China. East Asian states also do not wish to be caught in the middle of a China-U.S. competition, and they do not want to be forced to choose between the two countries.

East Asian peace, stability, and accommodation of China is a puzzle because international relations theorists have traditionally associated the rise of great powers with war and instability.[5] Indeed, those scholars who emphasize material power—both military and economic—have long predicted that East Asian states would fear China and balance against it. Realism in all its variants, with its emphasis on balance of power politics, has had the most consistently pessimistic expectations for East Asia. In 1993 Richard Betts asked, "Should we want China to get rich or not? For realists, the answer should be no, since a rich China would overturn any balance of power."[6] Twelve years later, John Mearsheimer confidently asserted that "China cannot rise peacefully . . . Most of China's neighbors, including India, Japan, Singapore, South Korea, Russia, and Vietnam, will likely join with the United States to contain China's power."[7]

Rival power–based theories have performed no better in their predictions. Those who argue that China's increased economic interdependence with the world will constrain its behavior are skeptical that this by itself can solve the security fears of East Asian states.[8] As John Ikenberry writes, "Economically, most East Asian countries increasingly expect their future economic relations to be tied to China . . . Can the region remain stable when its economic and security logics increasingly diverge?"[9] Although pragmatic interests are part of the explanation for East Asian stability, by themselves economic interests do not explain the variation in relations in East Asia. Indeed, increased economic relations between China, South Korea, and Japan have not had a noticeable impact on their political relations. Even power transition theorists argue that the most likely chance for conflict is in the context of a rapidly rising power. For example, Robert Powell writes that "rapidly shifting distribution of power combined with the states' inability to commit to an agreement can lead to war."[10]

In contrast to these power-based expectations, there is a vibrant body of work by scholars who specialize in East Asia that emphasizes the role of ideas in explaining aspects of East Asia international relations. Alastair Iain Johnston has argued that China is a status quo power, and that it is being socialized into the international system. Peter Gries explores Chinese nationalism and its effect on foreign policy, arguing that there is more to Chinese nationalism than merely memories of a "century of shame." Allen Carlson shows that Chinese conceptions of sovereignty have been changing during the reform period. Peter Katzenstein has studied East Asia's emerging regionalism and Japan's role within it, while Thomas Berger explores Japan's culture of antimilitarism. Studying Southeast Asia, Amitav Acharya has argued that a regional identity exists and has tangible consequences for regional cooperation.[11] As valuable as this work is, none of these authors have directly addressed what is arguably one of the biggest and most important issues for both scholars and policymakers in contemporary international relations: the consequences of China's rise in East Asia. This book aims to fill that gap.

Directly explaining why East Asian nations have accommodated China's rise, and why balance-of-power politics has not emerged, is important theoretically because it is interests and identity, not power, that are the key variables in determining threat and stability in international relations. Much scholarly discussion of China and East Asia has been unduly constricted in its explanatory power by remaining locked into a method that parses differences between various shades of realists and liberals, even as these same analyses emphasize factors such as historical memory, perceptions of China, and the beliefs and intentions of the actors involved. The debate over China's rise and what it means for international politics will most likely continue well into the future, and defining the terms of the debate is a critical first step in that process. The theoretical framework provided here helps to sharpen these seemingly endless paradigmatic debates by posing the central issues more clearly, isolating the important causal factors, and making falsifiable claims.

Identity is more than merely the sum of domestic politics; it is a set of unifying ideas that focus primarily how a nation perceives the world around it and its place within it.[12] Gilbert Rozman defines national identity as "a statement of the uniqueness of a particular nation-state, investing it with authority and separating it from other states that may seek to influence it."[13] National identities are constituted through two basic means: current interactions between countries, and the narratives that they tell about their national pasts.[14] That is, nations do not exist in myopic isolation from other nations, and identities are constructed in the context of their histories and current interactions. Thus ascertaining what is China's identity, what it cares about, and how other East Asian states view it is possible only by taking the East Asian experience on its own terms.

This book's central focus on identity does not preclude acknowledging other causal factors. Pragmatic interests over specific issues have an immediate impact on state relations, and I note their impact throughout the book. Military and economic power are also important, by providing the constraints within which states make choices. Indeed, some "defensive realists" are fairly optimistic about the future of East Asia, emphasizing nuclear deterrence and geography.[15] However, more important than power itself is what states want to do with that power. By incorporating the role of interests, identity, and power into our explanations, I build on an emerging tradition that looks for interconnections between causal factors, rather than isolating one factor at the expense of others. As Peter Katzenstein and Nobuo Okawara have written, "The complex links between power, interest, and norms defy analytic capture by any one paradigm. They are made more intelligible by drawing on different paradigms. . . ."[16]

Critics respond to explanations for East Asian stability by claiming either that East Asian states are too small to balance China, or that thirty years is not enough time to see balancing emerge.[17] Yet both these rejoinders are ad hoc arguments resting on an assumption of fear that is empirically unfounded; and they are an admission by realists that their theories do not explain East Asia. Most importantly, the assertion that small states inevitably fear larger states is contradicted by a large body of scholarship that probes whether and when this might be the case.[18] Empirically, small states rarely capitulate in the face of overweening power. North Korea continues to defy intense U.S. pressure, Vietnam fought China as recently as 1979 when their interests diverged, and the Japanese started a war with the United States they knew beforehand that they could not win, and continued to fight long after the outcome was certain.[19] At a minimum, the onus is on those who argue that East Asian states are too small to balance, to show empirically that these states actually fear China, that these states searched all available internal and external balancing options, and ultimately decided that capitulation was the best policy to follow. Anything less is not a serious analytic argument, but rather an admission by realists that their theories about balance of power do not apply.

The rejoinder that balancing will happen in the future has similar theoretical problems. Realists themselves argue that states are highly concerned with future possibilities and prepare for those contingencies today—indeed, the core of the security dilemma derives from fears of the future even if the present is peaceful.[20] In less than three decades China has gone from being a moribund and isolated middle power to being the most dynamic country in the region, with an economy that shows many signs of continuing to grow. By realist standards, China should already be provoking balancing behavior, merely because it is already so big and its potential rate of growth is so high. Yet as this book will show, this dramatic power transition has evoked little response from its neighbors. Five or even ten years of Chinese growth would be too early to draw conclusions; but as decades accrue, the argument that balancing is just around the corner becomes less plausible. Furthermore, this rejoinder—like that of "too small to balance"—also assumes fear on the part of smaller states, a highly questionable assumption in general and certainly with respect to East Asia. Beliefs of states must be empirically demonstrated, not asserted. As this book will show, fear is not the dominant attitude toward China. Thus it is a fair and important question to ask why East Asia has not already balanced China.

However, even though most major trends over the past three decades have led to more stability and cooperation in East Asia, there is no guarantee that those trends will continue indefinitely. Indeed, any discussion about China and East Asia's past and current relations invites speculation about what the future might hold. Most important for this book is to note that concerns about how China might act a generation from now center on identity, not power. That is, much of the speculation about China's future course focuses on the consequences that might follow if China becomes a democracy, how the Chinese Communist Party might evolve, and how Chinese nationalism and its interactions with other states will evolve—all of which are aspects of national identity. However, this book is not an attempt to predict the future, it is concerned with explaining outcomes of the past decades. The policies that China, the United States, and East Asian countries take today will affect how the region evolves. The security, economic, and cultural architecture of East Asia is clearly in flux, and how China and East Asian states might behave in the future when circumstances are fundamentally different is an open question, and an exercise with limited intellectual utility.

A final important issue is to actually define the region itself. This book takes as its locus of inquiry the East Asian region, defined as the states of Northeast Asia (mainly Japan, China, and the two Koreas) and Southeast Asia (mainly Taiwan, the states of ASEAN, and Australia and New Zealand). Defining what comprises the region is of more than semantic interest, because we would expect that the processes within the region would be different from those outside of it, and that states would interact differently with states inside or outside of the region. That is, the pattern I elucidate in this book is occurring only in East Asia, and extra-regional states such as India and Russia do not have the same basic views or interests as those within East Asia itself.[21] While extra-regional states often interact with those in East Asia, their main concerns and issues are different. As chapter 8 will discuss in greater detail, one major question about the United States is whether it is, in fact, an East Asian state, or whether it is a global actor with regional interests.

Events within the region can have an impact on states outside of it, but those events are not of primary concern to extra-regional states. Okawara and Katzenstein write that "regions are combinations of physical, psychological, and behavioral traits."[22] As Robert Ayson notes, "The widely inclusive membership of the Asia Pacific Economic Cooperation (APEC) is too wide to be analytically useful, including as it does Latin America as well as those states in East Asia."[23] Barry Buzan and Ole Weaver define regional security complexes as a set of "geographically proximate states . . . [characterized by] the relative intensity of security interdependence among a group of units, and security indifference between that set and surrounding units."[24] That is, in a region, the units are primarily focused on the interactions and issues that occur between the units, and relatively less concerned with issues that occur outside that set of states.

For example, some scholars have argued that India is an East Asian state.[25] However, India is first and foremost concerned with its relations in South Asia, most notably the Indo-Pakistani relationship. India, like other nonregional actors, has no direct impact on the major issues in East Asia, such as the future of Taiwan or the North Korea nuclear problem. Furthermore, although India has increasingly joined some East Asian regional institutions such as the East Asia Summit, its influence in the region remains peripheral at best. As will be discussed below, if Indian economic growth continues over the next few decades, it is possible that India will become a major actor in East Asia. For the time being, however, its influence is more prospective than actual, and thus we would not expect India to interact with China in the same manner as East Asian states, which must account for China directly and daily.

CHINA'S AMAZING RISE

Although China is unlikely to replace the United States as the most technologically advanced and militarily dominant country in the world within the foreseeable future, this does not mean China is weak. China is already very strong and very big, and centrally situated in East Asia. By virtue of its population, geography, economic growth, and military power, China is already a major actor in East Asia, and by some measures it is already the largest and most powerful.

Measuring China's size is difficult, and estimates vary widely. From 1978 to 2003, China averaged 9.7 percent growth, while Japan averaged 1.2 percent.[26] The World Bank estimates that from 1978 to 2005, Chinese economic growth lifted 402 million people out of poverty (defined as living on one dollar a day)—the largest poverty eradication in history.[27] The CIA uses a purchasing power parity estimate (PPP), which produces a 2005 Chinese gross domestic product (GDP) of $8.85 trillion, versus $4.01 trillion for Japan. PPP reflects the price of a commodity (or a bundle of commodities) that is the same between countries, when expressed in a common currency. The exchange rate used in converting GDP of one country to another for the purpose of inter-country comparison does not normally reflect the purchasing power parity (PPP), because many commodities are not traded internationally. Measured by exchange rates, China's economy in 2005 was $2.22 trillion, compared to $4.50 trillion for Japan.[28] Using exchange rates to compare across countries has its problems, as the Organisation for Economic Co-operation and Development (OECD) notes, "primarily because exchange rates reflect so many more influences than the direct price comparisons that are required to make volume comparisons."[29] Indeed, China has been under intense pressure by the United States to revalue the *renminbi*, and most economists believe that it may be undervalued by 15–40 percent. If so, the corresponding exchange rate measure of China's economy is also undervalued by a similar amount.

Hongkong and Shanghai Banking Corporation estimates that bank assets in China will surpass those in the United States in 2034, while Goldman Sachs estimates that China's GDP will surpass that of the United States by 2045.[30] Such predictions are speculative at best, and there exist any number of factors that could derail these predictions. However, China does not have to catch up to the United States in order to project influence. Richard Betts makes this argument clearly: "It is not inevitable that recent average rates will continue indefinitely, but if they do, the long-term prospects for the balance of power—global as well as regional—are staggering. If the country [China] ever achieved a per-capita GNP just one-fourth that of the United States, it would have a total GNP *greater* than that of the United States. Even by conservative estimates, the prospects of China as an economic superpower are not remote."[31]

In fact, by some conventional measures of great power status, China has surpassed Japan already. These measures include population, geography, military spending, and absolute size of GDP as measured by consumption. Angus Maddison has performed perhaps the most careful estimates of historical trends in GDP across countries.[32] He uses an approach developed by Roy Geary and Salem Hanna Khamis based on purchasing power parity and international average prices of commodities. By his estimates, China is already far larger than Japan, and historically, only during the Cold War was Japan's economy larger than China's (see Figure 1.1).

Another way to measure size is to use an aggregate of national power, which includes more discrete criteria than just a measure of the size of a country's economy as a whole. One dataset widely used by political scientists is the Correlates of War project.[33] This dataset on national material capabilities—the Composite Index of National Capability (CINC)—contains annual values for total population, urban population, iron and steel production, energy consumption, military personnel, and military expenditure of all states from 1816 to 2001. This measure of comprehensive national power shows that China far outstrips Japan in overall strength (see Figure 1.2).

China's growth as a technological and economic competitor to Japan is evident in other areas, too. China's share of world consumption overtook Japan's in 2005, notes economist David Hale.[34] Already China has displaced

FIGURE 1.1 JAPANESE AND CHINESE GDP, 1870–1994 (TRILLION 1990 GEARY-KHAMIS DOLLARS)

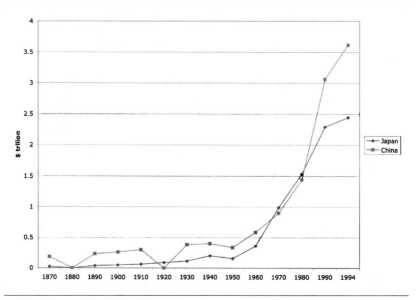

SOURCE: ANGUS MADDISON, *MONITORING THE WORLD ECONOMY, 1820–1992* (PARIS: DEVELOPMENT CEN-TRE, ORGANIZATION FOR ECONOMIC CO-OPERATION AND DEVELOPMENT, 1995), TABLE C-16A.

FIGURE 1.2 COMPREHENSIVE INDEX OF CHINESE AND JAPANESE NATIONAL POWER, 1860–2001

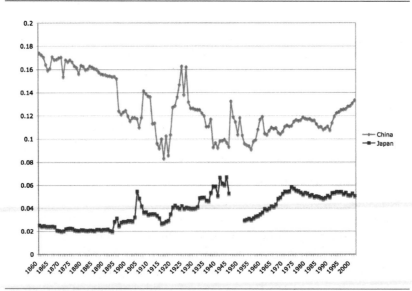

SOURCE: J. DAVID SINGER, "RECONSTRUCTING THE CORRELATES OF WAR DATASET ON MATERIAL CAPA-BILITIES OF STATES, 1816–1985," *INTERNATIONAL INTERACTIONS,* 14 (1987): 115–32, UPDATED DATASET AT THE CORRELATES OF WAR PROJECT, HTTP://WWW.CORRELATESOFWAR.ORG/.

Japan as the world's second-largest oil consumer.[35] In trade, China has rapidly closed the gap with Japan, and appears to be on course to overtake it as the leading exporter in Asia within the next few years.[36] The capitalization of China's stock market is the largest in Asia except for Japan's, despite being just a decade old. In fact, it has a larger capitalization than stock markets in Brazil, Hong Kong, India, Mexico, South Korea, and Taiwan.

By other measures, however, China remains a developing country far behind Japan. Gross capital formation is one such area. In the measure of manufacturing value added, Japan adds far more value than does China. Finally, in terms of per capita income, China remains a third-world country. Even when measured at purchasing power parity, Chinese per capita income is far smaller than that of Japan: $5,000 versus $28,000.[37] Using market rates, the World Bank estimates Chinese per capita income in 2002 at $944, compared to almost $45,000 in Japan.

On the other hand, China remains by most measures far ahead of India, another country that is often compared to it as a potential economic superpower. According to the World Bank, in 2005 China's GDP was $2.2 trillion, while India's was $785 billion, a difference of over $1 trillion.[38] From 1994 to 2004, China averaged GDP growth of 8.5 percent, compared to India's 5.6

FIGURE 1.3 CHINESE AND INDIAN EXPORTS, 1995–2004

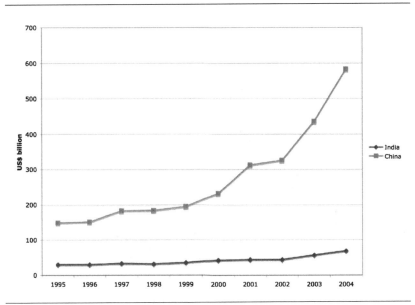

SOURCE: NATIONAL BUREAU OF ASIAN RESEARCH, STRATEGIC ASIA ONLINE, WWW.NBR.ORG

percent.[39] China's exports are more than five times those of India, and the gap is widening, not decreasing (see Figure 1.3). In other indicators of development, China also remains far ahead. China had an estimated 94 million Internet subscribers in 2004, compared to 14 million in India. China consumed three times as much energy in 2004 as did India. Chinese life expectancy in 2004 was 72.2 years, compared to 63.6 years in India, while literacy in China was over 90 percent, compared to 59 percent in India.[40] Thus, while India may at some point in time become a global competitor to China, at present India remains a regional economic power in South Asia, similar to Brazil's position in Latin America. India has not yet become a global economic force with a significant impact on other regions, such as East Asia.[41]

In sum, although China is not yet a mature, advanced economy, on a number of criteria important for international relations it is clear that China may soon be the dominant East Asian state. China is already a large presence in economic markets around the globe. Its population and landmass make it an important demographic power regardless of its level of development. China's nuclear arsenal and military are among the largest (although not most advanced) in the world, and exceed those of any other East Asian state.

ORGANIZATION OF THIS BOOK

The book is divided into three parts. Part I provides the theoretical basis for the argument, beginning, of course, with an overall examination of the Chinese "puzzle" above. Chapter 2 presents the theoretical ideas in more detail, and uses the previous six centuries of Asian international relations to show that balancing has not historically characterized East Asian international relations. Chapter 3 describes the situation in East Asia today. Focusing on East Asian state strategies toward China, chapter 3 concludes that states are accommodating China rather than balancing against it.

Part II examines why East Asian states are not balancing China. Chapter 4 asks what China wants, and shows that China has embarked upon a reassurance and engagement strategy with the rest of East Asia, precisely to mitigate fears in the other East Asian states over its intentions. Chapter 4 further discusses the complex issue of Taiwan's identity in East Asia. Chapter 5 explains why South Korea—one of the closest U.S. allies in the region and vulnerable to Chinese influence—is reconsidering its alliance with the United States and growing closer to China. Chapter 6 explains why most East Asian states believe China's claims, showing why the states of ASEAN are leaning toward China and avoiding an outright alliance with America. Chapter 7 explores Japan's identity problem, explaining why Japan—the largest potential balancer to China—is not challenging its emerging influence in the region.

Part III looks at the U.S. role in East Asia and draws theoretical and policy conclusions. Chapter 8 looks at the United States in East Asia and explains why it has not chosen to balance Chinese power. This chapter further explores whether it is the U.S. military presence that allows East Asian states to avoid balancing China. Chapter 9 revisits the theoretical basis for this book, and asks what the future may hold for East Asia.

CHAPTER 2

POWER, INTERESTS, AND IDENTITY IN EAST ASIAN INTERNATIONAL RELATIONS, 1300 TO 1900

Great powers rise and fall, and the causes and consequences of that have long been a central issue in the study of international relations. The general expectation is that rising powers cause instability by threatening neighboring states. Most of what scholars know about this issue, however, is based on the European experience from the seventeenth to nineteenth centuries, when five or more powerful states contended for domination of both Europe and the globe. While it is possible that the European experience will replicate itself in other regions of the world, it is important to pose this not as a certainty, but as a general theoretical question: When and under what conditions do rising, powerful states threaten smaller states?

Although military and economic power is clearly one factor in determining whether states are threatening, material capabilities do not necessarily lead straight to intentions. There are costs and benefits associated with rising powers, and while stronger states can do more than weaker states, their intentions may vary quite widely. For example, a powerful, revisionist China seething with resentment would prompt different responses from East Asian states than would a powerful, status quo China that desired peace and stability. As a result, states are constantly engaged in the process of deciding how to judge and interpret other states' actions for the meanings and intentions behind them.

This book places central causal emphasis on the role of national identities in shaping how states determine and respond to threats in international relations. Although an emphasis on the role of ideas is most commonly associated with constructivist theories, scholars working from diverse perspectives emphasize ideas as well. Although rationalists take preferences as given, while constructivists endogenize them, James Fearon and Alexander Wendt note that "the rationalist recipe . . . embraces intentionality and the explanation of actions in terms of beliefs, desires, reasons, and meanings. . . . there is little difference between rationalism and constructivism on the issue of *whether* ideas 'matter.'"[1] In fact, it is only the strictest of structural and material theories that ignore the importance of ideas, and those approaches have come under increasing criticism from a variety of theoretical perspectives.[2] As Robert Powell writes, "Although some structural theories seem to suggest that one can explain at least the outline of state behavior without reference to states' goals or preferences . . . in order to specify a game theoretic model, the actor's preferences and benefits must be defined."[3] The most sophisticated theoretical treatments from both the rationalist and constructivist paradigms have concluded that understanding preferences and identity is vital to being able to draw any conclusions about state behavior.

For example, Stephen Walt has argued that perceptions of threat are more important than pure power in determining threats and alliance behavior. Andrew Kydd has shown that trust and perception are the key variables affecting the intensity of security dilemma. Jacek Kugler emphasizes that the key variable in power transition and preventive war theories is satisfaction with the status quo.[4] Formal theorists have identified the information problem and the commitment problem as the two main causal mechanisms that could lead to interstate war—both of which are ideational.[5] In each of these cases, scholars have emphasized the importance of perceptions, beliefs, and intentions in the determination of threats.

INTERESTS, IDENTITIES, AND THREATS

To emphasize the importance of identities is only to recognize that interests and beliefs can vary widely. It does not preclude pragmatic interest-based foreign policy, but rather focuses research on determining which interests states judges as most important, and why. Powerful states pose both opportunity and threat, and the fundamental strategic conundrum confronting a smaller state when it faces a powerful neighbor is this: if the dominant state is essentially benign, the smaller state would prefer an accommodating stance that allows it to benefit from warm relations with its neighbor. The smaller state will be able to spend less on defense if it does not fear the larger state, and the smaller state can economically benefit from close ties to the larger and growing power. However, if the powerful state is essentially expansionist and dangerous, the smaller state would prefer to take a more cautious stance toward the more powerful state, in order to protect itself. The calculation about threats that a smaller state makes is thus a function of what it believes is the more powerful state's beliefs about its role and interests in international relations, and not necessarily the fact that its neighbor is powerful. It is quite possible that a powerful state will not pursue conquest and empire even if it has the potential to do so. For example, James Fearon notes that it is reasonable to assume that states pursue and satisfy safety, income for their citizens, and perhaps a number of other goals in addition to power.[6] In a system of unequal (or "unbalanced") power, it is not just security and economic relations, but also the intentions and preferences of both dominant and secondary states, that are the key to threat perceptions.[7] Formal theorists have devoted considerable energy to exploring the various ways in which states make assessments of intent, emphasizing problems such as information, commitment, and reassurance.[8]

Thus, a key question is, What are China's intentions, and how do East Asian states perceive them?

Although interests over specific issues are one component in determining a state's overall grand strategy, the process of enduring relations between states is longer, deeper, and broader. Over time, states base their assessments and subsequent strategies not only on specific goals of other states, but also on their deeper belief about what is that state's identity and what are appropriate actions in international relations.[9]

The myopic, arms-length transmission of information about interests is only part of what states face. Moving beyond interests is important for two reasons. First, preferences may not be fixed and unchanging. Although it may be analytically convenient to assume fixed and given preferences over one specific issue, in reality preferences may be malleable for any number of reasons. Second, preferences are issue-specific, but states have to develop grand strategies: that is, they have to decide how to interact with other states over time and across a range of known and unknown issues both current and future. States do not assess other states' preferences *de novo* over each issue—they also develop an overall assessment of the others' identities and beliefs.

An identity is how a nation defines itself in the world, what it thinks is an appropriate role and actions for itself and others, and is a "relatively stable understanding and expectation about self and others . . . [that is] socially constructed."[10] Although preferences may derive from identities (or beliefs), the relationship is not straightforward. Rather than being separate, strategy and choice are fundamental to the social construction of identity.[11] National identities are constituted through two basic means: current interactions between countries, and the narratives that nations tell about their national pasts.[12] States do not exist in isolation from one another; they interact constantly, deciding not only what they want, and what is appropriate, but also who they "are," and who others "are." To explain how states determine threats, we need to explore identities.

One way in which international relations theories incorporate identity into theories of threat in the context of a rising power lies in the distinction between status quo and revisionist states. Definitions of status quo and revisionist powers vary, but they tend to center on the satisfaction of a state regarding the current international order.[13] That is, the main driver of instability is the difference between the desired situation and the status quo: the greater the difference between the two, the greater the likelihood that a state will use force to redress the difference.[14]

James Lyall points out that the issue of status quo and revisionist states actually involves an identity variable: "theories [that] make extensive use of the distinction between status quo and revisionist states . . . rely heavily on pre-given and fixed identities to generate predictions about state behavior."[15] Alastair Iain Johnston writes that "convergence in the behavior of the participants in a social interaction may often have little to do with exogenous constraints and a lot to do with socialization."[16] Lyall notes that these beliefs are normative in nature—such as the "shared standards that govern membership in the international community . . . rules that govern the use of force . . . and the existing hierarchy, whether rooted in relative material strength or status (or both)."[17] Johnston measures status quo or revisionist powers by two main tendencies: 1) the rate and quality of a state's participation in international organizations and whether it tries to undermine or abide by existing rules and norms, and 2) a clear preference for the radical redistribution of material balance of power. Peter Katzenstein calls this the "social purpose of power."[18]

Thus another key question is, What are East Asian identities, can they accommodate China, and do they want to?

I measure identity in this book using widely accepted social science approaches. Opinion polls are one useful way to provide a view of a country's attitudes at one moment in time. Yet opinions can change, and polls do not measure the depth or durability of such opinions. Other measures, such as statements and speeches, are a good source for ascertaining the preferences and opinions of political and economic rulers. Finally, one must also look at what a country actually does in its military deployments, economic policies, and diplomatic relations.[19]

MATERIAL VIEWS OF INTERNATIONAL RELATIONS

A realist approach, which is a common alternative to the theoretical path followed in this book, emphasizes balance of power politics. In this view, intentions flow directly from capabilities, and the more powerful a state is, the more threatening it is. Although there are an almost infinite variety of "realisms," they tend to coalesce around a core argument that power is threatening (if not today, then potentially in the future), and that smaller states will group together to balance the power of the most powerful state.[20] As Kenneth Waltz writes, "hegemony leads to balance . . . through all of the centuries we can contemplate."[21]

However, recent scholarship has shed serious doubt on the balancing proposition as a default prediction in international relations.[22] Scott Bennett and Allan Stam subjected the realist balancing model to empirical testing across regions and over the past 150 years. Although the balancing model works well in Europe, they find that "significant differences in preferences for conflict exist across regions," and there is "no support for the argument that [Asian] behavior will converge on that of Europe. In fact, all of the regions outside of Europe appear to diverge from the European pattern [of classical balance of power]."[23]

There are sound theoretical reasons to doubt whether balancing behavior is homogeneously distributed across regions, and thus there is no theoretical reason to think that because Europe has a history of balancing, East Asia must see balancing in the future as well. Writing about different behavior across regions, Bennett and Stam note that "it is *not* that the actors are not rational, even though a universal model may fail. Rather, they simply are not playing the same game with the same preferences."[24] Without understanding states' identities and the nature of their interactions with other states, it is impossible to explain differential stability across regions.[25]

In addition to large quantitative studies, recent research on such disparate historical epochs as the Iron Age Fertile Crescent, Warring States China, pre-Colombian Mesoamerica, Ancient India, Greece and Persia, and ascending Rome has also shed doubt on the universality of the balancing proposition.[26] As Stuart Kaufman, Richard Little, and William Wohlforth conclude, ". . . the unipolar outcome is not necessarily an unstable one . . . [and] a survey of 7500 years of the history of international systems shows that balanced and unbalanced distributions of power are roughly equally common. There is no iron law of history favoring either a balance of power or hegemony."

In concert with this research, this book will show that the balancing hypothesis finds little empirical support in modern East Asia. Both power and preferences are important, and it is not helpful to view one factor in isolation from the other. The issue for the study of East Asian international relations is not whether stability can accompany China's rise, but rather why China's rise has thus far been peaceful, despite predictions to the contrary.

EAST ASIAN INTERNATIONAL RELATIONS, 1300–1900

To explain why East Asia has become increasingly stable since the late twentieth century, one must first examine how its states arrived there. This brief overview will show how power, politics, and ideas have worked in the historical context of East Asia, and set the stage for subsequent chapters that focus on the most recent three decades. History, and the manner in which it is interpreted in the present, are major elements in how states develop beliefs about themselves and the world.[27] If the interests and identities of the actors are important variables, then an ahistorical view of modern East Asia that merely considers capabilities and ignores the evolution of these states is likely to be profoundly misleading. Although much has changed in East Asia since the fourteenth century, it is worth asking whether and how states' interests and beliefs have changed and how they inform their goals and beliefs today. To ignore what the evolution of these states tells us about international relations is at best an oversight; at worst it reveals an unwillingness to engage the reality of East Asia's own dynamics. Whether the past has any bearing on the present is an open question, to be sure; but the debate should be held first, before one arrives at any conclusions.

Indeed, for too long international relations scholars have derived theoretical propositions from the European experience and then treated them as deductive and universal. This book builds on an important new line of research that corrects this scientifically indefensible parochialism.[28] However, even this research has paid little attention to a major historical epoch—the East Asian international system from 1300 to 1900. As a result, scholars may still underestimate the challenges a truly unbiased assessment of non-European international history presents to the conventional scholarly wisdom. For, whereas in many other international systems balance of power processes occurred but were overwhelmed by other causal forces, in the East Asian international system such processes barely registered in historical evidence. If balance of power theory is misleading in the other cases, in this case it is profoundly and fundamentally wrong.

Coming to grips with the historical East Asian system is important not only for theory but for contemporary policy analysis. Today's East Asian system is often discussed as if it emerged fully formed—like Athena from the head of Zeus—in the post–World War II and postcolonial era. To date, scholars have rarely described the main features of this system.[29] But if anything, many East Asian countries have been geographically defined, centrally administered political units for longer than those of Europe. To ignore the evolution of these states is at best an oversight; at worst it reveals an unwillingness to engage the reality of East Asia's own dynamics.[30] To explain East Asian international relations in the twenty-first century, we should begin by exploring how the region got to where it is today. Indeed, discussion of the contemporary global system might also benefit from comparison with this relatively recent example of political-military as well as economic hegemony. As Barry Buzan and Richard Little write, "existing frameworks in IR [international relations] are seriously crippled by their failure to build on a long view of history."[31]

In this section I introduce the international system of early modern East Asia, assess the role of balancing in the larger pattern of the system's interactions, and provide a theoretical explanation for the absence of balancing dynamics and the system's overall stability based on a logic of ideas that contradicts the core assumptions of neorealism.

The section is organized into three main parts. In the first, I describe the system and its constituent units. A generation ago, it might have been possible to dismiss the evidence concerning early modern East Asia as not truly probative for international relations theory because it was not a "real" system, the chief actors did not interact enough, or they were not state-like enough. This view is no longer tenable. New research tends to support the contention that this is a system to which international relations theory, and balance of power theory in particular, ought to apply.

Balance of power theory, however, cannot account for behavioral dynamics of this system, which I establish in the second section. Between 1300 and 1900, China's preponderant power never generated balancing behavior. If the system moved toward equilibrium, it was not as a result of balancing processes but rather as the outgrowth of domestic Chinese weakness. Other actors did not generally use these windows of opportunity to rein in Chinese power. Instead, Chinese decline led to periods of generalized chaos and conflict in East Asia. When China was strong and stable, order was preserved. Until the intrusion of the Western powers in the nineteenth century, East

Asian international relations were remarkably stable and peaceful, punctuated only occasionally by conflict between countries.

In the third section, I explain this behavioral pattern. The key is that East Asian international relations emphasized formal hierarchy among nations while allowing considerable informal equality. This system was materially based and was reinforced through centuries of cultural practice. With China as the dominant state and the peripheral states as secondary states or "vassals," as long as hierarchy was observed there was little need for interstate war. This contrasts with the Western tradition of international relations that consisted of formal equality between nation-states, informal hierarchy, and almost constant interstate conflict.

THE SYSTEM

In a study such as this, which covers a large, relatively understudied region over many centuries, it is important to be self-conscious about the limits and extent of the inquiry. In this section, I delineate the geographical scope of the Asian system, identify the key actors, assess the rough distribution of capabilities, and begin to establish the intensity of interactions among the system's constitutive actors.

GEOGRAPHICAL SCOPE

The geographical domain of East Asian international relations studied in this chapter begins with Manchuria in the north, the Pacific to the east, the mountains of Tibet to the west, and the nations of Thailand, Malaysia, and Indonesia running south. This study focuses mainly on the region comprising Japan, Korea, China, and Vietnam. Other countries that were sufficiently involved in the system to warrant discussion include Siam, Indonesia, the Philippines, the Ryukyus, and Malaysia. These countries were the major actors in the system (see Table 2.1).

This chapter focuses on the main political units that constituted the East Asian region from the fourteenth to the late nineteenth centuries. Some other actors existed, including the nomadic Uighurs and Mongols, and powerful pirate clans, but these will be discussed only in terms of their influence on great power relations. This study does not highlight these nonstate actors, for the same reason that studies of the European Westphalian system do not focus on Barbary pirates or Catalan separatists.[32] In addition, the time period

TABLE 2.1 EAST ASIAN POLITICAL SYSTEMS, 1200–1900

	CHINA	JAPAN	KOREA	VIETNAM	THAILAND	TAIWAN	MALAYA	JAVA	PHILIPPINES
1200	1279–1368: Yuan	1160–1333: Kamakura	918–1259: Koryo	939–1407: Champa and Nam Viet	1238–1350: Sukhothai	Thai domination	1222–1293: Singosari		
1300		1333–1573: Ashikiga	1392–1910: Choson		1350–1782: Ayuthia			1293–1520: Majapahit	
1400	1368–1644: Ming			1407–1427: Chinese rule 1427–1787: Le Dynasty			1402–1511: Malacca	Majapahit influence	
1500							1511–1641: Portuguese Malacca		1571: Spanish colony
1600	1644–1911: Qing	1603–1868: Tokugawa				1662–68: Dutch 1683–1895: Chinese	1641–1796: Dutch Malacca district		1619: Dutch colony
1700					1782: Chakri		1796: British colony		
1800		1868: Meiji		1802–1955: Nguyen Dynasty and French colony		1895–1945: Japanese colony			1898: U.S. colony

of this study is restricted to roughly the six centuries from 1300 to 1900—a period that covers the Chinese dynasties from the end of the Yuan, the Ming, and finally the Qing. China—and East Asia—has millennia of history, and this study no more attempts to explain earlier historical periods such as the "Warring States" period in China (481–221 B.C.) than a study that focuses on Napoleonic-era Europe would attempt to explain the foreign policy of third-century Visigoths.[33]

THE MAJOR ACTORS

Political units comprising the East Asian international system of the past millennium have been recognized sovereign entities with power over a geographic area. As Lien-sheng Yang wrote, "there is no doubt that China had at least a vague concept of state (*kuo*) by late Chou times (BC 400)."[34] Korea, Vietnam, and Japan historically have used the word for "country" (Korean *kuk*, Chinese *kuo*, Japanese *koku* or *kuni*, and Vietnamese *quoc*; all derived from the same Chinese character) to refer to each other and to China since well before the Song dynasty. Korea has a long history of sovereignty. Although Korea was occupied by the Han dynasty around 100 B.C., the Silla dynasty unified the peninsula in 668 A.D., and since that time Korea has existed separately from China and Japan.[35] The Korean embassies to Japan referred to the Tokugawa shogunate as *Ilbon kukwang* ("king of Japan"), while the Korean king was known as *Hankuk kukwang* ("king of Korea").[36] These three states together with Vietnam constituted the inner core of the Chinese-dominated regional system. In these four, the Chinese cultural and political influence was direct and major.

There were other states in the system that did not experience the same Chinese influence. Geographically more distant from China, states such as Siam, Java, the Ryukyus, and Burma engaged in extensive relations and interactions with the other states, and followed some Chinese norms and practices in dealing with other states, but were not directly influenced by Chinese culture and politics to the same extent as were Japan, Korea, and Vietnam.[37] Although not as tightly incorporated into the Sinocentric system, these states were deeply incorporated into the China-centered regional economy. Janet Abu-Lughod writes, "From the time the southern Sung [Song] first took to the seas in the late twelfth century . . . the petty kingdoms of the [Malacca] strait . . . changed from "gateway" to dependency . . . the Strait area must be conceptualized, at least in part and in the preceding centuries, as a dependency of China."[38]

In addition to the main political units that conducted international relations, there were other significant political or military actors in the region. Of these, the most important were powerful pirate clans, known in Japanese as *wako* (Korean *waego*, Chinese *wokou*). The *wako* were never considered a legitimate or alternative political entity, however, and they were never a political threat to Japan, Korea, or China. Indeed, dealing with the *wako* was one of the main factors that caused coordination among these countries—as the analogous problem of piracy eventually was to do among European states in the eighteenth and nineteenth centuries.

The *wako* had two major periods of activity—the mid-fourteenth century and the early seventeenth century. *Wako* ("invaders from Japan") were originally petty military families from the western islands in Kyushu. Bands of as many as three thousand intruders would pillage granaries, attack towns, take slaves in Korea and China, and interrupt trade. *Wako* roved as far south as the Yangtze Delta, Fujian, and Guangdong. The Chinese emperor Hongwu (reigned 1368–1398) warned the Japanese that he would send forces to "capture and exterminate your bandits, head straight for your country, and put your king in bonds" unless the *wako* raids were stopped.[39] The Koreans as well sought the cooperation of the shogunate to repress the *wako*, sending a number of embassies in the late fourteenth century to Japan. In fact, foreign relations between Japan and Korea at this time were essentially initiated because of the piracy issue.[40] The Koreans licensed a certain number of Japanese ships each year to trade with Korea; since trade was valuable, the Japanese had an incentive to rein in the *wako*.[41]

As Shoji Kawazoe writes, "the problem of suppressing piracy and the development of the tribute system that accompanied the founding of the Ming dynasty were the common threads running through Japan's relations with Choson, and Ming China."[42] Official relations between Korea and Japan covered protocols about how to deal with the return of Koreans or Japanese who were captured by pirates or those (known in Korean as "*Pyoryumin*") who accidentally landed in the other's country.[43] With the consolidation of the Ashikaga shogunate (1336–1573), the *wako* were severely weakened, and by the early fifteenth century, the *wako* had become more of a nuisance than a threat. However, a century later, a resurgent tide of pirates was afflicting Korea and China. Focused more on China than Korea, this later wave of *wako* attacked Fujian and other southern regions of China.[44] In large part, the resurgence of pirate raids caused the Ming to officially sever relations with Japan in 1621.[45] As the central governments of East Asia became more powerful and exerted great control, the *wako* eventually died out.

The main actors in the system were therefore national states that conducted formal, legal international relations with one another, and for whom international recognition as a legitimate nation was an important component of their existence. For example, the Korean Choson court divided foreign contacts into four grades, and several statuses within these grades. These grades corresponded not only to different diplomatic statuses and rights, but also entailed different trading and commercial rights. The highest-grade officials, for example, were allowed to outfit up to three ships for trade, "and also move an unlimited amount of that cargo . . . but Korean officials severely restricted the volumes of official trade permitted contacts in the two lower grades."[46] Entry into the country was governed by an official seal, and there are even reports of various attempts to forge diplomatic seals in order to gain better trading benefits. The other political actors such as pirates were a part of the system, but more as a cause of relations than a viable political alternative. Thus national states of varying size and technological capability existed in an international system based on formal recognition and regulated by a set of norms. As we shall see, from Japan to Siam, and for well over six centuries, this system functioned in essentially the same manner.

THE DISTRIBUTION OF CAPABILITIES

Material power was a major component of the medieval East Asian international system. China was the largest and most advanced country, and had the capability to move armies of hundreds of thousands of troops across water. In balance of power terms, it represented an existential hegemonic threat through most of the over half-millennium period discussed here.

China was by far the largest, most powerful, and most technologically advanced nation in East Asia, if not the world. China has historically been the economic, political, and diplomatic center of East Asia, as well as the center of technological innovation and cultural construction for the region. In 1750 China had a per capita level of industrialization equivalent to those in Western Europe, and twice that of the American colonies. China's output far exceeded that of Japan or any other country in the region. Paul Bairoch estimates that China produced almost one third of the entire global manufacturing output in 1750, while Japan produced less than 4 percent.[47]

Vietnam and Korea were dwarfed by China's size. David Marr writes that "despite the well known 'march to the south,' which brought them to the Mekong delta by the 17th century, the Vietnamese could never boast of controlling more people or resources than a single Chinese province."[48]

Korea and Vietnam, both part of the Asian landmass and sharing borders with China, were particularly vulnerable to Chinese conquest, had China wished to expand. Chinese military organization and technology also gave it the capability to project power over long distances. Indeed, China ruled Vietnam for almost a thousand years, from 112 B.C., when Vietnam was invaded by the emperor Wu of Han, until the fall of the Tang dynasty in 907.[49] Chinese military organization has been formidable since ancient times, and China had the military and technological capacity to expand through conquest further than it did.

As early as 624, under the Tang dynasty, emperor Taizong built an army of 900,000 men, the first standing professional Chinese army.[50] The limiting factor was not technological, but political—a decision by China not to pursue conquest. Although Japan was protected by water, it was a surmountable barrier, and China had the military capability to invade Japan throughout this period. The Chinese invasions of Japan in 1274 and 1281 involved up to 150,000 men and 4,400 Chinese naval vessels.[51] As to China's naval potential, the famous 1405 and 1433 expeditions by the Chinese admiral Zheng He (Cheng Ho) took 315 ships and over 28,000 men as far as Africa, bringing back elephants and other treasure to China.[52] The largest of these ships were 400 feet long and held nine masts, and seven-masted "supply ships" were 257 feet long and 115 wide.[53] The Ming navy consisted of 3,500 oceangoing ships, including over 1,700 warships. Abu-Lughod writes that "no naval force in the world at that time came close to this formidable armada."[54] When Japan invaded Korea in 1592 with intentions to conquer China, Japanese general Hideyoshi took 200,000 men, transported on 300 naval vessels.

TRADE AND THE LEVEL OF INTERACTION

The East Asian system, in short, featured smaller states existing under the shadow of a preponderant power with the material wherewithal potentially to conquer all or most of the system. In other words, it was a system primed for intense balance of power politics. We would only expect balancing dynamics to come to the fore, of course, if these actors were in sufficient contact with one another to truly constitute a system. I have already mentioned military interactions and below I will analyze political and diplomatic ones. Here I detail another important indicator of high interaction levels: trade.

Far from the West's bringing trade and interaction to a somnolent East Asia in the seventeenth century, there existed a vibrant East Asian economic trading system well before the West arrived. China and its tributaries had far more interaction with one another than has been traditionally acknowledged. Recent scholarship is finding that trade, both private and tributary, made up a significant portion of both government revenues and the national economies. The system was geographically quite wide, including trade from Japan to Java and Siam. Furthermore, trade with the West (mainly the Portuguese and the Dutch) in the seventeenth and eighteenth centuries was at most a minor portion of overall East Asian trade. The countries in this system were part of a thriving, complex, and vibrant regional order. As Abu-Lughod writes:

> The literature generated both in China and abroad gives the impression that the Chinese were "not interested in" trade, that they tolerated it only as a form of tribute, and that they were relatively passive recipients . . . This impression, however, is created almost entirely by a literal interpretation of official Chinese documents. . . . Upon closer examination, it is apparent that much more trade went on than official documents reveal, and that tribute trade was only the tip of an iceberg of unrecorded "private" trade.[55]

John Lee notes that "China since the sixteenth century was even more deeply involved than Japan in trade with the larger world. Few other places produced the commodities that were universally in demand in greater quantity or variety, and few others attracted foreign traders in the same number."[56] Gang Deng agrees: "China is often portrayed as a country isolated from the outside world, self-sufficient and insulated from capitalism . . . with marginal, if not non-existent, foreign trade. In fact, China needed foreign trade, both by land and sea, as much as many other pre-modern societies in Eurasia."[57]

As Deng explains, this activity belies the old "trade as tribute" view:

> Zheng Chenggong's Ming loyalist regime in Taiwan (1644–83) took part in triangular trade involving Japan, Vietnam, Cambodia, Indonesia, and the Philippines; his fleet to Japan alone comprised fifty ships a year . . . The total profit from overseas trade each year has been estimated at 2.3–2.7 million *liang* of silver . . . The tributary system was a form of disguised staple trade. Trade is also shown because of the fighting over the ability

by tributary states to pay tribute. Hideyoshi invaded Korea, a Ming vassal state, to force China to allow Japan to resume a tributary relationship, and threatened that a refusal would lead to invasion of China itself.[58]

During the late sixteenth century, trade between Manila and China was an estimated annual value of 800,000 *liang* of silver.[59] Table 2.2 shows the estimated number of ships that traded each year between China and Japan during the seventeenth century. Korea-Japan trade—between equals—was essentially pluralistic. *Daimyos* and rich Japanese merchants were involved, and, Etsuko Kang writes, "from the fifteenth century Japanese-Korean trade surpassed Japanese-Ming trade in quantity, and it had a greater impact on the daily life of the Japanese in western areas."[60]

During the Qing period, the Chinese built more than one thousand oceangoing ships each year. Deng concludes that "pre-modern China's long-distance staple trade reveals a system of international exchange, a prototype of division of labor transcending national/ethnic territories, and great manufacturing capacity with considerable technological advancement."[61]

TABLE 2.2 CHINESE DATA FOR SHIPS VISITING JAPAN, 1641–1683

YEAR	NUMBER OF SHIPS
1641–1645	310
1646–1651	220
1652–1656	259
1657–1661	238
1662–1666	182
1667–1671	185
1672–1676	138
1677–1681	126
1682–1683	53
Total: 43	1,711
Annual average	40

SOURCE: GANG DENG, "THE FOREIGN STAPLE TRADE OF CHINA IN THE PRE–MODERN ERA," INTERNATIONAL HISTORY REVIEW 19, NO. 2 (MAY 1997): 262.

Japan was deeply enmeshed in a network of foreign trade with other parts of East Asia at this period. Table 2.3 estimates Japanese silver trade in the mid-seventeenth century. Most notable is how small the Dutch portion of the silver trade actually was.

Stephen Sanderson writes that "trade with China and Korea became an important part of the Japanese economy. . . . During the fifteenth and sixteenth centuries foreign trade grew rapidly in intensity and trade ventures were extended to other parts of the far east, even as far as the Straits of Malacca."[62] During the Muromachi period, it is estimated that annual traffic between China and Japan was never less than forty to fifty ships annually.[63] Between 1604 and 1635, the Japanese recorded 335 ships sailing officially to Southeast Asia, and in the late seventeenth century, 200 ships arrived in Nagasaki every year.[64]

Even during the Tokugawa era, Japanese exports in the seventeenth century are estimated to have reached 10 percent of its GNP.[65] Indeed, China under the Qing was much more willing to consider private trading relations in the stead of formal tribute relationships. Richard Von Glahn writes that "Japanese trade with China grew substantially after the Tokugawa came to power in 1603. The Tokugawa *shogun* Ieyasu aggressively pursued foreign trade opportunities to obtain strategic military supplies and gold as well as silk goods."[66] Lee stresses the "undiminished importance of a trade relationship with China and, to a lesser extent, with Korea and the Ryuku" during the Tokugawa period.[67]

Using reports of Chinese ship captains as given to Japanese officials in Nagasaki during the Tokugawa era, Yoneo Ishii estimates that the junks that carried trade between China, Southeast Asia, and Japan had an average size of between 120 and 500 tons, with some capable of carrying as much as 1,200 tons of cargo.[68] Because of the dynastic transition between the Ming and the Qing during the 1670s and 1680s, direct China-Japan trade was difficult, so many of the junks originated in Taiwan, went to Southeast Asia, and then traveled to Japan. After the Qing court established full control of Taiwan in 1683, it lifted restrictions on shipping to Japan, and trade expanded dramatically.[69] "During the eighteenth century," Peter Klein tells us, "Japanese exports of precious metals over the isle of Tsushima into Korea and China actually surpassed the amounts of silver that had earlier been carried away from Nagasaki by the Chinese and Dutch."[70] The Tsushima profits from Korean trade during Tokugawa were enough to feed the entire population of Osaka at current rice prices.[71]

Trade served as a double-edged instrument of system consolidation, for it facilitated not only more intense state-to-state interactions but also the

TABLE 2.3 JAPANESE SILVER EXPORTS, 1648–1672 (KG)

YEAR	EXPORTS TO CHINA	EXPORTS TO THE NETHERLANDS	TOTAL SILVER EXPORTS	DUTCH SHARE (%)l
1648	6,727.50	23,332.50	30,060.00	77.6
1649	20,452.50	20,028.75	40,481.25	49.5
1650	25,605.00	14,775.00	40,380.00	36.6
1651	17,808.75	18,360.00	36,168.75	50.8
1652	21,326.25	21,446.25	42,772.50	50.1
1653	13,188.75	23,216.25	36,405.00	63.8
1654	30,678.75	14,430.00	45,108.75	32.0
1655	17,456.25	15,007.50	32,463.75	46.2
1656	19,653.75	23,212.50	42,866.25	54.2
1657	9,187.50	28,357.50	37,545.00	75.5
1658	41,358.75	21,150.00	62,508.75	33.8
1659	72,753.75	22,350.00	95,103.75	23.5
1660	75,566.25	16,008.75	91,575.00	17.5
1661	96,633.75	20,790.00	117,423.75	17.7
1662	48,536.25	22,350.00	70,886.25	31.5
1663	20,291.25	13,770.00	34,061.25	40.4
1664	62,490.00	20,895.00	83,385.00	25.1
1665	30,157.50	25,800.00	55,957.50	46.1
1666	27,135.00	14,913.75	42,048.75	35.5
1667	17,051.25	13,402.50	30,453.75	44.0
1668	12,806.25	0.00	12,806.25	0.0
1669	1,110.00	0.00	1,110.00	0.0
1670	1,481.25	0.00	1,481.25	0.0
1671	3,562.50	0.00	3,562.50	0.0
1672	33,615.00	0.00	33,615.00	0.0

SOURCE: RICHARD VON GLAHN, "MYTH AND REALITY OF CHINA'S SEVENTEENTH CENTURY MONETARY CRISIS," JOURNAL OF ECONOMIC HISTORY 56, NO. 2 (JUNE 1996): 443.

development of domestic state institutions. Southeast Asia illustrates both processes. From roughly 1400 to the eighteenth century, the expansion of international trade within Southeast Asia, and between Southeast Asia and China, Japan, and Northeast Asia, resulted in a regionwide process of territorial consolidation and centralization of royal authority.[72] As Andre Gunder Frank notes, "At least a half dozen trade dependent cities—Thang-long in Vietnam, Ayutthaya in Siam, Aceh on Sumatra, Bantam and Mataram on Java, Makassar on Celebes—each counted around 100,000 inhabitants plus a large number of seasonal and annual visitors."[73]

As in Northeast Asia, trade in Southeast Asia was regulated by royal monopolies. Thailand (Siam) is a case in point. The Siamese central civil administration had four working departments—Treasury, Palace, Land, and City. Treasury was in charge of overseeing foreign trade, and consisted of royal warehouses, factories, tax and duties collectors, and the "port master."[74] By the early eighteenth century, the number of Chinese ships calling at Siam had steadily increased. One European trader at the time wrote:

> The Chinese . . . bring them the most valuable commodities; and, at the same time, allow their own people to disperse themselves unto a great number of foreign parts, whither they carry their silks, porcelain, and other curious manufactures and knickknacks, as well as their tea, medicinal roots, drugs, sugar, and other produce. They trade into most parts of East India; they go to Malacca, Achen, Siam, etc. No wonder then that it is so opulent and powerful. . . .[75]

And, as Jennifer Cushman emphasizes, "Siam's exports should not be seen as marginal luxuries, but as staple products intended either for popular consumption or for the manufacture of consumer goods by the Chinese."[76]

Evidence on the relative importance of trade with the West suggests, moreover, that relations among Asian states continued to outweigh more sporadic interactions with outside powers. In contrast to Japan's continued incorporation into active trade in the region, Western trade—mainly Dutch and Portuguese traders—was simply never as important as has been believed. The annual Portuguese share of silver exports was usually less than 10 percent of total exports.[77] The Dutch were actually pushed out once the East Asian system stabilized by the end of the eighteenth century. Indeed, in 1639, the Tsushima *daimyo* told the Korean government that "because commerce with the Portuguese has been banned from this year, we must seek more broadly trade with other foreign nations besides them, and [the *shogun*] has ordered us to trade with your country even more than in the past."[78]

Thus Klein concludes that "during the eighteenth century . . . the East China Sea saw the re-establishment of its traditional self as it more or less retired from the world [European] market."[79] Numerous estimates compiled by researchers on different regions, periods, and markets show the overwhelming bulk of trade occurring within Asia as opposed to between Asian states and Europe.[80] Klein's assessment is typical: "European penetration into the maritime space of the China sea was marginal . . . weak and limited."[81]

It's clear, then, that the economic system of East Asia was far more integrated, extensive, and organized than the conventional wisdom allows. From at least the Song era of the tenth century to the end of the Qing dynasty in the nineteenth century, there existed a vibrant and cohesive trading and foreign relations system in East Asia that extended from Japan through Korea to China, and also from Siam through Vietnam and the Philippines. So extensive was this regional economic order that it had domestic repercussions, such as monetization of the Japanese economy. The Dutch and the Portuguese had less impact than is normally thought. It was only when China began to crumble in the nineteenth century that this system finally broke apart.

In sum, research on trade patterns indicates a high level of system interaction in East Asia that was relatively independent of the simultaneously developing European system. As Takeshi Hamashita contends, it is necessary to see "Asian history as the history of a unified system characterized by internal tribute/tribute-trade relations, with China at the center."[82] He stresses that a "fundamental feature of the system that must be kept sight of is its basis in commercial transactions. The tribute system in fact paralleled, or was in symbiosis with, the network of commercial trade relations; the entire tribute system and interregional trade zone had its own structural rules which exercised systematic control through silver circulation and with the Chinese tribute system in the center."

BEHAVIOR

Behavioral patterns in the Asian system are impossible to reconcile with balance of power theory. Most important, there is simply scant evidence of balancing. We do not see alliance formation against China, notwithstanding large fluctuations in Chinese capabilities that might have offered other states windows of opportunity to at least attempt to diminish Chinese dominance. To be sure, neighboring states did seek to emulate Chinese practices, but there is little evidence that the aim was to build up capabilities in order to match and rein in Chinese power. On the contrary, as I will discuss in more detail below, emulation actually had the opposite effect of ramifying the Chinese-dominated order.

Patterns of conflict, moreover, do not correspond to balance of power expectations. Balance of power theory is not a theory of war. Nonetheless, as a theory that explains systemic tendencies toward balance, it would predict that a system as dominated by one state as Asia was by China would be inherently unstable owing to underlying anti-hegemonic systemic forces. The theory expects that a state as dominant as China will likely seek further territorial expansion at the expense of weaker neighbors. This is, after all, why balancing is supposed to be the prime directive of states' foreign policies: to prevent a dominant state from expanding at the expense of the sovereign security of other system members. For this reason, the theory also expects those neighbors to fight to resist dominance, in this case by China, when possible. Neither of these expectations is borne out.

The most striking feature of the system was its comparative peacefulness. The contrast with Europe during the same time period is revealing (Table 2.4).

Overall, war between states was rare, and wars of conquest even more so; often centuries separated wars between the main political units. China did not seek to translate its dominant position into a system-wide empire by force of arms. China's last attempted invasion of Japan occurred in 1281. The Qing expeditions against the Korean Choson dynasty in the early seventeenth century were aimed more at consolidation, demarcation of borders, and reestablishment of the tribute system than with conquest.[83] For example, Seonmin Kim argues that the Qing expeditions against the Choson in the early seventeenth century were aimed at demarcating the border between the two states; "it was the wild ginseng growing in the borderland that initiated the border demarcation between China and Korea."[84] Kim quotes Huang Taiji (the Manchu emperor from 1626 to 1643 who laid the groundwork for the Qing dynasty) criticizing the Choson King Injo in 1631 for his trade policies, saying "the ginseng prices used to be sixteen liang per jin, but you argued that ginseng is useless and fixed the price at nine liang. . . . I do not understand why you would steal such useless ginseng from us."[85]

Conflict tended to occur not to check rising Chinese power but rather as a consequence of decaying Chinese order. As a Chinese dynasty began to come apart, the central power's attention turned inward and so conflict among the surrounding states would flare up. But it's nearly impossible to interpret that peripheral conflict as being meant to reinforce balance by checking China's potential to recover.

TABLE 2.4 EAST ASIA AND EUROPE OVER THE LAST SIX CENTURIES

	EUROPE	EAST ASIA
1492	Expulsion of Moors from Spain	(1392–1573) Ashikaga shogunate, Japan
		(1368–1644) Ming dynasty, China
		(1392–1910) Yi dynasty, Korea
1494	Charles VIII of France invades Italy	(1467) Onin War, Japan. Beginning of "The Age of the Country at War"
	Beginning of struggle over Italian peninsula by Spain and France	
1526	Bohemia and Hungary under Habsburg rule	
1527	Sack of Rome	
1552	Maurice of Saxony revolts against the Emperor	
1556	German-Spanish division of the Habsburg possession	
1562	French wars of Religion	
1572	Revolt of the Netherlands	
1580	Portugal united with Spain	
1588	Spanish Armada defeated	(1592, 1596) Hideyoshi invades Korea
1618	Thirty Years' War begins	(1600–1868) Tokugawa shogunate, Japan
		(1618) Manchus declare war on the Ming
1630	Countermoves by France and Sweden begin	(1627) Manchus invade northern Korea
1640	Portugal breaks away from Spain	
1642	English Civil War	(1644) Qing dynasty (Manchu)
1648	Peace of Westphalia	
1652	First naval war between Britain and Holland	
1667	War of Devolution: Louis XIV against Spain in the Netherlands	
1672	Second war, France against Holland and Spain	
1672	Second naval war between Britain and Holland	
1681	Vienna besieged by Turks	
1688	Third War (League of Augsburg)	
1710	War of the Spanish Succession	

TABLE 2.4 *(CONTINUED)*

	EUROPE	EAST ASIA
1720	Prussia acquires Western Pomerania from Sweden	(1709–29) Chinese intervention in unstable Vietnam
1722	Peter's war against Persia	
1733	War of the Polish Succession	
1735	Annexation of Lorraine to France assured	
1739	Britain at war with Spain in West Indies	
1740	First Silesian War, War of the Austrian Succession	
1744	Second Silesian War	
1755	Britain attacks France at sea	
1756	Seven Years' War	
1774	Crimea annexed to Russia	
1772	First partition of Poland	(1788) Chinese punitive expedition against Vietnam
1792	France declares war on Austria	
1793	Britain declares war on France, second partition of Poland	
1795	Third partition of Poland	
1799	War between France and the Second Coalition	
1801	Nelson's victory at Copenhagen	
1805	Trafalgar	
1806	Jena	
1808	Insurrection in Spain	
1812	Napoleon's Russian Campaign	
1815	Waterloo	
1815	Congress of Vienna	
1823	Absolute rule restored in Spain by France	
1830	July Revolution in France, Polish Revolution	(1839, 1856) Opium Wars in China
1848	Revolution in France, Italy, Germany	(1853) Commodore Perry lands in Japan
1859	War for Unification of Italy	

TABLE 2.4 *(CONTINUED)*

	EUROPE	EAST ASIA
1864	Denmark's war against Prussia and Austria	
1866	Austro-Prussian War	
1870	Franco-Prussian War	(1868) Meiji restoration
1878	Congress of Berlin	(1874) Japan annexes Taiwan
1899	Boer War	(1894) Sino-Japanese War
		(1900) Boxer Rebellion, China
1904	Russo-Japanese War	(1904) Russo-Japanese War

SOURCES: R. ERNEST DUPUY AND TREVOR DUPUY, *THE HARPER ENCYCLOPEDIA OF MILITARY HISTORY: FROM 3500 BC TO THE PRESENT,* 4TH ED. (NEW YORK: HARPERCOLLINS, 1993); PAUL K. DAVIS, *ENCYCLOPEDIA OF INVASIONS AND CONQUESTS: FROM ANCIENT TIMES TO THE PRESENT* (SANTA BARBARA, CALIF.: ABC-CLIO, 1996).

For example, at the beginning of the era under study, in 1274 and 1281, the Mongols under Kubalai Khan, having conquered northern China from the Song, attempted unsuccessfully to conquer Korea and Japan.[86] Eighty years later, with the consolidation of the Ming dynasty's control in China in 1368, Emperor Hongwu sent envoys to Annam, Champa, Koryo, and Japan announcing the founding of the Ming dynasty, and revived the policy of political relationships and an international order in which tribute missions were the main envoys between the surrounding states and the Chinese emperor.[87] The sole conflict that might be reconciled with a broad interpretation of balance of power theory occurred centuries later. As the Ming dynasty weakened, the Japanese general Hideyoshi attempted to invade China through Korea in 1592 and 1598, although he failed to take Korea.[88] However, as the Qing consolidated power early in the seventeenth century, conflict between the surrounding states ceased and relations between states were relatively peaceful for another two hundred years. Indeed, once the Tokugawa shogunate consolidated power in Japan, it chose not to challenge China's central position for almost three hundred years, despite being stronger than it had been under Hideyoshi.

For centuries the Chinese did face running border battles with the Mongols to the north, and at times employed 500,000 troops in an effort to secure that front.[89] In fact, the only successful invasions of China came from the north—Genghis Khan in 1215 and the Qing in 1618.[90] Despite successful conquest of China, however, change was not as lasting as it might have been. Genghis Khan ruled through the existing Chinese bureaucracy instead of supplanting the existing Sinic civilization. When the Manchus invaded the crumbling Ming dynasty and founded the Qing dynasty in 1644, they also adopted Chinese and Confucian practices.[91]

This brings up a final major difference between the Asia and contemporary Europe, and specifically a different systemic logic: in Asia major political units remained essentially the same after war. Boundaries and borders were relatively fixed, and nations did not significantly change during the time period under review. In 1500 Europe had some five hundred independent units; by 1900 it had about twenty.[92] In East Asia, the number of countries, and their boundaries, has remained essentially the same since 1200 A.D. With such a large central power in China, other nations did not wish to challenge China, and China had no need to fight.

In sum, the larger behavioral pattern is precisely what balance of power theory does not expect: stable system dominance by a materially preponderant state.

THE LOGIC OF ASIAN SYSTEMIC HIERARCHY

When China was stable, the regional order was stable. The dominant power appeared to have no need to fight, and the secondary powers no desire to fight. Why? Three overlapping explanations account for the system's stability: the distribution of power and benefits reinforcing Chinese dominance; culture and ideas supporting a stable hierarchy; and the diffusion of Chinese institutions and influence into the domestic politics of the other states comprising the system. The following subsections discuss each of these logics, and then a fourth subsection considers the case of Japan—which as the second-largest state is a crucial test case for the argument.

POWER AND THE COST-BENEFIT EQUATION

For most of the period under review, capabilities were distributed in such a way that it was very hard if not impossible for a balancing order to emerge. China was simply too strong, advanced, and central to counterbalance effectively. For simple realist reasons, therefore, all the usual impediments to balancing were exacerbated. In other words, one benefit of establishing subordinate relations with China was to ensure peaceful relations with it. For example, the Japanese Ashikaga shogunate (1333–1573) sought investiture by the Ming emperor in order to eliminate the insecurity caused by fear of another Chinese invasion. (Investiture will be discussed in more detail below.) As Kawazoe writes, "in order to [ensure peaceful relations with China], Japan had to become part of the Ming tribute system and thus cease to be the 'orphan' of East Asia. For centuries the Japanese had feared attack by the Silla (Korea), and the Mongol invasions had provided real grounds for fearing a Ming attack."[93]

China's strength also allowed it to provide security benefits to lesser states that agreed to play by the system's rules. Incorporation into the Chinese world provided protection from attack, and left the secondary states free to pursue domestic affairs and diplomacy with one another as they saw fit. For example, in 1592 the Chinese sent troops to Korea to attack Japanese general Hideyoshi's invasion force.[94] Jung Yak-yong, a prominent scholar of the nineteenth century, argued that Choson Korea after the Hideyoshi invasion had little fear of a second Japanese invasion both because Choson elites thought Japan's understanding of Confucianism was deep enough that it would not invade, and because they knew the Qing would come to Choson's aid in event of another Japanese attack.[95]

Other states bought into the Chinese role as system manager. In 1592, for example, King Naresuan of Siam learned of Japan's invasion of Korea, and sent a mission to China in October of that year, offering to send the Siamese fleet against Japan. Wyatt emphasizes: "This was no empty gesture. Naresuan understood the interconnectedness of international relations, and he wanted to maintain a balance of power favorable to open international commerce and to China's dominance in an orderly Asian state system."[96]

But this is only part of the explanation, for it cannot account for failure to balance when China was weak, for China's disinclination to expand further, and more generally for the system's astonishing stability. Another rationalist logic was at work: trade with China was a key element of international relations in the region. As detailed above, China was a lucrative and advanced market that tended to draw others into the system. Key here is that even "tribute" was more a hypothetical goal than reality, for the tributary nations gained as much in trade and support as they gave to the Chinese emperor. Tribute in this sense seemed as much a means of trade and transmission of Chinese culture and technology as it was a formal political relationship.

Japan is an important example. During the Song dynasty in China (960–1297), the Japanese economy was monetized because trade with China brought in so much coinage that the Japanese government was forced to legalize the use of coins. As Kozo Yamamura notes, this "had profound effects on the political, economic, and social history of Japan."[97] Despite three separate decrees by the Japanese *bakufu* to ban the use of coins, by 1240 they had allowed them in all but the northernmost province of Japan. Kawazoe notes that "many have since contended that it was the income that could be gained from missions to China that motivated Japanese king Yoshimitsu (Ashikaga shogun in 1403) to open relations with the Ming . . . the large gifts of copper coins, silks, brocades, and so forth that the Ming envoys brought to the shogunal court were certainly a major economic attraction. This tribute-gift exchange was in reality simply trade. . . ."[98]

IDEAS AND CULTURE

Being a client state brought economic and security benefits at a cost lower than engaging in arms races or attempting to develop a counterbalancing alliance against China. Sill, the rationalist calculus leaves a lot unexplained. After all, balance of power theory assumes rational actors, and the potential for mutually beneficial security and economic relations is frequently overwhelmed by problems of uncertainty and commitment that generate conflict. There are thus strong grounds for according ideational and cultural factors an important causal role in explaining Asian hierarchy.

The traditional international order in East Asia encompassed a regionally shared set of norms and expectations that guided relations and yielded substantial stability. In Chinese eyes—and explicitly accepted by the surrounding nations—the world of the past millennium has consisted of civilization (China) and barbarians (all other states). In this view, as long as the barbarian states were willing to kowtow to the Chinese emperor and show formal acceptance of their lower position in the hierarchy, the Chinese had neither the need to invade these countries nor the desire to do so. Explicit acceptance of the Chinese perspective on the regional order brought diplomatic recognition from China and allowed the pursuit of international trade and diplomacy.

The formally hierarchic relationship consisted of a few key acts that communicated information between actors. Most important was "kowtow" to the Chinese emperor by the sovereigns of the lesser states. Since there could be only one emperor under heaven, all other sovereigns were known as kings, and on a regular basis would send tribute missions to the Chinese capital to acknowledge the emperor's central position in the world. In addition, when a new king would take the throne in a lesser state, it was customary to seek the emperor's approval, a process known as "investiture." Although pro forma, investiture was a necessary component of maintaining stable relations between nations. Korea, Japan, the Ryukyus, Vietnam, Tibet, and other nations peripheral to China pursued formal investiture for their own rulers, sent tributary missions, and maintained formal obeisance to China.[99]

Kowtowing to China did not involve much loss of independence, since these states were largely free to run their internal affairs as they saw fit, and could conduct foreign policy independently from China. China viewed its relations with its subordinate states as separate from its internal relations, and generally did not interfere in the domestic politics of tributary states.[100] As the Ancestral injunctions noted, "if foreign countries give us no trouble and we move troops to fight them unnecessarily, it will be unfortunate for us."[101] For example, while Vietnam kowtowed to China it also went on to expand its territory in Southeast Asia. With Japan, as with Vietnam's relations with its Southeast Asian neighbors, China always had a policy of noninterference toward its tributary states, as long as its sovereignty was acknowledged and not threatened.[102] With regard to the Korea-China relationship, Gari Ledyard notes,

> Chinese "control" was hardly absolute. While the Koreans had to play the hand they were dealt, they repeatedly prevailed in diplomacy and argument . . . Korea often prevailed and convinced China to retreat from an aggressive position. In other words, the tributary system did provide for effective communication, and Chinese and Korean officialdom spoke from a common Confucian vocabulary. In that front, the relationship was equal, if not at times actually in Korea's favor.[103]

As for Vietnam, a brief Chinese interregnum (1407–1427) was brought about by turmoil in the Vietnamese court. After a ten-year struggle, the Le dynasty lasted from 1427 to 1787, existing uneasily beside China. Truong Buu Lam writes that "the relationship was not between two equal states. There was no doubt in anyone's mind that China was the superior and the tributary state the inferior. The Vietnamese kings clearly realized that they had to acknowledge China's suzerainty and become tributaries in order to avoid active intervention by China in their internal affairs."[104] As Marr notes:

> This reality [China's overwhelming size], together with sincere cultural admiration, led Vietnam's rulers to accept the tributary system. Providing China did not meddle in Vietnam's internal affairs . . . Vietnamese monarchs were quite willing to declare themselves vassals of the Celestial Emperor. The subtlety of this relationship was evident from the way in which Vietnamese monarchs styled themselves "king" (*vuong*) when com-

municating with China's rulers, but "emperor" (*hoang de*) when addressing their own subjects or sending messages to other Southeast Asian rulers.[105]

Culturally the Chinese influence was formative. Although both the Japanese and Korean languages are not Sinic in origin (generally they are thought to be Ural-Altaic, with more similarity to Turkish and Finnish), Vietnam, Korea, and Japan have used Chinese characters and vocabulary for over two thousand years.[106] Although the indigenous languages were used for everyday speech, formal communications were written in Chinese, and it was a sign of education to be conversant in Chinese literature and poetry.

CHINA'S LONG INSTITUTIONAL REACH

Many of the East Asian states were centrally administered bureaucratic systems based on the Chinese model. Centralized bureaucratic administration in China involved a complex system of administration and governance. Ming-era China was centrally organized into administrative districts down to the province level, with appointments made from the capital for most tax, commercial, and judicial posts.[107] In addition, since the Han dynasty, an examination system was used for selecting government bureaucrats, resulting in East Asia's region-wide focus on education. Anyone who passed the exam ensured both himself and his family a substantial increase in prestige and income. The states peripheral to China also had developed complex bureaucratic structures. Again, this form of government, including the bureaucratic system, was derived from the Chinese experience. The civil service examination in these countries emphasized knowledge of Chinese political philosophy, classics, and culture.

With the promulgation of the Taiho Code in 701, Japan during the Heian era (749–1185) introduced a Chinese-style government utilizing a bureaucratic system that relied heavily on imported Chinese institutions, norms, and practices.[108] Japan's university system in the eleventh century was based on a curriculum that studied the Chinese classics, the organization of Japan's bureaucracy was modeled after China's, and the capital city of Kyoto was modeled after the Tang dynasty capital in China.[109]

Japan, with perhaps the least centralized authority of the East Asian nations in this study, had a feudal tradition nominally overseen by an emperor. However, all countries in East Asia were essentially feudal in domestic social structure, and Japan was no exception. In addition, the domestic process of expanding centralized political control occurred in Japan just as it did in other countries in the region. Like all countries, Japan saw a waxing and waning of state power over the centuries, with a relative breakdown in central political control during the fourteenth century, but relatively firm centralized control both before and after. The Japanese emperor himself was a weak and nominal leader of the country. Most importantly for our purposes, Japan had a long tradition of being independently recognized as a single unit in international relations of East Asia.

Korea also used a bureaucratic system borrowed from the Chinese model and emphasizing the study of Chinese texts.[110] In Korea the examination system was used since the Silla dynasty of the seventh century, although it became fully incorporated into public life under the Choson (1392–1910) dynasty.[111] Indeed, Choson dynasty court dress was identical with the court dress of the Ming dynasty officials, with the exception that the identical dress and emblems were two ranks (in the nine-rank scheme) lower in Korea. That is, the court dress of a Rank I (the highest rank) Choson official was identical to that of a Rank III official at the Ming court.[112]

Although each country retained its own identity, the Chinese influence on family organization, education, culture, crafts, and arts was pervasive. The Sinicizing process included migration of Chinese to the Vietnam region, increased use of the Chinese language, the civil service examination system, the establishment of Confucian schools, the rise of Buddhism, Taoism, and Confucianism, Chinese-style clothing and marriage ceremonies, and a militia based on Chinese inventions and technology.[113]

Thus the Chinese influence on East Asia was pervasive.

JAPAN'S ROLE

The role of Japan is perhaps the most important to discuss, because for centuries Japan was the second-largest country in East Asia, although still considerably smaller and weaker than China. Did the system really encompass Japan? Until the Tokugawa shogunate (1603–1868), Japan followed essentially the same rules as other East Asian countries. The Japanese have traditionally described the world as *ka-I no sekai*, or "the world of China and the barbarians." Tashiro Kazui notes that "from the time of Queen Himiko's rule over the ancient state of Yamatai [183 to 248 A.D.] to that of the Ashikaga shoguns during the Muromachi period, it was essentially these same international rules that Japan followed."[114] In 1370, Prince Kaneyoshi of Japan presented a *hyosen* (*piao-chien*, a foreign policy document presented to the Chinese emperor) in which he referred to himself as "subject."[115] King Yoshimitsu's acceptance of Chinese suzerainty became a powerful legitimizing tool for his government.[116] Writing about the fifteenth century, Kazui notes that "both Japan and Korea had established sovereign-vassal relations (*sakuho kankei*) with China, joining other countries of Northeast Asia as dependent, tributary nations."[117] Key-huik Kim adds:

In 1404—a year after the ruler of Yi Korea received formal Ming investiture for the first time—Yoshimitsu, the third Ashikaga shogun, received Ming investiture as "King of Japan." The identical status assigned to the rulers of Yi Korea and Ashikaga Japan under the Ming tribute system seems to have facilitated the establishment of formal relations between the two neighbors on the basis of "equality" within the "restored" Confucian world order in East Asia.[118]

One common misperception in the scholarly literature is that Tokugawa-era Japan was a closed and isolated nation that operated outside the East Asian international system. However, in the last two decades, a revisionist view has become widely accepted, one which sees Tokugawa as deeply interested in, and interacting with, the rest of East Asia. There was a change in Japan's international status following its attempts in 1592 and 1598 to invade China through Korea. China essentially de-recognized Japan, forcing it outside the legitimate international order of the time. The Ming in 1621 expelled Japan from the Chinese world system, making it the "outcast of East Asia."[119]

Japan was forced to find an alternative way to conduct its foreign relations and trade. Although not fully reincorporated into the tributary system, Japan operated by essentially the same set of rules, following the function if not the explicit form of tributary relations with China. The key point is that Tokugawa Japan continued to accept the Chinese-centered system, even though formal tributary relations were never fully restored. Indeed, after the Hideyoshi invasions of Korea in 1592–1598, the Tokugawa shogunate recognized China's centrality and Japanese-Korean relations as equal. Kim writes:

The Tokugawa rulers understood and accepted the Korean position. Japan after Hideyoshi had no ambition for continental conquest or expansion. They tacitly acknowledged Chinese supremacy and cultural leadership in the East Asian world. . . . Although Tokugawa Japan maintained no formal ties with China . . . for all intents and purposes it was as much a part of the Chinese world as Ashikaga Japan had been.[120]

The Japanese called this new policy the *Taikun* (Great Prince) diplomacy, and some view this as having been a way for Japan to opt out of the Chinese system, because such a concept did not exist in the Confucian world order. It allowed the Japanese to conduct foreign policy without explicitly recognizing the Chinese emperor as superior, while still not provoking too harsh a response from the Chinese by formally challenging their position. However, the Tokugawa rulers remained integrated into East Asia, and made systematic efforts to gather information on regional affairs.[121] Trade was still conducted through Nagasaki, only by private merchants, and indirectly through Korea and the Ryukyus. Although the conventional wisdom was that the Tokugawa shogunate closed itself off from the rest of the world formally in 1633, a policy sometimes referred to as *sakoku*, the reality was that trade with China and the rest of the world continued to be an important part of Japan's economy. The more recent scholarship interprets *sakoku* as merely "maritime provisions" that were "simply a part of a sequential process rather than firm indications of new policy directions."[122] As noted previously, Japanese exports in the seventeenth century are estimated to have reached 10 percent of its gross national product (GNP).[123] This revisionist view sees Tokugawa foreign relations more as an expansion of state power and regulation in Japan rather than a policy of isolation. Indeed, it has been shown that the phrase *sakoku* did not exist historically, and is not seen in any Japanese sources, public or private, until a translation of a Dutch book about Japan.[124] These countries, even during Tokugawa and Qing, had extensive relations. During the Tokugawa period, the *bakufu* established formal and equal diplomatic relations with Korea, subordinate relations with the Qing, and superior relations with the Ryukus.

Klein notes that "by the end of the seventeenth century the Tokugawa regime had succeeded in maneuvering Japan into the center of a regional system of international diplomacy of its own making."[125] William Wray adds that "[Tokugawa] Japan had a distinctive policy for virtually every country or area with which it traded. There were far more Chinese than Dutch ships coming to Nagasaki. . . ."[126] Historians today interpret these maritime provisions more as examples of normal statecraft and the extension of Tokugawa control than as signs of paranoia or cowering anti-foreignism. Ronald Toby argues that Japan under Tokugawa had an "active state-sponsored program of international commercial and technological intelligence . . . that enhanced domestic sovereignty and enabled the state to regulate a desired foreign trade."[127]

CONCLUSION

Explanations consistent with realism, liberalism, and constructivism reinforce one another, generating a basic hierarchical logic in the East Asian system that is so strong that evidence of balancing processes over six centuries is hard to find. Consistent with hegemonic stability versions of realism, China's neighbors recognized the preponderance of Chinese power and accepted it instead of trying to balance against it. As liberalism would expect, the stability of the system was increased by substantial trading links among the major states. And as constructivism would suggest, the system was also stabilized by a complex set of norms about international behavior that was generally observed by the main political units. But both the outcome (stable hegemonic dominance) and the process evidence (no balancing and remarkable stability) decisively contradict balance of power theory.

The demolition of this regional order came swiftly in the mid-nineteenth century. The intrusion of Western powers and the inherent weaknesses of the East Asian states created a century of chaos. With the Western powers dividing up China and limiting its ability to act, the system broke apart. Japan was able to seize the initiative and attempt to become the regional hegemon. Much of Southeast Asia became embroiled in guerrilla wars in an attempt to drive out the Western colonizers, from Vietnam to the Philippines to Malaysia and Indonesia. The two world wars and the Cold War all muted East Asia's inherent dynamism. It was only in the 1990s that the system appeared to begin—once again—to resemble an East Asian regional system that is both powered and steered by East Asian states themselves.

Yet the causal factors that were important for stability in early modern East Asia remain worthy of attention. That stability was a function not only of power and size, but also of a complex set of norms about behavior that governed international relations between the main political units. East Asia from 1300 to 1900 was economically and politically important, and it was more stable and hierarchic than the European system. This observation is of great theoretical significance: there is a logic of hierarchy that can lead, and has led, to a stable, relatively peaceful hierarchical international system under (early) modern conditions. Further study of the historical East Asian international system should yield additional insights not only into its own dynamics, but also the dynamics of international systems more generally—including the contemporary one.

CHAPTER 3

DESCRIBING EAST ASIA

ALIGNMENT STRATEGIES TOWARD CHINA

To explain why East Asian states have increasingly accommodated China, one must first describe what East Asia actually looks like—that is, describe East Asian states' alignment strategies toward China in an empirically consistent and falsifiable manner. Doing this accurately is important, because there has been little sustained exploration of how these states interact with and view China, and so arguments about whether or not states are balancing China often rest on ad hoc and piecemeal empirical measures.[1] With the exception of Taiwan, no East Asian state fears the Chinese use of force. Indeed, the states in the region—even including Taiwan—are moving closer to cooperation with China on diplomatic and political relations.

Alignment is primarily military, but can also comprise economic and institutional components as well as a security component. Accompanying a lack of military preparations for conflict with China, and a concomitant absence of containment alliance behavior, East Asian states have moved toward China on economic and institutional matters. As China's economy has continued to grow in the past three decades, its neighbors have sought to benefit from that and have moved to expand economic and cultural ties, not limit them. Institutionally, the region has made rapid progress in creating a patchwork of multilateral institutions in East Asia that cover a range of issues and include China as a regular, active member. Furthermore, East Asian public opinion toward China reflects this trend. While publics throughout East Asia overwhelmingly expect China to become the major power center of East Asia in the near future, they also generally exhibit favorable attitudes toward China and assess bilateral relations as being close. In sum, most East Asian states view China's return to being the gravitational center of East Asia as inevitable and have begun to adjust their strategies to reflect this expectation. Furthermore, the rapidity with which East Asia and China have improved relations is striking.

These favorable attitudes may initially seem surprising. After all, China is already a great power in many ways and its economic growth seems set to continue into the near future, and therefore the potential costs of China's rise are fairly obvious. The richer China becomes, the more likely it can bully other states. And were China to provoke a war somewhere in East Asia, the effects could quite easily spill over to the rest of East Asia and have severe regional consequences. Even if a state avoids outright conflict with China, military balancing would be a costly endeavor.

However, the potential benefits from China's rise are also just as obvious. As both a consumer and a producer, the Chinese market is increasingly seen as shaping the future for many companies worldwide.[2] Individual companies, and countries, that have good relations with China stand to benefit from its economic emergence. Furthermore, stable relations with a dominant state can also reduce military fears and threat perceptions. Defense spending and arms races would drain resources and attention from the region-wide focus on economic growth, and the state would also forgo opportunities for economic cooperation with China and within the region.

This chapter first discusses the theoretical literature on alignment, arguing that a definition of balancing is most useful when it is tightly defined as referring to the possible use of force. I then show that East Asian states do not expect or plan to use force against China. I then explore other types of relations, including economic, institutional, and public opinion.

STRATEGIES AND ALIGNMENTS IN INTERNATIONAL RELATIONS

In outlining state strategies, the two most common concepts in the theoretical literature on international relations are balancing and bandwagoning. Although the literature often portrays states' alignment decisions as a stark dichotomy involving those two positions, they are only polar extremes. The traditional, most widely accepted measure of balancing is investment by states to "turn latent power (i.e., economic, technological, social, and natural resources) into military capabilities."[3] Balancing can be internal (military preparations and arms buildups directed at an obvious threat) or external (forging countervailing military alliances with other states against the threat).[4] Conversely, bandwagoning is generally understood to be the decision by a state to align itself with the threatening power in order to either neutralize the threat or benefit from the spoils of victory.[5]

Although these concepts seem straightforward, a furious scholarly debate has broken out over how to measure balancing. Because many states in the post–Cold War era are not engaged in obvious military balancing, as defined above, against the United States, an entire literature has introduced concepts such as "soft balancing" and "under-balancing" to explain why that "hard" balancing has not occurred.[6] For example, Robert Pape defines soft balancing as "actions that do not directly challenge U.S. military preponderance but that use nonmilitary tools to delay, frustrate, and undermine aggressive unilateral U.S. military policies . . . [such as] using international institutions, economic statecraft, and diplomatic arrangements."[7]

However, terms such as "soft balancing" and "under-balancing" make it virtually impossible to falsify the balancing proposition. That is, if "balancing" and the underlying theoretical argument that emphasizes power as essentially threatening can include obvious military and political attempts to counter a known adversary as well as more subtle disagreements that fall well short of war, it is almost impossible to provide evidence that could falsify this viewpoint. Furthermore, given that yet another escape clause lies at the extreme end of the spectrum—as referred to in chapter 1, some states are "too small to balance"—theoretical adjectives such as "hard" and "soft" balancing have limited analytic usefulness, and stretch the definition of that concept to the point of irrelevance. As Keir Lieber and Gerard Alexander write, ". . . discussion of soft balancing is much ado about nothing. Defining or operationalizing the concept is difficult; the behavior typically identified by it seems identical to normal diplomatic friction, and regardless, the evidence does not support specific predictions suggested by those advancing the concept." Absent a falsifiable claim that can be empirically verified, adding adjectives is merely an ad hoc attempt to retain a theoretical preconception.

What about economic balancing? Tariffs are not balancing if they are imposed generally and all states are equally affected. Even preferential trading blocs, although they discriminate against some countries, are not necessarily balancing. NAFTA (the North American Free Trade Agreement) discriminates against countries outside of one region, but this is nested in a larger effort to reduce tariffs worldwide. On the other hand, economic sanctions may be designed to weaken an adversary, the underlying cause being concern about the future use of force, and thus sanctions fit comfortably under balancing as it has traditionally been defined. So when assessing balancing behavior, the critical variable remains a state's concern about the use of force.

For the purposes of this book, I define balancing tightly, as preparations for the use of force, or "hard" balancing: military buildups and defense spending, or countervailing military alliances aimed at an adversary.[8] Bandwagoning, on the other hand, will refer to clear attempts to curry favor with a state through military alliances or economic and diplomatic cooperation. Between these two extremes lies a large middle area where states avoid making an obvious choice, and it is theoretically and empirically important to distinguish these middle strategies from the extreme polar opposites of balancing and bandwagoning.

Labels for strategies within this middle area include engagement, accommodation, hiding, and hedging, as well as numerous other similar strategies.[9] Within these middle strategies, the most important distinction is between those that represent more or less fear of a potential adversary. Countries may not balance but still be somewhat skeptical of another country, in which case they might prefer to hedge. Yet countries that do not fear a larger state do not hedge, even if they do not bandwagon. Those strategies can be called accommodation—attempts to cooperate and craft stability that are short of slavish bandwagoning. By defining and categorizing state strategies in this way, one can empirically derive variation along the dependent variable in a falsifiable manner (Figure 3.1).

While states often have sharp disagreements with one another over a range of issues, words such as "conflict" or "tension" do not help us sort out conflicts that are genuinely dangerous and could lead to war, those that are serious and could have consequences for diplomatic or economic relations between states, and those that may have domestic political currency but will not affect relations between states in any meaningful manner. Not all negotiations end in conflict, and not all conflicts end in war. As with measuring balancing behavior, the conventional distinction has been based on whether there is the possibility for the use of force.[10] Of paramount importance are the issues that could involve actual military confrontation.

There are issues between states that may not have the potential to escalate to actual military conflict but that still have real consequences for interactions between states—for example, economic disputes that could affect trade

FIGURE 3.1 SPECTRUM OF ALIGNMENT STRATEGIES

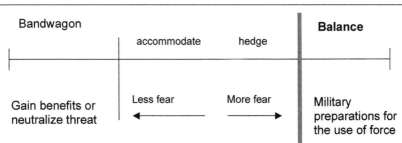

and investment flows. There are also those issues between states that do not have a measurable impact on actual interactions between states, but do have rhetorical or domestic currency. Paying explicit attention to what type of issue exists between states—issues that could involve the use of force, issues that may be consequential but not likely to lead to military conflict, and issues that are primarily domestic or rhetorical—will help us to better categorize and describe the salience of various issues in East Asia.

For example, as will be discussed in greater detail in the following chapters, the issue of Taiwanese independence is consequential and could easily lead to the use of force and a militarized dispute. Alternatively, contested ownership of the Spratly Islands is unlikely to lead to the use of force, but how the issue is resolved could have economic consequences for states in the region. Finally, diplomatic maneuvering and debate about which countries should be included in the East Asia Summit remains at the level of diplomatic squabbling, with little measurable impact on any state in the region.

ALIGNMENT IN EAST ASIA

Although the states in East Asia have complex and varied relations with one another and with China, it is possible to arrive at variation among the cases by exploring their alignment strategies toward China (see Figure 3.2). At one end, Vietnam is much smaller than China and has only recently normalized its relations with the United States, while North Korea is still formally at war with the United States and clings to China as its main ally. At the other end, Taiwan—although minuscule relative to China—relies almost completely on the United States to balance Chinese power. Japan as a major economic power is most skeptical of China and maintains close relations with the United States, but it is not engaged in military containment of China, and thus "hedging" would be an appropriate categorization of Japan's alignment strategy toward China. In the middle are states such as South Korea—whose relations with the United States and China are in flux—and the states of the Association of Southeast Asian Nations (ASEAN), such as the Philippines, whose relations with China continue to grow closer on a number of dimensions, and who are clearly not preparing for military balancing against China.

Some have argued that East Asian states do not fear China because they can rely on the U.S. military presence in the region to protect them. There is certainly an element of truth to that argument. As chapter 8 will discuss in more detail, all states, including China, desire good relations with the United States, and none is actively working against the United States. However,

FIGURE 3.2 ALIGNMENT OF SELECTED EAST ASIAN STATES TOWARD CHINA

North Korea	Vietnam, Malaysia	Philippines South Korea Japan	Taiwan
Bandwagon with China		Accommodation/hedging	Balance against China

American power is hardly the only or even the major reason that states do not fear China. As the rest of this book will show, most states do not fear conflict with China in the first place, and thus the U.S. presence is at most a form of generalized reassurance. In fact, most states are working assiduously to increase their ties with China, not limit them. Despite some skepticism within the United States, even that country has not chosen to balance or contain China. Thus it is not that surprising that East Asian states have not come to that conclusion, either.

SOUTH KOREA: THE PARADIGMATIC CASE

South Korea may be the clearest case of how China is reshaping foreign relations in the region. The Republic of Korea (ROK) has shown little inclination to balance China, and indeed appears on the whole to be moving enthusiastically—and some have argued, naively—to expand all manner of relations with it. South Korea and China have similar stances on a range of foreign policy issues, from the best way to deal with North Korea to concerns about the future of Japanese foreign policy. What makes the South Korean case even more vivid is that it has been one of the closest U.S. allies in the region for over sixty years. South Korea's embrace of China, and South Korea's overall changing strategic orientation, has led to open friction with the United States.

Although the U.S.-ROK alliance provides South Korea with a strong ally, South Korean planning has not been focused on a potential Chinese threat. South Korea has also shown considerable deference to China, especially in its reluctance to fully support U.S. plans for theater missile defense.[11] If South Korea considered China a threat, ostensibly its force structure would be different. Yet South Korea's defense spending has decreased by over a third, from 4.4 percent of GDP in 1990 to 2.8 percent of GDP in 2004. South

Korean naval and ground capabilities remained roughly the same over the decade. The number of main battle tanks, artillery, and surface combatants has remained roughly the same. South Korea did expand its tactical submarine force, but even here the expansion is modest. This shows that South Korea has not changed its military planning or procurement in any major direction, to face a land or sea threat. Thus, although South Korea still retains a strong military, it is clearly designed primarily to respond to a North Korean attack. A senior defense official said in 2006, "We are not planning on any type of conflict with China. The opposite, actually—we're increasing our cooperation with China in military exchanges."[12] The past decade has not seen any South Korean military adjustments that might deter China.

The engagement of China extends to the political sphere. In a survey of South Korea's National Assembly in 2004, the newspaper *Dong-a Ilbo* found that 55 percent of newly elected members chose China as the most important target of South Korea's future diplomacy, while 42 percent of "old-timers" chose China.[13] Jae-ho Chung notes that "despite the formidable threat that China may pose for Korea, no trace of concern for South Korea' security is evident in Seoul."[14] South Korea's 2004 National Security Strategy calls the Sino-ROK relationship a "comprehensive cooperative partnership" and calls for greater military exchanges between the two countries.[15] In 2006, a senior South Korean government official said that "China has no intention of threatening the Korean peninsula. China wants stability on its borders, and it has very good relations with us. We are also deeply intertwined on economic issues as well as cooperating on security issues."[16]

Thus, South Korea is one of the East Asian states that is moving most obviously to engage China and to embrace its emergence.

VIETNAM'S MILITARY AND SECURITY POLICY

Vietnam is another country that has moved quite far in its engagement of China. With normalization of ties between Vietnam and China in November 1991, cooperation has rapidly increased between the two neighbors. The two share a long history of deeply intertwined relations, and at present the two communist governments share similar goals of encouraging domestic economic reform while retaining political power. At present, Vietnam is neither currently arming nor actively defending its border against China, nor does it show signs of attempting to challenge China in the seas. In fact, the main trend of the past fifteen years has been a reduction in Vietnamese security fears and rapidly increasing Vietnamese military cooperation with China.[17]

Vietnam has significantly reduced its military personnel and spending since the late 1980s—with a major demobilization of 500,000 men in 1990.[18] In addition, Vietnamese defense spending has been cut by almost two-thirds since 1990. From 12 percent of GDP in 1991, by 2000 Vietnam was spending less than 4 percent of its GDP on defense. Furthermore, if Vietnam were preparing to fight China on the seas, it would be building up its naval capabilities. In fact, Vietnam's navy has been in a period of stasis.

Indeed, military exchanges between China and Vietnam have become frequent, and conducted at the highest levels. Table 3.1 shows a sample of high-level meetings between Chinese and Vietnamese military officials from 1991 to 2000. In 2001, the Chinese guided missile frigate *Yulin* paid a port call at Nha Rong in Ho Chi Minh City, the first ever by a Chinese naval vessel.[19] Traveling both ways, generals, defense ministers, and other military officials have begun to build strong relations between the two militaries.

Vietnam and China have formally delineated their land border and are making progress in resolving maritime issues. In October 2005, Chinese Defense Minister Cao Gangchuan and his Vietnamese counterpart Pham Van Tra signed an accord to conduct joint naval patrols of the Gulf of Tonkin area, which had been disputed by both sides. The two sides agreed to continue demarcation discussions of their shared border and said they hoped to finalize a border treaty that would also include neighboring Laos sometime in 2006.[20] In response to Chinese concerns that Vietnam might allow the U.S. navy access to Cam Ranh Bay, in 2002 Vietnam pledged to China that it would not provide access to foreign navies at the port, and only develop it for commercial purposes. As Major General Tran Cong Man said, "We will always live next to China. It is a demographic power. We must never confront them."[21]

The "Joint Vietnam-China Statement for Comprehensive Cooperation," signed in 2000 by Foreign Minister Nguyen Dy Nien and Foreign Minister Tang Jiaxuan, also aimed to promote "carrying out multi-level military exchanges in various fields to enhance mutual trust . . ." Compared to twenty-five years ago, or even the end of the Cold War, Vietnam's security situation is more stable and less dangerous. It has dramatically reduced its military spending and demobilized half its army, and now engages in close military cooperation with the Chinese.

SOUTHEAST ASIA

Cooperation between China and Southeast Asia is increasing, not decreasing, and none of the Southeast Asian states considers military conflict with

TABLE 3.1 EXCHANGE OF HIGH-LEVEL MILITARY DELEGATIONS BETWEEN CHINA AND VIETNAM, 1991–2000

DATE	FROM VIETNAM	DATE	FROM CHINA
July 1991	Le Duc Anh (minister of national defense)		
Feb. 1992	Maj. Gen. Vu Xuan Vinh	May 1992	Gen. Fu Jiaping
Dec. 1992	Gen. Doan Khu	May 1993	Lt. Gen. Chi Haotian
June–July 1993	Gen. Le Kha Phieu	March 1993	Gen. Yu Yongbo
April 1994	Gen. Dao Dinh Luyen	April 1995	Gen. Zhang Wannian
		Jan. 1995	Maj. Gen. Shen Binyi
		Jan. 1996	Lt. Gen. Zhou Yushu
July 1996	Lt. Gen. Pham Van Tra	Aug. 1996	Lt. Gen. Fu Quanyou
Oct. 1996	Nguyen Thoi Bung (deputy defense minister)	Nov. 1996	Lt. Gen. Xu Caihou
Oct. 1998	Maj. Gen. Nguyen Van Do	Feb. 1997	Gen. Wang Ke
April 1997	Gen. Dao Trong lich	June 1997	Lt. Gen. Liao Xilong
June 1997	Lt. Gen. Le Hai		
Oct. 1997	Maj. Gen. Nguyen Huy Hieu	Aug. 1998	Lt. Gen. Xiong Guangkai
June 1998	Senior Lt. Gen. Pham Van Tra		
Oct. 1998	Lt. Gen. Doan Chuong		
April 1999	Lt. Gen. Pham Thanh Ngan		
Nov. 1999	Gen. Hoang Ky	Jan. 2000	Lt. Gen. Zhang Wentai
July 2000	Gen. Fu Bingyao		
July 2000	Lt. Gen. Pham Van Tra (minister of national defense)		
Oct. 2000	Gen. Le Van Dung	Nov. 2000	Senior Lt. Gen. Yang Huaiqin
		Feb. 2001	Lt. Gen. Chi Haotian

SOURCE: CARL THAYER, "VIETNAMESE PERCEPTIONS OF THE 'CHINA THREAT,'" IN HERBERT YEE AND IAN STOREY, EDS., *THE CHINA THREAT: PERCEPTIONS, MYTHS, AND REALITY* (LONDON: ROUTLEDGECURZON, 2002), PP. 279–80.

China a possibility. Alice Ba characterizes the states' overall orientation toward China as one of "complex engagement," covering a "multiplicity of interactions—economic, political, and social; informal and formal; bilateral and multilateral—on a variety of issues."[22] Historically, Southeast Asian states have not seen China as a colonizer in the Western sense. That is, "demands for recognition did not result in the extinguishing of sovereignty the way Britain emasculated the Burmese monarchy."[23] Blair King of the Council on Foreign Relations summarizes Southeast Asian views of China's military thus: "it doesn't appear to me that [most Southeast Asian countries] sense a military threat from China."[24] The main orientation of Southeast Asian militaries continues to be control of the interior and borders, along with piracy and coastal defense, not preparations for military confrontation with China.[25] Singaporean commentator Janadas Devan has noted that "there is no discernible enemy (other than jihadists) on the other side. Why would Asian countries line up with the U.S. to confront replicas of themselves in China? . . . Asian states will line up with the U.S. if it drew a clear line? Hell, even the Australians won't."[26]

Indeed, this lack of balancing is reflected in Southeast Asian military procurement strategies. The only ASEAN country that has tactical submarines is Singapore, with 4, while China has 67. The National Bureau of Asian Research describes China's antisubmarine warfare (ASW) capabilities as "exceptional," while Singapore, Malaysia, and the Philippines have no ASW capabilities and Indonesia's are "limited." Singapore has 5 surface combatants, Indonesia 51, and China 149.[27] China has outspent ASEAN on defense for well over two decades. In 1985 China spent $21 billion on defense (in constant 2000 U.S. dollars), while the six major nations that now comprise ASEAN—Thailand, Indonesia, Malaysia, Singapore, the Philippines, and Vietnam—spent a combined $12 billion. By 2002, China had more than doubled its defense spending to $48 billion, while combined ASEAN spending had risen to only $19 billion.[28] In sum, Southeast Asia's militaries are not designed to face a major military conflict. Sheldon Simon writes that "the primary security concerns of ASEAN states (with the possible exception of Singapore) do not place global terrorism at the top of the list. Rather, a host of challenges emanating from within their societies and across their borders top the agenda."[29]

As the largest country in Southeast Asia, Indonesia could potentially view China as a rival. Yet Indonesia has only 300,000 troops to defend a population of 200 million and an area of land and sea that covers almost 10 million square kilometers.[30] Indonesia's security doctrine is "overwhelmingly inward-looking, with its navy geared primarily to coastal defense."[31] Although

Indonesia has more surface combatants than other Southeast Asian states, it lags far behind China, and Alan DuPont points out that it "still affords less attention to external security than probably any other state in Southeast Asia."[32] Some Indonesian observers actually view the United States as its greatest external threat, because the terrorist activity in Indonesia could prompt the U.S. to take preemptive military action against it.[33]

Indeed, Indonesia's 2003 *Defense White Paper* lists its potential future strategic threats as international terrorism, separatist movements, radicalism, and international crime. The white paper only mentions China once, in passing: "defense cooperation [with China] is currently at an early stage and it is important that this is continued."[34] Furthermore, military cooperation between China and Indonesia has increased. Reciprocal visits of Chinese and Indonesian senior military figures have taken place. As Michael Leifer notes, "Indonesia cannot be described as an enthusiastic advocate of engagement with China . . . however, outright containment of China has never been considered a realistic proposition."[35]

Malaysia has also rapidly improved its relations with China, even as its relations with the United States have become strained. Malaysia's main security concerns are domestic, focused on sovereignty and illegal immigration, and even "maritime terrorism and piracy are not Malaysia's highest priorities."[36] Since 1986, Malaysian defense planning has been based on a "no external threat" scenario, and Malaysia was the first ASEAN country to normalize relations with China, in 1974.[37] As Amitav Acharya writes, "While Malaysia may favor an 'engagement strategy,' it does not wish to be identified with an *American* engagement strategy."[38] Then–prime minister Mohammed Mahatir said in 1993, "We do not look at China as our potential enemy. We look at China as a country which has a great potential for becoming an economic power."[39] Yuen Foong Khong wrote that "Malaysian Prime Minister Mohamad Mahatir is impatient with advocates of containment and he has argued in public that engagement is a more appropriate policy. Mahatir's pro-engagement position is significant because China was probably Malaysia's chief strategic threat until recently."[40] Indeed, the reopening of the Bank of China in Kuala Lumpur in 2001 symbolized how far relations have come between the two states in recent years.

So clearly does Malaysia see a strong China as important for the region that then–foreign minister Abdullah Badawi said in 1998, "Talk of China as a threat presupposes it has a planned agenda. I don't think it has one. If China's economic reforms fail miserably, there will be no need for an agenda; the outflow of people will knock us all down."[41] The 1990s saw increased contacts between Malaysia and China, including visits by Chinese Premier Li

Peng in 1990. In November 1995, Malaysia and China agreed to expand bilateral military cooperation, including an officer exchange program and cooperation on defense industries.[42] In 2004, Malaysia announced that it would buy medium-range missiles from China, as well as short-range air defense technologies.[43] By March 2005, Malaysia rejected offers from both Japan and the United States to help patrol the Straits of Malacca.[44]

Australia has clearly stated it is not interested in joining a balancing coalition against China. Australian Prime Minister Alexander Downer said in 2006, "I think a policy of containment of China would be a very big mistake."[45] Kate Callaghan, a senior advisor to the shadow foreign minister of the Australian opposition party, said in 2006 that "Australia is welcoming China, not moving away from it. We know that we have to live with China, and we've developed a very good relationship with them. The idea that Australia would do any type of balancing against China is misplaced. Our relations with China are good and continue to improve. Even U.S. pressure to join a coalition is not going to succeed, because Australia values too highly its good relations with China, and we see no reason to unnecessarily harm those relations."[46] Milton Osborne, a former Australian diplomat, said that "China has now established itself as the paramount regional power in Southeast Asia."[47] Australia remains a close U.S. ally, and relations between the United States and Australia are solid. But this has not meant that Australia will refrain from engaging China. In fact, Australia has moved to expand ties with China on economic, military, and cultural fronts.

Although Singapore is widely viewed as America's closest ally in the region, it is also one of the countries that has moved furthest in its accommodation of China's emergence. Singapore is also the region's strongest advocate of engaging China. Yuen Foong Khong writes that "within ASEAN, the most articulate and explicit proponent of engagement [with China] was Lee Kwan Yew of Singapore . . . he cautioned America and others against pursuing a containment strategy because it would have few backers in East Asia."[48] For example, Singaporean Senior Minister Lee Kwan Yew said in 1993 that "China is seeking growth through trade, not territorial aggrandizement."[49] In 1994, Lee said that "for the world's stability and security, integrating China into an international framework is not a question of choice but of necessity. The world does not need another Cold War."[50] Singaporean Prime Minister Goh Chok Tong said in 2001, "It makes no sense to mortgage East Asia's future by causing the Chinese people to conclude that its neighbors and the U.S. want to keep them down."[51] Singapore's *National Security Strategy* of 2004 focuses almost exclusively on terrorism, border controls and piracy, and pandemics such as SARS. China is not mentioned in the document.[52] In

2006, China's Defense Minister Cao Gangchuan toured Singapore's Changi Naval Base.[53]

China-Philippine cooperation also continues to grow. In 2005, Gloria Macapagal-Arroyo was the first Philippine president not to make Washington her first official visit upon her election, traveling first to Beijing instead for a summit with Chinese President Hu Jintao. As one Manila newspaper noted, "Not even the United States can stop President Arroyo from further strengthening its bilateral relations with China."[54] In a meeting on December 11, 2005, President Arroyo noted that China-Philippine relations had entered a "golden period," as economic and military cooperation had steadily increased over the years.[55] In 2006, the Chinese People's Liberation Army (PLA) donated engineering equipment, including bulldozers and graders, to the Philippine Department of National Defense, leading Defense Secretary Avelino Cruz to mention several centuries of "strong affinity with the Chinese people . . . [which] is manifested in our nation's military history."[56] A Chinese missile frigate and supply ship made a port call to Manila in 2006, as well.[57] China has also donated $1.2 million in military aid to the Philippines, and the two sides plan to hold annual security talks.[58]

In 1995, Manila introduced the fifteen-year "Armed Forces Modernization Bill," which would allow the AFP to purchase multi-role jet fighters, twelve offshore patrol vessels, and new air defense radar.[59] However, trends in Philippine procurement have not been aimed at achieving the capability of actually containing China. Furthermore, Philippine defense spending has remained roughly the same over the past decade, even after the Philippines disallowed U.S. bases in its country in 1991. Although limited cooperation with the U.S. has resumed and a visiting forces agreement was signed in 1999, cooperation has focused on Muslim terrorists in Mindanao, not external balancing alliances. As Sheldon Simon concludes, "it is noteworthy that the U.S. presence in the Philippines [in 2006] has nothing to do with external defense, protecting the SLOCs (Sea Lines of Communication), or balancing China. The U.S. presence is focused exclusively on helping the Philippines to meet internal threats."[60]

Historically, Thailand's foreign policy orientation has emphasized a strategy to "go with strength" as the best means of preserving Thai security and independence. Thailand leaned toward the British in the ninteenth century, Japan during World War II, the U.S. during the Cold War, and now China during the latter's rise.[61] Thailand ordered the U.S. navy bases closed in 1975, and thus, in the space of a decade, China was "transformed from being a primary Cold War antagonist to being Thailand's main protector."[62] For example, Thailand and China shared strategic interests in limiting Vietnamese influence in Cambodia, and accepted Chinese intervention there in 1978.[63] As Evelyn Goh writes, "Thailand is the most sanguine of the original ASEAN member states regarding the rise of China."[64] Goh quotes a Thai Foreign Ministry official as saying that China is "a huge locomotive for growth that Thailand must try to harness to its own advantage."[65] Thailand refers to China as a "strategic partner," and has purchased ninety-six Chinese armored personnel carriers.[66] In 2005, Thai and Chinese destroyers held a joint naval exercise in the Gulf of Thailand.[67]

Thus, it is safe to say that none of the Southeast Asian states is actively attempting to balance or contain China through military means. Yuen Foong Khong concludes, "Judging from the position of the key ASEAN states on the 'engage-contain' China debate in the 1990s, it is safe to say that ASEAN would be content with a China that occupies its place as one of East Asia's great powers, but one that exerts its power responsibly."[68] Analyst Ian Storey argues, "Unlike the early Cold War era, Singapore and its ASEAN partners have collectively ruled out a policy of containment against China. The PRC [People's Republic of China] today is not perceived as a direct political-military threat."[69] Southeast Asian states are not opposing China's rise, but they are also not abandoning their ties to the U.S. and other states.

SKEPTICAL JAPAN

Japan is the East Asian country with the most potential to even contemplate a challenge to China, and indeed is the one country in the region expressing some concern about China's increasing size and military strength. For example, in 2006 Japanese Foreign Minister Taro Aso said of China, "It's a neighboring country with nuclear bombs, and its military expenditure has been on the rise for 12 years. It's beginning to pose a considerable threat."[70] Japan is currently in the process of deciding exactly how it views China, and the manner in which it desires to see China-Japan relations develop.

However, as chapter 7 will explore in greater detail, Japan is formulating its China policy within the context of a strong U.S.-Japan alliance. Michael Mastanduno sounds a note of caution: "As Japan has moved closer to the United States, it has become more isolated in the region . . . [and] it has perceived less of an incentive to expend the diplomatic effort needed to reassure and improve relations with its neighbors. The coming challenge for Japan is to continue improving relations with the United States along with, rather than at the expense of, its relations in a troubled neighborhood."[71] So, much of Japan's security stance toward China will be determined by the direction in U.S.-Chinese relations. If the United States does not attempt to contain China, it is highly unlikely that Japan will attempt such a feat by itself.

Indeed, there is little indication that Japan will attempt to balance China's military on its own terms, nor that Japan plans to pursue any type of independent security policy outside of the U.S.-Japan alliance. Robert Ross points out that "for almost its entire history, Japan has accommodated Chinese power . . . these [power] disparities might encourage Japanese bandwagoning or ambitious Chinese policy."[72] Thus many observers see no arms race is in the offing. Furthermore, the U.S.-Japan alliance is not yet aimed at China in any meaningful way.

Dispute over China's actual level of defense spending obscures the fact that Japan's military is already powerful and technologically advanced.[73] However, its budget has not increased from 1 percent of its GDP in three decades, while China's remained over 4 percent of GDP in 2004 (see Figure 3.3), and Richard Samuels notes that Japanese defense budgets "have been effectively flat since 1994, actually declining in nominal and real terms," and in 2007 the defense budget was reduced for the fifth year in a row.[74] The Japanese Defense Ministry has been asked to submit a list of "Cold War–oriented" equipment that can be eliminated.[75] Japan could easily spend far

FIGURE 3.3 CHINESE AND JAPANESE DEFENSE SPENDING, 1990–2004

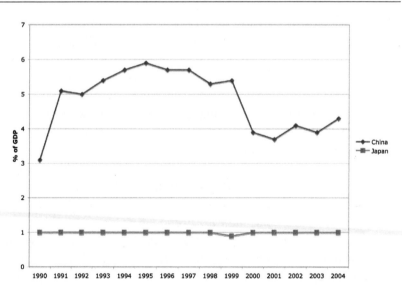

SOURCE: INTERNATIONAL INSTITUTE FOR STRATEGIC STUDIES, *THE MILITARY BALANCE 2004–05* (LONDON: IISS, 2005).

more than it does on defense, yet it has chosen not to. Thus it is difficult to make the "hard balancing" argument that Japan is responding to China.[76]

Japan's military, although already quite powerful, has not been reoriented to face China's increasingly powerful blue-water navy. Military exchanges between Japan and China are slowly increasing. Since Chinese Defense Minister Chi Haotian's 1998 visit to Japan (the first since 1984), Chinese and Japanese minister-level defense officials have met numerous times.[77] Furthermore, since 1993, Japan Defense Agency officials have met annually with their Chinese counterparts. In October 2000, for the first time Japanese defense officials toured Chinese military barracks, and working-level meetings are also steadily increasing.[78]

The recent shift in Japan's defense policy toward a closer alignment with the U.S. has been accompanied by changes to its military, although those changes are incremental.[79] In December 2004, Japan released its "National Defense Program Outline," the first major updating of their defense policy since the mid-1990s. However, while directly mentioning China for the first time, the guidelines also called for reductions in many types of procurement and staffing over the next decade. In 2005, Japan actually reduced its defense budget. For instance, the new guidelines show a planned reduction in total armed forces from a current level of 240,000 personnel to just 155,000 in 2015. The number of main battle tanks will be reduced by 40 percent, from 1,020 to 600, and artillery reduced from 870 to 600. Surface combatant vessels will be reduced from 54 to 47, although the number of submarines will remain constant at 16, compared to China's 69. Japan's combat aircraft will number 350, compared to China's 2,600. These numbers do not indicate the relative quality of the arms, and Japan will most likely have quality of arms equivalent to, or even more advanced, than those of China. However, the main point remains that Japan shows little signs of actually arming itself with an aim to balancing China.

Indeed, the message Japan gives out is mixed: although former Japanese Prime Minister Junichiro Koizumi was often associated with a more assertive stance regarding China, he also said that, "I do not subscribe to the view that China is a threat. The fact that the Chinese economy is becoming more powerful does not necessarily mean that it will pose any military danger."[80] The selection of Shinzo Abe as Japan's prime minister in September 2006 led to a new round of speculation about how Japan might interact with China under his leadership, although it is too early to discern his overall approach. However, Masaru Tamamoto, an editor at the Japan Institute for International Affairs, notes that "nobody wants a bad relationship with Beijing, but the political class is stuck," for domestic politics reasons.[81] Barry Buzan writes, "Without Japan being at the center of it, there could be no realistic Asian counter-China coalition, and there were no signs at all that Japan was interested in such a role, except as junior partner to the U.S."[82] While Japan is wary of Chinese growth, it has not yet engaged in direct balancing, either internally or through its alliance with the United States.

In sum, East Asian countries view China's rise more as an opportunity than a threat. East Asian states are not balancing China, and indeed hope to benefit from its rise. Although most states are not bandwagoning with China, they also are not balancing against it. As James Przystup writes, "it is highly unlikely that Japan or America's other allies in the region are prepared to join in a concerted containment strategy aimed at China . . . they have voiced their apprehension that actions taken in Washington could cause them to be confronted with difficult choices."[83]

INCREASED ECONOMIC RELATIONS WITH CHINA

As with East Asia–Chinese military relations, economic relations are growing closer, not more distant. No state in the region is attempting to limit economic exchanges with China in an attempt to slow or "balance" China's economic growth, but rather all states are moving to increase the ease with which companies and national economies interact with China. Later chapters will discuss in greater detail the nature of individual countries' economic interactions with China. Here I will briefly describe economic interactions with China that are already large and continue to grow. China is already the world's biggest market for many commodities, including cement and steel, and consumer goods, including cell phones and soft drinks.[84] In 2004, China was the world's third-largest consumer market. Paris-based retailer Carrefour has 240 stores in China, and plans to open 150 more store in 2005 alone, which would make it the fifth-biggest retailer in China. Other foreign retailers who have rapid expansion plans for the Chinese domestic consumer market include Wal-Mart (U.S.) and Metro (Germany).[85] As Gerald Curtis notes, "The entire region has become bullish on China. Businessmen and government leaders are hurrying to revise their view that economic relations with China amount to a kind of zero-sum game in which each Chinese success spells another country's defeat . . . private-sector and government policy are being driven more and more by the belief that relations with China can be turned into a win-win game."[86] That is, good relations with China also hold the possibility for regional stability and a spillover of increased economic and diplomatic cooperation.

The overall orientation toward closer economic relations with China does not mean that every individual company in the region is benefiting from China's economic growth. As future chapters will show, many companies face severe competition from Chinese firms, while others are prospering by entering or engaging in outsourcing with the Chinese market. However, the overall orientation of national governments is to increase opportunities for economic interactions with China, not to limit them. As yet there has been little national response in terms of trade barriers or other attempts to limit interactions with China. Indeed, the reverse is true: countries throughout the region are exploring numerous and varied ways of increasing their economic integration with China.

EAST ASIAN ATTITUDES: THE ABSENCE OF FEAR

Like government policy toward China, East Asian public opinion about China is generally positive, and reflects little of the fear hypothesized in the pessimistic theoretical literature. By fairly large majorities, publics in all East Asian countries see China as becoming increasingly powerful in the region both economically and militarily. Significantly, however, those same publics show a favorable orientation toward China and its growth. This is the opposite of what the conventional theories predict: that powerful states cause other states to fear them. To be sure, public opinion is both subject to change and far from a determining element in deciding foreign policy, especially in nondemocratic states or states that are transitioning to democracy. However, the role of public opinion is important in that it reveals basic attitudes and orientations of people in East Asia toward China.

The U.S. State Department conducted a particularly revealing poll in 2005. It covered over 1,000 residents in eight East Asian countries and was specifically designed to be cross-national.[87] Regarding East Asian attitudes toward China and the United States, Figure 3.4 shows that majorities in most countries held favorable opinions of both of them. However, the only two countries in which more people held favorable attitudes toward the United States than those who held favorable attitudes toward China were the Philippines, which held favorable opinions of both countries by very large margins (81 percent positive to China, 95 percent positive to the United States), and Japan, with only 29 percent favorable views of China versus 74 percent favorable to the United States. Figure 3.5 shows poll respondents' perceptions of a "good" bilateral relationship with China and the United States. Again, most countries held favorable perceptions of relations with both countries, and

FIGURE 3.4 EAST ASIAN ATTITUDES TOWARD CHINA AND UNITED STATES (% FAVORABLE)

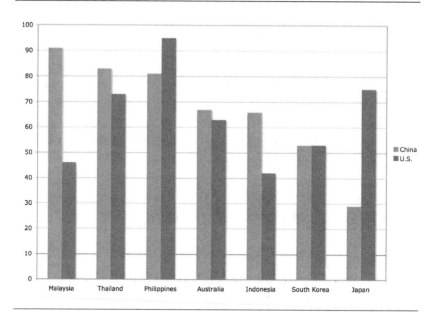

SOURCE: U.S. STATE DEPARTMENT, BUREAU OF INTELLIGENCE AND RESEARCH, "INR POLL: ASIAN VIEWS OF CHINA," NOVEMBER 16, 2005.

FIGURE 3.5 PERCEPTION OF BILATERAL RELATIONSHIP WITH CHINA AND UNITED STATES (% "GOOD")

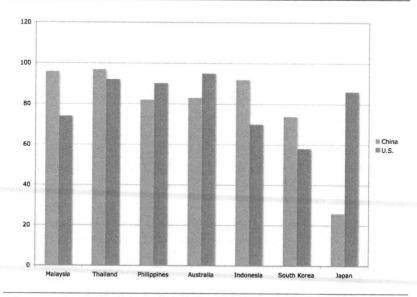

SOURCE: U.S. STATE DEPARTMENT, BUREAU OF INTELLIGENCE AND RESEARCH, "INR POLL: ASIAN VIEWS OF CHINA," NOVEMBER 16, 2005.

only Japan showed significantly more respondents feeling the U.S. bilateral relationship was good as opposed to those who felt the Chinese relationship was good.

When people were asked about future expectations, the results were even clearer. Asked which country would be the future power center of Asia in five to ten years, overwhelming majorities chose China (see Figure 3.6). The results are particularly interesting in Japan and South Korea, where dominant majorities chose China over the United States. Predictably, the Philippine populace remains convinced that the United States will be the power center of Asia, but they are clearly alone in this perception. Finally, when surveyed as to who the closest economic partner would be in five to ten years, the United States placed after both China *and ASEAN* in Malaysia, Australia, and Indonesia. In Japan, 48 percent of respondents felt the U.S. would be the closest economic partner, versus 37 percent who chose China (see Figure 3.7).

A BBC poll conducted in 2005 in 22 countries reveals similar favorable views of China. In answer to the question, "Is Chinese influence in the world mainly positive or negative?" few in Japan say China has a negative influence (25 percent), but at the same time, only 22 percent answered that China has a positive influence. Significantly, the majority of Japanese (53 percent) had no opinion. In the Philippines, 70 percent of respondents said China has a positive influence, and in Indonesia 68 percent said that China has a positive influence. When asked whether China's increasing economic power was mainly positive or negative, more Japanese responded positive than negative (35 percent and 23 percent), while Australians responded 52 percent positive and 38 percent negative, Philippines 63 percent positive and 31 percent negative, and Indonesians 65 percent positive to 21 percent negative.[88]

Even countries that have been staunch U.S. allies reflect this trend. An Australian opinion poll in April 2005 found that 69 percent of those surveyed had "positive feelings" toward China, while only 58 percent had positive feelings for the United States. Furthermore, 72 percent of respondents agreed with "Australian Foreign Minister Alexander Downer's expressed view that the United States should not automatically assume Australia's assistance in the event that US becomes embroiled in a conflict with China over Taiwan."[89] A Thai opinion poll conducted in 2003 found that 76 percent of Thais said China was Thailand's closest friend, 9 percent named the United States, and 8 percent named Japan.[90]

Public opinion is only one measure of public attitudes, and it would be unwise to make too much of poll results. Attitudes can change quickly, and polls rarely measure the intensity and depth with which opinions are held.

FIGURE 3.6 ASIA'S FUTURE POWER CENTER (%)

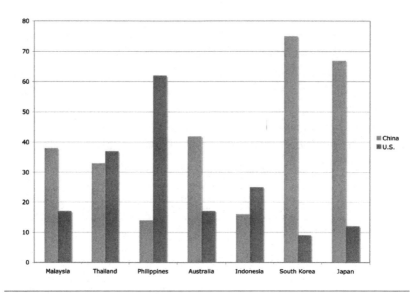

SOURCE: U.S. STATE DEPARTMENT, BUREAU OF INTELLIGENCE AND RESEARCH, "INR POLL: ASIAN VIEWS OF CHINA," NOVEMBER 16, 2005.

FIGURE 3.7 CLOSEST ECONOMIC PARTNER IN 5–10 YEARS (%)

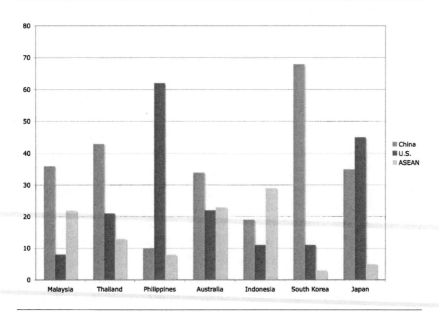

SOURCE: U.S. STATE DEPARTMENT, BUREAU OF INTELLIGENCE AND RESEARCH, "INR POLL: ASIAN VIEWS OF CHINA," NOVEMBER 16, 2005.

However, the evidence is fairly clear that, with the exception of Japan, the states and populaces in East Asia see China as increasingly important, and often view this rise favorably. There is little sentiment in East Asia for a confrontational approach toward China. Even the Japanese, although skeptical about China, see it as the future power center of East Asia.

MULTILATERALISM IN EAST ASIA

In addition to increasingly close bilateral relations between China and East Asian countries, in the past three decades East Asia has embarked on a path toward regional integration with increasing rapidity.[91] T. J. Pempel has identified two broad processes that are occurring in East Asia: regionalism and regionalization. Regionalism "involves the process of institution creation . . . when nation-states come together through top-down activities."[92] In contrast, "regionalization" is a process that "develops from the bottom up through societally driven processes . . . [such as] markets, private trade and investment flows, and the policies and decisions of companies."[93]

Three drivers have been important for the increased regionalism in the region. First, the end of the Cold War created permissive conditions for states to cooperate more closely with one another. Although some regionalism had developed during the Cold War, such organizations as SEATO (Southeast Asia Treaty Organization) were highly ideological, and even their own members were reluctant participants. Furthermore, the Cold War created divisions within the region that inhibited the development of regional institutions as the Soviets and Americans competed for influence.

Second, the 1997 Asian financial crisis spurred both an awareness of the interconnectedness of the region and also feelings that the United States was not as willing to aid East Asia as had been believed. Indeed, many East Asians felt that the U.S. was indifferent to their problems. Tsutomu Kikuchi has described "a feeling of humiliation shared by many East Asian countries" following the 1997 Asian financial crisis.[94] Donald Emmerson notes that "from within ASEAN . . . Washington was reproached for hostility, or indifference, or both—for torching the region's economies and then letting them burn."[95] Such sentiments were not helped by official U.S. pronouncements, as when Treasury Secretary Robert Rubin called the Thai currency implosion only a "glitch in the road."[96]

Third, the rapid economic growth in the region over the past half-century resulted in states that were more confident as well as increasingly interconnected. East Asian growth has been predicated on outward-looking, export-oriented development strategies that exhibit a measure of deep government involvement in the economy.[97] This model, often called "the developmental state," sets the conditions for states to enhance their interaction on economic matters.

Overall, East Asian governmental regionalism has grown dramatically in the past few decades.[98] In 1990, there were only Asia-Pacific Economic Cooperation (APEC), and ASEAN, which consisted of only six countries. By 2005, ASEAN had expanded to ten countries (Vietnam, Laos, Cambodia, and Burma joined during the 1990s). It has become the most visible group, and as regional identities have developed, the norms of consensus have often been dubbed "the ASEAN way."[99] At its heart, this principle covers the idea of state sovereignty, codified in Article 2 of the Treaty of Amity and Cooperation.[100]

Other organizations include CSCAP (Committee on Security and Cooperation in the Asia Pacific, 1993), ACFTA (ASEAN–China Free Trade Area, 2005), ARF (ASEAN Regional Forum, 1994), ASEAN+1 (ASEAN and China), ASEM (Asia-Europe Meeting, 1995), ASEAN+3 (ASEAN and Japan, China, and South Korea, 1997), and the East Asia Summit (2005). China also started the Shanghai Cooperation Organization (SCO), which comprises China, Russia, Kazakhstan, Kyrgyzstan, Tajikistan, and Uzbekistan. The SCO is focused on nontraditional security threats such as terrorism, but also includes confidence-building and force reductions along with increased economic cooperation among the states. At the 2003 annual meeting, Chinese Premier Wen Jiabao proposed creating a free-trade zone among the member states.[101] Alexa Olesen notes that "China is at least as powerful a force in Asia and within APEC as is the United States."[102]

China has shown a genuine desire to be an active member of these regional and international organizations, and this is perhaps best reflected in its considerable efforts to join the World Trade Organization (WTO).[103] Xinbo Wu notes that "the PRC understands that the best way to defend its interest is to make its own voice heard in the rule-making process"[104] by joining influential regional and international institutions.[105] Most notably, China has joined the WTO[106] and agreed to a sweeping set of reforms designed to bring its domestic economic practices in line with global standards.[107] China has also joined a number of other global institutions, such as the International Monetary Fund (IMF) and the World Bank, and is active in the United Nations, providing troops to peacekeeping missions and participating in global development forums such as UNESCO.

Financial cooperation is also increasing. In 1991, Japanese Foreign Minister Taro Nakayama proposed a security dialogue that would include ASEAN, China, Japan, South Korea, the United States, Canada, and Australia. U.S.

Secretary of State James Baker opposed the proposal, "because the United States wanted no regional framework that could jeopardize the hub-and-spokes arrangement it dominated."[108] It was only in 1997 that Japan began to take a more active regional role, through its proposal to create an "Asian Monetary Fund" similar to the IMF. Bowing to vigorous U.S. pressure, Japan abandoned the proposal.[109]

In June 2003, China and ten other East Asian countries agreed to establish an Asian Bond Fund of $1 billion that would create a regional bond market, funnel foreign exchange reserves back into the region, and respond to "economies in crisis," with a second bond fund established in December 2004 valued at $2 billion.[110] Another significant move was the Chiang Mai initiative—a currency swap arrangement among Asian states designed to help avoid the currency crisis that led to the 1997 crisis.[111] Between 1997 and 2003, local-currency East Asian bond markets tripled in size, with the Asian Development Bank supporting the ASEAN+3 (ASEAN and China, South Korea, and Japan) initiative.[112]

Although these multilateral institutions have experienced varying degrees of success, the region itself has seen a flourishing of intra-regional institutionalization and cooperation since the 1980s. It is far more integrated than many observers expected, with many of these multilateral institutions including China as a regular member.[113] In October 2003, China became the first large power from outside of ASEAN to sign the Treaty of Amity and Cooperation in Southeast Asia (India followed soon thereafter). The treaty includes pledges to avoid disputes and resolve by peaceful means those that do occur, and to refrain from even the threat of force.[114] Just as significantly, in November 2002 China signed the Declaration on the Conduct of Parties in the South China Sea, a memorandum that prohibits the use of force to settle rival claims over the oil-rich Spratly Islands.[115]

The other aspect of integration is "regionalization"—the increasing web of business and cultural relationships that are weaving East Asia together. Later chapters will discuss aspects of this regionalization in more detail. Regionalization in modern East Asia is characterized by three major strands of relationships. The first strand of informal regionalization was basically dominated by Japanese corporations—the so-called "flying geese"—built around Japanese capital and technology, which tied other East Asian states' economic fortunes into a Japanese corporate model.[116] The second strand was the reemergence of the Chinese diaspora that has spread throughout Southeast Asia, and increasingly ties China into the region. The third strand has been other East Asian business conglomerates, such as those from South Korea and Taiwan, which have increasingly invested not only in the United

States and Europe, but throughout East Asia as well. Furthermore, although much of this bottom-up regionalization has been economic in nature, regional cooperation also includes cultural flows of people and ideas. In 2004, over 4.4 million Chinese tourists visited Southeast Asia, and almost 3.5 million Japanese tourists did so. Culturally, South Korean television dramas are popular in Taiwan, Japan, China, and the Philippines (*hallyu,* or "the Korean wave"), while Japanese *anime* and pop music are known throughout the region, as well as Hong Kong movie directors such as Wong Kar-wai.[117]

Domestic political coalitions are also an important factor in explaining the development of regional integration. As noted earlier, the rapid economic growth in the region has been one of the defining characteristics of East Asia. States are not only focused primarily on this process of domestic economic and political development, but this also creates incentives to cooperate with their neighbors, especially because trade and foreign investment are such major aspects of the region's development. Etel Solingen notes that "take away markets and domestic politics that have produced them and one removes the most fundamental feature differentiating East Asia from other industrializing regions."[118] That is, political leaders use both material and cultural capital to argue for internationalization, and to build domestic coalitions. Solingen notes that the internationalist coalition emphasizes "domestic economic growth, cooperation and stability in the region, and dependable access to global markets, capital, investments, and technology." Such a coalition has little use for unproductive military defense spending based on external threats, or the protection of state-owned enterprises under the guise of national security.

The potential "backlash coalition" tends to comprise ethnic, religious, and civic groups threatened by internationalization, and inward-oriented sectors of the economy. Although this backlash coalition remains weak in most East Asian countries, regional instability can affect the balance of power between these opposing coalitions. To the extent that East Asian growth has been predicated on export-oriented sectors working with governments to expand integration in the world and regional economies, this economic growth has been a factor in driving the growth of regional institutions.[119] Throughout East Asia, the implicit—and sometimes explicit—social bargain consisted of high growth, employment, and investment combined with selective openness to international trade and finance, and direct investment. This involved regional stability and low defense expenditures, although occasionally leaders would attempt to use an external threat as a device for retaining power at home. Amitav Acharya notes that "the attainment of performance legitimacy through economic development is a key element of comprehensive security doctrines found in ASEAN."[120]

In East Asia, both regionalization and regionalism are occurring at a rapid rate, to the point where arguments about the relative underinstitution-alization of Asia made in the early 1990s are obsolete today. The question is not whether, but why, East Asia has become an increasingly integrated region, and what that means for security. Although East Asian institutions are not yet strong enough to constrain state behavior, the process has had an effect in providing information about intentions and strategies the states are pursuing.

A careful review of the evidence leads to the conclusion that East Asian states are not engaged in military balancing of China. No state other than Taiwan fears the Chinese use of force against it, and as will be discussed in chapter 4, even Taiwan is unsure about its strategy toward China. Most East Asian states are working to increase and improve their relations with China across a range of issues, from military cooperation and planning, to economic, diplomatic, and institutional relations. In terms of popular perceptions, East Asian publics see China as increasingly powerful and influential, but they also tend to have favorable opinions of China. Finally, regional institution building has progressed rapidly, picking up pace in the wake of the Cold War. This overall trend should not be seen as East Asian states bandwagoning with China—no state is abrogating relations with the United States. Indeed, no country wants worse relations with the United States, but they are also not relying on the America to deter China.

Since East Asian states' alignments toward China fly in the face of much conventional international relations theorizing, the rest of this book will focus on explaining why East Asian states are not balancing China. To that end, I focus on the role of East Asian identities. The next chapter will thus look at China's own view of its role and position in East Asia.

PART II
EAST ASIA RESPONDS TO CHINA

Talk of China as a threat presupposes it has a planned agenda. I don't think it has one. If China's economic reforms fail miserably, there will be no need for an agenda; the outflow of people will knock us all down

—MALAYSIAN PRIME MINISTER ABDULLAH BADAWI

CHAPTER 4

CHINA

IDENTITY, SOVEREIGNTY, AND TAIWAN

E xplaining the sources of stability and potential instability in East Asia first requires explaining China's identity. Identity is more than history and the narratives people tell about history; it is also formed by current interactions and pragmatic goals. This is true in all countries, including China. There is no immutable, essentialist, or primordial, unchanging Chinese identity. All identities are being constantly reinterpreted and defined, both by the myths people create to explain their past, and by their current interactions. China is no exception to this.

In fact, Chinese views of itself, its foreign policy, its goals, and its practices have changed often over the centuries. The Chinese state is different from the China of the Qing and Ming dynasties. The modern Chinese state has greater capacity to mobilize resources, has fostered greater national identification among its people, and has greater reach into their daily lives than ever before. The international context within which the Chinese state conducts its foreign policy has also changed, and the modern Chinese state is subject to more numerous external influences than ever before. So, in other words, as the international system has changed, so too has China. A premodern belief about the centrality of the Chinese civilization has given way to a strong identification with Westphalian norms.

Many scholars have emphasized, as central to Chinese identity and nationalism, feelings of a "century of humiliation" at the hands of Western powers, and a preoccupation with competition with the West and Japan. While these elements do exist, they are not in fact the only or even the key elements of Chinese identity. Of more importance for China and East Asia are two aspects to China's identity: an emphasis on sovereignty and the absence of territorial ambition. That is, to argue that Chinese identity is a critical variable in explaining China's foreign policy is not to ignore the importance of pragmatic interests in Chinese foreign policy. Identities are not the opposite of rational self-interest; in fact, identities in part determine which interests are important.

China's transformation from an ideologically driven, isolated state under Mao Zedong into an active regional and global player with deep international ties has been occurring for over thirty years, and so it is possible to draw some initial conclusions about China's preferences and beliefs. The evidence to date leads to the conclusion that China's foreign policy shows more signs of stability and a status quo orientation than worrisome signs of nationalism and aggression. There is an emerging consensus among scholars that for the foreseeable future China wants peace with its neighbors and economic growth at home. China poses little military threat to East Asia, but offers potentially enormous economic benefits to those countries with which it has good relations. Indeed, as China's power has grown, it has actually decreased its demands on its neighbors and become more involved in searching for cooperative and multilateral solutions to many issues. A major element of this grand strategy has been a conscious Chinese effort designed to reassure other states that China is a status quo power, the so-called strategy of "peaceful rise."[1]

As discussed in chapter 1, the one area where China claims it may use force is to retain Taiwan as an "integral" part of China. Significantly, Taiwan is not an instance of power politics, and few observers argue that control of Taiwan could tip the balance of power in the region. Rather, Taiwan has remained an issue because of competing conceptions of identity. Chinese view Taiwan as an issue of nation building, not of territorial expansion. The key question about Taiwan is whether, in fact, it is an independent nation-state, or whether it is merely a part of China. While the answer to many Chinese is obvious: Taiwan is not an independent nation-state; the answer to many external observers is precisely the opposite: Taiwan is clearly an independent nation. This disagreement over Taiwan's identity lies at the heart of the conflict, and is what differentiates Taiwan categorically from China's relations with other East Asian states.

This chapter is composed of three sections. The first section examines China's national identity. The second section explores China's interests and its strategy of "peaceful rise," and the extent to which that strategy is seen as a reflection of Chinese beliefs rather than as reassuring public relations. The third section discusses Taiwan.

CHINESE NATIONAL IDENTITY

There are numerous strands to Chinese national identity, and multiple traditions in Chinese history and experience that inform its current views. In modern times, scholars have tended to emphasize two of these aspects: a preoccupation with a "century of shame," and a virtual obsession with state power to compete with the United States, Japan, and Russia.[2] Michael Leifer reflects this viewpoint:

> The rising power in Asia-Pacific as the twenty-first century approaches is China, whose leaders harbor a historical resentment of national humiliations inflicted on their weakened state by a rapacious West. China's successful post–Cold War economic reforms have provided it with a historic opportunity to realize a sense of national destiny, which many regional states view with apprehension.[3]

Andrew Nathan and Robert Ross argue that, "in contrast to the self-confident American nationalism of manifest destiny, Chinese nationalism is powered by feelings of national humiliation and pride."[4] Nationalism and a focus on prestige has indeed arisen in China in recent years, as evidenced by such mass demonstrations that broke out to protest the 1999 U.S. bombing of the Chinese Embassy in Belgrade, and those that protested the Japanese soccer team at the 2004 Asian soccer championships held in Beijing. As Peter Gries notes, "if Sinologists continue to dismiss Chinese popular opinion, they will fail to grasp an essential component of Chinese politics." There is no doubt that nationalist sentiment appears to be on the rise in China, and the direction that such nationalism may take is not yet clear.

Although important, nationalism and resentment are only part of national identity. Chinese foreign policy has other traditions and elements. One of them is a pragmatic, realpolitik focus on national power and the international system, as opposed to an ideological, or idealistic, approach.[5] This involves not only recognizing that national power and self-interest are enduring aspects to international politics, but that the pursuit of these goals may take many forms.[6]

In fact, China's behavior over the past three decades shows a movement away from "righting historical wrongs" and toward crafting enduring relationships with its neighbors and the West. This transformation actually began with the end of the Cultural Revolution, when China began to reduce its Marxist-Leninist revolutionary rhetoric and develop a policy of reform.[7] In the 1980s, China began an active foreign policy designed to communicate its benign preferences and reassure the rest of Asia and the world. Much public discussion in China is about how to move beyond the long-held victim mentality (*shouhaizhe xintai*) that emphasizes 150 years of humiliation. Instead, analysts are increasingly discussing China's "great power mentality" (*daguo xintai*). Evan Medeiros and Taylor Fravel point out that "Chinese

officials now talk explicitly about the need to 'share global responsibilities,'"
while Peter Gries notes that Chinese nationalism is not inevitably dangerous, arguing that "much—but not all—depends on how the West interacts
with China."[8]

Yet perhaps the deepest lesson that the Chinese leadership learned over
the past century has been the importance of Westphalian norms, chief
among them sovereignty. This has combined with a traditional Chinese concern with territorial integrity, and the more recent struggles China faced in
the nineteenth century to preserve that territory against the numerous in-
cursions from outside powers. As Chinese rulers adjusted to the changing
nature of the international system, they came to identify sovereignty as a key
aspect of international relations.[9] As Michael Hunt noted, "like us [Ameri-
cans], the Chinese have had their enduring strategic concerns, although
their ability to secure their borders and culture against challenge has varied
over the millennia . . . this badly battered security line and an awareness of
the urgency and at the same time the difficulty of restoring it have been a
major legacy of the past to the PRC."[10] Samuel Kim observers that "China has
remained compulsively sovereignty-bound on most basic global issues and
problems."[11] That is, the past "century of humiliation," when outside powers
intervened and interfered at will in China, led to the lesson that national
unity and sovereignty were key aspects of modern international relations.
Allen Carlson notes that "the new emphasis in Beijing on cooperative international legal solutions to outstanding border disputes still represents a significant development in the overall Chinese stance . . ."[12]

Furthermore, conceptions of identity that emphasize nationalism and
historic resentment against the West provide little insight into how China
views its East Asian relations. As Lei Guang notes, "the dominant understandings of Chinese nationalism suffer from one major shortcoming: they
rely too heavily on our observations about China's antagonistic relations
with the West or Japan, the West's close ally. The strong Western-centric
quality of conceptualizations of nationalism in China may be one reason
why adding the prefixes 'anti-Japanese,' 'anti-American,' or 'anti-imperialist'
has little serious effect on the meaning of Chinese nationalism."[13] In particular, these sentiments do not necessarily affect the way China and East Asia
interact, or the way they view each other.

How does China view East Asia? There is scant evidence that China hopes
to reclaim a position of encompassing hegemony over the region—too much
has changed, in both China and East Asia. Steven Levine observed two decades ago that "it was neither feasible nor appropriate to China's new rulers
[the PRC] to simply resurrect, even in updated form, a foreign policy based

on the middle kingdom concept of late imperial China . . . this traditional world view had been eroded by the events of the late nineteenth century."[14] The states of East Asia today are more powerful and domestically consolidated than ever before, and thus China is no longer the sole model for political and economic organization it had been in past centuries. Furthermore, the globalized nature of economics and culture has meant that the region—and even China itself—is subject to a number of influential dynamics. This has led to a China that has neither the desire nor the capacity to attempt hegemony in the region.

In terms of territorial expansion, as this and subsequent chapters will show, although China has modified its tactics in dealing with East Asia its underlying conception has been one of stability and a lack of territorial ambitions. China's chief concerns have been regional, not global, and include securing its borders, delineating maritime claims along the eastern coast, and deepening economic relations within the region. The Chinese conception of "China" has been located around a geographic unit. Chiang Kai-shek said, "China's mountain ranges and river basins form a self-contained unit . . . there is no area that can be split up or separated from the rest."[15] Precise borders have been subject to dispute, the demarcation between China and its neighbors, but not the existence or legitimacy of other countries. Gilbert Rozman notes that China's view of East Asia is one not of expansion, but rather of stability: "it was common to identify greatness, the peak of the cycle, with China's ability to stabilize tributary relations with the peoples around its borders. In the absence of strong competing states, however, the Chinese empire tended to look inward."[16]

In sum, Chinese national identity is not fixed, but rather has changed as both China and the world have changed. Lessons of the past, and narratives about the past, do have an influence on Chinese outlooks, as they do on any country. Although some have emphasized the resentment that China feels for past wrongs, perhaps the most important lesson learned from the past is that the norm of sovereignty is a key part of modern international relations. Coupled with a historical lack of territorial aggrandizement, this has led to a focus on pragmatic and cooperative interactions with the rest of the world, so long as China's national interests are not threatened.

THE STRATEGY OF "PEACEFUL RISE"

There is increasing evidence that China has limited military aims, and much in China's behavior points to Beijing's desire to reach a modus vivendi with the region and indeed the world. The regime leadership has devised a fairly consistent strategy. Avery Goldstein writes that "this consensus in Beijing on a broad approach for dealing with the world, China's transitional grand strategy designed to sustain a peaceful environment for the country's rise to great power status, reflects not just China's capabilities and the constraints of a unipolar international system but also the hard lessons of experience learned during the Cold War and its immediate aftermath."[17] Although history and ideas are important elements to understanding China's preferences, the pragmatic interests, actions, and communications of today are equally important.[18] China's modern strategic priorities are to create a peaceful foreign policy environment while the PRC regime focuses on economic development and domestic political stability, preserve territorial integrity, calm regional fears about China's intentions, and increase China's regional and international influence and prestige.

Numerous high-level officials have reiterated this stance. Zheng Bijian, chairman of the China Reform Forum of the Central Party School and widely considered a major influence on the "peaceful rise" policy, said in 2006, "as for those who take it for granted that as a communist party, [China] will inevitably follow the Soviet-style route of seeking international expansionism and practicing domestic autocracy, those views are groundless."[19] The phrases used to describe the grand strategy have changed over the years as China has searched for a concept that best articulates its vision. In 1997, China unveiled a "New Security Concept" emphasizing peaceful coexistence, mutually beneficial economic contacts, dialogue among states to increase trust, and the peaceful settlement of disputes.[20] A year earlier, China accepted principles contained in a report by the ARF Inter-Sessional Support Group on Confidence-Building Measures, which advocated engaging in multilateral security organizations, Track II (informal) dialogues, and formal meetings among the participants as a way to reduce security fears in the region.[21]

Li Junru of the Central Party School wrote that "China's rise will not damage the interests of other Asian countries. That is because as China rises, it provides a huge market for its neighbors. At the same time, the achievements of China's development will allow it to support the progress of others in the region."[22] As Wu Baiyi, head of international politics at the Institute of European Studies, Chinese Academy of Social Sciences, has argued,

What China pursues now is a security of sustained development. The change is landmark . . . the nature of its security policy, therefore, is accommodative, rather than confrontational. Compared to past policies, the current concept signifies two major changes . . . For the first time, economic security is treated as equally important with those of "high politics." Second, it focuses more on the interrelationship between external and internal security challenges.[23]

This grand strategy provides a series of principles for managing China's foreign relations. Michael Swaine notes that the emerging strategy is similar to the Five Principles of Peaceful Coexistence articulated fifty years ago by Beijing.[24] As Avery Goldstein writes, "[China's grand strategy] comprises two components. One is diplomacy that focuses on establishing various types of partnerships with other major powers . . . the other component is an activist international agenda designed to establish China's reputation as a responsible member of the international community."[25] Thomas Christensen concludes that "there is little or no evidence that China's goal or expectation for the next two or three decades is to dominate East Asia militarily."[26] China's sense that its interests are safest going into the future under a grand strategy that emphasizes cooperation with its neighbors and the world, flows from its recognition both that its rise is potentially troubling and that it is not yet a mature great power.

DOMESTIC SOURCES OF GRAND STRATEGY

China's focus on sovereignty, nation building, and stabilizing its border is central to its grand strategy. Yet there are also domestic sources of China's foreign policy, chief among them the desire to create conditions that will sustain economic development. Chinese leaders face legitimacy problems, issues of regional separatism, a tenuous balance of power between the central and local governments, and extensive government corruption, as well as a host of other issues.[27] The Chinese communist party has few sources of legitimacy other than providing continued economic growth.[28] For that reason alone, China needs such growth in order to maintain regime stability, which has meant emphasizing not just stable political relations with other countries, but also stable and open economic relations around the world.

Economically, the central government also faces a number of problems, including how to raise the standard of living of China's vast rural population. Furthermore, the problems facing China's financial system are in many ways similar to those of East Asia before the Asian financial crisis: bank dominance of the financial system, a central bank subject to political pressures, weak or even nonexistent corporate governance standards, nonperforming loans, and a weak equity market that does not discipline capital.[29] In addition, as with East Asia a decade earlier, the international financial community sees China as an opportunity for explosive growth, and capital inflows into China have begun to approach bubble dimensions, where capital flows not because of a deep understanding and assessment of the opportunities in China, but rather because "everyone else is doing it." This does not mean China will inevitably face something like the 1997 Asian financial crisis (China has not yet floated the yuan), but it should lead to caution when assessing China's prospects for continued economic growth and ability to attract international capital through liberalization.

Capital constraints in the Chinese market result from overregulation and politicization, and from a lack of corporate governance, all of which have distorted equity markets. The current structure of banking regulation is intended to foster the growth of a Chinese banking industry through overt protectionism and the use of joint ventures with foreign firms to create a "training wheel" effect. However, the lack of liquidity and transparency has caused a bottleneck of capital, which has impeded growth of private industry and driven away risk-averse institutional investors. The state's position in the market is also a significant barrier to the development of functional equity markets. Risk premiums on existing instruments will not fall until the nonperforming loans (NPLs) hidden in the banking system are sold off as the bulky state-owned enterprises are dismantled, but privatization can proceed only as fast as is politically tolerable. Thus the extent to which capital markets can develop in the short term will be largely determined by the approach taken in selling off state-owned shares as privatization and restructuring proceed.

Furthermore, the "big four" banks (the Bank of China, China Construction Bank, Agricultural Bank of China, Industrial and Commercial Bank of China) are widely considered "too big to fail," leading to the sorts of moral-hazard problems that have been well identified in the literature.[30] The Bank of China admits that 28.8 percent of its assets are currently nonperforming. Other estimates are far higher. Indeed, as is widely known, when NPLs on the state's books are factored into calculations of government debt, the ratio of government debt to GDP is 70 percent. Pieter Bottelier estimates that the big four may have NPLs as high as 40–45 percent of their combined assets.[31] Standard & Poor's estimates the cost of bailing out China's banks would be between 47 percent and 86 percent of GDP.[32] It is estimated that the total size of NPLs (including rural credit cooperatives) in China is between $800 billion and $1 trillion, or almost half of GDP.[33] In contrast, before the Asian financial crisis of late 1997, South Korea's NPLs accounted for 16 percent of bank assets, while they were 15 percent in Thailand.[34] Thus the economic problems facing China are significant and could have a severe impact on its ability to lead internationally or regionally.

Despite these problems, an assessment of the Chinese economy also reveals a number of positive developments. Indeed, Chinese management of its economic reform to date has been remarkably successful. So smooth and rapid has been China's economic growth that it's easy to forget how rare it is when countries actually manage the reform feat. Indeed, given the chaos of the decade-long Cultural Revolution (1966–1976) and the disastrous Great Leap Forward (1958–1960), China's subsequent policymaking is even more remarkable. China during the 1960s never grew at more than 2.1 percent, and the social and economic dislocations of the Cultural Revolution affected the entire country.[35]

The central government in China has navigated the reform process fairly well.[36] The Chinese Communist Party has learned to manage the economy and begin implementing the WTO standards with considerable speed. In assessing China's eleventh five-year plan of 2005, economist Barry Naughton notes that "[the plan] takes the context of China's high speed economic growth as a market economy for granted . . . and provides [goals] that are clear-headed, and indeed are fundamentally accurate. In fact, they reflect the best of current world thinking about what the process of development entails."[37] Minxin Pei writes that "conservative macroeconomic management, despite several episodes of high inflation, is another much-praised policy adopted by the Chinese government in maintaining a stable pro-growth environment."[38] In its military planning, China has also exceeded predictions. Kurt Campbell, deputy assistant secretary of defense for Asian and Pacific Affairs during the Clinton administration, offered this assessment in 2006: "You look back on those intelligence studies, and it's only been a decade. China has exceeded in every area of military modernization that which even the far-off estimates in the mid-1990s predicted."[39] Thus for both international and domestic reasons, China is following a grand strategy of reassuring its neighbors, focusing on economic growth at home while expanding economic relations abroad, and stabilizing relations on its periphery.

CHINA'S INTERACTIONS WITH EAST ASIA

A grand strategy, however, needs to be more than a concept; it needs to be expressed in concrete actions. The evidence to date reveals that China is increasingly conforming with, and adapting to, international standards and norms, rather than attempting to subvert them. One way in which scholars have asked this question is to explore whether China is a status quo or a revisionist state.[40] Perhaps the most careful study of China's behavior is by Alastair Iain Johnston, who writes that "it is hard to conclude that China is a clearly revisionist state operating outside, or barely inside, the boundaries of a so-called international community. Rather, to the extent that one can identify an international community on major global issues, the PRC has become more integrated into and more cooperative within international institutions than ever before."[41]

As noted in chapter 3, China's more active diplomacy includes growing trade relations with East Asia, the signing of numerous cooperative agreements, joining and proposing multilateral, bilateral, and informal ("Track II") institutions and forums, resolving its borders disputes, and increased high-level military and diplomatic visits to numerous countries. As one observer has described it, "During the past few decades, China's foreign policy has undergone a remarkable transformation."[42] This is even more striking when put in a historical context. In the mid-1980s, analyses of Chinese foreign policy emphasized China's preference for bilateral relations and its disdain for multilateral or cooperative institutions.[43] Yet as China increasingly interacted with the rest of the world and with East Asia in particular, it came to realize that such multilateral cooperation was necessary and that it could be beneficial.

As China has grown more powerful, it has also engaged in more international actions, not less, and has moderated its rhetoric. We noted in chapter 3 that instead of abjuring multilateral cooperation, China has joined a range of institutions, from the WTO to the ASEAN Regional Forum to the ASEAN-plus-China negotiations over a free trade area. Indeed, Evan Medeiros and Taylor Fravel note that "in the last ten years, Chinese foreign policy has become far more nimble and engaging that at any other time in the history of the People's Republic."[44]

Johnston points out that China is more involved in international organizations than other states at its similar level of economic development. Moreover, Johnston tells us, China is increasingly embracing and complying with international norms, as it did on the issues of free trade and sovereignty in the 1990s. Johnston quotes a 2001 U.S. General Accounting Office assessment that reported that China had "shown considerable determination" to build the legal infrastructure required under the WTO.[45] On other issues, however, such as human rights, China is widely considered to be less in compliance with international norms.

In terms of military cooperation and exchanges, the PLA (People's Liberation Army) has also rapidly increased its military diplomacy in the past two decades. In July 1998, China published its first defense white paper, *China's*

National Defense, and has followed with new editions every two years. The 2000 edition commented, "China holds that the ARF [ASEAN Regional Forum] should continue to focus on confidence-building measures, explore new security concepts and methods, and discuss the question of preventive diplomacy."[46] Although the defense white paper has much less of the transparency and detail one finds in those published by other East Asian states, such moves were the first sustained attempt at creating some transparency regarding the PLA's goals and capabilities.[47] The 2004 edition comprised ten chapters and seven appendices, describing both China's national defense policies and the army's modernization process.

The PLA has also become much more active in supplementing state diplomacy through a wide range of activities. In the past two decades, China has sent more than 1,000 military delegations abroad, and hosted more than 2,000 military delegations from other countries.[48] The number of delegations in the 1990s was double that of the 1980s. Most senior PLA leaders make at least one and often more international visits each year. Port calls by the PLAN (PLA Navy) have rapidly increased, with return hostings increasing as well.[49] China has signed state-to-state military protocols with contiguous nations, such as the 1996 Agreement on Confidence Building in the Military Field Along Border Areas, which it approved with Russia, Kazakhstan, Kyrgyzstan, and Tajikstan. China has also engaged in numerous Track II (unofficial) initiatives, such as the Committee on Security and Cooperation in the Asia Pacific (CSCAP).[50]

Taylor Fravel's careful study of China's resolution of territorial disputes provides a useful overview of its increasingly stable borders. China has tended to negotiate compromises about its frontiers, often in very unfavorable terms for itself, while remaining staunchly unwilling to compromise on what it views as its homeland. Even when China's regime has faced internal struggle it has been willing to compromise. Fravel points out that this often helps internal stability. Solving border disputes can seal borders, deny internal dissidents refuge or material, gain a regime promises that the foreign powers will not intervene, and affirm its sovereignty over the unrest in the region.[51] For example, China's settlement of its border dispute with Burma ended with China accepting only 18 percent of the disputed land, only 6 percent of the disputed land with Nepal, and 29 percent of the disputed land with Mongolia. China and North Korea demarcated their border in 1962, with North Korea controlling the majority of Baekdusan, an important cultural icon in Korea.

In the past four decades China has resolved territorial disputes with its neighbors, again, often on less than advantageous terms.[52] David Shambaugh notes that "China has managed to peacefully resolve all of its land border disputes except one (with India), having concluded treaties that delimit 20,222 kilometers of its boundaries."[53] These include Afghanistan, Burma, Kazakhstan, Kyrgyzstan, Mongolia, Nepal, Pakistan, and Russia. India and China have developed a number of confidence-building measures that have reduced the tension along that border, and in early 2005 agreed to begin negotiations to finally demarcate it.[54] China has also resolved its disputes with Cambodia and Vietnam, renouncing its support for the Khmer Rouge and embracing the Paris Peace Accords of 1991 that brought elections to Cambodia, and normalizing relations and delineating its border with Vietnam.[55] All Asian countries except Cambodia, North Korea, and Thailand have signed the United Nations Convention on the Law of the Sea, which helped to institutionalize disputes between many of the countries over fishing rights, trade routes, and other matters.[56]

China does have unresolved territorial disputes with ASEAN over the Spratly Islands, with Japan over the Senkaku (Diaoyu) islands, and with India.[57] As will be discussed in chapter 6, China is not unique in this regard. Many other Asian nations also have unresolved territorial issues, and this is much more the result of a century of change, and increasingly legalistic practices among states, than it is evidence of simmering hostility. For example, Japan has yet to resolve either its dispute with Russia over the Northern Territories, or its dispute with Korea over the Dokdo Islands. Malaysia and Indonesia have had recurring border issues, and six major states have unresolved claims to the Spratly Islands. Furthermore, in 2002 China signed a declaration on the code of conduct for the Spratlys in which it abjured the use of force. Importantly, the code of conduct included most of the language ASEAN provided, and little the Chinese wanted.

Thus territorial disputes by themselves are not an indicator of Chinese ambitions.[58] Indeed, the rapid pace at which it resolved its territorial disputes is strong evidence that China wants to resolve these issues, not use them as a pretext for initiating conflict on its periphery. Given China's deep interest in sovereignty, and its resolution of territorial disputes, it is hard to see that it would reopen these claims or use them as a pretext for expansionism.

THE USE OF FORCE AND CHINA'S MILITARY MODERNIZATION

Although China engaged in military conflicts on its borders during the Cold War and provided limited support to communist insurgencies in Southeast Asia, it has generally limited the use of force in the past twenty-six years.

During the Cold War, all of China's military conflicts occurred on its periphery: Korea (1950), India (1962), Russia (1969), and the last major military conflict, with Vietnam (1979). None of these clashes were wars of conquest; all were attempts by China to protect its borders and stabilize its relations with countries along its periphery.

Vietnam's 1978 occupation of Cambodia—under Soviet tutelage—"undermined China's credibility as guarantor of regional peace and stability."[59] Furthermore, the Chinese felt that Vietnam had betrayed them: having supported Ho Chi Minh's fight against the French and the U.S. by providing arms, money, and 100,000 Chinese military volunteers, the Chinese felt that Vietnam should not undertake aggressive policies toward the Chinese-backed Cambodian government. At the same time, the Vietnamese felt that China was too aggressive and imperious, and that the Cambodian state was destabilizing the region. To stabilize its borders, Vietnam invaded Cambodia.

In response to Vietnam's occupation of Cambodia, Beijing attacked the six northern provinces of Vietnam. The short but bloody 1979 war a classic punitive expedition. Although the Chinese had perhaps 75,000 casualties, either killed or wounded, the war had a profound effect on Vietnam. Within a month, the PLA captured Lang Son, a provincial capital on the final hills before the plains open up to the Red River Delta and Hanoi. Beijing immediately announced its intention to withdraw, and within two weeks all Chinese troops were pulled out.[60] Following the 1979 war, the six Vietnamese border provinces were under constant harassment by the Chinese, and the Vietnamese had to divert enormous resources in order to protect their border. Yet as we will see in chapter 6, since that time China and Vietnam have normalized relations and settled their border disputes, and cooperation between the two countries is rapidly increasing.

China and India also fought a brief war over the contested border between the two nations in 1962. It is also worth noting that India started the conflict, not China. China achieved early success and India was in no shape to counterattack, yet the Chinese halted their own attack. This was limited and careful use of force by the Chinese. Gerald Segal writes that "India . . . launched a local offensive on 14 November [1962]. It was easily rebuffed by China and Beijing moved to deliver the final crushing part of its military lesson. By 18 November the PLA forces broke through Indian lines again. With the Indians in panic, China declared a unilateral cease-fire and withdrew its forces to the lines it had originally proposed."[61]

Although the border remained undelineated after the 1962 war, China and India have made significant progress in stabilizing this relationship. In April 2005, the two nations signed an agreement focused on resolving the fifty-three-year-old border dispute. On April 11, 2005, Chinese Premier Wen Jiabao and Indian Prime Minister Manmohan Singh released a joint statement pledging to establish an "India-China strategic and cooperative partnership for peace and prosperity."[62] China officially recognized the Himalayan territory of Sikkim as part of India, and reached agreement with India about how to resolve the rest of their boundary dispute, offering at one time to take only 29 percent of the disputed land.[63] The comprehensive agreement also covered areas including civil aviation, finance, education, and tourism. Evan Medeiros and Taylor Fravel conclude that as a result of China's efforts, "China's long land border, the site of many of the country's major wars, has never been more secure."[64]

China continues to modernize its military, but it is not necessarily focused on power projection, and rather is mainly concerned with Taiwan.[65] As Bates Gill and Michael O'Hanlon write, "Most of the Chinese aims that run counter to U.S. interests are in fact not global or ideological but territorial in nature, and confined primarily to the islands and waterways to China's south and southeast."[66] China has no plans to create carrier battle groups, it has built few destroyers capable of operating in the open ocean, it is not building long-range bombers, and most importantly, the PLA has not adopted an overall military doctrine that would allow force projection capability—rather, the PLA's doctrine is one of "peripheral defense."

The effort is mainly focused on the potential for conflict across the Taiwan Strait. David Shambaugh concludes that "the PLA does not seem to have made much progress in enhancing its power projection capabilities, nor do these seem to be a priority."[67] China did buy one aircraft carrier from Ukraine, the *Varag*, although it is not combat-ready.[68] Indeed, the PLA anchored the carrier in Macao and turned it into a recreation center.[69]

Some analysts believe that China is aggressively pursuing a submarine force as its main force projector, and that this force is mainly aimed at Taiwan. In terms of its missile capabilities, for four decades, China has made a conscious decision to confine itself to a relatively modest second-strike nuclear force, although this could change depending on United States actions regarding missile defense.[70] Currently China has some twenty nuclear-capable DF-5 ICBMs with an estimated range of 13,000 miles. China has also deployed 600 short-range ballistic missiles across the Taiwan Strait.

In 2006, a mid-career naval officer who monitors the Chinese military said, "This is just one aspect of the overall PLA modernization effort that has been underway during the 10th Five Year Plan . . . [is this aimed at] Taiwan? You bet. Japan? Possibly, but I really don't think Hu and the 'center' leaders want to ever have to use these forces. However, my Clausewitzian mind tells me that sometimes other factors overcome 'good' intentions."[71]

In sum, China in the past thirty years has come quite far in establishing peaceful relations with its neighbors and the world, and in reassuring others of its intentions. China's chief concern for sovereignty and stabilizing its borders derives quite clearly from its national identity. Furthermore, domestic instability and the need to sustain economic development have also led China to emphasize stable working relations within the region. Concerns over whether this is tactical and temporary, or strategic and enduring, miss the point that for China this is the grand strategy that it appears set to follow for the foreseeable future.

IS TAIWAN A NATION-STATE?

The only situation in which there is the clear possibility of Chinese use of force is the dispute over Taiwan. Yet the key issue regarding Taiwan is whether it is an independent nation-state, or whether it is a part of China. While China has been publicly and formally willing to reject the use of force to settle other issues, such as the Spratly Islands dispute, it has steadfastly been unwilling to do so in the case of Taiwan and indeed has been doing everything possible to make credible its threat to use force in order to stop Taiwan from declaring independence. Yet, as has been discussed in brief earlier, Taiwan is not an "exception" to the argument put forth in this book about the peaceful nature of Chinese intentions. That is, Taiwan is not an instance of Chinese expansionism. Rather, Taiwan-China relations are categorically different in Chinese eyes than are relations between China and the other East Asian states.

It needs to be emphasized again that the Taiwan issue is not about power but about identity. China claims Taiwan not because it will move China's military influence ninety miles further into the Pacific Ocean, or because Taiwan's value as a military asset can have any appreciable impact on the regional balance of power. Indeed, Taiwan is militarily insignificant. China claims that Taiwan is a part of China, and that Taiwan is an issue of nation building and an internal matter, and that Taiwan must never be allowed to declare independence. Conversely, the United States is concerned about the loss of Taiwan not because it believes Taiwan could tip the balance of power, and not even because there is any U.S. belief about a potential "domino effect," whereby the loss of Taiwan could lead to further losses. No, the U.S.

cares about Taiwan because of its identity as a thriving capitalist democracy. Thus the critical issue is whether Taiwan is a nation-state.[72]

This question is important for theoretical as well as policy reasons. The issue of Taiwan does not fit easily into Western conceptions of sovereignty. Although the United States treats Taiwan as a de facto sovereign state, *de jure* it is not. This ambiguity has an impact on whether states fear China or not, because East Asian states do not use China's actions toward Taiwan as an indicator of how it would behave toward the rest of the region. This is in contrast to the predominant perspective in the United States, where some see Chinese attitudes toward Taiwan as prima facie evidence that China is a destabilizing and revisionist power. The contrast between these assessments of Chinese preferences highlights the different ways in which the United States and East Asian states interpret China's actions, and helps explain why East Asian states do not fear China as much as many Western theories predict that they should.

The United States formally and legally does not recognize Taiwan and thus it is not officially a sovereign nation to the United States. With U.S. diplomatic recognition of China in 1979, and the formal de-recognition of Taiwan, the United States explicitly agreed to the "one China" principle.[73] In fact, as of early 2007, only twenty-four states held formal diplomatic relations with Taiwan; the most important state that recognizes Taiwan is probably the Holy See. No other European state recognizes Taiwan, nor do any of the major East Asian or Latin American states.

Despite this lack of formal recognition, the United States treats Taiwan as a de facto nation-state, even though *de jure* it is not. Thus, the United States sees the Taiwan issue as a major indicator of whether China is a status quo or revisionist state. For example, Secretary of State Colin Powell said in a November 2003 speech that "whether China chooses peace or coercion to resolve its differences with Taiwan will tell us a great deal about the kind of role China seeks with its neighbors and seeks with us."[74] As Evan Medeiros writes, "For many U.S. policymakers and analysts, Taiwan is the litmus test of China's future role in global affairs. China's resolution of the Taiwan situation is one of the most important indicators of how China will use its growing economic influence, diplomatic skills, and military might to shape international affairs in the future."[75]

However, while the U.S. answer to the question of whether or not Taiwan is a nation-state is essentially "yes," the Chinese answer is exactly the opposite.[76] China views Taiwan as an internal problem, similar to Northern Ireland for the United Kingdom or Chechnya for Russia. Xu Dunxin, former Chinese ambassador to Japan, expresses a common Chinese refrain: "The

Taiwan issue is China's business. It is China's internal affair. No country, including the U.S., has a right to concern itself with this issue."[77] Although such announcements tend to be dismissed in the West, the Chinese have had a consistent policy toward Taiwan, and it is perhaps premature to argue that China is not sincere in expressing this attitude.[78] As one Chinese academic noted, "The United States fought a civil war to keep its country unified. Why would they expect Chinese to behave any differently?"[79]

Indeed, in contrast to the assurances that China signals to the rest of East Asia, China is sending clear signals about how it views Taiwan and the actions it will take to keep Taiwan from declaring independence. These actions include military exercises, massing of short-range missiles aimed at Taiwan on the Chinese coast, and legal actions such as passing the "Anti-Secession Law" of March 2005, which authorizes use of force in event of a Taiwanese declaration of independence.[80] China is doing everything possible to convince the rest of the world that it will use force under certain circumstances.

The Chinese view Taiwan as an internal issue because they claim that Taiwan has always existed as an informal part of China. Taiwan historically was not a formal province of China, but was considered either a part of Fukien province, or was administered by Chinese officials assigned from Beijing. Official Chinese records in the eighteenth century refer to Taiwan as a "frontier area."[81] Although clearly a "part" of China, Taiwan was not considered a part of Han China, and yet it was also not a separate political entity like Korea and Vietnam. Thus, although nominally independent, Taiwan was a part of China. Furthermore, Taiwan has traditionally served as a refuge for the losers of mainland strife. In 1644 the Ming loyalists retreated to Taiwan to harass the triumphant Qing.[82] Led by Admiral Koxingga, the Ming loyalists used Taiwan as a base from which they hoped to oust the Qing. Although the Qing eventually subdued the Ming loyalists on Taiwan, Taiwan was not made a formal province of China until 1886.

Taking this Chinese view seriously also means recognizing that a Western conception of sovereignty on China may be missing the point. The nations of East Asia have made an implicit pact with Taiwan: exist as a quasi-nation and enjoy the benefits of the international system. It should be emphasized that this has been the traditional solution to the Taiwan issue.[83] As long as Taiwan was willing to abide by these rules and be a quasi-nation, the benefits of being a nation-state were available to it. Taiwan's leaders could travel the world and play golf and perform quasi-diplomatic functions, Taiwan's firms could trade and invest overseas, and its status was not threatened, even by China. But while Taiwan could act like a nation-state, it could not officially become a nation-state.[84]

China has a complex view of international relations. Although adopting much of the Western rhetoric regarding sovereignty, in its practices the Chinese also incorporate many non-Westphalian elements.[85] For its part, China is more comfortable with a loose definition of "nation" than are many Western states. China has already agreed to a "one nation, two systems" approach with respect to Hong Kong. The Chinese attempt to derive an identity that allows for the "one-country, two-systems" principle with Hong Kong is one example of how identities can be reconfigured to accommodate this looser definition of sovereignty.

THE DEBATE IN TAIWAN

The question of whether or not Taiwan is a nation-state is complicated by the fact that Taiwanese themselves are undecided about this issue. Truly indigenous Taiwanese comprise less than 1 percent of the population. The rest are of mainland descent, the main dividing line being whether they came to Taiwan before or after 1949. Taiwanese themselves are not sure whether they are 1) culturally Chinese but with a distinct identity, 2) basically Chinese, or 3) something else. What has become clear is that only a very small minority of Taiwanese support immediate independence; the vast majority advocate the status quo indefinitely.

Economically, there has been a gradual change in Taiwan's stance toward the mainland. For decades the government of Taiwan engaged in an attempt to restrict economic ties between China and Taiwan. Until 2001, the Taiwanese government placed heavy restrictions on Taiwanese investments into China that were larger than $50 million. This was an attempt to restrain the Taiwanese business community from emphasizing China as either a market or a production base.

However, the economic logic of creating cross-strait ties was too powerful to ignore, and the result of these restrictions was that many Taiwanese companies simply set up corporations in third countries and funneled the money indirectly into China.[86] With the lifting of restrictions, Taiwanese trade with and investment in China expanded rapidly, and by 2005 over forty thousand Taiwanese companies had made investments in the mainland, employing 10 million people. The Taiwanese central bank estimates that total Taiwanese investment in China is perhaps $80 billion, with private estimates putting that figure at over $100 billion.[87] Sixty-seven percent of Taiwanese foreign direct investment went to China in 2004, and almost 30 percent of total trade, despite rising political tensions. Thirty-eight percent of Taiwanese exports—over $70 billion—went to China in 2005.[88] Thus the economic future and vitality of Taiwan is increasingly tied to the mainland. Over one million Taiwanese have moved to the mainland since 1985. In the past few years, Taiwan and China have discussed opening direct tourism links, joint sea rescue drills in the Taiwan Strait, and linking ferries and direct shipping.[89]

Not surprisingly, the business community in Taiwan has become increasingly opposed to the idea of independence for Taiwan, simply because the economic importance of China is too strong. In one of the most striking examples of this, in March 2005, Hsu Wen-lung, the founder of Chi Mei Optoelectronics Corporation and who has extensive investments in China, wrote an open letter to the Taiwanese press in which he indicated his support for "one China" and his opposition to Taiwanese independence.[90]

The Taiwanese electorate itself does not want independence. Opinion polls regularly show that 80 or 90 percent oppose declaring immediate independence.[91] A poll conducted in February 2006 by the Taiwanese Institute for National Policy Research found that 67 percent of respondents preferred maintaining the status quo, 12 percent favored unification, and only 17 percent favored independence.[92] As a result of sentiments like this, President Chen Shui-bien's approval ratings hover in the low teens, while likely Kuomintang presidential candidate (and current Taipei mayor) Ma Ying-jeou has approval ratings of 80 percent.[93] Ma's 2006 visit to the United States, where he publicly opposed independence, was hailed in Taiwan. While in the United States, Ma said he would pursue the "Five Dos": resume negotiations with China on the basis of the "1992 consensus," reach a peace accord with confidence-building measures, facilitate economic exchanges with the aim of eventually establishing a common market, work with China to boost Taiwan's presence in international bodies, and boost educational and cultural exchanges.[94] In the "1992 consensus" that Ma supports, both China and Taiwan agree that there is one China, although they have their own interpretation of what that "one China" is.

Militarily, China can already devastate Taiwan. In fact, the U.S. Defense Department's fifth annual "Report on the Military Power of the People's Republic of China" concluded that the military balance across the Taiwan Strait has already tipped in China's favor.[95] As a result, Taiwan is not even defending itself anymore. The Legislative Yuan in Taiwan has allowed the "special arms procurement budget" to remain inactive for over three years, and has avoided purchasing arms the United States has already agreed to sell to Taiwan.[96] The *Economist* notes, "Legislative opposition in Taiwan [to the U.S. defense package] has sparked concerns in the U.S. that the island is not willing to contribute seriously to its own defense."[97] This is particularly telling because the military balance is shifting in China's favor. In 2005, an unofficial U.S. assessment of the military balance over the Taiwan Strait concluded that "some analysts in the United States fear we are on the cusp of a tipping point where the PLA develop[s] [the] capability to attack Taiwan and accomplish its political objectives in a speedy enough manner that the U.S. could not reasonably expect to get to the fight in time, even in the event of a political decision to engage."[98] Lee Kwan Yew, Singapore's former prime minister, forcefully pointed out to Taiwan in the 1990s that it must defer to China because it has no other choice. "Whatever weapons the West can supply Taiwan, the array on the mainland side will become so massive in any confrontation that Taiwan must talk."[99]

Taiwan has balanced China with U.S. help since its inception in the late 1940s. In the 1950s, tensions were high across the Taiwan Strait, and in both 1954 and 1958 there was the possibility of serious escalation of conflict between China and Taiwan.[100] China was deterred by an explicit U.S. military protection of Taiwan backed with veiled threats of nuclear weapons. By the 1970s the global geopolitical situation had changed; the U.S. had begun to approach China in an attempt to isolate the Soviet Union, and in 1979 it normalized ties with China at the expense of Taiwan. Taiwan was quickly ousted from a number of international organizations, including the U.N. However, Taiwan's survival at that time still depended on the United States as an ally that could provide safety against the mainland.

Today, however, Taiwan cannot realistically defend itself. This has led to a potential schism in Taiwanese domestic politics, where the economic future of Taiwan depends on close ties with China, and yet the political future is an increasingly vibrant democracy with a population that views mainland China with concern. As Yu-shan Wu has said, "China's economy is too large to ignore, and it is too natural that our businessmen would prefer to do business there. There is no escaping China. Our only hope is that we change China before it changes us."[101]

EAST ASIAN AND AMERICAN VIEWS OF TAIWAN

Considerable ink has been spilled in speculation about how East Asian states would react to a war over Taiwan. If Taiwan is a sovereign nation, then conflict between Taiwan and China, and China's actions toward Taiwan, provide information about how China views its position in the world and how it might act toward other states either regionally or globally. Conversely, if Taiwan is not a sovereign nation, then we would draw different conclusions about what Taiwan means for stability in the region. Thus the issue of China and Taiwan poses an interesting dilemma for international relations theorists. Is the dispute between China and Taiwan a dispute between nation-states? If not, how do we make sense of the conflict?

Most significantly, it is clear that East Asian states want peace and stability and are working to achieve that outcome. Furthermore, one sees the hypothetical nature of the debate over Taiwan. Speculating about what might happen in East Asian states' response to a hypothetical war over Taiwan is ultimately of little analytic value, because so much of states' responses will be determined by the actual specifics of how such a conflict occurred and how China, Taiwan, and the U.S. ended up reacting in that time.

Even U.S. officials have cast doubt about whether the United States would use force to defend Taiwan in all circumstances. In 1996 the United States did send two aircraft carriers to the Taiwan Strait after China engaged in a series of provocative missile launches. This strategy of "strategic ambiguity" by the United States centered on the goal of leaving doubt in both Taiwan and China as to whether America would intervene, in order to forestall either adventurous tactics by the Chinese or a unilateral declaration of independence by Taiwan.[102] Although President George W. Bush's presidency in 2000 marked a tougher line toward China and more favorable statements regarding the U.S. willingness to defend Taiwan, the United States also made it clear that it does not support Taiwanese independence when it pressed Taiwanese President Chen Shui-bien in 2004 to restrain his rhetoric.[103]

In 2006, Senator John Warner, R-Va., chairman of the U.S. Senate Armed Services Committee, said that if "conflict were precipitated by just inappropriate and wrongful politics generated by the Taiwanese elected officials, I'm not entirely sure that this nation would come full force to their rescue if they created the problem."[104] Richard Armitage, former deputy secretary of state, pointed out on a trip to Taiwan in the winter of 2006 that the "Taiwan Relations Act does not commit us to defend Taiwan . . . [the word 'resist'] doesn't necessarily mean militarily."[105]

Most states in East Asia see the China-Taiwan issue as an internal matter, and do not view Chinese actions against Taiwan as an indicator of how China will act toward any other state. ASEAN, and all its members, recognize China and officially consider Taiwan to be a province of China. Although most Americans view China as the destabilizing power with respect to the Taiwan issue, most Asian elites and their public view Taiwan as the cause of friction with China.[106] Southeast Asian states are comfortable with a Taiwan that can for all intents and purposes be independent, but that de facto remains a part of China. The furor over the 1996 and 2000 Taiwanese elections, and then-president Lee Teng-hui's 1996 statements in particular, revealed the consequences of breaking this understanding. Although much of the response emphasized the destabilizing nature of the Chinese threats and hailed the democratic elections in Taiwan, there was caution as well.

The reaction to the Chinese military maneuvers of 1995–1996 was especially telling.[107] U.S. concern was directed almost exclusively at China for being provocative. However, the rest of the Asian states were muted in their responses to Chinese military intervention, and informally extremely upset at Taiwan for provoking China. The informal feeling among other Asian states has been that "Taiwan broke the pact."[108] Thus Southeast Asian nations do not view China's actions and intentions toward Taiwan as an indicator of deeper revisionist Chinese preferences about the region itself, nor do they view Chinese actions toward Taiwan as an indicator of how China would act toward other East Asian states.[109] If this is the case, then East Asian states do not fear China as much as the U.S. expects them to.[110]

While much of the reaction in East Asia was sympathetic to the Taiwanese and the American view, there was also another perspective. The *Singapore Straits Times* wrote, "Yes, the [Taiwanese] people want their space and wealth, but they know in their guts that they have to be reunited with the mainland someday. When and how, that is the question—not if."[111]

Given this perspective, can the United States construct a coalition of states willing to be involved in a U.S.-led military effort to defend Taiwan in the event of a Chinese attack? Numerous U.S. officials have commented on the strategic importance of the Philippines, Japan, and South Korea in having potentially well-situated bases to use in such a conflict. However, this possibility has raised concern among the Southeast Asian states and puts them in a difficult position relative to China. They have all said that their defense treaties do not necessarily include military conflict in Taiwan.[112] For example, in March 2001, Philippine Foreign Undersecretary Laura Baja Jr. expressed concern about Taiwan as catalyst for a war in which the Philippines would be involved but would have had no interest in fighting.[113] Even in private conversations, Japanese and Korean defense and military officials would not make a definitive statement about whether they would allow their militaries, or even their military bases, to be used in the event of a conflict between Taiwan and China.[114]

Australia, one of the closest U.S. allies in the region, has also dodged questions about whether it would allow its bases to be used in the event of a China-Taiwan conflict.[115] The Australian fracas over whether it would be involved in a conflict over Taiwan is worth describing in detail, because it shows how little other East Asian countries wish to be involved in a war. In

August 2004, Foreign Minister Alexander Downer suggested that Australia might not fight alongside the United States in a conflict over Taiwan, which immediately created an uproar. In an interview on Australian television on August 20, 2004, Prime Minister John Howard answered questions about Downer's statement:

INTERVIEWER: Just to get this clear, would Australia automatically back Washington in a war between China and Taiwan?

JOHN HOWARD: Well, that's a hypothetical question.

INTERVIEWER: But Mr. Downer did raise it, regardless of being hypothetical.

JOHN HOWARD: I'll give you my answer. My answer is that we are working very hard to stop any conflict between the United States, China, and Taiwan, and actually for all the talk, relations between China and America are quite good at the present time. There is tension over Taiwan. We have a one-China policy. We think some of the statements that have come out of Taiwan in recent times have been a little bit provocative. We want stability and cooperation between China and Taiwan and we certainly don't want conflict between the United States and China. That is not in our interest.

INTERVIEWER: But the awkward question remains—has the foreign minister redefined the terms of the ANZUS treaty [the 1951 Tripartite Security Treaty between Australia, New Zealand, and the United States] and in doing so created problems between Australia and the United States?

JOHN HOWARD: Well, our obligations are clear under the ANZUS treaty, but I'm not getting into a hypothetical question. There's no conflict between the United States and China.

INTERVIEWER: But if they're clear, what are they?

JOHN HOWARD: Well, we have to consult and come to each other's aid when we're under attack or involved in conflict. That's the situation.

INTERVIEWER: Do you agree that that contradicts what Alexander Downer said?

JOHN HOWARD: No, I don't. I simply say that the issue of conflict between China and the United States is hypothetical.[116]

In fact, it is not even clear what Japan would do in the event of a military conflict between China and Taiwan. Although this is hardly unique (no one is sure exactly what the United States would do in such a circumstance, either), it probably depends very much on the nature and causes of such a conflict.[117] As Gregory Noble writes, "While there is significant ambiguity about what Japan would do if a crisis erupted, and no doubt much would depend upon the specifics of the case, analysts increasingly suggest that

Japan (like another crucial regional ally, Australia) would not necessarily follow the U.S. lead."[118] What is clear is that Japan—like most of the other East Asian states—views Taiwan as a "Chinese" matter, and that it views Taiwanese statements about independence with concern.[119] Although Japan did publicly mention Taiwan for one of the first times in its joint statement with the United States on February 19, 2005, that statement merely called for the parties to resolve the Taiwan issue in a "peaceful manner," and said that Japan looks forward to cooperating with China. As Ralph Cossa notes, this mention "hardly constitutes a demonstration of Japan's willingness to confront the rapidly growing might of China."[120]

In sum, the Taiwan issue is important for two reasons. First, the only potential source of conflict between the United States and China exists because of the ambiguous nature of Taiwan's identity, not because of power. Second, substantively, the Taiwanese themselves are unsure of whether or not they are Chinese. Other East Asian states appear extremely reluctant to commit themselves to one side or the other, preferring that the matter be resolved peacefully. Indeed, even the official U.S. position is that the substance of the resolution is not important, but that the two sides must not use force to decide the issue.

CONCLUSION

China's concern for sovereignty and its lack of territorial ambition are central aspects of its identity. While potentially aggressive nationalist sentiment does exist within China, this has not stopped China from crafting a grand strategy that is largely peaceful, multilateral, and cooperative. The one area in which China has claimed it will use force is to keep Taiwan from declaring independence, and this is an issue of identity, not power politics.

China is already a powerful country that offers potentially large economic and political benefits to other countries that have stable relations with it. China has managed almost three decades of economic modernization with overall domestic cultural and political stability, and shows little sign of revisionist impulses in international relations. Furthermore, China is cognizant that its actions will prompt a reaction from other states, and has increasingly attempted to communicate its desires with the rest of East Asia. China's strategic priorities are focused on preserving regime security through continued economic growth while also preserving territorial integrity.

Some have questioned whether this Chinese grand strategy is merely a pragmatic and tactical ploy while China is still relatively weak, and wonder whether it will continue if China actually achieves unquestioned great power status a generation from now. This is the wrong question to ask, however. Pragmatic interests lead China to search for economic growth, secure borders formally recognized by treaties, and increased economic and diplomatic integration with the world. Although such ties in and of themselves do not guarantee that China will always be peaceful, it does reflect how important assessments are of China's goals and intentions. That is, the question about China's future course arises because of concerns about Chinese identity, not about its power. Furthermore, as chapter 9 will explore in greater detail, it is simply not possible to do anything more than speculate about what any country will be like a half century from today, and the Chinese themselves have little idea.

CHAPTER 5

SOUTH KOREA

EMBRACING INTERDEPENDENCE IN SEARCH OF SECURITY

South Korea presents perhaps the clearest example of the changing nature of East Asian international relations. Conventional power politics perspectives would expect South Korea to fear a rapidly growing, geographically and demographically massive authoritarian and communist China that sits on its border. Not only does China already have the military capability to threaten the peninsula, but the power disparity is widening. China also maintains close relations with North Korea—South Korea's main external threat since 1945. Furthermore, the United States and South Korea have enjoyed a close alliance for over a half century, and it was only U.S. military action that prevented the North (in concert with the Chinese) from conquering the South in 1950. Since that time, the United States has stationed military forces in South Korea to prevent a second North Korean invasion. For all these reasons, the conventional perspective would expect that South Korea cleave closely to the United States and against China and North Korea.

However, over the past fifteen years South Korea has not only drawn closer to China, it has also been embracing North Korea while apparently being content to let its relations with the United States—its longtime ally and protector—unravel. Furthermore, South Korea has had increasing friction with Japan, a capitalist democracy that shares an alliance with the United States. Indeed, South Korea appears more worried about potential Japanese militarization than about Chinese militarization. This has caused both confusion and sometimes even anger in the United States, as some wonder why South Koreans are ungrateful to the United States despite its long history of supporting South Korea. Although the U.S.-ROK alliance remains strong, the United States is no longer the main focus of South Korea's foreign policy. There is little evidence that South Korea will attempt to balance China, and even less evidence that South Korea fears China. As Chung-min Lee writes, "for the first time since the bilateral alliance [with the United States] was forged more than a half century ago, more Koreans are at least *entertaining* the specter of closer political, security, and economic ties with China."[1]

There are pragmatic reasons for South Korea to draw closer to China and North Korea, to be sure. South Korea's economic development over the past half century was predicated on international trade and investment, and this strategy is finding its logical extension as South Korea emphasizes its economic and cultural ties with both China and North Korea. South Koreans also view the potential costs and chaos that could occur from rapid regime change in North Korea as unacceptable, and there was fear, particularly at the height of the second nuclear crisis in 2002–04, that the United States might start a preemptive war against the North that would devastate both sides of the Demilitarized Zone (DMZ). Furthermore, China is not a realistic military threat to the peninsula—the military threat arises because of the unresolved division of Korea itself.

Yet South Korea's foreign policy orientation reflects more than merely the triumph of economic interdependence over power politics. South Korea's identity is another key reason that its foreign policy is changing. This identity has two fundamental strands. Most important is an intense desire for unification of the peninsula, which is South Korea's overriding foreign policy goal. Second, Korea has a long history of stable relations with China, and a much more recent and conflicted history with Japan and the United States. This identity, long masked by the Cold War and a succession of military governments, is increasingly asserting itself in South Korea.

The ultimate goals of each country are also different. The United States has consistently made eliminating North Korea's nuclear and missile programs its primary goal on the peninsula, while many in South Korea view their primary goal as unification with the North, whether or not it has nuclear weapons. China shares this goal of peaceful change in North Korea. Perhaps because of these shared goals, the current interactions between South Korea and China have been largely positive, from cooperation over the North Korean issue to expanding economic and cultural ties between the South and China. To be sure, there are domestic divisions within South Korea, and many conservatives are skeptical of both engagement with the North and a too-optimistic approach to China. Still, despite these divisions, on the whole South Korean attitudes support these two trends.

This chapter will examine South Korea's changing foreign policy, and explain why the U.S.-ROK alliance has come under strain. The first section examines South Korea's national identity, emphasizing the twin aspects of unification and historical narratives about Korea's relations with large powers. The second section explains the divergent strategies pursued by the United States and South Korea over the North Korean nuclear issue and explores the long-term South Korean goal of reintegrating North Korea into the region. The third section explores the Korea-China relationship, showing that South Korea, although wary of a powerful China, is moving closer to China on political, economic, and cultural fronts. The fourth section explains why the U.S. and South Korea have experienced tensions in their relationship.

KOREAN NATIONAL IDENTITY AND ANTI-AMERICANISM

National identity is composed of both current interactions and national narratives about the past. For Koreans, an overriding aspect to their identity is the idea of a unified Korean peninsula. Koreans often cite five thousand years of history and a unified language, culture, and history. Furthermore, Koreans claim to "share a single blood-line," regardless of geography, and believe that North Koreans "are of the same Korean ethnic-nation."[2] While these beliefs are demonstrably false, this "myth" of Korean homogeneity has real consequences for the conduct of politics and foreign policy. As Gi-wook Shin notes, "a sense of ethnic unity has served Koreans in a variety of ways from being an ideology of anticolonialism to that of national unification."[3]

This idea of a unified Korean nation with a shared bloodline is to the foundation of South Korea's foreign policy toward North Korea. That is, Koreans on the whole do not question the ethnic unity that includes both North and South Korea. South Koreans overwhelmingly desire unification with the North. Shin writes, "Koreans regard the current division as temporary . . . [T]hough the two sides diverge over the form and strategy of unification, their proposals rest on the premise that Koreans will be reunified because they belong to the same ethnic nation/race."[4]

Conceptions of history are also important for national identity. The overriding element of Koreans' national identity is their perception that they are surrounded by much larger powers. A common Korean phrase is "when the whales fight, it is the shrimp that get hurt" ("*gorae saumae, saeoo tojinda*"). Of the large powers surrounding Korea, China has perhaps the most positive image in Korean eyes. Korea's current relationship with China, and Korea's long history as one of China's closest allies, has led to a narrative that emphasizes their peaceful relations. Historically, the Korea-China relationship was often called *sadae* ("serving the great") or, more pejoratively, *sadae-juui* ("flunkeyism").[5] In this view, Korea recognized that China was a greater power but also benefited from close relations with it. From the end of the Chinese-dominated regional system in the late nineteenth century until normalization of relations in 1992, Korea had little interaction with China. Thus South Korean views of China are based largely on historical memories of the distant past.[6] In the short time that has elapsed since ties were renewed, interactions have mostly been positive, as will be seen below.

This largely positive national narrative about Korea-Chinese relations contrasts with the largely negative one of Korea-Japan relations. Japan's colonization of Korea from 1910 to 1945 was particularly harsh, ultimately involving the forced Japanization of Koreans, such as the ban against Korean language and the forcing of Koreans to take Japanese names.[7] Resentment of Japan's colonization remains palpable in Korea. Examples abound, from protests over forced sexual slavery during World War II ("comfort women") to popular songs claiming that the disputed islands in the East China Sea are Korean, not Japanese.[8] While economic relations with Japan continue to rapidly improve, and while some political leaders have succeeded in developing good working relationships with their Japanese counterparts, South Korean resentment and hostility over issues such as Japanese colonization and ownership of the disputed Dokdo Islands exist just below the surface.

Between relatively positive Korean views of China and relatively negative views of Japan lie South Korean views of the United States.[9] Although South Korean sentiment about the United States is often labeled as purely "anti-Americanism," it is more complex than that, and even those who oppose American actions tend to view America itself fairly positively. Although some feel that relations have only recently deteriorated, Daniel Snyder notes that there is a "myth of the golden age" regarding the U.S.-ROK alliance. Relations between the two have always been contentious, never completely harmonious.[10]

For their part, some Americans selectively emphasize certain aspects of the U.S. involvement in Korea, for example its defense of South Korea during the 1950 Korean War, seeing this involvement as essentially absolving the United States of responsibility for its other actions. More than 33,000 U.S. troops died in the Korean War, and with the armistice, the military alliance came into formal existence with the signing of the 1953 bilateral defense treaty.[11] The core of the alliance has always been U.S. military deployments in South Korea, which at their height comprised 100,000 troops and nuclear-capable Lance missiles and even today includes nuclear-capable forces of over 30,000 troops, sophisticated airbases, and naval facilities that guarantee U.S. involvement in any conflict on the peninsula. The military alliance provides that operational control of selected ROK armed forces will be given to the U.S. commander of the ROK-U.S. Combined Forces Command (CFC) in wartime. Given these security arrangements and the extensive American economic support for recovery after the war, many Americans view the U.S. role in South Korea as basically positive.

Yet many Koreans have a perspective on the historical U.S. role in Korea that is far more complex. Although virtually unknown in the United States, U.S. President Theodore Roosevelt brokered the 1905 peace treaty that ended the Russo-Japanese war. That treaty—part of the negotiations known as the Taft-Katsura Agreement—essentially acknowledged Japanese primacy in Northeast Asia, including dominance over Korea, in de facto exchange for Japanese acceptance of U.S. domination over the Philippines.[12] Indeed, during negotiations in 2006 over the proposed U.S.-ROK free trade agreement, a South Korean negotiator made reference to the Taft-Katsura act.[13] The U.S. role in dividing Korea in 1945 is another source of concern to some Koreans, who note that the Franklin Roosevelt administration in 1943 took the position that Korea should be free and independent "in due course" after liberation from Japan.

The issue that most severely divided South Koreans in their perceptions of the United States was the furious debate over whether the United States had implicitly or explicitly supported Chun Doo-hwan's suppression of dissidents in Kwangju in 1980. This remains an intensely emotional issue in South Korea, since much of the South Korean population remains convinced that Chun Doo-hwan could not have suppressed the Kwangju uprising without at least implicit U.S. consent.[14] The Kwangju massacre, more than any other single incident, led to a basic shift in opinions among many South Koreans. Anti-Americanism and anger at what was perceived as U.S. arrogance and high-handedness began to grow noticeably from that point onward.[15] Finally, as this chapter will elaborate, there are disagreements over how best to deal with North Korea. Thomas Kern notes that "it appear[s] to many South Koreans that the United States is interested in maintaining the political *status quo* on the peninsula at all costs."[16] With perceptions of steadfast U.S. support for four decades of authoritarian governments, many South Koreans came to distrust the United States' intentions on the peninsula.

Tensions between the United States and South Korea did exist during the decades of South Korean military rule, but they were manipulated and contained by the ruling elite. The advent of increasingly liberal democratic governments since 1987 enabled dissidents to express their concerns more freely. Regarding Anti-Americanism in particular, Katharine Moon writes, "Anti-Americanism as a social movement is both a consequence of rapid democratization and a catalyst for democratic consolidation in the area of foreign policy within South Korea; and this social movement's particular traits, such as methods of protest and coalition behavior, are informed both by the legacy of authoritarianism and more current efforts at democratic consolidation."[17]

In sum, South Korean identity is focused primarily on national unification of the peninsula. Beliefs about China are largely positive but based more on ancient history than any critical appraisal of the current Chinese regime. Conversely, negative views about Japan are a reflection of more recent history. South Korean views of the United States are mixed: while there are elements of anti-Americanism, there is also widespread goodwill.

NORTH AND SOUTH KOREA

The changing nature of South Korea's overall foreign policy is most visible in its strategy for solving the North Korea problem. U.S. and South Korean policies were in relatively close accord during the entire Cold War period and well into the first North Korean nuclear crisis of 1993–1994. And as recently as the mid-1990s, South Korea viewed North Korea primarily as an imminent military threat.[18] Yet the past decade has resulted in a major change in how South Korea views itself, North Korea, and the ROK's own preferred method for resolving the issue of a divided Korean Peninsula. The 2002 crisis over North Korea's nuclear programs showed how far South Korea and the United States had drifted apart in their foreign policies and perceptions. South Korea increasingly fears that the United States could initiate a conflict on the peninsula that would devastate the ROK.[19]

The United States has continued to view North Korea primarily in military terms and is worried about North Korean military strength, in particular Pyongyang's nuclear weapons and missile programs.[20] The United States is concerned over the potential sale of either nuclear material or missiles to terrorist groups such as Al Qaeda, which would in turn use such weapons against the United States. Furthermore, although from 1999 to 2006 Pyongyang had placed a voluntary moratorium on tests of its ICBMs, its unsuccessful test of a Taepodong-2 missile in July 2006 heightened fears throughout the region about its weapons programs.[21] In response, the United States has generally attempted to isolate North Korea and avoided negotiating directly with the North, choosing instead to negotiate only through a multilateral process composed of a complex mix of negotiation and coercion in an attempt to convince it to halt its nuclear programs.

By contrast, South Korea has come to view North Korea primarily as an issue of national reunification, and view it in economic and cultural terms.

South Korea's much deeper long-term question has proven more complex: how best to manage and ultimately solve the North Korean issue—even if nuclear weapons are no longer a factor. As a result, although managing the nuclear issue has been a necessary step to reintegration, South Korea's foreign policy over the past decade has reflected this more fundamental goal of unifying the peninsula.

South Koreans believe that North Korea can be deterred and are worried instead about the economic and political consequences of a collapsed regime. To put the matter in perspective, should North Korea collapse, the number of refugees could potentially exceed the entire global refugee population of 2004.[22] Even assuming a best-case scenario in which such a collapse did not turn violent, the regional economic and political effects would be severe.[23] Alternatively, were a war to break out, the consequences could potentially devastate the region. The commander of U.S. forces in Korea estimated that a war could result in $1 trillion in industrial damage and over one million casualties on the peninsula.[24]

South Korean engagement resulted from more than merely pragmatic reasons. In actively moving toward unification, South Korea has embarked on a path of economic interdependence and political reconciliation with North Korea. Begun a decade ago, this new policy will most likely continue to be South Korea's primary foreign policy direction. The goal is to slowly change and to promote reform in North Korea—the Democratic People's Republic of North Korea, or DPRK—through increased economic and cultural ties.

South Korean engagement of North Korea actually began under the Kim Young-sam government (1993–1998), when South Korean nongovernmental organizations, most of which were Christian-based, ignored governmental prohibitions against sending aid to North Korea during its famine.[25] With the Kim Dae-jung administration (1998–2003) and continuing with the Roh Moo-hyun administration (2003–08), South Korean official policy changed as well. Kim had long criticized the conservative military governments for both excessively politicizing the North Korean threat and impeding inter-Korea reconciliation efforts. As president, Kim called for a "Sunshine Policy" that would engage North Korea and begin the reconciliation process.

The Sunshine Policy reaped an important political and psychological benefit—the first sustained exposure to the DPRK and the regime's reclusive leader, Kim Jong-il. The unprecedented summit in June 2000 between the ROK and North Korean heads of state resulted in a flurry of political, commercial, and social exchanges, including reunions between families separated by the Korean War. The summit marked the culmination of a change in South Korean attitudes toward North Korea. South Koreans were paralyzed with excitement, with newspapers and television devoted almost exclusively to the summit. This was especially true among baby boomers who had not experienced the horrors of the Korean War and the brutality of North Korean forces killing innocent South Koreans during their occupation of ROK territory. Conservatives, especially those who had experienced the Korean War, were more wary of these developments. Four decades of rapid economic development has created a generation of young South Koreans who have nothing more than book knowledge about the Korean War, poverty, or a genuine North Korean threat. South Korea thus began to pursue economic and cultural engagement with North Korea and turned away from its previous policy of competition and hostility.

Official ROK policy toward North Korea is explicitly based on the idea that trade and interdependence can promote peace and stability on the peninsula, and so encouraging the North to continue economic reforms and to open itself up more to the international community is a means to achieve this. For example, when speaking of the increasing economic and cultural ties between the North and South, the South Korean Ministry of Unification stated that "with the peaceful use of the demilitarized zone, [and] the eased military tension and confidence building measures, the foundation for peaceful unification will be prepared."[26]

For almost a decade, South Korea has consistently pursued a policy of economic engagement toward North Korea designed to encourage North Korean economic reforms. Following the shift to the Sunshine Policy, South Korea rapidly increased its relations with the North: North-South merchandise trade has exploded over the last five years, increasing 50 percent from 2004 to 2005 and exceeding $1 billion for the first time.[27] Commercial trade amounted to 65 percent of total North-South trade in 2005, while noncommercial (government) trade accounted for less than 35 percent. Thus while the government is supporting the economic integration of the two Koreas, private firms are also heavily involved. Trade with South Korea accounted for 20 percent of North Korea's trade in 2004, while South Korea's $256 million worth of economic assistance comprised 61 percent of total external assistance to the North.

South Korean conglomerates rapidly expanded their activities in the North with the official approval of both South and North Korean governments. Perhaps the most notable success has been the Kaesong Industrial Park, a special economic zone just north of the DMZ in the ancient capital city of Kaesong. Designed to use South Korean capital and North Korean labor, the zone includes roads and a rail line connecting North and South through the DMZ.[28] The first products from Kaesong, North Korean–made iron kitchen pots, became available in Seoul in December 2004, and they sold out in one day.[29] Currently shoes, clothes, electronic products, machinery, and some semiconductors and communication equipment are being produced at Kaesong, and production exceeded $100 million for the first time in 2006.[30]

Kaesong in some ways represents the most visible success of the South's engagement policy of the North. The actual economic benefit of Kaesong at this initial stage is minimal—it is estimated that the North earns less than $20 million annually in rent and taxes, and few of the South Korean companies currently operating (less than twenty) are profitable. However, the South Korean government planned to license another twenty firms to operate in Kaesong by the beginning of 2007, and Kaesong was explicitly excluded when the South reduced its aid to the North following the latter's missile tests of July 2006.[31]

South-North negotiations have covered a wide range of issues, such as reconnecting the railroads through the DMZ, repaving a road through the DMZ, creation of joint sports teams, family reunions, economic assistance, and most significantly, military discussions.[32] In 2004, the two sides agreed to the establishment of a hotline between North and South Korea, held the first high-level meeting between North and South Korean military generals since the Korean War, and halted the decades-long propaganda efforts along the DMZ.[33] The South Korean *2004 Defense White Paper* downgraded North Korea from the South's "main enemy" to a "direct and substantial threat to our military." In 2005, North and South Korea established three hundred direct telephone lines linking the South with the Kaesong Industrial Park, the first such link since Soviets troops severed telephone lines in 1945.

Growing contacts with the North reinforced the perception in South Korea that North Korea was more to be pitied than feared, and interactions between the North and South have increased in a number of noneconomic areas as well. The Hyundai group established a tour of Mount Kumgang on the east coast of North Korea, which more than 275,000 South Koreans visited in 2005; over 1.1 million have visited since 2000. In 2005 alone, more than 10,000 Koreans held cultural and social exchanges in the North, along with 660 separated family members.[34] Meetings between divided families have occurred on an intermittent basis, and both countries agreed to march together in the Olympics under the "unification flag."[35]

To be sure, there is much skepticism about Kim Jong-il's intentions and the extent of North Korea's market-socialism reform policies.[36] For example, Peter Hayes notes that "the regime is investing in minerals development, niche markets for exporting cheap labor or embodied labor, a bootstrapping sector, and real estate development on the DMZ that combined, represent a long-term and slowly growing economic foundation for a nuclear-armed DPRK."[37] Alternatively, Marcus Noland has an "essentially pessimistic" view of the North Korean reforms: "it is fair to say that the reforms have been a mixed bag, not delivering as expected and contributing to increasing social differentiation and inequality."[38]

The 2002 South Korean presidential election showed the degree of distance between the United States and South Korea on how to deal with the North. In large part, the election came down to a referendum on South Korea's stance toward North Korea and the United States. By a vote of 49.8 to 48.1 percent, voters chose Roh Moo-hyun, who favored continued engagement with the North, over more conservative Lee Hoi-chang, whose stance toward North Korea—suspending assistance until it cooperates on issues like arms control—more closely reflects America's. In electing Roh Moo-hyun by the largest share in modern Korean political history, voters voiced their displeasure with the Bush administration's inflexible stance.[39] Soon after his election, in January 2003, Roh Moo-hyun said that "South Korea ranks 12–13 in world economy and I want to preside over our strong nation as its strong president. All I am asking is an equal partnership with the United States."[40]

South Korean popular support for an engagement policy appears to be deeply rooted, and reflects the changing nature of South Korea's national identity. In the past decade, South Korea began to formulate a positive image and role for itself by rethinking its relationship to North Korea. After decades of demonizing the North, the South no longer defines itself as its opposite, but rather has begun to define itself as the North's "distant relative." In a way, it is not surprising that South Korean national identity has begun to change with respect to North Korea. Not only do both sides believe that they share a common history and culture, but by any measure—economic, political, cultural, or diplomatic—South Korea won the competition with the North. Thus it is relatively easy for South Korea to be magnanimous.

Although some argue that it is only the younger generation of South Koreans who support engagement, this is not in fact the case. Indeed, discussion about a generational rift in South Korea is somewhat overstated.[41] In reality, there is widespread agreement among the South Korean populace that engagement is the proper strategy to follow. For example, an opinion poll by South Korean newspaper *Dong-a Ilbo* found in March 2005 that 77 percent of Koreans supported the use of diplomatic means and talks with North Korea in response to the latter's nuclear weapons development and kidnapping of foreign civilians. Significantly, even those from the "older generations" were solidly in favor of engagement. Of those in their sixties or older, 63.6 percent supported diplomatic means.[42] In 2005, a Korean Institute for National Unification poll found that 85 percent of the general public and 95 percent of opinion leaders approved of North-South economic cooperation.[43]

In fact, a leftist (or "progressive") strand of South Korean politics is not new. Though masked during the Cold War, a long-running leftist element has existed in South Korean politics since the 1940s. Kim Kyung-won, a former ambassador to the United Nations and the United States under Chun Doo-hwan, made the following statement:

> South Korea has always had a deeply-held leftist strand of politics. Back in the 1940s it was probably stronger than the conservative forces, and only the U.S. military government allowed the right to win power. We thought [this strand] had disappeared under the military governments, but it did not. And now, it is back, reasserting itself.[44]

This leftist strand of politics was so strong that Park Chung-hee was forced to declare martial law from 1972 to 1979, during which time he temporarily closed the universities because of extensive student protests. After a coup d'etat in 1980, the entire city of Kwangju rose up in protest, and the demonstrations were only put down by the direct use of South Korean military units that were pulled off the DMZ.[45]

Given widespread South Korean popular support for engagement with the North, for electoral purposes both the opposition and ruling parties back that stance, too. In 2005, for example, the opposition Grand National Party—often considered more hard-line toward the North than the ruling Uri Party—submitted a proposal to establish a special economic zone along the entire border with North Korea to foster inter-Korean economic cooperation. The proposed zone would extend the current Kaesong industrial zone to Paju in Kyeonggi province in the South, with plans to expand the economic boundary from Haeju in the North to Incheon in the South as a joint inter-Korean project similar to the Kaesong zone.[46]

South Koreans could have arrived at a policy of coercion in their desire for unification. Yet a number of factors have combined to support an engagement strategy. First was the belief that outside powers—mainly the United States—were both exacerbating the division against the wishes of Koreans and also increasing the possibility of a devastating war on the peninsula. Second was the actual progress that has been made through the engagement strategy, however minimal. Events such as joint North-South athletic teams and tourist visits to the North have had a profound psychological impact in South Korea, emphasizing the commonality of Koreans on both sides of the DMZ.

Even in the wake of the North Korean nuclear tests of October 2006, South Koreans remained far more suspicious of U.S. motives, and more supportive of engagement, than many other countries. An opinion poll conducted in South Korea after the nuclear test found that 43 percent of South Koreans "blamed the U.S." for provoking a North Korean test, 37 percent blamed North Korea, and only 13 percent blamed South Korean engagement policies.[47] The South Korean Catholic Bishops Conference released a statement that week denouncing the nuclear test, but also reiterating support for its programs in the North: "For the recent several years, the South and the North have maintained peaceful exchanges, through which the two Koreas came to recognize the other not as an enemy but as one people, the same brethren . . . no one should block the way of reconciliation which the South and the North have paved through all efforts, nor should turn back the streams of the peace and unity running through the Korean peninsula."[48] Even the conservative opposition party, while calling for reductions in aid, remained willing to engage the North under more restrictive circumstances.[49] Although it imposed a few symbolic sanctions on the North, the South Korean government steadfastly refused to let U.N. Resolution 1718 significantly affect the Kaesong and Mount Kumgang joint economic ventures between the two countries.

In sum, unification through interdependence with North Korea is the keystone of South Korean foreign policy. Managing the nuclear issue has been a necessary step to reintegration, but South Korea's foreign policy over the past decade has reflected the more fundamental goal of unifying the peninsula. There is widespread popular support for an engagement policy, and this support show little signs of abating. Indeed, until national reconciliation is achieved, North Korea will be the overwhelming first priority of South Korean foreign policy.

CHINESE RELATIONS WITH THE KOREAN PENINSULA

The goal of integrating North Korea back into the region, and even eventual unification, is still only part of the strategic problem South Korea faces. South Korea—and a unified Korea—must find a way to live in a region with two massive countries (Japan and China), and a global superpower with interests in the region (the United States). There are no easy choices. To that end, this section assesses the degree of South Korea–Chinese economic cooperation and the degree to which Seoul welcomes or accepts increased Chinese regional influence in Northeast Asia. In both respects, developments in the past few years have arguably edged Korea closer to China.

THE LURE OF THE CHINA MARKET

Much like every other country in the region, South Korea increasingly sees its economic fate tied to the future of the Chinese economy. The potential benefits are large, especially given the two countries' geographic proximity and cultural similarities. Though there are clearly worries in South Korea over the rapid rise of Chinese manufacturing and technological prowess, this concern has not stopped the headlong rush of South Korean firms into China. Nor does the South Korean government resist regional moves— mostly initiated by China—to foster economic integration and open borders.

In terms of economic cooperation, China's attraction to South Korea was exemplified in 2003 when the PRC surpassed the United States as the largest export market for South Korean products—a position the United States had held since 1965.[50] Figure 5.1 shows total trade (imports and exports) between South Korea and China, Japan, and the United States. It is most notable that China has become the largest trading partner of South Korea and that that transition has taken place quickly.[51] In 2003 South Korea invested more in China than did the United States ($4.7 billion to $4.2 billion). In that same year, ROK exports to China increased 35 percent, to $47.5 billion, far surpassing South Korean exports to the United States, which increased 7 percent, to $36.7 billion.

Over 25,000 South Korean companies now have production facilities in China.[52] South Korea's Woori Bank has a 150-member research group focused on China, and by 2004 all the major South Korean banks had opened branch offices in China.[53]

China's increased importance to South Korea is evident not just in economic interactions. For example, the number of Chinese language schools in South Korea increased 44 percent from 2003 to 2005.[54] Over 1.6 million South Koreans visit China each year, and the numbers continue to grow.[55] In 2003, there were 35,000 South Koreans studying at Chinese universities (comprising 46 percent of all foreign students in China), while over 180,000 South Koreans had become long-term residents in China.[56]

FIGURE 5.1   SOUTH KOREA'S MAJOR TRADE PARTNERS, 1990–2005

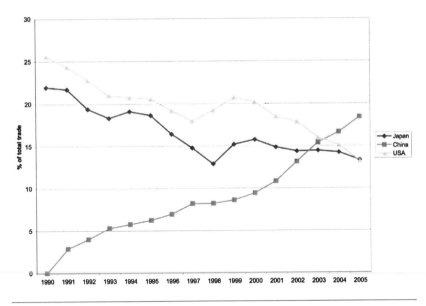

SOURCE: STRATEGIC ASIA ONLINE, HTTP://STRATEGICASIA.NBR.ORG/.

As noted in chapter 3, South Korea–China relations are warm and only becoming more so. Public opinion reflects this trend. For example, an April 2005 poll conducted by *Dong-a Ilbo* newspaper in South Korea revealed the extent of South Korean perceptions about the United States and China. Asked which country was most important for South Korea to have good relations with, 35.5 percent chose North Korea, 28.7 chose the United States, and 22.1 chose China. Similarly, 17.3 percent of respondents saw the United States as the most threatening to Korea, while only 6.7 percent saw China that way. When asked about potential concerns relating to China, 26 percent chose negative economic consequences, and only 8 percent chose China's military buildup.[57]

ROK-China relations have not been completely smooth, however. In recent years the two countries have clashed verbally over the nature of the ancient kingdom of Koguryo (37 B.C.–668 A.D.), with both sides claiming that Koguryo was an historical antecedent to their modern nation.[58] This dispute does not, however, appear likely to have any substantive effect on relations between the two countries, in part because it does not involve official Chinese government policy but rather comes from unofficial claims by Chinese academics.[59] China and North Korea formally delineated their border in

1962, with China ceding 60 percent of the disputed territory. In contrast to South Korea's territorial dispute with Japan over the Dokdo/Takeshima islands, which has never been formally resolved, the dispute over Koguryo is restricted to claims about history, and at no time has the Chinese government made any attempt to abrogate the 1962 treaty or renegotiate the actual border.[60]

Of more relevance is the fact that individual South Korean firms are increasingly finding themselves in direct competition with Chinese manufacturers. Korea's technological lead over Chinese firms has shrunk more rapidly than was anticipated even a few years ago. Currently, South Korean firms have an estimated 3–5 years lead on their Chinese counterparts, down from a 10-year margin just a few years ago.[61] While it is unlikely that in the immediate future this will become a source of trade friction between the two countries, it serves to remind South Koreans that close relations with China are not an unmixed blessing.

CHINESE INFLUENCE

China's recent influence over the North Korea–U.S. standoff is further evidence of its emerging role in the region. Much of the conventional wisdom has viewed China's role in the "six-party talks" (involving Russia, China, Japan, North and South Korea, and the United States) as a temporary matter, and expect that any Chinese influence will recede when the crisis is resolved. However, it may be just as likely that East Asian states are witnessing China emerge (or reemerge) as a leader in the region, with (perhaps unwitting) U.S. assistance. Chung-min Lee writes that "the growing role of China vis-à-vis the North Korean nuclear crisis . . . is resulting in a reevaluation of China's overall relationship with the two Koreas. On-going complications and tensions in the R.O.K.-U.S. alliance have also contributed to a more open view of possibilities in South Korean–Chinese relationship."[62]

The difference between regional perspectives and that of the United States became pronounced during the second nuclear crisis. During the six-party talks, policymakers from China, Russia, South Korea, and even occasionally Japan began to implicitly or explicitly criticize U.S. policies as being too confrontational, and all four urged some degree of economic engagement and diplomatic restraint. Most significantly, China and South Korea began to privately and publicly advocate positions that were more moderate than the American position. For example, in June 2004, Zhou Wenzhong, China's deputy foreign minister, said, "We know nothing about [North Korea's] uranium program. We don't know whether it exists. So far the U.S. has not presented convincing evidence of this program. . . . The United States is accusing North Korea of having this or that, and then attaching conditions [to negotiations]. So it should really be the U.S. that takes the initiative."[63] As one experienced member of a nongovernmental organization that has deep ties with North Korea noted recently, "China is essentially pushing aid and economic relations over the border to the North. They have far more access to the North than South Korea does, and this is worrying the South Koreans as they look to the coming years."[64]

In fact, Chinese trade and investment into North Korea outstrips even that of South Korea—almost two thirds of total North Korean trade in 2005 was with China, nearly double the amount of inter-Korean trade.[65] Without Chinese cooperation, a U.S. attempt to isolate the North will be difficult, if not impossible, to bring to success. Indeed, Kim Jong-il's nine-day visit to Chinese industrial zones in January 2006 was evidence that China continues to have warm relations with the North, and that China intends to continue its engagement policy, showing no signs of taking a more coercive stance toward the North.

Furthermore, as the stalemate dragged on, Chinese officials made public pronouncements urging a conciliatory line to the North, and arguing that North Korea was on the path to reform. In January 2005, Li Bin, the Chinese ambassador to South Korea, argued, "To think that North Korea will collapse is far-fetched speculation. The fundamental problem is the North's ailing economy. If the economic situation improves, I think we can resolve the defector problem. The support of the South Korean government will greatly help North Korea in this respect."[66] Other Chinese commentators have echoed this sentiment. In early 2005, Piao Jianyi of the Institute of Asia Pacific Studies in Beijing said that "although many of our friends see it as a failing state, potentially one with nuclear weapons, China has a different view. North Korea has a reforming economy that is very weak, but every year is getting better, and the regime is taking measures to reform its economy, so perhaps the U.S. should reconsider its approach."[67]

As one newspaper report put it in June 2004:

Mr. Bush appears to have been pushed by those allies, at least according to the accounts offered up by Asian officials—and confirmed by some but not all—of their American counterparts. For months, diplomats from China, Japan and South Korea have worried that the talks with North Korea were going nowhere, and they have described Mr. Kim and Mr. Bush as equally stubborn.[68]

One scholar characterizes current trends this way: "gazing into the crystal ball, this is what [experts] see: the withdrawal of the 37,000 troops currently stationed in the South; a strong Korean peninsula threatening Japan; a tilting balance of regional power—in China's favor; and the United States in direct confrontation with China."[69] Jae-Ho Chung writes, "China's growing influence over the Korean peninsula is real. The bottom line for Seoul is not to antagonize China; in this regard, South Korea being sucked into a U.S.-China conflict over Taiwan or elsewhere must be avoided."[70]

In sum, despite some tensions in the ROK-China relationship, on the whole China has rapidly become an extremely important economic and diplomatic partner for South Korea. South Korea has warm and increasingly close relations with China along a range of security, economic, and diplomatic issues and does not want to be forced to choose between Beijing and Washington. Although there is little sentiment in Seoul to replace the United States with China as South Korea's closest ally—and despite Seoul regarding Beijing's influence in Pyongyang as worrisome—continued improvement in Seoul's relations with Beijing means that South Korea's foreign policy orientation is gradually shifting. Though still important, the United States is no longer the only powerful country to which South Korea must pay attention.

The events of the past few decades have led to a fundamental shift in South Korea's foreign policy orientation, its attitudes toward the United States and China, and its own self-image. However, in a process that Jae-ho Chung calls "the choice of not making choices," although South Korea and China have increasingly close economic and cultural ties, and share a similar foreign policy orientation toward North Korea, South Korea has not bandwagoned with China, nor does it wish to abandon its close ties with the United States.[71]

As Victor Cha writes:

> The net assessment therefore is that in terms of grand strategic choices, South Korea has edged down the path of being cut "adrift," [moving away from the U.S. and closer to China] but not yet by definitive leaps and bounds. . . . The fact that no clear direction has been set out over the past year is testament to the genuine state of flux in the ROK's strategic direction.[72]

THE CHANGING U.S.-ROK ALLIANCE

The U.S.-ROK alliance is under greater strain than ever before. While South Korea has clearly not abandoned the United States for the embrace of China, and while cooperation and interaction is still deeper with the United States than with China, South Korea has moved in the direction of warmer ties with China and less dependence on the United States. This has been a slow process, but the events of the past few years have accelerated the trend. Indeed, it is increasingly possible that the U.S.-ROK alliance will change in a fundamental way. In part this is a natural evolution, but it also reflects starkly different perspectives between the two countries on major international issues. As Scott Snyder notes, "the alliance appears demonstrably less important to both Americans and South Koreans than it was during the Cold War."[73]

The U.S.-ROK alliance has succeeded beyond expectations in maintaining peace at the strategic crossroads of Northeast Asia, promoting South Korean economic development, and helping one of East Asia's most vibrant and successful democracies emerge. The United States, of course, pursued mutual U.S.-ROK security interests in maintaining regional peace, which was the prerequisite for South Korean development. These Koreans overwhelmingly value the U.S.-ROK alliance and welcome a U.S. military presence in their country—indeed, there remains deep appreciation and warmth for the United States. George Washington University professor Kirk Larson notes that there continues to be "substantial support for the alliance and a continued U.S. military presence in South Korea."[74]

Contrary to public perceptions, both sides value the alliance and their long-standing relationship, and the ROK has sought to cooperate with the United States in many diverse areas in hopes of strengthening the alliance. For example, South Korea provided the largest contingent of troops to Iraq after the United States and United Kingdom. The relocation of U.S. military bases outside of Seoul proceeded with minimal protest, and U.S. and South Korean negotiators are holding discussions about a free-trade agreement between the two countries. [75]

The most central aspect in the relationship is the military alliance that has been in effect since 1953. However, this alliance is embedded within a much larger U.S.-ROK relationship that has grown dramatically in the past half century. With bilateral trade of over $55 billion in 2002, South Korea is a major trading partner of the United States. U.S. firms invested almost $5 billion in South Korea in 2004.[76]

There are real differences, and real changes in perceptions and attitudes, between the United States and South Korean people regarding the U.S. role in South Korea, policy toward North Korea, and the U.S. and South Korean roles in East Asia. Understanding the history of the U.S.-ROK alliance, and more broadly the interaction between the United States and Korea over the last century, sheds light on the context in which South Koreans view the United States and how the bilateral relationship has reached its current state in 2007.

There are domestic divisions in South Korea over the utility of the U.S.-ROK alliance, over policy toward North Korea, the global "war on terror" being pursued by the United States, and South Korea's relations with the other powers in the region.[77] While differences over how to deal with North Korea are nothing new, these were often tactical, resolved in large part because of the common perception that North Korea represented a serious security threat. In recent years, however, Seoul finds the Bush administration's apparent interest in fostering Pyongyang's collapse or in using military force to be unacceptable, since both events would threaten progress made over the past three decades. Magnified by other tensions in the relationship—increasing South Korean self-confidence and pride, anti-Americanism, and concerns about U.S. unilateralism—the Bush approach to North Korea has become the prism through which many South Koreans view the security relationship. Eric Larson notes, "The ongoing nuclear crisis and what is perceived as a harsh position on the part of the U.S. toward North Korea seems to have led to growing concern among many South Koreans that U.S. actions could pose as great a threat to South Korea as North Korean ones."[78] A September 2003 *JoongAng Ilbo* poll found that the United States was simultaneously the most-liked and the second-most-disliked country in South Korea.

The split in the two countries' approaches to North Korea became clear soon after the election of George W. Bush in 2000. The Bush administration began adding new conditions to the Agreed Framework (AF) early on in its tenure. The AF was signed between the United States and North Korea in October 1994, as a means of resolving concerns about North Korea's nuclear facilities, and involved reciprocal steps that both sides would take to allay each other's concerns. Yet on June 6, 2001, the White House included conventional forces in the requirements it wanted North Korea to fulfill, saying, "The U.S. seeks improved implementation [of the AF], prompt inspections of past reprocessing . . . [and] a less threatening conventional military posture." On July 3, 2001, a senior administration official said, "We need to see some progress in all areas . . . we don't feel any urgency to provide goodies to them [the North Koreans]."[79] Given South Korea's engagement of the North, many in the South began to worry that the increasingly hard-line U.S. stance was actually provoking the North.

With the October 2002 crisis over a second North Korean nuclear program, U.S. and South Korean positions openly diverged. The South Korean populace and leadership urged restraint, while the Bush administration took a harder line. In his 2002 State of the Union address, President Bush included North Korea in the "axis of evil" along with Iraq and Iran, and later offered other choice negative personal opinions about Kim Jong-Il (referring to Kim as a "pygmy" and how he "loathed" him), after which many speculated a dark future for U.S.-DPRK relations.[80] As the crisis intensified, Colin Powell refused to consider dialogue with the North, remarking, "We cannot suddenly say 'Gee, we're so scared. Let's have a negotiation because we want to appease your misbehavior.'"[81] The South Koreans were concerned that the Bush administration's open embrace of preemptive war as an instrument of national policy would make North Korea a potential target, with Seoul—and South Korea—being the victims and bearing the brunt of the devastation that would follow.

On the other hand, many in the United States were skeptical as to the wisdom of South Korea's policy on North Korea. Indeed, South Korea's adamant refusal to take a harder line toward North Korea has led some analysts to call its foreign policy "appeasement," thus increasing friction with the United States. Nicholas Eberstadt of the American Enterprise Institute called South Korea "a runaway ally," arguing that the U.S. ought to "work around" the Roh administration.[82] The Cato Institute called for an "amicable divorce" between South Korea and the United States, and researchers Ted Galen Carpenter and Doug Bandow suggested that the alliance should be dissolved.[83] In the *Wall Street Journal*, Bruce Gilley even advocated that China invade North Korea in order to force regime change.[84]

In 2005, President Roh Moo-hyun made some unusually direct comments on U.S. policies toward North Korea. The United States had begun to publicly pressure his country to take a more active stance against the North's illegal financial activities, such as counterfeiting U.S. money. Roh said:

> I don't agree (with) some opinions inside the US that appear to be wanting to take issue with North Korea's regime, apply pressure and sometimes wishing for its collapse. If the US government tries to resolve the problem that way, there will be friction and disagreement between South Korea and the US.[85]

When the United States released a press statement through the U.S. Embassy in Seoul "urging" South Korea to take action against North Korean financial transactions, the South Korean Foreign Ministry released a response calling the U.S. press release "inappropriate."[86]

The South Korean Embassy in Washington argued that "a more confrontational U.S. policy approach is not likely to bear fruit. North Korea has never succumbed to external pressure over the past fifty years, despite the wishes of foreign ideologues."[87] In Seoul, the liberal newspaper *Hankyoreh Shinmun* editorialized that "the Koreans should resolve their own problems, including the nuclear issue."[88] Over one hundred respected figures in Korean society, including Catholic Cardinal Stephen Kim, sent an open letter to the U.S. Embassy in Seoul, urging the U.S. ambassador to reject military options.[89]

Most of the South Korean public clearly opposes the U.S.-led efforts. Only 15 percent of South Koreans surveyed in the summer 2002 considered terrorism to be a national priority.[90] Victor Cha writes that 72 percent of South Korea opposed the U.S.-led war on terrorism (Table 5.1). In the run-up to the war in Iraq in March 2003, 81 percent of the general public opposed U.S.-led military action against Iraq and only 9.7 percent supported it; 75.6 percent opposed the deployment of ROK combat troops to Iraq and only 16 percent supported it.[91] A survey of South Korean college students in October 2003 found that 88 percent believed the U.S. initiated a war against Iraq without justifiable cause and only 4.7 percent thought the U.S. justified in its actions.[92]

While South Korea—and perhaps even a unified Korea—will continue to seek good relations with the United States, it is also becoming clear that South Korea will not blindly follow the U.S. lead in the future. With increasing ties to China, and with a younger generation that is not interested in kowtowing to the United States, South Korean is perhaps the strongest example that the world does not fear China the way we think it should.

The U.S.-ROK alliance is still strong, and China has not yet become the regional leader in Northeast Asia. However, compared to fifteen years ago, the U.S. influence is diminished, and China's influence has clearly increased. Over the long run, the United States has not articulated any fundamental strategy toward the region other than ridding North Korea of nuclear weap-

TABLE 5.1   AMERICAN AND SOUTH KOREAN VIEWS OF THE "WAR ON TERROR"

	SOUTH KOREANS	AMERICANS
View terrorism as a "very big" or "moderately big" problem	44%	87%
Favor U.S. war on terrorism	24%	89%
Agree with U.S. military action in Afghanistan	43%	88%

SOURCE: ADAPTED FROM ERIC LARSON AND NORMAN LEVIN, *AMBIVALENT ALLIES? A STUDY OF SOUTH KOREAN ATTITUDES TOWARD THE U.S.* (SANTA MONICA, CALIF.: RAND, 2004), P. 72. ORIGINALLY SOURCED FROM PEW CENTER FOR PEOPLE AND THE PRESS, JUNE 2003; PEW CENTER FOR PEOPLE AND THE PRESS, DECEMBER 2002; GALLUP INTERNATIONAL, DECEMBER 2001.

ons. This means that if and when the nuclear issue is resolved, South Korea and the U.S. may not have the same interests in how the region should look, in who should be the leader, and may not be able to agree on where the threats are. Even the conservatives in Seoul recognize that the traditional Cold War alliance with the United States will inevitably change, and they hope to find some way of dealing with China while retaining their U.S. relationship.

Moreover, China's rise is forcing South Korea to confront a region radically different from the past fifty years. While most international relations theory, and indeed, most American policymakers, see the United States as the most obvious and benign ally with which South Korea should ally, China's proximity and its massive size mean that South Korea can no longer ignore it. Far from being threatened by China, South Korea in fact shares similar policy orientations on short-run issues such as the best way to solve the nuclear crisis.

Furthermore, South Korea shows no signs of security fears regarding China, and even is willing to let China take the lead on some regional issues, such as how to resolve the second North Korean nuclear crisis. Even those South Korean conservatives do not advocate a balancing posture against China. Thus, while there may be a transition occurring in East Asia, it is clear that the pessimistic predictions regarding China's rise have not begun to manifest themselves on the Korean peninsula. Rather than fearing China, South Korea appears to be adjusting to China's place in Northeast Asia.

CHAPTER 6

SOUTHEAST ASIA

ACCOMMODATING CHINA'S RISE

The states of Southeast Asia have moved further to create multilateral institutions and to accommodate China than have those in Northeast Asia. Furthermore, the tight military alliances that exist between the United States and Japan and Korea are absent in Southeast Asia, and Southeast Asia is ethnically more integrated with China than is Northeast Asia. Even some states that previously had close relations with the United States, such as the Philippines, have begun a process by which the United States becomes no longer the main focus of their foreign policies. These states are increasingly taking both the United States and China into account. Like Japan and South Korea in Northeast Asia, however, Southeast Asian states also want to avoid a zero-sum choice between either China or the United States. They hope instead for a situation in which they benefit from rising Chinese economic power but also continue to maintain good relations with the United States.

This strategy of accommodating China while staying close to the United States arises because of the potential benefits that come from engaging China, and also because of the efforts that China has itself made to engage these countries and reassure them of its intentions. China and the Southeast Asian states place a high value on respecting sovereignty and pursuing nation-building, and this similarity of perspectives has been a key reason why China and Southeast Asia have managed to adjust and learn to cooperate over numerous issues. These states also view the likelihood that China will use military force in the region as low. They prefer a strong and active China to a weak and preoccupied China, they see continued economic growth as beneficial for the region, and they have moved to include China in a number of bilateral and multilateral institutions.

This trend toward cooperation is especially apparent when compared to the dynamics in the region thirty years ago. The end of the Vietnam War marked the end of a period of instability in Southeast Asia. There were exceptions—Cambodia and Burma, for example—yet on the whole, an era notable for its economic growth and domestic nation building began. More recently, the U.S. actions during the 1997 Asian financial crisis, and its policies during its "global war on terror," have led many in Southeast Asia to question the legitimacy of U.S. actions and leadership. As a senior Singaporean diplomat concluded in 2004:

> The balance of influence is shifting against the United States. In the last decade the Chinese have not done anything wrong in Southeast Asia. The Japanese have not done anything right, and the U.S. has been indifferent. So already Thailand, Laos, Cambodia, and other states are defining their national interest as "Finlandization" with respect to China. The U.S. will never be shut out of Southeast Asia completely, but there is less room for it now than in the past fifty years.[1]

In this chapter, after an overview of the "ASEAN way" in the first section, we will focus on China's actions toward Southeast Asia, showing how in the past three decades the Chinese have actively engaged the region and attempted to reassure these states through a variety of measures. The next section examines Southeast Asian perspectives of China, concluding that these states are more inclined to accommodate rather than balance. The fourth and fifth sections present two short case studies of the Philippines and Vietnam. The Philippines is the closest U.S. ally (and a former U.S. colony) in the region, and Vietnam only normalized relations with the United States recently. Thus both their foreign policy strategies can shed particular light on the conundrums facing Southeast Asian states. A sixth section examines the U.S. role in Southeast Asia, emphasizing the different U.S. and Southeast Asian views of the Asian financial crisis and the global war on terror.

THE "ASEAN WAY"

Policymakers in Southeast Asia emphasize that the Association of Southeast Asian Nations (ASEAN) has developed in order to manage complexity in the region, not to balance any particular outside power. Southeast Asia comprises a number of overlapping subgroups, including the small states such as Singapore and the Pacific island states, the continental states such as Vietnam and Thailand, and the Islamic states such as Indonesia and Malaysia. They vary politically, economically, ethnically, religiously, and culturally. Yet they also form a distinct region, one that is already deeply interconnected and integrated, and growing more so as time passes. As Andrew Shearer of the Australian Embassy in the United States remarked, "this plethora of overlapping and multiple systems has led to a functional, bottom-up approach to regionalism, with multiple views and systems depending on the specific issue at hand."[2]

Scholarship on Southeast Asia that emphasizes the role of ideas is well developed, and takes as its main focus ASEAN. Going beyond realist notions of power, a group of scholars have argued that explaining ASEAN's emergence and influence in regional affairs is not possible without reference to the norms and identities that have existed in Southeast Asia. This scholarship emphasizes the "ASEAN way," a set of norms that emphasize security cooperation in East Asia, noninterference in domestic issues, respect for sovereignty, and nonconfrontational dialogue building.[3] Amitav Acharya defines the ASEAN way as a "process of regional interactions and cooperation based on discreteness, informality, consensus building and non-confrontational bargaining styles" that stands in contrast to the "adversarial posturing, majority vote and other legalistic decision-making procedures in Western multilateral organizations."[4] Indeed, Southeast Asian states have always had a tendency to avoid balancing coalitions. For example, the U.S.-led SEATO (Southeast Asian Treaty Organization) had comprised only four Southeast Asian countries—Thailand, the Philippines, Australia, and New Zealand.[5]

This set of norms, and in particular the concern for national sovereignty, came about partially because Southeast Asia has undergone tremendous change in the nineteenth century, when only Thailand avoided being colonized by Western powers. Southeast Asian countries only regained their independence in the post–World War II era. Of the larger Southeast Asian states, the Philippines first achieved independence, in 1946. Indonesia followed in 1949, and Malaysia (and Singapore) in 1957. With the unification of Vietnam and the end of the Vietnam War in 1975, the states of Southeast Asia all experienced varying degrees of peace, economic prosperity, national consolidation, and participation in flourishing regional integration.[6] Given the ethnic, religious, and racial divisions within each of these heterogeneous states, their main objectives included domestic political unity, nation building, and protecting their national sovereignty from external interference. As Acharya writes, "it was during the 1960s that the moderate nationalist leaders of Southeast Asia saw regionalism as a way of preserving their state security and regime survival not from neo-colonial pressures, but from the twin dangers of Cold War superpower rivalry and domestic communist insurgencies."[7]

Thailand, Malaysia, Singapore, Indonesia, and the Philippines founded ASEAN in 1967 with the aim of preventing major powers from using the region as a battleground.[8] The founding ASEAN-5 were originally supportive of active U.S. containment of communism in Southeast Asia. For example, none of the original members had normalized ties with China (Indonesia had normalized ties with China in 1950, only to suspend them in 1967 over suspicions of Chinese support for the Indonesian communist party).

Placed in the historical context we examined in chapter 2, Southeast Asian states' suspicions regarding China were relatively new, resulting mainly from China's post-1949 policies, and most notably over suspected Chinese support for internal communist movements.[9] Before 1949, Southeast Asian nations had had stable and deep relations with China, whereas during the Cold War, the Chinese were occasional supporters of the communist parties in Malaysia, Indonesia, and Vietnam. For its part, after the end of civil war in 1949, China became relatively isolated in international affairs.[10] On the whole, China during the Cold War focused more on internal problems, and was not actively involved in the world economy due to trade embargoes from Western and many Asian nations. China was preoccupied with domestic factional struggles, the Great Leap Forward of the late 1950s, the Cultural Revolution of 1966–1976, and its troubled relations with the Soviet Union. By the late 1960s, China's foreign policy had become much less radical, even though relations with Southeast Asia remained cool.

As the United States and China moved toward rapprochement in the early 1970s, as the Vietnam War wound down and the U.S. military presence diminished in Southeast Asia, and as China began to reintegrate itself into the world, the Southeast Asian nations began to normalize relations with China. Malaysia did so in 1974; Thailand and the Philippines, in 1975. Singapore and Indonesia did not normalize relations with China until 1990.

CHINA'S FOREIGN POLICY TOWARD SOUTHEAST ASIA

China has increasingly sought to reassure Southeast Asian states about its intentions. China has had deep historical trading ties throughout the region, and builds upon this long history as well as its current interactions.[11] Brantley Womack points out three Chinese policies that have helped to create a nonthreatening diplomatic environment in Southeast Asia for it. The first policy itself encompasses China's "Five Principles of Peaceful Coexistence," from the Bandung conference of 1955. These relatively noncontroversial principles are mutual respect for sovereignty and territorial integrity, mutual nonaggression, noninterference in one another's internal affairs, equality and mutual benefit, and peaceful coexistence. China's concern for sovereignty and noninterference fit well with ASEAN's similar concerns. The second policy is one of economic reform and opening that China has pursued for the past three decades. Finally, China's policy of multipolarity in the 1990s helped assuage Southeast Asian fears of Chinese aggrandizement.[12] As noted in chapter 4, China's own preoccupation with maintaining its sovereignty and with internal nation building fit quite well with Southeast Asia's devotion to the same goals. Both the Southeast Asian region and China had experienced extensive external interference in their affairs for over a century, and both were focused on the task of solidifying and strengthening their countries.

In the past two decades, China actively pursued preventive diplomacy in what it viewed as a multipolar world, and in particular it began to engage and court states in Southeast Asia. This strategy became pronounced following the Tiananmen Square incident in 1989, in which Chinese authorities used force to suppress a protest in Beijing that had drawn worldwide attention. Realizing that other states viewed China with suspicion, Beijing began to actively cultivate better relations with its Southeast Asian neighbors. In 1990, Chinese Premier Li Peng visited Indonesia, Singapore, Thailand, Malaysia, the Philippines, and Laos. These moves included normalization within two years of Chinese relations with Singapore, Vietnam, Indonesia, Brunei, and South Korea.

Beijing began participating in multilateral forums, something it had previously avoided. Foreign Minister Qian Qichen's visit to the 24th ASEAN Foreign Ministers Meeting in July 1991 marked the first formal contact with ASEAN.[13] Although originally Beijing had attempted to negotiate with the Southeast Asian states on a bilateral basis, when ASEAN stood firm China adjusted, and worked cooperatively with ASEAN itself. Most significantly, Beijing began to discuss the Spratly Islands dispute in these multilateral settings, while also reaching bilateral accord with Malaysia and the Philippines over the islands.[14] Womack writes that "frustrated by the west, and duly noting the respectful silence of Southeast Asia and South Korea, China began sustained efforts to improve regional relations."[15] China became a dialogue partner of ASEAN in 1996, and in 1997 joined "ASEAN+3" (China, South Korea, and Japan). China and ASEAN also pursued the ASEAN-China Free Trade Area (ACFTA), portions of which began implementation in 2005.[16]

China's unwillingness to take advantage of the Asian financial crisis of 1997 furthered Southeast Asian views of China as a responsible actor in the region. China did not devalue its currency at the time, and this was interpreted by ASEAN as a sign of goodwill. China pledged $1 billion to Thailand to help assuage its foreign exchange problem; it also pledged $400 million to Indonesia in standby loans as part of the IMF package, and further extended Indonesia $200 million in export credits.[17] In 1998, then-ASEAN Secretary-General Rodolfo Severino, Jr., said that "China is really emerging from this [crisis] smelling good. We still have a territorial problem with China, but otherwise things here are going well between ASEAN and Beijing."[18] Malaysian leader Mohammed Mahatir said in 1999:

China's performance in the Asian financial crisis has been laudable, and the countries in this region . . . greatly appreciated China's decision not to devalue the yuan. China's cooperation and high sense of responsibility has spared the region a much worse consequence. The price China has to pay to help East Asia is high, and the Malaysian people truly appreciate China's stand.[19]

Chinese efforts to reach out to Southeast Asia continued in the 2000s. In Bali in October 2003, China became the first large power from outside of ASEAN to sign the Treaty of Amity and Cooperation in Southeast Asia. The treaty includes pledges to avoid disputes and to resolve those that do occur, by peaceful means, and renounces the threat of force.[20] In 2004, Chinese Prime Minister Wen Jiabao described China as "a friendly elephant," recognizing its size, but arguing that it poses no threat to Southeast Asia.[21] Zheng Bijian, a close advisor to China's top leadership, said that "if China does not provide economic opportunities in the region, it will lose the opportunity for a peaceful rise."[22] Chinese President Hu Jintao said in 2004 that China would seek security dialogues with all the Southeast Asian states. Hu said that "China is ready to set up a military-security-dialogue mechanism with other Asian countries and actively promote confidence building in the military field."[23] One Chinese diplomat who worked for three years in Southeast Asia during the 1990s told me,

China today is not the same as it was before. From 1949, sometimes they [Southeast Asian nations] even thought we were exporting revolution to their countries. But today we want good relations for our own economic growth. Southeast Asia doesn't know us that well, but more and more, as we interact, they come to see us for who we are. They will always have problems with China just because of our size, but they also see the value in good relations. China is not that ideological anymore. The United States is more ideological than we are.[24]

Chinese actions indicate more than just a reassurance strategy. They reflect China's view of itself and the region. Southeast Asian states, long wary of external interference in their affairs, and focused on economic development and political consolidation, have seen that China does not have imperial aims in Southeast Asia, and is in fact moving on political, economic, and cultural fronts to improve relations with that region.

SOUTHEAST ASIA'S APPROACH TO CHINA

Southeast Asian states see their economic future as heavily influenced by China's economy, and trade and investment between ASEAN and China has been rapidly increasing. Yet the ties involve more than trade. Southeast Asian states are culturally and ethnically linked with China, and this, combined with a long history of stable relations, helps shape how they view China. There is still caution about China and its role, if only because the region itself has undergone so much change in the past half century. Nevertheless, the trend is clearly toward greater cooperation.

In the past thirty years, China has become an important economic actor in Southeast Asia. And in the past five years alone, China-ASEAN trade has increased at rates of over 30 percent annually.[25] While U.S. total trade (exports and imports) with ASEAN ($148 billion in 2005) remains marginally greater than Chinese total trade with ASEAN ($130 billion in 2005), the gap is closing quickly (see Figure 6.1). As recently as 2000, total Chinese trade with ASEAN was only $39 billion. In 2005, Chinese exports to ASEAN exceeded U.S. exports to ASEAN for the first time.[26] Indeed, in July 2005, China, Brunei, Malaysia, Myanmar, Singapore, and Thailand implemented reciprocal tariff reductions on over 7,455 types of goods and commodities, as part of progress toward an ASEAN-China Free Trade Zone.[27] In 2005, China pledged $3 billion in economic assistance to ASEAN countries.[28]

China and Southeast Asia have also taken a series of steps to increase intra–Southeast Asian cooperation, and this has been part of a wider effort by both parties to expand cooperation regionally and globally. By 2006, China and ASEAN had established 46 dialogue mechanisms at different levels, including 12 at the ministerial level.[29] Although these multilateral institutions have experienced varying degrees of success, the region itself is not the

FIGURE 6.1 ASEAN TOTAL TRADE WITH UNITED STATES AND CHINA, 2000–2005

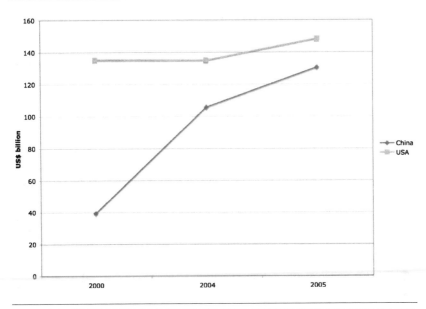

SOURCE: DATA COMPILED FROM BRUCE VAUGHN AND WAYNE MORRISON, *CHINA–SOUTHEAST ASIA RELA-TIONS: TRENDS, ISSUES, AND IMPLICATIONS FOR THE UNITED STATES* (WASHINGTON, D.C.: CONGRESSIO-NAL RESEARCH SERVICE, 2006), PP. 10–12.

same as it was in 1990. In addition to explicitly economic ties, ASEAN-China relations include the ASEAN-China Senior Officials Consultations, ASEAN-China Joint Cooperation Committee meetings, and ASEAN-China summits. Another significant move was the Chiang Mai initiative—a currency swap arrangement among Asian states designed to help prevent the currency crisis that led to the 1997 Asian financial crisis. Although ASEAN signed a "Strategic Partnership for Peace and Prosperity" with China, it has also signed an ASEAN-Japan "Strategic Partnership," an ASEAN–South Korea "Comprehensive Cooperation Partnership," and an ASEAN-India "Partnership for Peace, Progress, and Shared Prosperity."[30] Thus, China is increasingly important, but Southeast Asian states are also focused on a wide range of cooperative mechanisms with states around the globe.

Jose Almonte, former director general of the Philippine National Security Council, noted that "East Asia's greatest single problem is how to incorporate China into its regional arrangements—how to 'socialize' the country."[31] He wrote in 1997, "Southeast Asians are more ready to accept that China will sooner or later become a great power, and that it is unrealistic for outsiders to prevent such a development."[32] Singaporean Prime Minister Goh Tok Chong said that "it makes no sense to mortgage East Asia's future by causing the Chinese people to conclude that its neighbors and the U.S. want to keep them down."[33] Singapore has most actively moved to engage China, and has the most clearly articulated engagement policy. For example, in 1994, Goh said,

> It is not preordained that China's military power will turn into a threat, or that it will behave like the former Soviet Union . . . [But] China must show through its attitude and action that, big as it will be, it intends to be a responsible member of the international community.[34]

Southeast Asia's orientation toward China is reflected in its numerous actions. Singapore has a policy to lure Chinese companies to the island, offering generous terms for listing on the stock exchange. For its part, Indonesia has signed memoranda of understandings with China over defense technological cooperation, tsunami relief, economic and technical cooperation, and other issues.[35] China's energy companies have invested into Indonesian oil and gas fields in Java and Papua, and Indonesian exports to China increased 232 percent in 2005.[36]

Of Thailand, a report by the Congressional Research Service concludes that it "appears to be relatively comfortable with expanding ties with China."[37] After the U.S.-China "spy plane incident" of 2001, Thai Prime Minister Thaksin Shinawatra offered to broker talks between the two superpowers, emphasizing that the Thais and Chinese have a relationship that goes back centuries. Shinawatra added, "economically, China is also a big market and Thailand must have a good relationship with her." Gaye Christofferson noted that "Thai newspapers reflected a Chinese tilt. One article claimed that 'most Thais regard China as more of a friend of Thailand than the United States or Japan.'"[38] Indeed, Chinese Defense Minister Chi Haotian held talks with Thailand's defense minister in June 2001, two months after the incident.

Thus, on political and economic relations, the states of Southeast Asia are also moving closer to China.

THE CHINESE "BAMBOO" NETWORK

Southeast Asian relations with China rest on more than just the pragmatic creation of economic ties and cooperative institutions, however important those may be. Southeast Asia's integration with China is as much a result of the webs of ethnic Chinese throughout Southeast Asia who have rapidly reestablished their historical trade and investment relationships with China as it is of more formal institutional relations. These ethnic links, often referred to as the "bamboo network," or "greater China," are weaving Southeast Asian and Chinese economies and societies tightly together.[39] Ethnic Chinese make up 10 percent of Thailand's population, 3 percent in Indonesia, 2 percent in the Philippines, and almost 20 percent in Malaysia. Furthermore, the ethnic Chinese in Southeast Asia tend to be economically well positioned relative to the indigenous populations. As Gerald Curtis writes, "It is not simply a matter of China's becoming an important export and FDI [foreign direct investment] destination for other countries in Asia. The pattern of trade and investment is creating production process networks that crisscross the region . . . the consequence is not only growing economic interdependence but the beginnings of significant economic integration."[40]

Dajin Peng notes that "the core of the ethnic Chinese business network consists of relatively tight relations cemented by kinship and lineages."[41] Singaporean banks and investors are a major part of this—Singapore's DBS bank bought shares of banks in Thailand and Hong Kong and the Philippines.[42] As T. J. Pempel writes, "By the mid-to late 1990s . . . a dense web of networks in manufacturing and banking was crisscrossing East Asia. Corporations with quite different types of internal organization and varying degrees of flexibility were involved."[43] Hongying Wang has shown that informal personal relationships based on *guanxi* (personal connections) have facilitated FDI into China.[44] Ethnic Chinese firms are thus an important aspect of Southeast Asian economies, linking them to each other, as well as to China (see Table 6.1).

From 1979 to 1997, over two-thirds of all foreign capital into China came from ethnic Chinese. In specific industries, the impact of the diaspora is even greater. For example, in 2000, 72.8 percent of China's information production was actually Taiwanese production based in China.[45] By 2000, 72

TABLE 6.1   STOCK HOLDINGS OF MAJOR FIRMS IN FOUR ASEAN NATIONS BY OWNERSHIP TYPE (%)

NATION	GOVERNMENT	OTHER	FOREIGN	CHINESE
Malaysia	48.0	22.6	4.1	25.3
Indonesia	67.1	7.4	3.1	22.4
Thailand	13.2	9.9	45.6	31.3
Philippines	31.4	16.9	29.5	22.2

SOURCE: DAJIN PENG, "INVISIBLE LINKAGES: A REGIONAL PERSPECTIVE OF EAST ASIAN POLITICAL ECONOMY," *INTERNATIONAL STUDIES QUARTERLY* 46, NO. 3 (SEPTEMBER 2002): 432.

percent of all investment into ASEAN and China was into China. By 1999, total external trade from the "Chinese" region of China, Taiwan, and Hong Kong (after removing trade within these three countries) was greater than that of Japan: $810 billion to $731 billion.[46] These networks are not necessarily exclusive, however. It is common for a Taiwanese firm to manage a Thai electronics factory that uses Japanese technology for production.[47]

These ties are more than just business relations. For example, two-thirds of the Thai parliament in 2006 was of Chinese origin, as were the last three prime ministers.[48] The Thai queen spent ten days in China in 2001, during which the "Chinese leadership reportedly paid rare and constant attention to the royal party," and Thai Princess Sirindhorn studied at Beijing University.[49] Southeast Asians are also increasingly turning to China as a source of training for their future intellectuals and elites. In 2003, there were 77,628 foreign students studying in China, and David Shambaugh notes that 80 percent of them came from other Asian countries.[50] In 2005, more Chinese than Japanese visited Australia, where Chinese is the most widely spoken foreign language.[51] Chinese tourists to Southeast Asia now outnumber Japanese tourists to the region.[52] In sum, Southeast Asian relations with China continue to strengthen, driven in part by the rich mix of ethnicities and ethnic affinity in Southeast Asia.

THE SPRATLY ISLANDS

The only issue that might lead to armed conflict in the region is the dispute over the ownership of the Spratly Islands.[53] However, the possibility is low. Furthermore, the Spratlys dispute is primarily one of "boundary setting" and the resolution of previously undemarcated borders among all the Southeast Asian states, rather than a case of Chinese expansionism—China is only one of many claimants.[54] The disputed islands are too small to provide bases for power projection, and it is still unclear whether they contain any significant natural resources.[55]

Competing claims over the Spratlys have been made for at least four decades. In 1971 the Philippines had claimed islands in the South China Sea and garrisoned eight of them, calling the zone "Kalayaan" (freedom).[56] In 1974 and 1988, China clashed with Vietnam over the Spratlys, and in 1995 China evicted Philippine fishermen from the Mischief Reef. These clashes involved patrol boats and were not major military mobilizations, and Vietnam and Malaysia, not just China, have made claims to the Philippines' stated exclusive economic zone. Vietnam has also occupied the Barque Canada Reef, which is also claimed by Malaysia. In the 1990s, China erected "military bases" on Mischief Reef that were in fact little more than semisubmerged huts. Indeed, Greg Austin points out that "the [Chinese] occupation of Mischief Reef could scarcely be seen as a new military threat to the Philippines . . . China's record in the South China Sea is little different from that of other countries."[57] It is worth noting that Taiwan claims the largest island in the area, and that Malaysia claims the largest number (twelve) and occupies six.

Despite the complexity of the competing claims, the parties involved have made progress in finding a resolution. Most significantly, in November 2002, China signed the Declaration on the Conduct of Parties in the South China Sea, a memorandum that prohibits the use of force to settle rival claims over the oil-rich Spratlys.[58] As one senior Singaporean diplomat noted, "The Spratlys issue is not resolved, but nobody wants to go to war there. There are a number of codes of conduct and there has been a decrease in the armed clashes. China's moves over the Spratlys in 1994–1995 had the potential to bring a pall to China's relations with all of ASEAN. In order to avoid this, China worked out resource sharing agreements without giving up their claims. China's goals are internal, not foreign policy. China is building up its navy because of Taiwan, not ASEAN."[59]

U.S. assessments of the region have also not seen the Spratlys as a major issue. The Department of Defense's 1995 *Strategic Framework for the Asian Pacific Rim* mentioned the Spratlys only in passing, and the 1998 report did not mention the South China Sea at all.[60] Vietnamese and Chinese leaders have met annually since the normalization of their relations in 1991 despite the Spratly Islands issue, and relations have improved steadily over time. Ang Cheng Guan writes that "it is unlikely that the two countries [Vietnam and China] will engage in another military clash over their South China Sea dispute."[61] Indeed, in 2006 the second meeting on implementation of the Code of Conduct was held in Hainan, China, by the China-ASEAN working group, discussing relevant cooperation projects and deciding on a working plan for 2006.[62]

Cooperation over the Spratlys has continued to increase. In March 2005, Vietnam, the Philippines, and China agreed to jointly explore oil exploration in the South China Sea.[63] This agreement calls for the China National Offshore Oil Corporation, the Vietnam National Petroleum Corporation, and the Philippine National Oil Company to conduct three years of "joint marine seismic work" over an area of 140,000 square kilometers in the Spratlys.[64]

In conclusion, compared to the situation just after World War II, when weakly institutionalized, newly independent states feared for their survival,

Southeast Asian states in 2006 are in a far more secure international and domestic situation. All states in the region have made significant progress in settling border claims and delineating boundaries. That the Spratlys can be seen as the most likely source of conflict in the region is in itself an indicator of how much progress has been made. These states are overwhelmingly focused on economic development and domestic political consolidation. Furthermore, they face no significant external threats to their survival, and the various countries are deeply interlinked with one another through ethnic ties, trade and investment relations, and cultural history. Within this context, their rapid embrace of China is not that surprising.

THE PHILIPPINES

The Philippines and Vietnam are particularly relevant case studies for illustrating the changing regional dynamics. The Philippines, a former U.S. colony, has always been most closely aligned with the United States in Southeast Asia. Conversely, among those same Asian states Vietnam has had the most distant relations with the United States. Yet the Philippines and Vietnam are both moving steadily toward China on a number of fronts, while still retaining good relations with the United States. Similarly, both countries want to avoid a situation in which they are forced to make a stark choice between one superpower or the other.

As noted in chapter 3, Philippine-China relations are warm, and getting even warmer. Trade and investment between the two countries is rapidly increasing. From 2000 to 2005, total bilateral trade between the two countries went up annually at an average rate of 42 percent.[65] Total trade between China and the Philippines was $17 billion in 2005, roughly the same as U.S.-Philippine trade of $18 billion.[66] In June 2006, Chinese Commerce Minister Bo Xilai visited Manila and agreed to a series of investments in agriculture, fishing, tourism, mining, and energy that could be worth up to $32 billion.[67] State-run schools in the Philippines are required to offer Mandarin Chinese as an elective.

Compared to its tight alignment with the United States during the Cold War, the Philippines has moved away. Although the Philippines has no desire to have poor relations with the United States and has no intention of renouncing the mutual defense treaty, the Philippines also has a looser relationship with the United States in 2007 than it did in 1990. For example, when a U.S. EP-3 plane collided with a Chinese jet over Hainan Island in 2001, most Southeast Asian nations publicly hoped for a negotiated settlement and none of them backed the United States. The Philippines did not postpone the third meeting of the China-Philippines Experts Working Group on confidence-building measures in the South China Sea, which convened at the same time as the incident.[68] Furthermore, Philippine President Gloria Macapagal-Arroyo stated that the incident was between two "elephants" and did not involve other, smaller countries.

The most direct evidence of this changing relationship was the Philippine decision in 1991 not to renew an agreement that permitted U.S. military deployments at Clark and Subic Bay bases. At its height Subic was the largest naval facility in the world outside of the United States, a major element of U.S. force projection in the region and even outside of the region. The Philippine government's official position on the bases was that "the Philippines faced no external enemies or threat, and that threats arising from both communist insurgency and the right-wing military rebels could not be addressed by U.S. military presence in the country."[69] Although after the terrorist attacks of September 11, 2001, the Philippines increased its military cooperation with the United States in a limited fashion aimed at domestic terrorist insurgencies, cooperation remains well below pre-1991 levels.[70]

The conventional explanation for why the Philippines did not renew its bases treaty with the U.S. is based on domestic political considerations. For example, Yuen Foong Khong writes that "by 1989 it became obvious that the negotiations had become entangled with a fierce domestic political debate within the Philippines. The surge in Filipino nationalism derailed the negotiations."[71] Barton Brown emphasizes the different cultural milieus in the Philippines and the United States, arguing that "from the start of negotiations, the security partners danced to different tunes . . . arguing over rights and duties of allies, friends, partners, patrons, and clients."[72] The situation came to a head in 1991. The Philippine senate voted against a treaty to renew the basing agreement with the United States on September 16, and the largest naval base outside of the United States—Subic—was closed the following year, along with Clark air force base. Ironically, in 2004 China gave the Philippines $1 billion in soft loans and investments, some of which will be used to develop the Subic-Clark area as a logistics hub for Southeast Asia.[73]

Since 1992, the Philippines and the United States have increased military cooperation. In 1998 Philippine President Fidel Ramos signed a visiting forces agreement that compromised Philippine stances over criminal jurisdiction on status-of-forces. The Philippines signed a new agreement with the United States in May 1999 that allows U.S. troops back into the Philippines for training and other activities.[74] However, the United States and the Philippines never made clear whether this agreement would include a U.S. security guarantee for the Philippines regarding the South China Sea.[75] Significantly, however, despite four different Philippine presidents (Cory Aquino, 1986–1992; Fidel Ramos, 1992–1998; Joseph Estrada, 1998–2001; and Gloria Macapagal-Arroyo, 2001–present), none have raised the possibility of returning the alliance to the level of having permanent U.S. bases in the Philippines.

Most importantly, however, renewed U.S.-Philippine military cooperation is focused almost exclusively on the "war on terror" and geographically concentrated on the southern Mindanao region of the Philippines.[76] The sporadic deployment of U.S. forces through the Philippines is a less obvious and clear commitment to the defense of the Philippines than permanent basing. The Philippines is increasing its military cooperation with the United States in a limited fashion, but it has not returned to anywhere close to the levels of cooperation of pre-1991, and is focused on domestic terrorist insurgencies, not a China threat. [77]

The Philippines did send a small medical contingent of fifty-one peacekeepers to Iraq as part of the "Coalition of the Willing." However, Philippine public opinion was solidly opposed to the U.S. war in Iraq—in three opinion polls conducted over two years, the proportion of Filipinos favoring a "neutral" stance on Iraq remained well over 60 percent, with only single-digit support for the United States if it lacked U.N. support.[78] With the kidnapping of a Philippine truck driver in Iraq, and with extensive negative Philippine public opinion against the troop deployment, the Philippines pulled its troops out earlier than planned, in July 2004. In response, U.S. Chargé d'affaires Joseph Mussomeli said that U.S.-Philippine ties face "erosion" if further problems occur in the relationship.

In sum, the Philippines has actively moved to increase the breadth and depth of its relations with China, even as it tries to retain strong ties with the United States. Long the closest U.S. ally in Southeast Asia, the Philippines in the twenty-first century is widening its foreign policy focus beyond the United States in an attempt to maintain good relations with China, as well as the other ASEAN states.[79]

VIETNAM ACCOMMODATES CHINA

Vietnam deserves special attention because it is the Southeast Asian state that is furthest along the spectrum of alignment toward China rather than the United States. The United States clearly plays little role in reassuring Vietnam against possible Chinese aggrandizement. Vietnam is the only

ASEAN state to which the United States has not granted permanent normal trade relations status. In fact, Vietnam only normalized relations with the United States in 1995, and memories of the U.S.-Vietnam war are still very much alive in both countries. Furthermore, Vietnam also shares a land border with China, and the two countries fought a short but sharp war in 1979. If any country should be worried about Chinese intentions, it is Vietnam— yet Vietnam and China continue to develop normal relations, and the Vietnam-Chinese border is not fortified.

Vietnam is only cautiously and slowly deepening its relations with the United States, while it has moved quickly to repair and deepen relations with China. Although Vietnam is in some ways hedging its bets against China, it is also accommodating and adjusting to its larger neighbor. Vietnam is conducting its foreign policy in an historically consistent manner: adjusting to China while attempting to keep as much autonomy as possible. As one Singaporean diplomat described it, the Vietnamese are "supreme pragmatists. The question of balancing is simply absent. The question for the Vietnamese is how do you preserve flexibility on the periphery of a large and rising China?"[80]

As Henry Kenny argues, Vietnam is lapsing back into a "cultural tradition that tends to favor Vietnamese submission to China in exchange for Chinese benevolence and, if needed, protection of Vietnam against hostile outside forces."[81] For its part, China is undertaking a series of actions designed both to reassure Vietnam of its intentions and to further stabilize their relationship. Kim Ninh writes, "This love-hate, dependent-independent relationship with China is a fundamental factor in the Vietnamese conception of security."[82] Furthermore, both ruling regimes are communist dictatorships that are attempting to follow a path of economic reform while retaining political power.

Like most countries in Asia, Vietnam went through a period of upheaval during which colonialism, anticolonialist movements, and outside powers severely distorted and limited its national coherence. Divided into North and South Vietnam in 1954, Vietnam began its "modern" era in 1975 with unification and the final ousting of outside powers. Even when Soviet-Vietnamese relations were at their warmest after 1975, this was not the central relationship for the Vietnamese, but rather it was the Chinese who most occupied Vietnam's attention. In large part, the Vietnamese were using the Soviets as a hedge against China's influence at the time.[83] Ang Cheng Guan quotes Ho Chi Minh as recognizing the central role of China in Vietnam's foreign policy: "[in 1960] Ho Chi Minh appealed to Khruschev to accede to the Chinese because, according to Ho, China was a big country . . . Khruschev retorted that the

Soviet Union was by no means a small country. Ho replied, 'For us it is doubly difficult. Don't forget, China is our neighbor.'"[84]

During the 1980s, repairing relations with China became the main goal of Vietnamese foreign policy, and relations between the two states slowly improved.[85] Vietnam made concessions to China by withdrawing its military forces from Cambodia and Laos, demobilizing half its regular army, and "adopting a defensive posture, including a policy of non-provocation towards China."[86] Vietnamese officials visited China more often during that decade, pointedly noting their desire to emulate the Chinese model. As one Vietnamese official recently pointed out, "Remember that after defeating the Chinese, we always sent tribute."[87] In February 1985, Vietnamese General Secretary Le Duan declared that he was "firmly convinced that friendship between China and Vietnam would have to be restored."[88] Martin Stuart-Fox writes, "Burma and Vietnam have historically defeated Chinese armies, only to ensure their security by reinscribing in the Chinese world order. This was in no way humiliating, it was a sensible course of action."[89]

Vietnam's main political and economic model is China. For example, Vietnamese Foreign Minister Nguyen Dy Nien stated in 2001 that relations with China were the priority in Vietnam's foreign policy. Visitors to Vietnam that year included the Chinese defense minister; Vice Chairman of the Central Military Commission Chi Haotian (for six days), and Chinese President Hu Jintao. "The consistent message that emerged from these meetings was that the Vietnam-China relations should continue to be guided by the principles of 'long-term stability, orientation towards the future, good neighbourliness and friendship, and all-round cooperation.' As agreed upon by [then–Vietnamese General Secretary] Le Kha Phieu and [then-President of China] Jiang Zemin when they met in Beijing in February 1999."[90]

Rapprochement began during the 1990s with resolution of border disputes; since then, cooperation has increased rapidly across all areas. Vietnam-China agreements included the "Treaty on the Land Border between the SRV and the PRC," the "Agreement on the Demarcation of Waters, Exclusive Economic Zones and Continental Shelves in the Bac Bo (Tonkin) Gulf between the SRV and the PRC," and the "Agreement on Fishing Cooperation," which are of profound historical significance.[91] The "Joint Vietnam-China Statement for Comprehensive Cooperation," signed in 2000 by Foreign Minister Nguyen Dy Nien and Foreign Minister Tang Jiaxuan, called for regular high-level meetings to promote cooperation. The range of issues covered in that agreement was comprehensive, including promotion of economic, commercial, and investment ties, as well as communications, transport, and environmental protection. Furthermore, the statement said that "the two sides commit to strengthening the cooperation and coordination at multilateral, regional, and international forum[s] including the United Nations, ASEAN Regional Forum, APEC, [and] ASEM." The Chinese PLA Navy (PLAN) and the Vietnamese navy have conducted joint search-and-rescue missions and joint exercises designed to counter smuggling.[92]

Carl Thayer notes that

> there are at least two contending schools of thought within the Vietnamese leadership about how Vietnam should manage its relations with China. One group, centered on the military, but including ideological party conservatives, advocates going beyond mere normalization and developing close military and security ties. The military, in particular, has pursued its own discussions with their Chinese counterparts . . . [yet] Vietnam has eschewed pursuing the path of confrontation or dependency. Instead, Vietnam has been sensitive to the nuances of China's regional and global status.[93]

Kim Ninh writes that although "China remains the biggest external security threat to Vietnam . . . Vietnam is doing its best to cultivate friendly bilateral relations and is engaging in talks over a number of contentious issues between the two countries."[94]

VIETNAM'S ECONOMIC RELATIONS

After unifying Vietnam in 1975, the Vietnamese leaders attempted to pursue an economic strategy that emphasized state ownership of the means of production and independence from the rest of the world. The results, typical for a centralized and planned economy, were disastrous. Vietnamese leaders noted that "sovereignty and independence" was an empty slogan without economic growth.[95] Although China began a policy of economic reform in 1978, for the first decade after unification the Vietnamese leaders did not follow that path.

However, by the sixth party congress of the Vietnamese Communist Party in 1986, the economy was in a crisis. Unemployment was over 20 percent, inflation had spiraled out of control, and poverty and malnutrition were widespread.[96] In response, Hanoi's leadership began a process of *doi moi*, or "renovation," which led to reforms that increased agricultural production. From those initial steps, the economy has come a long way. By the early

1990s, border incidents between Vietnam and China had mostly disappeared, and unofficial border trade had begun to develop.[97]

In this path of renovation, the Vietnamese have been heavily influenced by the Chinese model of reform. This was not initially the case: in the mid-1980s the Vietnamese economic planners looked for potential models to follow in Singapore and Taiwan, as well as China itself.[98] Yet by the early 1990s, it was clear that Vietnam would emulate China. Across a range of issues, from developing the Tonkin Gulf to technical cooperation, both China and Vietnam began to show the political will to improve relations. Since 1991, trade and other forms of economic cooperation have developed steadily between the two countries. By 1997, this trade totaled $1.44 billion, and China had invested an estimated total of $102 million in Vietnam.[99] In 1999 the two countries signed a tourism cooperation plan, allowing Chinese nationals to enter Vietnam without having a visa.[100] China also signed an economic agreement with Vietnam in 2000, providing $55.254 million to upgrade the Thai Nguyen Steel Company and other industrial plants in Vietnam.[101]

In 1999, Vietnamese General Secretary Le Kha Phieu visited China and said that "since its establishment, and especially during 20 years of reform and open-door policies, China has obtained great achievements. I would like to seize the opportunity of my trip to study China's experiences in building socialism with Chinese identity."[102] At a meeting at the Chinese Academy of the Social Sciences on economic reform in 2000, Vietnamese party General Secretary Le Kha Phieu said, "If China succeeds in its reform then we'll succeed; if China fails, we fail."[103] The United Nations International Development Organization representative in Hanoi said in 2001 that "the Vietnamese are very keen to follow development in China."[104] Formal visits between China and Vietnam at the vice-minister level or above have increased steadily since the 1990s, with over 80 in 1999 alone.[105] By 2004, there were about 100 working visits at the vice-ministerial level or higher each year.[106]

In 1999, Vietnam postponed its trade agreement with the United States until China had signed its own agreement with Vietnam. One observer noted, "If Vietnam got a trade agreement with the U.S., they would see it as upstaging China. It's not that China told them not to sign it. It's just that they didn't want to upset China."[107] Bilateral trade between China and Vietnam is expected to reach $10 billion in 2006, up from $8 billion in 2005.[108] Thus indications are that Vietnam and China are developing a stable relationship with each other.

Although Vietnam has been cautiously cultivating warmer ties with the United States, and normalized diplomatic relations in 1995, it has shown no hurry to rapidly improve relations. The major achievement following normalization was the 2002 implementation of a bilateral trade agreement, which served to increase economic ties between the two countries.

When Vietnam joined ASEAN in 1995, Vietnam's deputy foreign minister explicitly told reporters that his country's entry should not worry China.[109] Vietnam joined ASEAN in 1995, and has been a strong advocate of the organization. One Singaporean diplomat said that "with China, it is not just a question of building an army or finding an ally. Those are not enough. As the Vietnamese learned with the Soviets, a strong external ally is not necessarily sufficient without domestic reforms. So you still need external allies (ASEAN), and there is no point in quarreling with the U.S. But Vietnam also realizes that you can't rely on the big powers. They abandon you."[110] Allen Goodman argues that "ASEAN is not SEATO and the Vietnamese are not anxious to see it converted into a military alliance of any sort, especially one that threatens China."[111]

In the spring of 1997, Vietnam and China clashed over Chinese drilling sixty-five miles from Vietnam's coastline. Vietnam protested to China and also called on ASEAN, and the Chinese withdrew the rig. David Wurfel notes that "the Vietnamese press, however, barely mentioned this apparent diplomatic victory. There was a reason for their reticence; they had boldly played the ASEAN card and wanted to avoid antagonizing China further by gloating over their success. This marked a new stage in Sino-Vietnamese, and in ASEAN-Vietnamese relations."[112] Indeed, as noted earlier, all parties to the disputed Spratly Islands have made significant progress toward setting up multilateral institutions by which to resolve their differences. By 2005, Vietnam and China had agreed to joint development of oil and natural gas in the Tonkin Gulf. Chinese President Hu Jintao and Vietnam Communist Party General Secretary Nong Duc Manh signed a framework agreement to jointly explore natural gas and oil reserves there.[113]

Although Vietnam and China have a long history of difficult and complex relations, Vietnam is accommodating and even emulating China across a range of areas, from the military to the economy to culture.[114] Vietnam is not fortifying its border, it is expanding military cooperation with China in both maritime patrols and border control, and is increasingly economically integrated with China. At the same time, the Vietnamese have a proud history of independence and resisting foreign aggression.

This nuanced, accommodationist strategy toward China has deep historical roots. That the Chinese have worked hard to reassure Vietnam is also evident. Although relations between Vietnam and China are filtered through a cultural and historical lens, much of the reassurance comes from the actions that the Chinese leadership is taking today.

THE UNITED STATES IN SOUTHEAST ASIA

In contrast to China's increased presence in Southeast Asia, over the past thirty years the United States' diplomatic and military presence has significantly diminished. In particular, the 1997 Asian financial crisis and the "global war on terror" have caused Southeast Asian states to reconsider their relations with the United States. Although all countries in the region want to maintain good relations with America, the latter's influence is less pervasive now. Noting this trend, two former U.S. ambassadors to the region wrote in 2005 that the U.S. presence in Southeast Asia is receding, lacks coherence, and that "the current U.S. approach to the area has been spasmodic: some counter-terrorism effort here, a bit of development financing there, an occasional presidential visit, and frequent statements about the glories of ASEAN."[115]

Gradual economic success in some of the Southeast Asian states in the 1980s had caused the United States to begin to pressure them for greater economic concessions and to become less willing to subsume economic relations to geopolitical considerations.[116] This hinted at the beginnings of a divide between the United States and its ASEAN allies. The ASEAN states began to explore alternative or complementary security arrangements to the United States, such as the ASEAN Regional Forum (ARF). At the 1987 ASEAN summit, ASEAN had made clear its interest in exploring "possible relations with additional third countries [i.e., not the U.S.]," with a view toward mitigating its dependence on the U.S.[117] As Andrew MacIntyre and Barry Naughton observe, "The United States had economic interests that conspicuously conflicted with those of [East Asia], and it prosecuted these interests through other channels, with muscular approaches to bilateral economic relations and multilateral agreements . . . if the United States was a goose, it had a very different flight path."[118]

The United States, although an important actor in the region, is also absent from much of the integration that is taking place. For a long time the United States resisted most proposals by East Asian states to form coalitions. In 1989, Australia proposed the creation of APEC as a purely "East Asian" framework that excluded the United States. Then–Secretary of State James Baker protested strongly to Australia's Foreign Minister Evans in 1989. The United States also opposed a proposal by Malaysia leader Mahatir Mohammed in 1990 to create an East Asian economic grouping.[119] In 1997, the United States opposed a Japanese proposal to create an East Asian monetary fund, an action that might have lessened the shock of the crisis.[120] The United States is either dismissive of, or excluded from, many of these institutions.[121]

That such vibrant institutionalization and integration of the region is occurring relatively unnoticed in the United States is significant.

In terms of overall presence and leadership, despite being welcomed in some areas the United States has also managed to provoke resentment in Southeast Asia. The U.S. presence in the region has been shaped fundamentally in the past decade by two major events—the Asian financial crisis that swept through the region in 1997, and the "global war on terror" (GWOT) that began after the terrorist attacks of September 11, 2001. In both cases, the United States has widened a gulf in attitudes and perceptions between it and the Southeast Asian states.

Although the causes and consequences of the 1997 Asian financial crisis have been hotly debated, it is worth noting that Western and East Asian perceptions of these causes and consequences tend to be at odds with each other.[122] Western analyses have tended to emphasize the poor business practices of East Asian firms ("crony capitalism"), putting blame for the crisis on the countries themselves.[123] In contrast, East Asian analyses tend to emphasize the indifferent attitude of the International Monetary Fund (IMF) and the U.S. government in particular as the most important causes of the crisis.[124] Donald Emmerson notes that "from within ASEAN . . . Washington was reproached for hostility, or indifference, or both—for torching the region's economies and then letting them burn."[125] More important than the reality of what caused the crisis is noting that these different perceptions exist, and have shaped the way in which some countries in Southeast Asia have viewed their relations with the United States. As Marcus Noland has noted, "the crisis served to make Asian countries more aware of their Asian identity."[126]

Furthermore, there was widespread wonder in Southeast Asia about why the United States, having pushed Thailand to open its capital markets, did not help when it got into trouble.[127] There was also speculation that the United States was secretly pleased with the crisis, because it allowed American banks to advantage themselves, and created more opportunities for U.S. companies abroad. Jagdish Bhagwati even introduced the phrase "Wall Street-Treasury complex" to denote the American interests that relentlessly press for increased capital mobility to open other countries to highly competitive U.S. financial firms.[128] The IMF—under strong pressure from the U.S. Treasury Department—prescribed very different remedies for Southeast Asian states than it did for Latin American states or for Mexico.[129] The first bailout package, to Thailand in August 1997, comprised $17.2 billion. The United States did not contribute any money to this bailout, although Japan, the IMF, the World Bank, and the Asian Development Bank contributed to the package. This contrasts with the $50 billion bailout by the IMF and the prompt action of the United States to Mexico in 1994, and created the impression that the United States was indifferent to Asia's problems. The Americans did contribute $3 billion to Indonesia's package in November 1997, although that was less than the $5 billion that Japan and Singapore each contributed.

With the IMF's resources largely depleted, the U.S. Congress refused until October 1998 to appropriate the funds to replenish them. A senior Thai diplomat said, "the American attitude is driving us closer to Japan and China."[130] As the former executive director of APEC, William Biddle, noted, "There was considerable disenchantment among the Asians who felt they didn't get the financial help from the U.S. they thought they should."[131] In a speech strongly positive about China's role in Southeast Asia, Singapore's ambassador to the United States noted in 2006 that "the U.S. response or failure to respond to the Asian financial crisis in 1997 strengthened China's standing in the region. . . . when the Clinton Administration chose not to bail out Thailand . . . it left a deep impression on Thailand and the rest of ASEAN . . . the bitter medicine prescribed by the IMF was seen to be an American prescription."[132] It's clear, then, given reactions like these, that many in Southeast Asia view the Asian financial crisis and the U.S. response to it as an instance of America using its power to the detriment of regional actors. This perception was furthered by the seeming U.S. indifference to, or even hostility toward, Southeast Asian regional and multilateral institutions.

The second major recent event that has affected U.S.–Southeast Asian relations is the U.S. "global war on terror." While these states are all concerned about terrorism, some states—especially those with large Muslim populations—are also concerned with the possibility of unilateral American actions in the region, the possibility that the U.S. might even take preventive military action against them, and the possibility that the United States would use the GWOT as cover to creating a containment coalition against China. Although the United States has close working relations with many countries in the region, the GWOT "caused severe damage" to U.S.–Southeast Asian relations, notes Blair King, and "had a very negative impact on the image of the U.S. military in the region."[133] Singaporean Ambassador Chan Heng Chee noted, "Some ASEAN countries felt that all the U.S. cared about was the war on terrorism . . . democracy and human rights proved to be also complicating issues between the U.S. and some ASEAN nations. A further warming up to China and other powers as a result of the discomfort with the U.S. cannot be discounted."[134]

This hesitance on the part of many Southeast Asian nations to embrace the U.S. war on terror is further evidence that Southeast Asian states are not "hedging" against China. Were they concerned about China, an ideal way in which to increase the U.S. presence in the region would be under the guise of antiterrorism activities. Indeed, there was suspicion in Southeast Asia that the United States was pursuing precisely a containment strategy against China. For example, two Malaysian researchers noted that "the pressure exerted by the US on the littoral states [to allow a U.S. military presence] is enormous," and noted a "worst case scenario" in which the U.S. would use the threat of terrorism and piracy to limit China's access to the straits.[135] However, although Southeast Asian states welcome increased U.S. technical assistance and aid, aside from Singapore and Australia, they have been generally hesitant to allow the United States any increased military role in the region. As Donald Weatherbee notes, "it remains to be seen beyond the counter-terrorism effort, how fungible the American military presence is in terms of future political influence as compared to an economic presence."[136]

Some Indonesian observers have even viewed the United States as the greatest external threat to Indonesia, concerned that it would undertake preemptive military action against Indonesia because of the terrorist activity there.[137] Indonesian analyst Andi Widjajanto wrote in 2003 that "Indonesia must try to provide a counterbalance to the preemptive doctrine of U.S. President George W. Bush."[138] This concern was echoed in Malaysia. As Helen Nesadurai tells us, "Malaysia also regarded the strategy of 'pre-emption' to be highly threatening to its sovereignty, because that meant the U.S. might be tempted to intervene in any way it saw fit if the Malaysian government was seen to be incapable of acting against terrorists and other actors who threaten US security."[139]

Many Southeast Asian states have large Muslim populations (Indonesia is the world's largest Muslim nation), and they walk a delicate line in supporting the U.S. war on terror and yet not alienating their domestic constituencies. The Pew "Global Attitudes Poll" taken in 2003 showed that 74 percent of Indonesians were either "very worried" or "somewhat worried" about a potential U.S. military threat, while only 15 percent of Indonesians had a "favorable" attitude toward the United States.[140] Former Malaysian Prime Minister Mahatir Mohammed was particularly critical of the U.S. decision to invade Iraq.[141] Even Thailand and the Philippines, although they had each initially supported the GWOT and even sent token troop contingents to Iraq as part of the "Coalition of the Willing," pulled out their troops out of Iraq as the situation bogged down and domestic opposition mounted. Rodolfo Biazon, chairman of the Philippine Senate's National Defense and Security Committee, said in 2006, "There's a perception of negligence or indifference on the part of the United States. Terrorism is the only effective link we have. On defense, economics, everything else, there isn't much interest."[142]

A good example of the hesitance with which Southeast Asian states view the GWOT has been their resistance to join U.S.-led initiatives that exist outside the United Nations or regional multilateral organizations. Singapore, Thailand, the Philippines, Australia, and New Zealand all joined the "proliferation security initiative" (PSI), designed to coordinate activities aimed at "halting the spread of WMD [weapons of mass destruction] by sea, ground, and air."[143] However, China, Indonesia, and Malaysia have not joined, because they view the PSI's international legality as dubious and because they fear that the PSI may legitimize preemptive interventions on sovereign territory.[144]

Another indicator of ASEAN states' views of a U.S. military presence came in disagreements over how best to combat terrorism and piracy in the Strait of Malacca. On March 31, 2004, the head of the U.S. Pacific Command, Admiral Thomas Fargo, testified before Congress about the U.S. "regional maritime security initiative" (RMSI), saying that "[in the Strait of Malacca] we're looking at things like high-speed vessels, putting special operations forces on high-speed vessels, putting, potentially, marines on high-speed vessels."[145] Admiral Fargo further claimed that "there's very large, widespread support for this initiative."[146] In response, both Malaysia and Indonesia "emphatically rejected the suggestion."[147] Even Thailand turned down a U.S. request in 2004 to set up a military base in Thailand, and also declined a U.S. offer of Special Forces that would help fight Islamic violence.[148] Although these states are willing to accept U.S. technical assistance, they have all denied U.S. requests to use their countries as military bases, or even to preposition equipment.

The United States was forced to scale down the RMSI, and instead proposed providing logistical support to Malaysia and Indonesia, but without military units deployed in the strait or any American bases in the region. ASEAN subsequently moved forward with its own arrangements and institutions to combat terrorism and piracy, including ARF (the ASEAN Regional forum) and ASEAN plus three (China, South Korea, and Japan). In 2005, China and Singapore signed an agreement to cooperate over strait security, as did China and Malaysia.[149] In July 2004, Singapore, Malaysia, and Indonesia agreed to "trilateral coordinated patrols," with the codename of "MALSINDO."[150] Indonesian Chief Marshal Djoko Suyanto later emphasized that the involvement of countries other than those three would be limited to the provision of equipment.

Southeast Asian states have also worked to include China in regional arrangements, along with Japan and South Korea, too. China and South Korea have joined Japan and seventeen other Asian countries in investing in capacity building, communication, and other navigational aids.[151] ReCAAP (the Regional Cooperation Agreement on Combating Piracy and Armed Robbery against Ships in Asia), an initiative originally begun by Japan within the ASEAN plus three (ASEAN and Japan, China, and South Korea, or "APT") framework, was ratified by twelve of sixteen countries including India and Sri Lanka, and came into force on September 4, 2006.[152]

Even stalwart U.S. allies such as Australia are unwilling to embrace the United States at the expense of good relations in the region. In 2006, the former Australian defense force chief, Admiral Chris Barrie, said "the [Australian] relationship with China will become hugely more important for economic and social reasons . . . and Australians will likely feel resentful and untrusting of traditional alliances . . . pressures on the ANZUS alliance relationship between the U.S. and Australia . . . could even lead to a fracturing of the alliance."[153] U.S. Secretary of State Condoleezza Rice traveled to Australia in spring 2006, cautioning the region about China's potential to become a "negative force" and urging a common position by the United States, Australia, and Japan on how to deal with China. In response, Australian Foreign Minister Downer pointedly downplayed the trilateral meeting, stressing that its purpose was not to contain China.[154]

There have been moments of success, however. The rapid U.S. response to the tsunami that swept through Southeast Asia in December 2004 was widely seen as rebuilding trust in the United States. Furthermore, it was pointed out that only the U.S. had the military and logistical capability to provide quick and comprehensive aid throughout the region.[155]

On the whole, U.S. influence in the region has declined from its height during the Cold War. Some Southeast Asian nations are even more concerned about the potential for unilateral U.S. actions than they are about a Chinese military threat. One writer called the U.S.–Southeast Asia differences "a growing disconnect between the U.S. and its closest allies in Asia," noting that analysts worry that "the growing gap between the U.S. and its friends in Asia could begin to undermine security alliances that have bolstered stability in the region since the end of World War II."[156]

Southeast Asia is a region undergone rapid transformation, and the evidence in 2007 points to accommodation of China's increased presence in the region. The states of Southeast Asia are more secure, and more stable, than they were three decades ago. As the U.S. role has greatly diminished, the Chinese presence has increased. To be sure, Southeast Asia still faces a number of issues, such as piracy, territorial disputes over the Spratly Islands, ethnic minorities, and potential terror attacks and domestic instability in a number of countries. Yet the states of Southeast Asia, although by no means bandwagoning with China, are clearly moving closer to China and away from pure reliance on the United States.

This trend does not mean Southeast Asia is without caution about China's intentions, or that these states wish to abandon relations with the United States. Rather, Southeast Asian countries want stable relations with *all* the major powers, and China is one of those. Lacking any reason to fear China, they have moved closer to it as a means of embracing stability and economic growth. As Singaporean Prime Minister Lee Hsien Loon said in 2005, "China's emergence is the single biggest event of our age . . . [but] ASEAN does not want to be exclusively dependent on China, and does not want to be forced to choose sides between China and the U.S."[157]

CHAPTER 7

JAPAN

A NORMAL IDENTITY

The question of Japan's identity has manifested itself most obviously in a long-running debate over whether, and how, Japan can become a "normal" country.[1] Postwar Japan was considered abnormal because its military and diplomatic presence did not match its economic prowess. Standard realist theories would expect a much more assertive Japan, and yet for six decades Japan defined its national security comprehensively, covering a range of military and nonmilitary issues. As Richard Samuels notes, "the consensus is that postwar Japanese planners made a strategic choice . . . the United States would provide deterrence, and Japan did not need, nor would it seek, to act like a great power."[2] Attempts to describe this foreign policy included terms such as "semi-sovereign," "reluctant" realism, "mercantile" realism, and "anti-militarism."[3] The difficulty that scholars have faced in categorizing Japanese foreign policy reflects the underlying uncertainty—in East Asia and within Japan itself—about how Japan views itself, its neighbors, and its role in the region.

In the 1990s the domestic Japanese consensus behind this comprehensive foreign policy began to unravel, and today Japanese grand strategy is in a state of flux. Although the U.S.-Japan alliance is closer than ever before, Japan is slowly removing barriers to its foreign deployment of its self-defense forces (SDF) and investing in advanced weaponry. Domestically, politicians have begun to advocate modifying Article IX of the Japanese constitution, the famous "peace article," in which Japan renounced war forever. One main factor causing this reappraisal has been the rise of China. Japan remains the richest and most advanced country in the region, and has the most potential to challenge China for regional influence, and thus it is not surprising that the dominant strategic issue in Japan over the past decade has been how to respond to the opportunities and threats posed by China.

Despite uncertainty about Japan's future course, it is still possible to discern two fundamental traits to Japanese foreign policy. First, Japan has shown little desire or capacity to lead East Asia. When China was strong, Japan did not challenge China, nor did it harbor designs on East Asian dominance or leadership. From its sporadic and unsuccessful attempts to dominate East Asia in the past, its reluctance to provide public goods during its era of high growth in the post–World War II era, its acceptance of U.S. predominance during the Cold War, and to its increasingly deep enmeshment in its U.S. security alliance in the twenty-first century, there is little in Japan's domestic institutions, history, culture, or the structure of the region that leads to the conclusion that Japan will challenge China.

Second, the U.S.-Japan alliance remains the sine qua non of Japanese foreign policy, having been successful beyond expectations in ensuring Japanese and American interests in the region while simultaneously reassuring Japan's neighbors about Japan's intentions. The possibility that Japan might pursue a truly independent security policy outside the confines of the alliance remains remote, and it is within this context that Japan can pursue a dual hedge: a security policy focused on the U.S. alliance, and economic and commercial engagement of China.[4] Although there are elements to the Japan-China relationship that provide evidence of both competition and cooperation, outside of the U.S.-Japan security alliance it is unlikely that Japan would challenge China. It is only in the context of the U.S.-Japan relationship that Japan can take an assertive and skeptical stance toward China. Already China is Japan's most important economic partner; militarily Japan is already strong but gains little from competing with China.

Yet the success of the U.S.-Japan alliance also brought with it unintended consequences: Japan was merely frozen in place after World War II, and for other East Asian states it is not clear whether the alliance has restrained an unrepentant Japan or that the past sixty years represent a genuine and enduring change in how Japanese view themselves and the region. With an American policy in the past few years that has seemed to move from restraining Japan to actually pushing Japan to be more assertive, East Asian states' concerns about Japan's true intentions and beliefs have been exacerbated. Although change in Japan's grand strategy is still overwhelmingly cautious and incremental, and despite sixty years of a responsible and restrained foreign policy, John Ikenberry notes that this "identity crisis" exists because "without finding a way to put the history issue to rest, Japan will continue to be a diminished regional player, isolated and incapable of helping to shape East Asia that is transforming with the steady rise of China."[5] Although unease about Japan's increasingly muscular foreign policy is often manifest in terms of conflicts about Japan's historical role, the issue also reflects unease about Japan's current intentions and beliefs.

This chapter first explores that historical role of Japan in East Asia, showing that even during the heyday of economic growth in the postwar era, Japan only reluctantly took on leadership positions in the region. It then explores the issue of what type of power Japan is, showing that the U.S.-Japan alliance is the central pillar of Japanese foreign policy. The third section argues that Japan's conflicts with its neighbors over history is as much about current intentions and beliefs as it is about the actual historical facts; a fourth section directly examines the hot and cold nature of China-Japan relations.

JAPAN'S HISTORICAL ROLE IN EAST ASIA

From an historical perspective, it is not that surprising that Japan does not challenge China. As shown in chapter 2, Japan only attempted East Asian dominance when China was weak. When China has been strong, Japan has not challenged it. As the Ming dynasty was decaying in the late sixteenth century, Japan invaded Korea, only to be repulsed by combined Ming-Choson forces. Three hundred years later, in the late nineteenth century, Japan again faced decaying and despotic Chinese and Korean monarchies, a regional power vacuum, and extra-regional threats from Western nations. Robert Ross notes that even in the early twentieth century, "Japan's bid for self-reliance failed not only when the international circumstances were most favorable, but also when its domestic system was uniquely oriented toward strategic expansion."[6] Today Japan's situation is the opposite: strong and stable Chinese and East Asian states are experiencing rapid economic growth, Japan faces no external threat, domestic Japanese institutions are deeply democratic, and Japanese public opinion is highly skeptical of overly assertive foreign policies.

In fact, Japan has historically aligned itself with what it perceived to be the world's dominant power, although as Richard Samuels notes, "Tokyo's historical penchant for bandwagoning has never been unqualified."[7] Consistent with its historical pattern, after recovering from defeat in World War II, Japan did not challenge U.S. regional dominance, but instead crafted a close working relationship with the United States. This in itself is a major problem for power-based theories, because by the late 1970s, Japan was the second-largest economy in the world and clearly in a position to challenge the United States had it chosen to do so. Yet in the post–World War II era, Japan defined its security in explicitly comprehensive terms, covering military, economic, external, and internal dimensions.[8] This security policy included an unwillingness to rearm its military forces beyond those necessary for coastal defense despite U.S. pressure to do so, a strong commitment to and focus on multilateral international institutions such as the United Nations, extensive overseas official development assistance (ODA) to countries around the region, and a domestic and international emphasis on economic growth and development.[9] Peter Katzenstein and Nobuo Okawara note that "Japan's security policy is formulated within institutional structures that bias policy strongly against a forceful articulation of military security objectives and accord pride of place instead to a comprehensive definition of security that centers on economic and political dimensions of national security."[10]

For almost six decades that foreign policy was peaceful, responsible, and restrained, and rested on a domestic consensus characterized by the Yoshida doctrine and the 1955 system. The Yoshida doctrine, named for Yoshida Shigeru, Prime Minister during the early postwar era, emphasized economic growth while relying on the American security alliance and Article IX.[11] The "1955 system" was characterized by stable and conservative rule by the Liberal Democratic Party (LDP), which has held power essentially from 1955 to the present day.[12] Domestic Japanese support for Article IX was so thorough that any revision of the constitution had remained beyond discussion by any serious politician well into the 1990s. This overall foreign policy stance was led by a group of politicians throughout the Cold War era who were internationally cautious, open to improving relations with China, and peace-oriented. Geography, population, economics, and a firm U.S.-Japan alliance meant that Japan benefited from a stable regional and international order as it stayed relatively safe from military threats. Even when Japan was the richest and most economically dynamic country in the region, during its era of high growth in the 1970s and 1980s, it only sporadically attempted any form of regional leadership, and those efforts were often unsuccessful.[13]

One concrete manifestation of the Japanese difficulty in providing leadership was its economic development strategy. Often referred to as the "developmental state," Japan's focus has been on protecting domestic industries from foreign competition and investment, and nurturing exports.[14] While this strategy was very successful, it led to numerous conflicts with the rest of the world. In contrast, China has been remarkably open to foreign direct investment and the arrival of foreign multinational corporations, which leads other countries to see a stake in China's continued development.[15]

The East Asian regional economy after World War II was a Japan-dominated system, in which superior Japanese capital and technology formed the basis of production networks that centered on Japanese multinational companies. Often referred to as the "flying geese" model, the system in this period was characterized by a clear economic hierarchy with Japan as the dominant economy.[16] With the bursting of Japan's economic bubble in 1990 and the increasing dynamism in China's economy, Japan's dominant position began to fade. Throughout the era of Japanese high growth, however, Japan was generally unenthusiastic about taking on a leadership role in its foreign economic policy that was commensurate with its economic power. As one longtime investment banker from the region noted, "Japan did not have an Asian strategy, it had a Washington strategy. Asia was an afterthought."[17] Of all the traits that an economic leader provides that Charles Kindleberger identified long ago—stable long-term lending, relatively stable exchange rates, coordination of macroeconomic and particular monetary economic policy, an open market for world goods, and acting as lender of last resort by discounting or otherwise providing liquidity in a financial crisis—Japan provided these reluctantly, if at all.[18]

In East Asia in particular, Japanese capital became the largest source of foreign investment during the 1980s, and Japanese banks became the leading regional creditors. Given that Japanese firms accounted for the bulk of traded goods, and Japanese overseas development assistance was far larger than that from the United States, the Japanese yen would have become the natural reserve currency, not the U.S. dollar. However, Japan's financial institutions resisted such a role, and resisted taking a leadership position in regional economic affairs.

In fact, Japan's policies exacerbated the precarious international economic situation of other East Asian nations. Japan's central bank kept interest rates extremely low during the 1980s and 1990s, in a policy mainly aimed at invigorating domestic demand.[19] As a result, cheap Japanese capital flooded East Asia and indeed the world—but this capital tended to be dollar-denominated, not yen-denominated. With the yen depreciating against the dollar because of the Plaza Accords of 1985, East Asian states initially benefited from the policy, but when the dollar began to appreciate against the yen in 1994–1995, their loans suddenly became much more costly. Peter Katzenstein writes, "At the root of Asia's reliance on the dollar lies Japan's traditional unwillingness to internationalize its currency and to explicitly exercise monetary leadership, not only in Asia but worldwide."[20]

In addition to Japan's unwillingness to undertake an East Asian leadership position on economic matters, the manner in which Japan's political economy was—and continues to be—organized also led to tremendous friction with other countries, among them the United States.[21] With massive trade surpluses, and almost insurmountable barriers to foreign firms attempting to export to or invest in Japan, many countries and companies felt that "Japan Inc." was playing an unfair game. Thus Japan's economic development came at the cost of friction with countries around the world. Indeed, one of the main foreign policy issues in the United States during the 1980s and 1990s was an attempt to get Japan to open its markets to foreign—mainly American—access. From the "voluntary" export restraints on Japan's automobile exports in the early 1980s, the Plaza Accords of 1985, the Structural Impediments Initiative of the late 1980s, to George Bush's infamous 1991 visit to Japan, U.S. frustration at Japan's unwillingness to allow foreign penetration of its markets was high. It was only when Japan entered a period of economic downturn that friction with the rest of the world subsided.[22] Michael Mastanduno writes that "Japan attempted to deflect the resentment and pressure. It concluded bilateral agreements yet dragged its feet in implementing them."[23]

Japan's economic development strategy was predicated on a close working relationship between the government, business, and politicians. Often called "the iron triangle," Japan's large business conglomerates—*keiretsu*—organized themselves around a core bank that funneled capital to a wide array of subsidiary companies covering a wide range of sectors.[24] Behind high protectionist barriers that kept out foreign competition, and working closely with governmental bureaucracies such as the Ministry of Finance and the Ministry of Trade and Industry, these firms focused on exporting goods around the world and were able to rapidly dominate international markets in sectors ranging from automobiles to consumer electronics and shipbuilding.

This led to friction because countries feared that Japanese firms would quickly wipe out domestic businesses in a range of industries. As Japanese firms expanded overseas through both production and sales, domestic companies came under extreme competitive pressures. Whole industrial sectors were wiped out by the advent of Japanese products. In Southeast Asia, Japanese firms quickly set up production and commodity chains, and although the Southeast Asian countries benefited from Japanese investment, control of the technology and processes tended to remain in Japanese hands, creating a two-tier sector. Although Japanese foreign direct investment (FDI) was a key factor in East Asian states' development, high and often impenetrable Japanese trade barriers meant that Japanese FDI also brought even greater trade deficits with Japan, and greater Japanese penetration of local markets without corresponding access to Japan itself.[25]

Furthermore, Japanese firms did not exit mature industries, and kept a tight control over their technology. As Dajin Peng observes, "as a result, hierarchical regional networks of production highly dependent on Japan emerged."[26] Indeed, Walter Hatch and Kozo Yamamura have shown that Japanese multinational corporations retained tight control over their membership within the Japanese *keiretsu* network, and also retained tight control over their technology.[27]

Although Japanese technology transfer was critical to both South Korea's and Taiwan's economic takeoff—accounting for over half of technology imports in those countries during their years of initial economic growth—Japanese firms "made other East Asian countries dependent on Japan's technology and equipment."[28] Richard Doner notes that few East Asian firms aligned with Japanese firms were able to reduce their dependency on the Japanese multinationals.[29] Bernard and Ravenhill note that "the industrialization of Korea and Taiwan has been marked by a far greater and longer-lasting dependence on important technology, primarily from Japan." They cite a study that 36 percent of Korean electronics industrial components came from Japan.[30] Korean and Taiwanese firms have been forced to engage in reverse engineering in order to reduce their dependence on Japanese technology. This has changed in the past decade as a few South Korean and Taiwanese firms have become technology innovators, but the process was long, and was not nurtured by the Japanese. Ironically, some major Japanese companies such as Sony are now partnering with Korean companies such as Samsung in an attempt to remain competitive in world markets.[31]

With the Asian financial crisis of 1997, Japanese corporations continued to pull back from East Asia. Honda cut production in Thailand by 40 percent in 1998, while Toyota suspended its production entirely (although it resumed it later). Japanese FDI into East Asia declined as well. In 1996, there were 856 Japanese firms entering China, ASEAN, and East Asia. By 1998, that number had dropped to 210.[32] From 1992 to 2001, Japan's share of Asian trade also dropped from 45 percent to 30 percent, while China's share rose from 6 percent to 21 percent—15 percent shifted from Japan to China in less than a decade.[33] Andrew MacIntyre and Barry Naughton show that Japanese bank lending to East Asian countries peaked in 1994, and by 2000 was at the same level as in 1986. They note that "with Japanese economic dynamism slipping, the critical element in the conception of a Japan-centered system was removed, while . . . the Chinese economy gained strength."[34]

The Japanese developmental state pursued a strategy that was in fact quite different from the one that China has been pursuing. As shown in chapters 4 and 6, China's development strategy, in contrast to Japan's, has been predicated on being open to foreign capital, firms, and imports. FDI into China is predominantly East Asian, and indeed from the Chinese diaspora. This "reintegration" of the Chinese core with its East Asian periphery is both economic and cultural, stitching together the region. China is already more integrated into East Asia than was Japan during its era of high growth. Economically, culturally, and ethnically, China's presence in East Asia has already exceeded that of Japan's. Chinese growth is East Asian growth, in a way that growth never was for Japan.

China's liberalization of its command economy in 1978 led to a massive influx of foreign capital, initially from overseas Chinese living in Taiwan, Hong Kong, and Southeast Asia, but rapidly followed by an influx of capital from the rest of the world. Relying on a combination of cheap domestic labor and foreign capital, China's development is highly dependent on open capital markets and international trade of both imports and exports. Although China's rapid increase in exports has led to friction with the United States, and although concerns over the protection of intellectual property rights continues to be a source of concern, this friction is different, and lower, than it has been with Japan. Foreign countries and firms can see mutual benefit in working with China and its economic development, while Japan's growth was more zero-sum.

This different approach to development manifested itself in a variety of ways. For the past two decades, foreign direct investment into China has far outstripped that of Japan. In fact, total FDI into Japan since World War II has amounted to a little over $100 billion; China since its opening three decades ago has already attracted over $660 billion of foreign investment.[35] Furthermore, trade of both imports and exports comprises a larger proportion of Chinese GDP than in Japan. In this sense, China's economy is more similar to the United States than it is to Japan. The United States has generally been welcoming of foreigners, foreign trade, and multinational investment. China's economy is increasingly open to foreign penetration.

Japan's foreign relations and its domestic economic and political institutions are deeply intertwined. In the past, Japanese attempts to influence or control the East Asian region have been met with resistance, and led to resentment in East Asia. In the post–World War II era, although Japanese security policy was restrained, its foreign economic policy resembled the overall historical pattern: little attention to the region, and less influence than was commensurate with its economic strength.

THE DOMESTIC DEBATE OVER JAPAN'S INTERNATIONAL ROLE

Japan's era of high growth ended abruptly in 1991 with the twin crises of a stock market crash and a savings and loan crisis. In the fifteen years since then, Japan averaged only 1.1 percent annual growth. In terms of forgone wealth, if Japan had averaged even modest percentage growth over that time period, it would be trillions of dollars more wealthy than it is today. As Michael Green wrote, "What a decade it might have been . . . Japan might have emerged as a new kind of superpower."[36] The decline in its economic fortunes forced Japan to confront the constraints and tradeoffs in its grand strategy as it shapes military, development, and economic policies.

In addition to the "lost decade" of lost economic growth, Japan also faces a declining demographic situation. Japan's birthrate fell to 1.29 in 2005, well below the 2.2 replacement rate that would keep the population stable at its current level of 130 million. Without a dramatic change in immigration policy, it is estimated that Japan's population could contract between 25 and 30 percent by the year 2050, resulting in a Japan with a population of around 100 million.[37] A Japanese Ministry of Health, Labor, and Welfare study concluded that although there were four active workers for every elderly person in 2002, by 2050 there would be only 1.5 workers for every elderly person.[38] This would have serious implications for Japan's economy and military capability. Perhaps more importantly, a population decline of such magnitude would have severe cultural repercussions as well. In response, Japanese are asking whether to allow massive inward migration—much of which would surely be Chinese—and deal with the cultural and social disruptions that would inevitably accompany it. Tokyo Governor Shintaro Ishihara forcefully argued for immigration, saying that "regardless of how one feels about immigration, it is necessary for Japan's future and it is good for Japan's future."[39] However, as Michael Mastanduno notes, "Japan is not the United States; a commitment to national homogeneity has brought with it a resistance to immigration on a meaningful scale."[40]

Although Japan's national identity and actions derive partly from its international interactions, much of its foreign policy also derives from domestic Japanese institutions and politics. Fifteen years of economic malaise and halting reforms, Japan's difficulty in dealing with its historical relations with other East Asian states, and its attempts to act on the international stage all manifest a set of domestic institutions that were very stable but whose very stability also limited Japan's flexibility in dealing with new situations.[41] In the 1990s, a bursting economic bubble, declining population, unease over growing Chinese power, and questions about the U.S. alliance all combined to cause Japanese to question what type of power they are and how Japan should act in international relations. Support for the Yoshida doctrine and the 1955 system began to whither, and Japan began to take hesitant steps away from its avowedly pacifist stance of the preceding five decades.[42] Those steps included naming China as a potential threat in the future, the dispatch of troops to the Middle East to support the U.S.-led war on terror and stabilization of Iraq, the 2004 National Defense Program Outline (NDPO) that outlined Japan's new security policy, and increasingly frequent discussions by prominent politicians regarding the modification of Article IX of the constitution.

Yet change has still been modest. Although the 2004 NDPO was perhaps most notable for naming China as a potential threat, the overall tenor of the document emphasizes economic interdependence and the "fundamental principles of maintaining exclusively defense-oriented policy and of not becoming a major military power that might pose a threat to foreign countries . . . Japan will continue to uphold the basic policies of securing civilian control, adhering to the three non-nuclear principles, and building a modest defense capability on its own initiative."[43] As noted in chapter 3, although the 2004 NDPO contained much that expanded Japan's security commitments, it also called for reductions in many types of procurement and staffing over the next decade. The NDPO recognized the problems that Japan faces in the future, saying that "while roles which the defense capability has to play are multiplying, the population of the youth of Japan keeps decreasing from low birth rate, and the fiscal conditions continue deteriorating."[44]

There is also widespread public support for Article IX and the values that it symbolizes. Given the LDP's overwhelming majority in the Diet as of 2007, most observers expect Japan to modify Article IX in the near future. Yet opinion polls have consistently found that the Japanese public opposes revision. In May 2001, the *Asahi Shimbun* found that 74 percent of Japanese opposed revision.[45] Three years later, an *Asahi Shimbun* poll of April 2004 found that 60 percent of Japanese opposed changes to Article IX, with only 31 percent in favor.[46] A *Nikkei Shimbun* poll of April 2005 found that Article IX was not the largest cause of concern about the current constitution. In fact, 35 percent of respondents cited the lack of clauses on environmental and privacy rights as the main problem with the current constitution, while 26 percent cited Article IX, 23 percent chose clauses on the organization of the Diet, and 22 percent cited vague restrictions on governmental powers.[47]

Given this generally apathetic reaction to nationalism, the LDP softened a patriotism clause which it had included in a draft of a potential revised constitution. Masaru Tamamoto observes, "With only a tenth of the people polled agreeing that their government reflected popular will, patriotism was going to be a hard sell."[48] Michael Mochizuki concludes that "the only way a constitutional amendment permitting the use of force in international security activities and the exercise of the collective self-defense right will win public acquiescence is one that also requires such military activities to have clear international legitimacy either through the United Nations or another multilateral mechanism."[49]

In domestic politics, opposition to increased assertiveness has waned over the past two decades. The main opposition party in the post–World War II era was the Socialists. Strongly committed to a pacifist approach, and opposed to the U.S.-Japan alliance, the Socialists were staunchly opposed to the conservative LDP. However, with the electoral reforms of the early 1990s, their Social Democratic Party of Japan (SDPJ) made a serious miscalculation that some have even called "suicide."[50] In 1994, the Socialists entered into a coalition with the LDP which allowed the Socialists' leader, Tomiichi Murayama, to become prime minister in Japan. Yet in so doing, the Socialists abandoned five decades of opposition to the U.S.-Japan security treaty and to the Self-Defense Forces.[51] The result was that the Socialists held power in a coalition government for less than two years and effectively removed itself from national politics. Meanwhile, the LDP emerged without any serious political party on the left to halt its rightward slide.

The position of main opposition party has been taken by the Democratic Party of Japan (DPJ), formed in 1996. During the 2005 Diet elections, the DJP put forth a foreign policy platform that placed top priority on repairing relations with Japan's East Asian neighbors and reducing reliance on the United States. However, the election, mainly a referendum on then–Prime Minister Junichiro Koizumi's domestic economic reforms, saw an historic victory for the ruling LDP.[52] The LDP itself has changed, as well. Koizumi managed to weaken much of the foundations of the old LDP ruling system—factions, policy caucuses, and local organization—and centralized control in the party headquarters. Thus, a key uncertainty is how Japanese domestic politics will evolve over the next decade. Koizumi has potentially radically altered Japanese domestic politics, and his transformation of the LDP may mark an enduring change. With the election of Shinzo Abe as Prime Minister in September 2006, it appeared that Japan's more assertive foreign policies would continue. It is notable that Abe's first international trip, weeks after his election, was to Beijing and Seoul, not Washington, and the trip was widely judged a success. However, it remains to be seen whether the LDP will evolve, whether Koizumi is an exception to institutionalized rule in Japan, and how and to what extent the Japanese electorate will welcome a more assertive Japan internationally. The evolution of Japan's foreign relations with both the United States and East Asia depends in part upon how well Japan's leaders balance numerous competing pressures.

The diversity of opinions reflects this unsettled and fluid debate. Japan is thus dealing with a number of issues, such as how to balance economic prosperity with military power, how closely to hew to the United States or Asia, and what type of power Japan should be. Some argue that Japan is a middle power, and that attempting to compete for great power status would be self-defeating. Takeshi Hamashita has developed an argument linking Japan to the traditional Sinocentric Asian hierarchical order, while Yoshihide Soeya has argued that Japan is a middle power and as such should formulate policies consistent with that status.[53] Soeya has said that the difference in Article IX reflects the "twisted roots" of Japan's postwar foreign policy:

> The postwar taboos [Article IX, the military] are gone, so everything is being discussed. But the changing discourse doesn't really inform actual policy changes. In fact, the changes reflected in the 2004 NDPO indicate that Japan is becoming a full-fledged middle power. It's not a military document, because the document really focuses more on international security— peacekeeping, multilateral institution building, and other aspects of international politics. Japan in the future will be more like Canada or Australia, and in that sense, Article IX has become a liability, not an asset.[54]

Akiko Fukushima, who was an advisor to Koizumi on foreign affairs issues, said in 2006 that "most Japanese politicians and policymakers know that we cannot compete with China or the United States. We know that we are actually a middle power, and we are just trying to come to terms with that . . . we have two main goals. First, to maintain the U.S.-Japan alliance. The second is to be a responsible and reliable actor in Asia . . . our question is how to conduct our foreign policy while realizing our constraints."[55]

The other mainstream perspective consists of those who wish Japan to become a "normal nation," exemplified by a strong military and a close U.S.-Japan alliance. Ichiro Ozawa was an early advocate, arguing for Japanese deployment of military forces, revision of the constitution, and a more balanced Japanese foreign policy.[56] Koizumi and Abe both come from this perspective. They view China as a potential threat, and although they advocate a military buildup, Richard Samuels notes that they "have eschewed identifying Japan as a great power . . . they continue to hew to the Yoshida rhetoric of Japan as a peace-loving nation."[57] Among this strategy's supporters are the Japanese Defense Agency, conservative newspapers such as the *Yomiuri Shimbun*, and other elements in the Ministry of Foreign Affairs, all of whom firmly support a close U.S.-Japan military and diplomatic relationship. Christopher Hughes concludes that "the collapse of the 1955 political system has precipitated a fundamental shift in Japanese elite political attitudes toward security policy. Japan's two major political parties are now committed to the maintenance of the U.S.-Japan alliance and increasingly equate Japan's future international security contribution with some form of JSDF [Japan Self-Defense Force] overseas dispatch and the exercise of military power."[58]

Two other perspectives exist on the margins of this domestic debate. The extreme right wing in Japan (typified by Tokyo Governor Shintaro Ishihara), although relatively marginalized, has become more influential in the past few years. This group, whom Samuels labels "neo-autonomists," harbors resentment against both China and the United States. They believe that Japanese military power is important for its own sake, as national prestige, and doubt the depth of the U.S.-Japan alliance, as exemplified by a speech by Ishihara in 2005. He claimed that "if tension between the United States and China heightens, if each side pulls the trigger, though it may not be stretched to nuclear weapons, and the wider hostilities expand, I believe America cannot win," and added that the security treaty between Japan and the United States is "so undependable."[59] They view nuclear armament as a necessity, and view Japanese apologies for past militarism as an affront. While these views are not yet completely legitimate in Japan, they have gained increasing currency over the years.

Pacifists—those who seek a reduced or eliminated military, and more distance in the U.S.-Japan alliance—are the weakest segment at this point. As noted earlier, the Socialists severely weakened themselves with disastrous political calculations in the mid-1990s, and with the rise of regional issues such as the North Korea problem, their argument that a Japanese military was detrimental to Japanese wealth and security became less convincing. Pacifism has lost its resonance in Japanese domestic discourse, and although a strand of the population still hews to these values, it is the least powerful of the four major viewpoints.

Japanese domestic politics and discourse is in a state of change. The old Cold War consensus has largely dissipated, and a new one has not yet arisen. It does seem safe to conclude that Japan is considering how much more muscular its foreign policy should be, and how best to achieve a number of goals within a changed domestic and international context. Its future course is still unclear.

THE U.S.-JAPAN ALLIANCE

Japan's recent movement in the direction of a more muscular foreign policy can only be understood within the context of a deepened U.S.-Japan alliance.

Even with Japan's increasing assertiveness, it remains difficult to conceive that it would pursue a security strategy independent of the United States. Yet support for the alliance is not unalloyed; Japanese policymakers have a persistent concern about the endurance and depth of the U.S.-Japan relationship. On the one hand, Japan fears being entrapped by a United States that has lost influence in the region and is moreover embarking upon ventures that may not reflect the goals or desires of the Japanese people. On the other hand, Japan fears abandonment by the United States, and wonders about the American commitment to Japan's own security.

To that end, Japan appears to be hedging its relationship with the United States, although not to the extent that it is hedging its relationship with China. In fact, the Prime Minister's Task Force on Foreign Relations in 2002 released a document outlining "Basic Strategies for Japan's Foreign Policy in the 21st Century," which reiterated that the "United States is the most important country for Japan . . . [yet] it is impossible that the Japan-U.S. relationship will become like the one between the UK and the U.S."[60] Reflecting Japan's omnidirectional hedging, the prime minister's report of 2000 recommends that Japan "build creative relationships with Asia while continuing to use the Japan-U.S. relationship as an invaluable asset."[61]

Koizumi drew closer to the United States on a number of initiatives—participating in the U.S. Proliferation Security Initiative to control weapons of mass destruction, sending 500 troops to Iraq to participate in the "Coalition of the Willing," and supporting a generally more coercive American approach to North Korea.[62] Japanese officials have also agreed to revise the defense cooperation guidelines to allow for Japanese rear-area support of U.S. military operations in areas "surrounding Japan." In 2006, the Japanese central government agreed to cover more than half the costs of relocating 6,000 U.S. Marines from their bases in Okinawa to Guam. Japan has joined the United States in its missile defense initiative, and deployed Japanese non-combat troops to Iraq and the Indian Ocean.[63] In February 2003, Japanese Defense Minister Shigeru Ishiba even argued that preemption was allowed under the Japanese constitution, saying, "Attacking North Korea after a missile attack on Japan is too late."[64]

Yet the actual change in Japan's foreign policy has been incremental, not wholesale. While widening its use of force, Japan is still very conservative compared to the roles that other states assume without controversy. Indeed, the Japanese troop deployment to Iraq required that Australian troops guard them, to ensure that no Japanese casualties occurred. As a senior Bush administration official said in 2005, "we've made sure the Australians are surrounding the Japanese forces, because even one casualty would cause Koizumi major difficulties with the Japanese electorate. We [the U.S.] decided the symbolic support was more important than the practical difficulties of protecting them."[65]

The United States is clearly hoping that Japan can be the linchpin of its broader East Asian presence. Samuels notes, "Washington's exhortations that Tokyo expand its security footprint have never been so strident or grandiose."[66] Christopher Hill, assistant secretary of state for East Asian and Pacific Affairs, said that "in many ways, [the U.S.-Japan alliance] is a model for what we hope many countries around the world can and will achieve."[67] Former assistant secretary for East Asian and Pacific Affairs James Kelly said in congressional testimony that "over the next few years, we hope to build with Japan an enhanced strategic dialogue," while the U.S. *National Security Strategy* of 2002 said the Bush administration would "look to Japan to continue forging a leading role in regional and global affairs."[68]

Tokyo's willingness to go along with Washington's desire for a more assertive Japan has sparked a reaction within East Asia and Japan itself. However, Tamamoto comments, "America's Japan handlers had wishfully chosen to ignore the nationalist baggage that comes with 'normal state' advocacy. The United States is the only country possessing leverage over both Japan and China, and Washington has arguably squandered that advantage."[69] John Ikenberry writes, "Complicating matters, the United States has urged Tokyo along the course of great power 'normalization.' . . . [Yet] 'normalization' and 'historical reconciliation' are working at cross-purposes."[70]

Japan's alliance with the United States is hardly the only cause for this unresolved relationship between Japan and its neighbors. However, whereas previously the alliance was viewed as reassuring other states about Japan's intentions while simultaneously protecting Japan, it is now the United States that is urging Japan to become more active both globally and within the region. Wu Xinbo observes, "For years, many Chinese analysts regarded the U.S.-Japanese alliance as a useful constraint on Japan's remilitarization. Developments since the mid-1990s . . . however, have convinced them that the alliance has become an excuse for Japan to pursue a more active security policy."[71]

U.S. officials, although they view the warmer alliance differently, do recognize this possibility. For example, a senior U.S. administration official said in 2005 that "we see changing Article IX as meaning Japan can be more involved in peacekeeping operations, anti-piracy, and anti-terrorism. We have no indications or fears that Japan would militarize. The question is whether East Asian countries would see it the same way."[72] As Eugene Matthews has noted, "fear [of Japanese nationalism] stems from two basic concerns: first, that if Japan's military is given too much power it could against cause the country great pain and, second, that the Japanese public itself could again embrace militarism."[73]

Even those who view the U.S.-Japan alliance as critical for Japanese security note that the United States is not necessarily a reliable or desirable ally. There have been persistent fears in Japan that either they would be "entrapped" by the United States into conflicts they did not wish to participate in, or that they would be abandoned when Japanese and American interests diverged. Although Japanese security is linked to the United States, Japanese public opinion is not unequivocally behind U.S. global foreign policy objectives. The *Asahi Shimbun* found that before the U.S. attack on Iraq in 2003, 78 percent of Japanese opposed a war, and 70 percent felt that the Bush administration's policies were arrogant or destabilizing.[74] Samuels concludes, "Tokyo sees [Washington's] diplomatic vigor, moral authority, and economic allure as already waning, particularly in Asia."[75]

Despite these concerns, the Japan-U.S. alliance remains the central pillar of Japan's grand strategy. As Mochizuki notes, "the possibility of Japan breaking out militarily by acquiring offensive capabilities and nuclear weapons and by adopting a doctrine of pre-emption is slim."[76] As noted in chapter 3, the closer U.S.-Japan alliance has created conditions under which Japan can actually confront China with more confidence. However, the least likely future scenario is one in which Japan decides to confront China itself, outside the confines of the alliance. As Leonard Schoppa has said, "It is only within the context of the alliance that Japan can confront China. Because of the American security blanket, Japan can get away with [provocative statements]. Without the U.S. alliance, Japan would follow the same course as the rest of Asia—accommodating China's rise."[77] Eugene Matthews speculates that "counterintuitively, Japan and China could also draw closer together if Japan decides to reassert itself—if, that is, both countries recognize the risks of an escalating arms race."[78] Although there is uncertainty about what Japan would do without its U.S. alliance, the fact that such questions can be asked shows the unresolved nature of Japan's national identity, and the lingering suspicions about how it might act.

In sum, the U.S.-Japan alliance has succeeded admirably in providing for Japanese security and projecting U.S. interests in the region, while simultaneously reassuring other East Asian states about Japan's intentions. However, six decades of a close relationship between Japan and the United States did not resolve the fundamental question about Japanese identity. In fact, the alliance merely froze Japan in place, and neither Japan nor its neighbors has yet resolved their fundamental relationship. As a result, both Japanese and

East Asians have become frustrated. Japanese see six decades of peaceful and restrained foreign policy as proving that the days of Japanese imperialism are over. They are frustrated at continued Chinese and Korean suspicions about their intentions, and are tired of constantly "kowtowing" for the actions of their ancestors. East Asians see a Japan that is a junior partner to the United States, one that, if it pursued a truly independent foreign policy, could potentially behave irresponsibly and become a disruptive force within the region. They see six decades of grudging Japanese reticence marked by insincere apologies backed by little or no substantive change in the Japanese mind-set.

HISTORICAL NARRATIVES AND THE ISSUE OF JAPANESE IDENTITY

The issue of Japanese identity has most often manifested itself in renewed friction over "history." In the past few years, disagreements between Japan and China, Russia, and South Korea have erupted over a number of issues, many of which derive from questions about how Japan remembers or avoids remembering its imperialist behavior in East Asia during the first half of the twentieth century. For example, China and South Korea regularly object to the content of Japanese junior high school textbooks that purportedly gloss over Japanese imperialism. They also criticize Japanese politicians when they visit the Yasukuni shrine—a Shinto shrine dedicated to worship of soldiers who died in service of the emperor, and which houses the remains of some World War II Japanese soldiers who were convicted of war crimes. The Japanese treatment of "comfort women" (East Asians, mostly South Korean and Filipinos, who were forced into sexual slavery during World War II by the Japanese) is also an issue, as is the Japanese treatment of the 1937 "Nanjing massacre," when Japanese troops ransacked Nanjing. Territorial disputes also exist between Japan and Russia, South Korea, and China about ownership of various islands, further inflaming passions in Japan and in the region.[79]

However, to call these disputes "historical" is a mischaracterization and obfuscates more than it illuminates. While some dispute is actually about historical facts, such as whether the Nanjing massacre actually occurred, much is not about historical fact but rather about the meaning of those facts. That is, historical disputes have arisen from the changing, and unresolved, identities and political relationships in the region, and the manner in which national narratives have dealt with history. The debate is over how history is remembered, and how it is characterized in the present; the dispute is thus the most obvious indicator of how Japan and its neighbors view one another, and themselves, and their roles in the region. Indeed, the issues would be much easier to solve if they really were about history: just find better historians and archeologists. But while history is the proximate cause of this friction, the ultimate cause is the underlying mistrust between the neighboring countries about not only the others' intentions, but also their underlying identities. Because of the unresolved political relations, it is not surprising that history is resurfacing as an issue.

For example, territorial disputes are not about who owned the islands first. First, were one side be somehow able to definitely prove initial ownership, it would not make the slightest impact on the beliefs of the other side. Second, and more importantly, the issue arises because historically, sovereignty over uninhabited rocks was not an issue, and thus border demarcation among the ancient kingdoms was categorically different than it is today. Applying modern concepts of territorial sovereignty deep into the past has little utility, because these concepts did not exist back then. Finally and most importantly, the issue could easily be resolved if political relations in the present were stronger—since they are not, historical issues take on a resonance that is greater than its actual significance.

There are a number of reasons why these historical issues have returned after a few decades in which they were less salient. First, Japan has not felt as threatened by its neighbors, and in particular, by China, until recently. When Japan was clearly the most powerful country in East Asia, it was easier for it to avoid provoking its neighbors. As China has become more powerful, Japanese have begun to feel that their efforts to reassure their neighbors have been unduly rebuffed, and Japanese resentment toward China has begun to increase.[80] Second, as noted above, the U.S.-Japan alliance put Japan's conception of its national identity into suspension. Although it was not clear what Japanese identity was, at least with the U.S. Cold War alliance, Japan was stable. As that domestic Japanese consensus has begun to weaken, a question is emerging in both Japan and the region as to Japan's future course.

For China, this tension with Japan is not particularly surprising. China's leadership faces the difficult balancing act of both developing a modus vivendi with Japan, while at the same time controlling Chinese nationalism that in many cases is more virulently anti-Japanese than is that of the leadership. China as well is also suspicious of what Japan's tone-deafness means. Wu Xinbo writes, "Japan's actions on all these issues [textbooks, Yasukuni shrine, and the Pacific War] affected partly by its unique cultural tradition and partly by its rising political conservatism, only fuel the Chinese belief that Japan is fundamentally incapable of behaving as a responsible power and achieving genuine reconciliation with its neighbors."[81]

South Korea's troubles with Japan are somewhat more surprising. While China remains an authoritarian, communist country, South Korea and Japan are both advanced capitalist democracies with long-standing alliances with the United States. Furthermore, both countries are deeply intertwined in their economic relations. As such, the bickering over ownership of the Dokdo/Takeshima Islands and prime ministerial visits to the Yasukuni shrine is all the more anomalous. In part these issues resonate because of domestic politics: leaders on both sides have been pandering to their domestic constituents, and getting worked up over a meaningless set of rocks is easier to do than concentrating on divisive and difficult issues such as North Korean nuclear proliferation, free trade agreements, and how to deal with the United States and China. Partly it is a lack of leadership on both sides: while former Prime Minister Koizumi and South Korean President Roh Moo-hyun could have worked to resolve these issues, they were both content to ride the wave that is focused on history. When Shinzo Abe became prime minister in September 2006, he quickly visited both China and South Korea, signaling a willingness to improve relations with both countries. However, it is still too early to tell how Abe will ultimately handle these issues, or what his basic approach will be. Finally, these disputes are a convenient excuse for other frustrations the two sides have with each other: South Korea is concerned about Japan's moves to change its military stance, while Japan is frustrated that South Korea continues to engage rather than contain North Korea. These frustrations form an explosive mix of sentiment and anger.

Gilbert Rozman notes, "In particular, Japan has failed to bolster its claims to leadership by 1) setting a high moral tone in its treatment of history; 2) forming networks and exchanges where moral issues are addressed; and 3) developing a vision of regionalism capable of winning confidence from others."[82] Yet Tamamoto pointed out in May 2006, "Those in favor [of Yasukuni visits by the Prime Minister] say that China should not dictate what Koizumi should do. Those against say that Koizumi should not upset China . . . what is curiously missing in the popular discussion is the significance of Yasukuni itself."[83]

Clashing national identities, linked to problems in national narratives about historical events, are the primary problem. For example, on the occasion marking the eighty-seventh anniversary of the March 1 Independence Movement in South Korea, Roh advised Koizumi that an act of a nation's leader should be judged by the standard of whether it is proper in light of universal conscience and historical experience. His remarks on Japan's moves with regard to a revision of the pacifist constitution—that an "ordinary country" does not have to entail a military buildup—were followed by Koizumi's advice to Roh that he should take a close look at Japan's footprints in the sixty-year postwar period and its efforts toward a friendly relationship.[84] While the leaders of both nations were busy giving each other advice, the issues threatened to spiral out of control.[85]

On the subject of the Dokdo Islands dispute, one South Korean diplomat noted, "it is not the islands themselves that is upsetting. It's what Japan's actions tell us about Japan's mind-set. The Yasukuni shrine visits, Dokdo, and the textbooks are all evidence that not much has fundamentally changed in Japan, and they view the world the same way they did a hundred years ago. For a country that wishes to take a role of real responsibility, that is worrisome."[86] In 2006, Roh said that "Japan has already apologized. We do not demand that they apologize once again. We demand that they put their apology into practice. If Japan aspires to become an 'ordinary country' and even a 'leading nation' of the world, it should try to earn the trust of the international community by acting in conformity with universal standards of conscience and decency."[87]

The difficulties that Japan has with its neighbors were not confined to China and Korea. Japan has also not resolved its disputes with Russia over territory, and indeed clashes arose between Russia and Japan in summer 2006 over the disputed Kuril Islands, with Russian security forces killing a Japanese fisherman and arresting three others. Since 1994, Russia has seized thirty Japanese fishing boats and wounded seven Japanese fishermen.[88] Negotiations between Russia and Japan over the four disputed islands have been at an impasse since World War II, and in the spring of 2007 negotiations were still deadlocked, with the Japanese proposing "all or nothing" solutions, while the Russians were asking what Japan would give in return for the islands.[89] Noted Joseph Ferguson, "as long as the historical issues of World War II remain unresolved in East Asia . . . Japanese-Russian bilateral relations will continue to tread the familiar path of mistrust and misunderstanding."[90]

In early 2006, Japanese Foreign Minister Taro Aso claimed that Japanese colonization is the cause of high educational levels in Taiwan. This had the unique effect of uniting both China and Taiwan in denouncing his stance. The Chinese foreign ministry said it amounted to "overtly glorifying invasion history that made Taiwanese people suffer," while a Taiwanese deputy education minister said that educational levels are attributable to Chinese cultural traits; parents "would sell their land so their children could go to school . . . [Educational success] has nothing to do with Japan's colonization," he said.[91] Hugo Restall wrote, "Japan has mishandled its World War II past for so long, and botched its transition to being a 'normal nation' so badly, that it is becoming diplomatically marginalized in its own region."[92]

Even some Southeast Asian states have not been so sanguine about Japan's moves. Speaking in 2006 in Tokyo, former Singaporean Prime Minister Lee Kuan Yew said "there's this underlying fear that the Japanese drive for perfection and supremacy will once again lead to unhappy clashes."[93] As Keiichi Tsunekawa notes, "in China, South Korea, and some Southeast Asian countries, distrust of and animosity toward Japan persist, based on historical memory."[94] Lee Kuan Yew has likened Japan to an alcoholic who merely has not had a drink in sixty years. When Japan sent peacekeeping troops to Cambodia in the early 1990s, Lee said, "To let an armed Japan participate [in peacekeeping operations] is like giving a chocolate filled with whiskey to an alcoholic."[95]

Ryutaro Hashimoto recounted that while he was prime minister of Japan in the late 1990s, Singapore's Lee complained to him that although Japanese tourists were common in Singapore, they had virtually no idea of Japanese actions there during World War II, and he asked Hashimoto to do something about that.[96] In another reminder of the past being kept alive, the *Mainichi Shimbun* reported that despite the fact that Southeast Asian countries benefit from trading relations with Japan, the country's image at the 2005 ASEAN annual meeting had been "tarnished" by repeated criticism of Koizumi's visit to the Yasukuni shrine.[97]

Yet it is important to keep these diplomatic disputes over history in context: very few of them had actual consequences for policies between Japan and its East Asian neighbors. As noted in chapter 3, these disputes are important, and hinder the creation of enduring and stable relations. But the possibility of the use of force is absent, and even economic relations between Japan and its neighbors have not been unduly affected. In 2005, Japanese investment into China hit a record high of $6.5 billion, rising 19.8 percent over 2004. Koji Sako of the Japan Overseas Trade Organization noted that the economic relationship between Japan and China is now sufficiently compelling and mature to overcome occasional political flare-ups. Said Sako, "The Japanese market is flat and the population is declining. China is therefore very important."[98] Two thousand overseas Chinese entrepreneurs held a conference in Kobe, Japan, in September 2006, sponsored by the Chinese Chamber of Commerce in Japan, with strong support of the Japanese Ministry of Foreign Affairs.[99]

Although Roh's frigidly polite interaction with Koizumi at the East Asia Summit was noted throughout the region, most policies between Japan and

South Korea are unchanged. Their economic interaction proceeds apace, and the long-discussed free-trade agreement between the two countries is a victim not of sentiment regarding history, but of much more mundane domestic politics and an unwillingness by either side to give ground on agricultural issues. In fact, absolute trade and investment flows between the two countries continue to increase, even though the relative share of Japan's total trade with South Korea declined. Indeed, total trade between Japan and South Korea increased almost $30 billion between 2001 and 2005.[100] Japan and South Korea have also continued to work together on a number of other issues. For example, in 2005 the two countries signed the bilateral currency swap deals at the Bank of Korea. The agreement, worth $3 billion, will help stabilize their financial markets and provide for the lending of short-term capital to the other party when one runs short of foreign currency. Nobuhiro Hiwatari notes that "there has been little complaint from Japanese multinational corporations that their businesses have been hurt in Korea."[101] Economist Andy Xie notes that China-Japan economic relations are flourishing even though the two governments are "barely on speaking terms."[102] Japanese policy toward North Korea was stalled in 2007; but that was because the six-party talks themselves had seen only limited progress. Thus, although diplomatic relations were hardly warm, these disputes remained the province of rhetoric and domestic showmanship.

Resolution of these issues—such as territory and textbooks and, more broadly, the entire issue of "history"—will take sustained attention and energy from the leaders of all countries in the region. Masaru Tamamoto observes that "for the Japanese to cure their amnesia, to grasp why Asia is so suspicious of them, it is also necessary to recapture their history, to connect the present with the past."[103] Instead of riding popular sentiment, it will take leaders who decide to create a genuine stable relationship with one another, and are willing to devote political capital to such an end. Until that happens, and as long as both sides pander to popular sentiment instead of confronting it, these issues will keep resurfacing as major events.

JAPAN AND CHINA: COLD POLITICS, HOT ECONOMICS

China-Japan relations show both elements of cooperation and competition, often referred to in Japan as "*seirei keinetsu*" (cold politics, hot economics). Economic relations have become steadily closer at both the governmental and firm levels, and Japanese firms are increasingly sourcing their production into China. Economic cooperation, efforts at economic institution building, and interdependence between China and Japan have been growing. Politically, however, the two countries have a stable working relationship marred by sporadic disputes at the rhetorical level.[104] Disputes over territory, textbooks, and the Yasukuni shrine episodically occur, although these have remained as minor diplomatic squabbles for quite some time now. Although military conflict between Japan and China—or even any major disruption in their economic or diplomatic relations—remains unthinkable, Japan and China have not completely arrived at a stable equilibrium in their relationship, and in some ways the overall relationship has deteriorated over the last decade.

HOT ECONOMICS

The economic relationship between these two countries is deep and growing deeper. Already the transformation of China has allowed it to take an important position in the regional economy, and Japan's influence has summarily receded, although it remains substantial. Yet not only has Japan not shown overt fear of China, it is moving closer to China and the two economies are becoming more integrated. There is even evidence that Japan realizes and accepts that China may eventually dominate the region. As Saadia Pekkanen writes, "A wide range of Japanese academics, trade bureaucrats, lawyers, judges, and especially businessmen say with stunning pragmatism that debate is over—China has already passed Japan politically and will pass Japan economically; Japan has always been number two, first globally vis-à-vis the United States and soon also regionally with respect to China."[105] Pekkanen argues that Japan's increasing focus on regional free-trade agreements is a direct strategy "designed to ensure its economic security—long the most consistent and dominant of goals for the Japanese government, and the least likely to ever go away."[106]

From the normalization of ties between Beijing and Tokyo in 1972, on into the late 1990s, Japan's overall approach to China emphasized the positive economic aspects to its relations. Japan supported and encouraged China's emergence into the world community, provided China with extensive official development assistance despites China's export of arms, and supported China's bid to join the World Trade Organization. During the 1990s, Japanese economic relations with China intensified. In 2004 China became Japan's largest trade partner, and in 2005 two-way trade between China and Japan grew 12.4 percent to 24.9 trillion yen, larger than U.S.-Japan bilateral trade of 21.8 trillion yen, which only grew 6 percent.[107] In 2002, China passed the United States as the largest exporter to Japan, and total Japanese trade with China is rapidly closing the gap with total U.S.-Japan trade (see Figure 7.1).[108] Japan does twice as much trade with China as does the United States, and Japanese trade with China is growing faster than U.S. trade with China.[109] In fact, between 2000 and 2004, trade with the United States actually decreased, from 23.2 trillion yen in 2000 to 20.5 trillion yen in 2004.[110] China is also the largest recipient of Japanese investment in Asia.[111] Japan accounted for two-thirds of all China's receipts of bilateral aid from 1980 to 2000, while the United States did not give any aid to China.[112] Japanese investment in China continues to expand, and over 32,000 Japanese companies had operations in China as of 2006. Koizumi said in 2002, "I see the advancement of Japan-China economic relations not as hollowing out of Japanese industry but as an opportunity to nurture new industries in Japan."[113]

In cultural flows as well, China has rapidly become a major source and destination for Japan. For example, 1.5 million Japanese tourists visited China in 2000, an increase of 41 percent in three years, and by 2003, more Chinese students were studying in Japan than in the United States.[114] As Pekkanen notes, "it is difficult perhaps for Americans to appreciate just how much—in perception and also increasingly in fact—the U.S. has slipped and China has loomed on the Japanese trade policy horizon."[115] More than 150,000 Chinese

FIGURE 7.1 JAPANESE TOTAL TRADE WITH CHINA AND UNITED STATES, 1980–2005

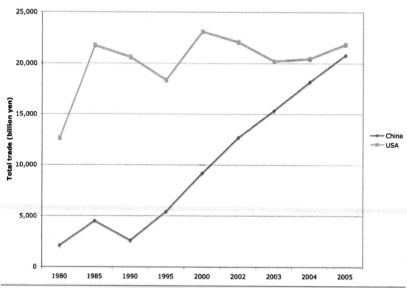

SOURCE: *JAPAN STATISTICAL YEARBOOK 2007* (TOKYO: MINISTRY OF INTERNAL AFFAIRS AND COMMUNICATIONS, 2007), HTTP://WWW.STAT.GO.JP/ENGLISH/DATA/NENKAN/INDEX.HTM.

students attend Japanese universities, and ten million Chinese work for Japanese companies in China. In turn, it is estimated that 100,000 Japanese lived in Shanghai in 2005, and Japanese investment in China reached $ 31.5 billion in 2005.[116] Furthermore, 9.2 million Chinese work for the over 32,000 Japanese companies with operations in China, and Japan has created a $10 billion endowment to pay for 1,100 Chinese schoolchildren each year to conduct homestays with Japanese families.[117]

China and Japan have institutionalized their relationship in other ways as well. The Japanese and Chinese prime ministers meet several times each year, although that was disrupted in the final years of Koizumi's rule. The leaders of the two countries meet at the annual APEC summit meeting, the ASEAN+3 summit, the Sino-Japan summit (since 1998), the trilateral summit between China, Japan, and South Korea (since 2000), and the Boao Forum (since 2002). As Eric Heginbotham and Richard Samuels note, "the China-Japan relationship has already become more institutionalized than most analysts have expected."[118]

Cooperation at the working level is more stable than at the highest political levels. Despite the antagonism between China and Japan over various issues, companies and government officials from both countries have good working relations, and this cooperation often involves South Korea, too. For example, in the summer of 2005, the Chinese, Japanese, and Korean coast guards participated in a short series of rescue and antiterrorism exercises off the coast of China.[119] In 2006 the ministers of China, Japan, and South Korea who are in charge of tourism held their first-ever meeting to boost the number of visitors among the three countries to 17 million in five years, 5 million higher than the present level, and agreed that they would meet annually, taking turns as hosts. Their "Hokkaido Declaration" expressed the importance of peace and stability in East Asia through strengthened interactions and joint promotion campaigns, and promised to remove obstacles to tourism exchanges. Another inaugural trilateral meeting of the transportation ministers was held in 2006, aimed at creating a "seamless logistics system" in Northeast Asia, with plans to meet annually and the goal of eventually evolving into an intergovernmental cooperative channel. Finally in 2006, finance ministers of South Korea, Japan, and China met and agreed to start joint research at a government level to study the prospects for a single regional currency.[120]

In addition to this working-level cooperation, Japan is moving quickly to increase East Asian institutionalization. Japan approved China's entry into the WTO four months earlier than the United States. Moreover, Gen Nakatani, Koizumi's defense minister, suggested in February 2002 that Japan and

China work towards the creation of an "Asian NATO," which is a departure from Japan's traditional focus on the U.S.-Japan alliance. In 2004, the Japanese Ministry of Economy, Trade, and Industry created a permanent division of Economic Partnership, taking an unusually large staff of over eighty-five personnel, while the Ministry of Foreign Affairs created a similar Economic Partnership division of forty staff members. Both divisions are aimed at expanding Japan's regional and economic integration into the region.[121]

Japan is also engaging in regional institution building. This is in part spurred by China's active foreign policy in this area. In November 2000, China proposed the creation of an ASEAN-China free trade area, which ASEAN accepted, and which prompted Japan to follow suit and propose a similar ASEAN-Japan free-trade area the very next day. That Japan was reacting to China's initiatives has not gone unnoticed in Southeast Asia. As Heginbotham and Samuels note, in 2000 and 2001 China's move "challenged Japanese economic leadership in the region. Japan . . . stumbled along as China set the pace, shape, and direction of regional trade institution building."[122] Pekkanen comments, "it is instructive that for decades while the U.S. and Europe pursued such pacts, Japan did nothing. It was only when its emerging powerful neighbor began to show interest in the idea (of regional pacts) that Japan began to get more serious."[123]

LUKEWARM POLITICS

While economic, cultural, and institutional relations between Japan and China have rapidly gained both density and scope, political relations between the two have not seen the same progress. Still, while political relations are probably not "warm," and the public squabbling between leaders has received much of the attention, there has been stability in their bilateral relations, and both sides have worked with care to manage the relationship and keep those diplomatic squabbles from overwhelming the economic relationship and sidetracking diplomatic efforts.

Japan normalized diplomatic relations with China in 1972, six years earlier than the United States. In 1978, China and Japan signed a treaty of friendship, and the following year Deng Xiaoping visited Tokyo, while Japanese Prime Minister Masayoshi Ohira visited Beijing. A decade later, after the Tiananmen Square incident in 1989, it was Japan that put pressure on the United States not to enact an embargo against China.[124] In 1994, while the United States was pressuring China over human rights, Japanese Prime Minister Morihiro Hosokawa visited Beijing and publicly distanced Japan from the United States, saying that it was not wise for one country to try to impose its democratic values on another.[125]

Ever since the 1972 China-Japan Joint Statement that there is one China, and the de-recognition of Taiwan, Japan has continually reiterated its support for the "One China policy." Over the years, Japanese prime ministers and other government officials have consistently reaffirmed the 1972 statement. For example, in 1995, Prime Minister Keizo Obuchi signed a joint statement with President Jiang Zemin that "Japan promised to abide by its stance on the Taiwan issue as contained in the China-Japan Joint Statement, and reiterated that there is only one China."[126] In 2002, the Japanese Foreign Ministry persuaded Keio University to withdraw an invitation to Taiwan's former president, Lee Teng-hui, a Keio alumnus.[127]

However, the "honeymoon" in Japan-China political relations began to cool in the 1990s. The revision of the U.S.-Japan Mutual Defense Treaty Guidelines in 1997 actually made Japan's military role in Taiwan even more ambiguous. The revision expanded the scope of defense cooperation to include the "surrounding areas" of Japan.[128] When pressed for clarification by China, the official Japanese response was that "surrounding areas" is not a geographical concept, but a situational one.[129]

Japanese public opinion regularly rates trade disputes and concern over official development assistance from Japan to China as more important than military or political issues.[130] Jian Yang cites Japanese opinion poll data showing that in 2001 the number of those who think China friendly dropped from 75.4 percent in 1985 to 47.5 percent.[131] A *Mainichi Shimbun* poll in 2004 asking about "countries threatening Japan" found that North Korea ranked first (50 percent), China second (24 percent), and the United States third (11 percent).[132] In terms of major problems in Sino-Japanese relations, a 2004 poll conducted by the Japanese Ministry of Foreign Affairs found that trade issues, crimes by Chinese in Japan, and maritime disputes were three of the top four issues cited by respondents (the other being "historical consciousness"). Military issues were fifth, and Taiwan was sixth. Another Ministry of Foreign Affairs poll found that in "areas of concern regarding China," economic development far outranked military capabilities as the top concern, with 61.8 percent of respondents citing economic development, while only 32.6 percent cited military capabilities.[133] Poll numbers continued to show the Chinese military threat a distant second behind North Korea. A 2005 *Asahi Shimbun* poll found almost identical results: North Korea by far was considered the most threatening country to Japan, with China and the United States a distant second and third.[134] The Japanese Cabinet Office's opinion survey of April 30, 2006, revealed that 63.7 percent of respondents referred to the situation on the Korean peninsula as the great concern to Japan's peace and security, while 46.2 percent cited international terrorist organizations, 36.3 percent China's military buildup, and 29.6 percent arms control of weapons of mass destruction and missiles.

Reflecting Japan's dual hedge, public opinion polls regularly reveal that the Japanese public, although wary of China, is almost as wary of the United States. For example, when asked about overall opinion of the United States, a 2005 *Asahi Shimbun* poll found that 22.8 percent of Japanese respondents held favorable opinions, 14.7 percent held unfavorable opinions, and 61.0 percent had a neutral opinion. This compares with Japanese views of China—where 9.9 percent held favorable opinions, 27.6 held unfavorable opinions, and 59.8 percent were neutral. Those same respondents felt China was the most important for Japan's economy in the future, at 39.1 percent, compared to 32.8 percent citing the U.S. Asked about China's economic growth, 45.6 percent thought China's growth would have a favorable effect on Japan, while 31.7 felt it would have a negative impact.[135] However, although observers often focus on occasional surges in Japanese negative feelings about China, Masaru Tamamoto notes that "between 1990 and 2004 the proportion of Japanese who said they liked or disliked China hovered around 30 percent . . . in other words, a large majority of Japanese do not normally harbor any distinct feeling toward China."[136]

Michael Wills comments, "Japan and China have refrained from engaging in a direct interactive military competition . . . concerns on both sides do not add up to an arms race."[137] The National Defense Program Outline of 2004 did mention China, saying it "continues to modernize its nuclear forces and missile capabilities as well as its naval and air forces. . . . We will have to remain attentive to its future actions."[138] One year later, on February 19, 2005, the "Joint Statement of the U.S.-Japan Security Consultative Committee" noted that common strategic objectives of Japan and the United States include "developing a cooperative relationship with China, welcoming the country to play a responsible and constructive role regionally as well as globally."[139] It is difficult to read anything into this other than an attempt by the United States and Japan to cooperate with China. As Ralph Cossa notes, this mention "hardly constitutes a demonstration of Japan's willingness to confront the rapidly growing might of China."[140]

The fact that in the past Japan has followed a restrained grand strategy has led scholars to view even the smallest of changes in its foreign policy as a sign of major militarization. However, such small steps are exactly that—small and marginal steps, not major changes. As Gregory Noble notes, "some of Japan's most important security concerns can be addressed most effectively by maintaining good relations with China."[141] Tokyo has chosen to embrace China economically and hedge against China militarily. Japanese are worried about China—and their embrace of the U.S. security alliance is their way of hedging the opportunity and threat that arise from China's emergence. At this point, economic interdependence has not had spillover effects that ameliorate or resolve political disputes.

Over the past half century, Japan's international political role did not keep pace with its economic importance. This has begun to change in the past decade. First under Prime Minister Koizumi, and continuing under Prime Minister Abe, Japan is deepening its alliance with the United States, considering building its military beyond its present levels, and discussing whether to modify Article IX of the constitution. Yet Japan's search for a way to "normalize" its foreign policy and strengthen its relations with the United States has exacerbated unresolved relations with its East Asian neighbors, precisely because of uncertainty in the region about Japan's identity and its ultimate place in the region. Indeed, discussion over whether or not Japan can become a "normal country" exemplifies both the central importance of identity in East Asia, and Japan's unresolved role in East Asia. What is normal and what is not, and how Japan defines its role in the region, are all issues of identity, not power.

Japan's unresolved identity is both reflected in, and exacerbated by, Japan's close alignment with the United States. Japan's willingness to ally with the United States since World War II reflects a long-standing Japanese tendency to rarely challenge a dominant, stable power. At the same time, Japan and the United States tended to reinforce each other's distaste for multilateralism in the region, and the alliance was in part what prevented Japan from crafting a stable relationship with the rest of East Asia; it allowed both Japan and the other East Asian states to avoid dealing with difficult political issues that divide them. Economic interdependence has also had little effect on political relations in the region; they have instead moved in parallel with each other. In fact, Japan has not crafted enduring ties with Russia, China, or the Koreas, despite the increasing economic relations. To that end, identity, rather than military or economic power, is the driving factor behind Japan's foreign policy, and how it develops will have a central role in shaping that foreign policy in the future as well.

Japan is hedging in a number of directions. Although its chief concern is China, it is also worried about the depth and reliability of the U.S. alliance. These two concerns are not symmetric—Japan and the United States have a strong alliance, and that alliance appears set to endure well into the future. Although the consensus behind the postwar Yoshida doctrine has evaporated, Japan has not yet arrived at a new consensus about its grand strategy for the twenty-first century. It does appear, however, that such a grand strategy will involve elements of the omnidirectional foreign policy that is has pursued in the past.[142]

PART III

EAST ASIA AND THE UNITED STATES

One night it came to me . . . that there was nothing to do but to take them all, and to educate the Filipinos, and uplift and civilize and Christianize them as our fellowmen.

—PRESIDENT WILLIAM MCKINLEY, 1898

Dewey could have gone about his affairs elsewhere and left the competent Filipino citizens to set up the form of government they might prefer and deal with the friars and their doubtful acquisitions according to the Filipino idea of justice and fairness—ideas which have since been tested and found to be of as high an order as any that prevail in Europe or America.

—MARK TWAIN, 1898

CHAPTER 8

THE ROLE OF THE UNITED STATES IN EAST ASIA

The United States is not balancing China, and thus it is no surprise that the rest of East Asia is not, either. Debate over whether or not to view China as a threat is increasing in Washington, but so far there is little consensus. The business community is strongly in favor of building durable relations with China, while the military establishment is more skeptical. There are also those who are willing to take a "wait and see" attitude, hoping that over time, developments can assuage U.S. fears about future Chinese intentions.

Threats to the United States in East Asia do not arise from the traditional sources of great power rivalry and conflict. Rather, the greatest threats to the United States in the region could arise from the actions of the smallest and weakest countries, Taiwan and North Korea. Furthermore, these threats are also not direct threats against the United States, but instead they arise indirectly—from a U.S. decision to defend Taiwan, or from the possibility that North Korea could sell nuclear weapons to a Middle Eastern terrorist group that would use it against the United States. Aside from these indirect threats, the United States, like most East Asian countries, faces no direct military threat to its security.

Yet U.S. interests in the region are as much economic as they are military. Economic growth, not military conflict, has been the hallmark of the modern East Asian region, and U.S. economic ties to the region are deep and growing deeper. The United States has traditionally interacted with East Asia through a series of bilateral arrangements, known as the "hub and spoke" model. When U.S. power was at its height during the Cold War, this strategy was largely successful at promoting U.S. interests and fostering growth and stability in the region. Now, however, this strategy is under increasing strain. While relations with Japan have grown closer, most other U.S. bilateral security arrangements in the region are in the process of evolving or being scaled back. At the same time, the rise of regional multilateral cooperative institutions, while hardly in a position to replace the role of the United States, are creating alternate pathways to cooperation. Combined with China's rise and increasingly active diplomacy, the United States is now increasingly in the position of reacting to changes in East Asia, rather than instigating them.

Despite these deep ties to the region, however, the United States is not an East Asian nation; rather, it is a global power with regional interests. The United States is only intermittently attentive to the region; Washington often deems problems elsewhere in the world as more important than issues in East Asia. It will mainly intervene in the region when it is in its interests to do so. This has implications both for U.S. policy in the region, and for how East Asian states view the U.S. presence. The United States remains by far the most powerful and important country in the world, and all East Asian states would like more, not less, American attention to the region, even if they also know they cannot rely on, nor expect, unquestioned U.S. support. Still, most of the states welcome or accept U.S. leadership, in other words, are satisfied with the status quo: a U.S. military presence that is not unduly intrusive, in addition to stable economic relations with China.

To that end, the United States faces a difficult path in the future. It can try to remain the most important and influential country in the region, but this will require more sustained attention to the region and a more equal relationship with many countries than has been the case in the past. Or, the United States can allow East Asian cooperation to develop, with it occasionally being included and occasionally being absent. How U.S. policy develops will have key implications for stability in the region. If the United States and China ultimately begin to balance each other militarily, the region as a whole will become increasingly unstable. If the two great powers find a modus vivendi, even if that is not outright partnership, the region will more likely be stable.

IS THE UNITED STATES AN EAST ASIAN NATION?

As noted in chapter 1, regions are defined by ideational as well as material factors. The processes within the region may be different from those outside of it, and states may interact differently with states inside or outside of the region. The United States has been deeply involved in East Asia for more than a century, but involvement—even war—is not the proper criterion for determining whether a state is within or outside of a region. Rather, as Barry

Buzan has argued, it depends much more on whether the issues within the region are the primary ones upon which the state focuses.[1] By this definition, the United States is a global actor that has regional interests. In defining the United States in this way, I build on the work of scholars such as Thomas Christensen, Christopher Layne, and others, who define the United States as an "offshore balancer" in East Asia.[2]

Popular opinion in the United States sees America as European, not East Asian. Culturally and ethnically, the dominant narrative about American identity focuses on its European and Protestant roots. As recently as 1928, Al Smith was the first legitimate Catholic presidential candidate, and it was not until 1960 that a non-Protestant became president. Indeed, concern about immigration of non–northern European immigrants has existed since the founding of the Republic, beginning with worries about southern European immigration and followed by the Chinese exclusion act of 1882 and other measures in the early twentieth century; today a debate rages about immigration, focused mostly on Hispanics.[3] As Tony Horwitz recently noted, "Coursing through the immigration debate is the unexamined faith that American history rests on English bedrock, or Plymouth Rock to be specific."[4] Scholars regularly group the United States with European countries, categorizing them as "Western" or even "Anglo-American."[5] Ethnically, African-descended Americans make up three times the population than do Asian-descended Americans, 12.8 to 3.8 percent, and yet few would call the United States "an African nation."[6]

Culturally and ethnically, then, it is clear that the United States is not an East Asian nation. Yet politicians regularly assert that, because of its interests in East Asia. However, the key is not whether a state has interests in a particular region, but rather the priority of those interests. The United States has global interests, and can choose to withdraw from any region. Indeed, one enduring strand of U.S. identity is the "isolationist" urge to pull back to the North American continent.[7] This contrasts with the East Asian states, which, despite their global interests and concerns, are principally focused on issues that arise from interactions among themselves.

The Iraq war and the North Korean nuclear issue are good examples of this. While the states of East Asia have been concerned in recent years primarily with North Korea, the United States has focused more on Iraq and events in the Middle East, attempting to manage the North Korean issue here and there. As Admiral James Fallon, commander of U.S. forces in the Asia-Pacific, said in 2006, "[U.S. policymakers] are intensely focused on the Middle East, so I tend to business out here."[8] Were any crisis to develop on the Korean peninsula, the United States would have the option of getting involved or not, while Japan,

China, and the Koreas would have no choice but to deal with that situation. For example, a war or a regime collapse in North Korea would unleash a flood of refugees to the surrounding countries. The United States, however, could choose whether to allow in refugees, and how much money it would want to devote to the aftermath of radical change in North Korea. It's worth remembering that during the Cold War, one of the chief South Korean fears was that the United States would not involve itself in a crisis.[9] It is thus unlikely that the United States will start paying consistent attention to the region, even though East Asian states want more, not less, of that. As Brantley Womack notes, "U.S. participation in [East Asia] is episodic and issue-driven," rather than continual and encompassing.[10]

Still, the United States is the most powerful country in the world—it has been called a "hyper power"—and its power is so much greater than all others that few dare even compete.[11] All states in East Asia—including North Korea and China—want good relations with America; the economic, diplomatic, and military benefits of that relationship can be extraordinary. Furthermore, no East Asian state in the region, even China, wants to exclude the United States from the region.

Although East Asian states are continually developing their own regional institutions, engaging in informal cooperation, and increasingly trading and investing in one another, this is more a natural progression than it is an attempt to exclude the United States. For the past fifty years, the United States was the unquestioned dominant military and economic power in the region, so it was possible to ignore the nascent East Asian attempts at cooperation. However, China now seems more willing to work with multilateral regimes than is the United States. The United States has not signed ASEAN's Treaty on Amity and Cooperation, while China has. The United States refuses to sign the UNCLOS (U.N. Convention on the Law of the Sea), which forms the basis of ASEAN maritime cooperation, while China has signed it. The United States is belatedly beginning to negotiate free-trade agreements in the region. As mechanisms other than the "hub and spokes" become more institutionalized, the United States will have to face up to the fact that it is deciding not to be involved. In fact, it has historically been dismissive of East Asian regional attempts at creating multilateral institutions and other forms of cooperation, believing that such efforts were both unlikely to succeed, and absent American participation, unlikely to be effective.[12] The "hub and spokes" model for U.S. relations in East Asia has come under pressure.

Yet the fact that the United States is not an East Asian country means that as the region continues to integrate economically, politically, and institutionally, the United States will be increasingly facing a dilemma: to pay more attention to the region in order to remain more involved, or to allow East Asia to develop on its own with only occasional and intermittent U.S. participation. As Dennis Blair and John Hanley noted in 2001, "the fundamental security challenge in the Asia-Pacific region is to transform the balance of power approach . . . into one that instead aims to produce security communities."[13] Given America's global interests, it appears that this tension will be difficult to resolve.

THE UNITED STATES IS NOT BALANCING CHINA

There are some in the United States who are skeptical about China's emergence. However, the United States itself is not balancing China, and a basic direction of American policy toward China has not yet emerged. The debate in Washington is between those who see economic interdependence with China as beneficial for the United States, those who are more skeptical of China view and hence feel that balancing Chinese power is the prudent policy, and those who believe it is possible to socialize China into global values. As Thomas Christensen notes, "Especially if one uses the United States' containment policies toward the Soviet Union as a basis of comparison, the [argument] that the United States has been dedicated to a grand strategy of containment of China as a general policy to maintain U.S. hegemony—is, for the most part, divorced from reality."[14] Michael O'Hanlon points out that "many attributes of U.S. power are changing only slowly, and most U.S. interests are changing little in Asia."[15]

Those in the United States who view economic interdependence as binding their country and China together tend to come from the business community. They view the economic relations as so deep and important that threatening these ties would be dangerous for both countries. As Stephen Cohen writes, "The United States' international power position has not been enhanced by the domestic economy's increased dependence on the kindness of strangers with cash to lend. On the other hand, the Asian super-creditors have gained little real leverage over their biggest borrower."[16] Of a $263 billion increase in U.S. imports from East Asia between 1995 and 2005, China accounted for almost $200 billion, and between 1981 and 2005, U.S. imports from China increased more than 10,000 percent. Furthermore, the Asian creditor countries have compiled almost $2 trillion worth of U.S. debt in the past decade, and six Asian countries account for 53 percent of the total foreign holdings of U.S. Treasury securities in 2005.[17] Wal-Mart alone bought $18 billion worth of Chinese goods in 2005, and U.S. companies are investing in China and increasingly outsourcing production to China (and other areas of the globe).

The depth of this economic relationship has led some to argue that U.S.-Chinese interdependence is so deep that the two cannot compete in traditional terms. Niall Ferguson noted that of twelve competitive Senate seats in the 2006 elections, "Not one of the candidates [was] willing to play the anti-China card."[18] Ferguson goes on to note that "American voters just don't see China as a problem . . . 22 percent of voters see Iraq as the country's top concern, 10 percent give first place to the economy, 7 percent cite unemployment. Trade is nowhere."[19] Former National Security Agency senior director for Asian affairs Michael Green and China analyst Bates Gill wrote in a 2006 opinion piece that "Mr. Bush must try to prevent China-specific trade legislation and punitive executive branch action against China."[20] Political scientist Xiaobo Lu has said, "To understand China-American ties, just look at the amount of American debt held by China."[21] When Chinese President Hu Jintao visited Seattle in 2006, Boeing CEO Alan Mulally's reaction was to exclaim, "China rocks!"[22] Gary Locke, former governor of Washington State, said that "the U.S.-Chinese relationship is stronger and better than ever before . . . but even if there are some disputes with China, the relationship is much better than ten years ago, much better than 30 years ago."[23]

But while the business community sees China as an opportunity, the military establishment is far more suspicious. The Pentagon's 2006 *Quadrennial Defense Review* said that China has the "greatest potential to compete militarily with America," and that Chinese military modernization "already puts regional balances at risk."[24] It advocates deploying six aircraft carriers and 60 percent of U.S. submarines to the Pacific to "support engagement, presence, and deterrence."[25] The Heritage Foundation's John Tkacik, Jr., writes that "'hedging' has become the watchword in China relations in Washington. It's about time."[26] Despite being concerned foremost with the ongoing U.S. involvement in the Middle East, long-term military planning is increasingly suspicious of China's diplomatic and military moves in East Asia.

Yet the question is not as stark as economic versus military interests: a vigorous debate has broken out in Washington over Chinese identity as well. And although the debate is rarely couched using this academic term, there are those who believe that it is possible to socialize China. Others, who are more skeptical, believe that Chinese power is all that matters. For example, the Bush administration's 2002 *National Security Strategy of the United States* declares, "The United States welcomes the emergence of a strong, peaceful, and prosperous China."[27]

The U.S. military has also increasingly called for engagement and interaction with its Chinese counterparts, in part to establish just what kind of a country China is. U.S. Pacific Fleet commander Admiral Gary Roughead said in 2006, "We're interested in increasing transparency with the PLA Navy. Its increasing capability is at a rate commensurate with the country's economic growth . . . by engaging them, we hope to gain some insight into that."[28] In 2006, during a four-city tour of Chinese military bases, Admiral William Fallon, commander of U.S. forces in the Asia-Pacific, said that "the more they are like us, the easier it will be . . . it's when you don't know, you assume everyone's out to kill you . . . This is one area where the secretary of defense [then, Donald Rumsfeld] in particular has been pro-engagement."[29] Chinese Defense Minister Cao Gangchuan said to Fallon, "I'm looking forward to seeing you here, sir, once a year."[30] Later, Fallon said that confidence building measures and exchanges of lower-level military officers were important: "I believe we need to start moving down this road, and the sooner we do it, the better off we will be."[31] The United States and China have also discussed establishing a military hotline and conducting joint naval drills.[32]

Indeed, much recent American policy analyses of China recognize that China's rise depends on China's identity and how that develops over time. The strand of thinking that argues that the United States can "socialize" China, and that China can and should be an upstanding international citizen, are arguments about China's identity and its beliefs. The 2006 *National Security Strategy* called for a policy to "encourage China to make the right strategic decisions for its people while we hedge against other possibilities."[33] In December 2005, then–Deputy Secretary of State Robert Zoellick called on China to become a "responsible stakeholder" in international affairs, and "This concept has spurred a useful debate in China about its role in the world."[34] In a subtle critique of China's behavior, Zoellick later said, "For America's own future, I always find it unfortunate when we blame others for our own problems. So we also have to focus on things we need to do."[35]

This U.S. attempt to change China's identity has been under way for many years. Alastair Iain Johnston noted, "The Clinton administration's strategy of constructive engagement was, for some, aimed at pulling China into the 'international community,' and exposing it to new norms of the market and domestic governance."[36] Clinton's Defense Secretary William Perry had made similar claims a decade earlier, arguing that, "engagement is the best strategy to ensure that as China increases its power, it does so as a responsible member of the international community."[37] Others have harshly criticized China precisely because of its values, citing human rights abuses and its authoritarian government as reasons why it is both dangerous and unpredictable.

In sum, the United States has not decided how to view China or what overall U.S. policy toward it should be. The United States is deeply entwined with China's economy, and that relationship continues to grow, while the security situation has not yet reached a stable equilibrium. Of key importance is the realization that much thinking in the U.S. emphasizes Chinese identity. Many who are skeptical about China point to the authoritarian nature of the Chinese Communist Party and Chinese nationalism. Those who are more optimistic hope that China over time will be increasingly socialized into international norms and values. Robert Ross concludes, "The United States and China are the two great powers of East Asia. They will not be strategic partners."[38]

DOES U.S. POWER REASSURE EAST ASIAN STATES?

That the United States is not balancing China provides a perspective on two common explanations for why East Asian states too are not doing so. That is, some scholars have argued that some states are "too small to balance," and that East Asian capitulation to, or bandwagoning with, China is largely a foregone conclusion. Others emphasize the role of the United States as an offshore balancer, arguing that it is the U.S. presence that allows East Asia to remain relatively unconcerned about China's rise.[39] These two arguments are logically incompatible, although they are often used together. That is, if small states can rely on an offshore balancer in the face of a rising power, then they are not inevitably doomed to capitulation to that rising power. At the same time, if the United States is not balancing China, that reassurance to East Asian states is limited.

As noted in chapter 1, the argument that small states capitulate in the face of overwhelming power actually finds little empirical support. Many small states do not submit even when the odds are strongly against them, if they care about the issue strongly enough. Indeed, the record of past U.S. military conflict is replete with wars against states that by purely material standards should have capitulated immediately. For example, since 1991, Iraq twice defied the United States instead of succumbing, despite a massive disparity in their relative power positions. The Taliban regime in Afghanistan did not give in to U.S. demands that it turn over Osama bin Laden in 2001, despite the obvious intent by the United States to use force if the Taliban did not comply. By basic measures of power, North Vietnam during the 1960s as well should never have chosen to resist the United States. These examples should give pause to those promoting the notion that East Asian states will simply capitulate in the face of rising Chinese power. That is, states make a choice about whether to capitulate, and overwhelmingly they choose not to. Thus an explanation for stability in East Asia that emphasizes East Asian states' inability to balance China needs to be shown, not asserted.

The problem with arguing that East Asian states will capitulate in the face of Chinese power is even harder to sustain because if these states truly feared China, one obvious option is to seek closer U.S. relations by which to balance China. The argument that U.S. power reassures East Asian states and allows them to avoid balancing is widely held, particularly in the United States. Richard Betts argued in 1994 that while Japan will probably not balance Beijing in the short term, that possibility becomes relevant "if Russia and the United States ceased to provide strategic counterweights to China."[40] At the same time, Aaron Friedberg wrote, "For the time being, Japan and South Korea have chosen to continue their Cold War policies of taking shelter beneath the U.S. nuclear umbrella, although their willingness to continue doing so will depend on the intensity of the threats they perceive and their faith in American security guarantees."[41] There is no doubt that the United States is the most powerful military presence in the region, and indeed around the globe. It is also true that these countries in general are comfortable with that presence.

As we saw in chapter 4, if Taiwan, with only 23 million people and close geographic proximity to China, could choose to balance because of a U.S. military umbrella, then all the other states in East Asia could as well. Hypothetically, were states such as Vietnam or Malaysia genuinely afraid of China, they would be working much harder to improve their relations with the United States. That is, they would be actively attempting to engage the United States on a range of issues, most notably military ones. It is significant that many states have chosen not to do that, and in some cases are even resistant to a greater U.S. military presence; it tells us about their perception of China, and indicates the U.S. military presence may not be as central to their security thinking as is generally believed.

Although the United States does not have the same military footprint in East Asia that it did at the height of the Cold War, it does remain by far the most powerful military in the region. And there have been occasional new American deployments. In March 2001, Singapore completed construction of a deep-water port at Changi Naval Base. In the first year after its opening, five U.S. carriers docked there. Singapore also is closely cooperating with the U.S. in its counterterrorism efforts, notably the Proliferation Security

Initiative and the Container Security Initiative. Thailand has worked closely with the United States on counterterrorism, enough so that the United States declared Thailand a "major non-NATO ally" in 2003.[42] The two countries conduct an annual joint military exercise known as "Cobra Gold," which focuses on counterterrorism and counter-crime efforts.[43] Indonesia offers limited repair and port visit facilities to the United States in the port of Surabaya. Malaysia hosted over fifteen U.S. naval ship visits in 2005, and also allows U.S. Navy SEALs to train in the jungles.[44]

Yet these collaborations do not mean that East Asian states are using U.S. power to balance China; they do not necessarily view these sporadic U.S. deployments as a hedge against growing Chinese power. As was shown in earlier chapters, many East Asian states are hesitant about further U.S. deployments, in some cases precisely because they fear the United States may be setting the stage for a potential containment policy against China. While the U.S. military presence is one factor involved in East Asian states' alignment strategies, it is not the only one—and indeed is probably one of the less important factors—behind East Asian accommodation of China. As the preceding chapters have noted, East Asian states have little if any threat perception from China in the first place, and are moving closer to China, not father away. While the Philippines, South Korea, Japan, Taiwan, and Singapore might be able to imagine some U.S. support against China under special circumstances, it is hard to envision the United States defending Vietnam or Indonesia or Malaysia against China. The evidence that East Asian states rely on a U.S. military presence to hedge against China is often misplaced.

The U.S. handling of the Asian financial crisis, and even its war on terror, has been received with muted enthusiasm in some parts of East Asia, and in some cases outright hostility. A Pew Research Center poll in 2003 revealed that only 15 percent of Indonesians had a positive view of the United States.[45] Australians were also heavily opposed to sending military deployments in Iraq, while throughout the region there was skepticism about U.S. intentions both in the Middle East and the implications for U.S. policy in the region itself.

Reflecting these sentiments, the Malaysian *Business Times* editorialized in 1996 that "this is not to belittle the role of the U.S. forces in the region . . . yet one has to also question the consistency of the United States in rendering help . . . there is no guarantee that a U.S. presence means a U.S. commitment to safeguard the security of every nation in this region."[46] The Thai newspaper *Siam Post* also editorialized in 1996 that "the swift U.S. military response to the China-Taiwan crisis made Asian-Pacific countries feel somewhat secure, though most were well aware that the deployment of the U.S. naval forces was just for show because the American people would never approve of their engaging in real combat."[47] Malaysian leader Mohammed Mahatir has been one of the most vocal critics of U.S. policies in the region. He publicly argued that the rise of China should not be the cause of a U.S. containment policy in the region, and called the U.S. naval presence in East Asia "a waste of money as there was nothing to fear from either Japan or China . . . I don't think the U.S. military presence guarantees security in Asia . . . If we are invaded it is not certain that the U.S. would extend a helping hand."[48]

Other ASEAN states, while incrementally increasing their military cooperation with the United States, have done so out of a concern over terrorism and local security issues, not because of fears over China. With the exception of Taiwan and South Korea, none of the U.S. military deployments around the region are aimed at defense or deterrence against a specific external threat, and instead are aimed at internal stability, border control, and terrorism. While many Southeast Asian states are cooperating with the United States, it is important to note that the nature of this cooperation is qualitatively different from its Cold War alliances of the 1970s. None of these agreements cover military cooperation against third-party threats, and none have provisions of a political nature necessary for actual deterrence against those kinds of threats. As noted in chapter 6, Thailand rejected a U.S. request to preposition military equipment on ships in the Gulf of Thailand.[49] Nikolas Busse writes, "Balance of power is about deterrence more than anything else. Thus, conceiving of FPDA [Five Power Defense Arrangements] or similar arrangements as tools for balancing seems difficult if they lack proper mechanisms of deterrence."[50]

East Asian states view U.S. power and presence as they view Chinese power—a fact of life to be accommodated, benefited from, and adjusted to as much as possible.[51] The region is concerned primarily with economic growth, and the states are not overly focused on external threats to their survival. To that end, both the argument that states are too small to balance, and that the United States reassures them against Chinese aggrandizement, are difficult to sustain empirically.

The United States has deep economic ties with China and East Asia, and although there is some suspicion of China, the United States has not yet chosen to balance China. Indeed, there is little direct threat to American interests in East Asia—the biggest threat to American interests comes from the weakest state, North Korea. Even that threat is not a traditional military one, but rather stems from the fear that a weak North Korean regime might sell one or two of its suspected nuclear weapons to terrorist groups that might use them against the United States.

There are many other nontraditional threats that could arise—certainly the Asian financial crisis of 1997 had a global impact on financial markets. Economic meltdown in China would have direct repercussions on the U.S. economy. Furthermore, pandemics such as avian flu could hurt the United States, and drug running and illicit trafficking of humans occurs in the region. To that end, the United States' interests in the region are similar to those of other East Asian states—not primarily military in focus, but rather economic and arising from nontraditional sources. For these reasons alone, the United States is welcomed in the region as a country that can potentially provide both leadership and resources to help to solve or at least mitigate these problems.

However, close scrutiny of East Asian attitudes toward the United States and China reveals that there is little regional appetite for an outright containment or balancing coalition against China. The discussion in the United States that emphasizes China's military modernization and potential threats a generation from now has little resonance in the region. Thus how U.S. foreign policy evolves will have a major impact on stability in the region. If the United States and China manage their relationship and coexist, even if they never develop warm relations, it will be stable. If the United States ultimately decides to view China as a threat, or if China's own actions make it reasonable to consider it a threat, the region can veer toward instability.

More generally, the United States faces a difficult challenge—how to remain deeply involved in a region that is rapidly transforming, often without U.S. action. Given its global concerns, it is unlikely that the United States will ever make East Asia its top priority. But as the region develops on its own, the Cold War "hub and spokes" model for U.S. relations in the region is coming under increasing strain. While all countries in the region desire more U.S. involvement and attention, they also are increasingly willing to craft security and economic arrangements on their own.

CHAPTER 9

CONCLUSIONS AND IMPLICATIONS

The rise and fall of great powers, and whether those things happen peacefully, has long been a preoccupation for students of international relations. Over the past half millennium in Europe, war and instability have accompanied the rise and fall of major states. Because Europe was the primary locus of both war and economic development over that time, it has been natural to conclude that the European experience is the norm in world politics.

Now China is in the middle of what may be a long ascent to global great power status. Indeed, it may already be a great power, with the only question being how much bigger China may become. The rise of China, and whether it can peacefully find a place in East Asia and the world, is thus one of the most important issues in contemporary international politics. Given the European historical experience, many conclude that China cannot rise peacefully. Others, attempting to assess China's current actions and goals, believe that it is possible for China to emerge without causing instability. This debate will likely continue well into the future, and thus defining the terms of the debate and isolating the central issues is an important step.

Jeffrey Frieden and David Lake argue that "progress in the study of international politics . . . depends on more, not less, rigorous theory and more, not less, systematic empirical testing."[1] This book has attempted just such a task. A main aspect of this project has been to sharpen our theories in an attempt to more accurately describe East Asian state strategies toward China and the main sources of stability and instability in the region. The evidence provided here leads to the conclusion that no East Asian state is actively balancing China. East Asian states see substantially greater economic opportunity in China than they do military threat, and hence East Asian states accept, rather than fear, China's expected emergence as a powerful and perhaps the dominant state in East Asia. They prefer China to be strong rather than weak, and although the states of East Asia do not unequivocally welcome China in all areas, they are willing to defer judgment about what China wants.

Explaining how this has come about—and China has already peacefully managed thirty years of rapid economic and political growth—is also an important task. I have argued that pragmatic interests combine with national identity to explain the variation in state behavior in East Asia. This argument builds on a number of traditions in the study of international relations, from formal theorists to constructivists, that are sensitive to the role of ideas and that explore the microfoundations of state behavior within a specific context.

Much of East Asia's increasing stability is a result of material factors: strong states, military and economic development, and the decline of crisis points in the region. The last war of conquest was World War II; the Korean and Vietnam wars were both civil wars between nations divided by superpowers, as is the Taiwan issue. Furthermore, the hallmark of East Asia over the last half century has not been military conflict, it has been economic development. The domestic institutions and populations of East Asian countries are oriented toward economic growth, and there is little appetite within these rapidly developing countries for risky and far-fetched military adventures.

However, just as important as these material factors in explaining East Asia's increasing stability are identity and interests. East Asia has enjoyed thirty years of relative stability even while accommodating China's rapid emergence because of a shared understanding among East Asian states that although China will most likely reemerge as the regional core, its aims are limited. Calculations about alignment strategies on the spectrum between the extreme positions of balancing and bandwagoning are far more complex than simple measures of relative power would suggest, and although threat perceptions depend on the costs and benefits that the rising power poses, just as important are states' assessments about the identities and preferences of that rising power.

On the whole, East Asian states believe that China has peaceful intentions, which includes stable and peaceful relations with its neighbors, domestic stability, and an emphasis on economic growth and economic relations. There is a regional understanding about China's goals and its appropriate role in regional affairs. China has already experienced rapid economic growth for three decades, and it is increasingly reclaiming its position as the regional core in East Asia that it has historically occupied. East Asia is already deeply intertwined with China, both culturally and economically.

There are other stabilizing factors in East Asia, as well. The region is more integrated than ever before, and the states in the region are busily building numerous bilateral and multilateral institutions across a range of cultural, economic, and political issues. As recently as a decade ago, it was widely considered that East Asian regionalism was so scarce as to be unimportant. However, in the face of the rapid progress made in creating multilateral institutions in East Asia, today that view is more difficult to uphold. Furthermore, economic interdependence on the whole is rapidly stitching the region together, and although world markets remain important, the East Asian region itself is becoming an economic nexus in its own right. Finally, regional states themselves are increasingly legitimate and prosperous, and many have made a democratic transition. Although some states remain relatively weak—among them Cambodia and Myanmar—the majority of East Asian states have become more politically stable and legitimate over the past generation, not less.

In addition, Japan is the only East Asian state that might potentially compete with China for political influence, but it appears unlikely to do so, and such competition would occur only in the context of a U.S.-Japan alliance. Japanese grand strategy is in flux, and Japan remains the most skeptical of Chinese motives. However, even if Japan-China competition occurs, competition is unlikely to be military in nature, especially given that the economies of both countries are increasingly deeply intertwined. Japan is hedging on all fronts—it is embracing Chinese economic vigor while remaining alert to the possibility that Chinese political power and influence may move against its interests. Japan is also deepening its alliance with the United States while beginning to create the domestic and international institutional and political linkages that would allow that relationship to become more of a choice than an obligation.

Regarding the United States and China, there is also no issue that appears poised to inevitably drive conflict between these two states. Their interests are aligned in many areas—stabilization of the North Korean issue, concerns about terrorism, and pandemics. On the most important economic issues, Chinese and American interests are also increasingly intertwined, as both benefit from a vibrant regional trading order. Although in security strategy the two powers have not wholly reached a stable modus vivendi, a clash is also not inevitable. The United States and China are maritime and continental powers, respectively, and China has not yet chosen to directly compete with the U.S. military.[2]

If at some point the United States decides to move from a strategy of accommodating China's emergence to a strategy of outright balancing, a key question will be how East Asian states respond. The answer to this question is not as obvious as some might expect. If East Asian nations do not balance

China as realists expect, an American attempt to construct a balancing coalition to contain China using East Asian states will be highly problematic. The research presented in this book leads to the conclusion that many East Asian states will be extremely reluctant to choose sides. As one respected scholar wrote just before taking a position in the U.S. government in 2006, "U.S. policies designed to slow China's economic growth or isolate Beijing diplomatically in the region . . . would undercut the U.S. diplomatic position with everyone else in the region, including U.S. allies."[3]

Furthermore, if forced to choose, many East Asian states may not choose the United States. As Singaporean Ambassador to the United States Chan Heng Chee said in 2006, "many countries are comfortable with the status quo . . . with the United States as the dominant pole . . . [however] whether these sentiments are retained in the coming decades depends on what the United States does in alliance maintenance and what the U.S. does in foreign and economic policy internationally."[4] Her reminder, that East Asian states assess American actions and motivations as much as they assess China's actions and motivations, emphasizes that East Asian states are active regional participants in their own right. Others offer even more blunt assessments: Martin Stuart-Fox writes that:

> How are the states of Southeast Asia likely to respond to the rising power of China in the face of U.S. determination to maintain its unchallenged position of the world? Will they side with the world superpower? Certainly not in the case of the mainland states, and probably not in the case of Malaysia and Indonesia. . . . This would not just be because of geography, but also because history and ideas predispose the countries of Southeast Asia to draw on their own experience of the benefits of deference to status in working out their relations with China.[5]

Even if U.S. power recedes significantly from East Asia, the region may not become as dangerous or unstable as is generally believed, because other nations may continue to adjust to China's central position in East Asia. Indeed, the importance of the United States has been receding relative to regional influences for the past thirty years: although the United States still retains overwhelming power in the region, already its scope and influence is considerably smaller than it was at its height at the end of the Vietnam War. Furthermore, East Asian states have grown significantly stronger, richer, and generally more stable over the past generation, and multiple centers of stability have begun to emerge, from increased economic interdependence, nascent regional institutionalization that continues to gather momentum, and overlapping and multiple identities and interests. That the United States plays an important security role in East Asia is relatively uncontroversial. Whether a significant United States withdrawal would be deleterious for the region is far more questionable. Historically, it has been Chinese weakness that led to chaos in East Asia. When China is strong and stable, order has been preserved. The picture of East Asia in the twenty-first century that emerges is one in which China, by virtue of geography, power, and identity, is becoming the core state. In response, Asian nations are likely to accommodate, rather than balance China, even if the United States reduces its presence in the region.

However, although East Asia has become increasingly peaceful and stable over the past three decades—and trends are generally indicating more accommodation of China, not less—China is in the middle of its emergence and evolution, and is a long way from being a mature and stable country. As important as the past three decades have been to East Asian stability, China's ultimate intentions in the distant future are still unclear. If present trends continue, China may ultimately be a strong, reassuring, and stabilizing force in international politics. Alternatively, it is also possible that if China actually becomes the most powerful state in East Asia, it could increasingly pressure and intimidate other states. That is, China currently confronts the "commitment problem" identified by formal theorists: even if a state claims benign intentions today—and even if others believe it today—once circumstances change, a state's commitment to benign goals may change, as well.[6]

Although it is impossible to draw any firm conclusions about China's future path, the argument advanced in this book provides some guidance as to the important factors that are likely shape China's future course. Most significantly, concerns about future Chinese intentions are partly concerns about how Chinese national identity will develop. Will other states find credible a rising power's claims? The answer involves what the other states believe its intentions and values are, not just how powerful it is. Debate about whether China can remain unified, whether China can become a democracy, and how its nationalism develops, are essentially arguments about the future course of Chinese identity.

Chinese—and East Asian—identities are still in the process of being determined. Little is fixed, and there is no immutable "Chinese mind-set," just as there are no immutable perceptions of China. The actions that states take in the present will have an effect on what intentions and identities develop. How China acts, how East Asian states act, and how the United States and other global states act will affect the prospects for stability and peace in the region, and what identities ultimately form. As Avery Goldstein writes, "The future will depend on the policies China and others choose to embrace once its current strategy has run its course, the transition is complete, and China has risen to the ranks of the great powers. At that time, different leaders in Beijing will make choices that reflect their country's new capabilities and transformed international constraints that cannot be confidently foreseen . . . speculation is premature at best and unwisely provocative at worst."[7]

Indeed, any prediction a generation into the future is mere speculation. How Chinese identity and power will develop is unknowable, and speculation is neither a satisfying nor interesting scholarly exercise.[8] What might be Chinese goals and beliefs a generation from now is at best a wild guess—so much will change between now and then, within China itself, within the region, and around the globe. In 1945 it would have been remarkable to think that thirty years into the future, the United States would be withdrawing from Vietnam, that China would be not only communist, but lost in the throes of a "cultural revolution" lasting a decade, or that a country like South Korea would be capable of economic growth making it the eleventh-largest economy in the world. In 1975, most observers thought the United States and Soviet Union would be locked into their rivalry well into the next century, and would have scoffed at the notion that China could manage an economic transformation that would dwarf that of South Korea's. Thus as the twenty-first century unfolds, it is probably wise that we remain cautious in our predictions about the future.

Making sense of a region as vast, ancient, and dynamic as East Asia is a monumental task. It is true that East Asian states have been increasingly "socialized" into a Western, Westphalian set of norms and beliefs about how the world works. International politics has become increasingly globalized, and all states are connected more tightly today than ever before. However, it is important to recognize that this convergence has been neither total nor unidirectional. That is, although all states must care about sovereignty, global norms, and the consequences of economic interdependence, they also retain their own historical experiences, regional concerns, and judgments about how what is of primary importance and what is secondary.[9] Thus East Asian states have adapted and taken some of these "Western" norms and practices, but not all of them.[10] Furthermore, these states are becoming increasingly influential in international politics. No longer just passive recipients of Western influences, they are active participants as well.

The United States has generally viewed its foreign policy and grand strategy as global, whether during the Cold War or now in its fight against terrorism. Yet most politics is actually more local than global, and the United States has also not been very good at understanding the nuance and complexity of the diverse regions in which it has interests. China's rise in East Asia has global implications, to be sure. Yet perhaps more importantly, the East Asian region has its own internal dynamics, shared history, culture, and interactions—many of which occur without any attention to the larger world, and many of which are not well understood by Americans. To argue that a regional view of China's rise is critical does not mean that the search for basic, underlying factors is futile, or that social science cannot illuminate important issues in East Asia. Quite the opposite—if anything, this book emphasizes the need for rigorous and systematic study. How China and the East Asian region evolve in the coming generation will have a major impact on regional and global relations, and if all sides manage their relations with care, the future has the potential to be more peaceful, more prosperous, and more stable than the past.

NOTES

1. THE PUZZLE AND CHINA'S AMAZING RISE

1. Chan Heng Chee, "China and ASEAN: A Growing Relationship," Speech at the Asia Society Texas Annual Ambassadors' Forum and Corporate Conference, Houston, Texas, February 3, 2006.
2. Muthiah Alagappa, "Managing Asian Security," in Alagappa, ed., *Asian Security Order* (Stanford: Stanford University Press, 2003); David Shambaugh, "China Engages Asia: Reshaping the Regional Order," *International Security* 29, no. 3 (Winter 2004–2005), pp. 64–99; Carl Thayer, "China's 'New Security Concept' and Southeast Asia," in David Lovell, ed., *Asia-Pacific Security: Policy Challenges* (Singapore: Institute of Southeast Asian Studies, 2003); Brantley Womack, "China and Southeast Asia: Asymmetry, Leadership, and Normalcy," *Pacific Affairs* 76, no. 4 (Winter 2003–2004): 526; and David Kerr, "The Sino-Russian Partnership and U.S. Policy Toward North Korea: From Hegemony to Concert in Northeast Asia," *International Studies Quarterly* 49 (2005): 411–37.
3. Avery Goldstein, *Rising to the Challenge: China's Grand Strategy and International Security* (Stanford: Stanford University Press, 2005); Robert Ross, "China's Grand Strategy: A Kinder, Gentler Turn," *Strategic Comments* 10, no. 9 (November 2004).
4. Stephen Brooks, *Producing Security: Multinational Corporations, Globalization, and the Changing Calculus of Conflict* (Princeton: Princeton University Press, 2005).
5. Robert Gilpin, *War and Change in World Politics* (Cambridge: Cambridge University Press, 1981); Paul Kennedy, *The Rise and Fall of Great Powers: Economic Change and Military Conflict From 1500 to 2000* (New York: Random House, 1987); Charles Kupchan, *The Vulnerability of Empire* (Ithaca: Cornell University Press, 1994).
6. Richard K. Betts, "Wealth, Power, and Instability: East Asia and the United States after the Cold War," *International Security* 18, no. 3 (Winter 1993): 55. See also Aaron Friedberg, "Ripe for Rivalry," *International Security* 18, no. 3 (Winter 1993/94): 5–33; Denny Roy, "Hegemon on the Horizon? China's Threat to East Asian Security," *International Security* 19, no. 1 (Summer 1994): 149–68; Thomas Christensen, "Posing Problems Without Catching Up: China's Rise and Challenges for U.S. Security Policy," *International Security* 25, no. 4 (Spring 2001): 5–40; Arthur

Waldron, "The Chinese Sickness," *Commentary* 116, no. 1 (July/August 2003): 39–46; Christopher Layne, "The Unipolar Illusion: Why New Great Powers Will Rise," *International Security* 17 (Spring 1993): 5–51; Kenneth Waltz, "The Emerging Structure of International Politics," *International Security* 18 (Fall 1993): 56, 65, 164; U.S. Department of Defense, *The United States Security Strategy for the East Asia-Pacific Region*, November 1998, p. 62; Richard Bernstein and Ross H. Munro, "The Coming Conflict with America," *Foreign Affairs* 76, no. 2 (March/April 1997): 18–32; and Gerald Segal, "The Coming Confrontation Between China and Japan," *World Policy Journal* 10, no. 2 (Summer 1993).

7. Zbigniew Brzezinski and John Mearsheimer, "Clash of the Titans," *Foreign Policy* 146 (January/February 2005): 47. See also Mearsheimer, *The Tragedy of Great Power Politics* (New York: Norton, 2001), p. 400.

8. Joseph Grieco, "China and America in the World Polity," in Carolyn W. Pumphrey, ed., *The Rise of China in Asia: Security Implications* (Carlisle, Pa.: Strategic Studies Institute, 2002), pp. 21–48; Paul Papayounou and Scott Kastner, "Sleeping with the Potential Enemy: Assessing the U.S. Policy of Engagement with China," *Security Studies* 9, no. 1 (Fall 1999): 164–95; Ming Wan, "Economic Interdependence and Economic Cooperation: Mitigating Conflict and Transforming Security Order in Asia," in Alagappa, ed., *Asian Security Order*, pp. 280–310.

9. G. John Ikenberry, "American Hegemony and East Asian Order," *Australian Journal of International Affairs* 58, no. 3 (September 2004): 353–67.

10. Robert Powell, "The Inefficient Use of Power: Costly Conflict with Complete Information," *American Political Science Review* 98, no. 2 (May 2004): 231. See also Douglas Lemke, *Regions of War and Peace* (Cambridge: Cambridge University Press, 2002); and Henk Houweling and Jan Siccama, "Power Transitions as a Cause of War," *Journal of Conflict Resolution* 32, no. 1 (March 1988): 87–102; Jack Levy, "Declining Power and the Preventive Motivation for War," *World Politics* 40, no. 1 (October 1987): 82–107; Woosang Kim and James Morrow, "When Do Power Shifts Lead to War?," *American Journal of Political Science* 36, no. 4 (November 1992): 896–922.

11. Alastair Iain Johnston, *Social States: China in International Institutions, 1980–2000* (Princeton: Princeton University Press, forthcoming); Peter Gries, *China's New Nationalism: Pride, Politics, and Diplomacy* (Berkeley: University of California Press, 2004); Allen Carlson, *Unifying China, Integrating with the World: Securing Chinese Sovereignty in the Reform Era* (Stanford: Stanford University Press, 2005); Peter Katzenstein, *A World of Regions: Asia and Europe in the American Imperium* (Ithaca: Cornell University Press, 2005); Thomas U. Berger, *Cultures of Antimilitarism: National Security in Germany and Japan* (Baltimore: Johns Hopkins University Press, 1998); Amitav Acharya, *Constructing a Security Community in Southeast Asia: ASEAN and the Problem of Regional Order* (London: Routledge, 2001), and Acharya, *The Quest for Identity: International Relations of Southeast Asia* (Oxford: Oxford University Press, 2000).

12. Alexander Wendt, "Collective Identity Formation and the International State," *American Political Science Review* 88, no. 2 (June 1994): 384–96; Katzenstein, *A World of Regions*; Jeffrey Checkel, "The Constructivist Turn in International Relations," *World Politics* 50, no. 2 (February 1998): 324–48.

13. Gilbert Rozman, "China's Quest for Great Power Identity," *Orbis* 43, no. 3 (Summer 1999): 384.

14. Peter Gries, *China's New Nationalism*, chapters 2 and 3.

15. Goldstein, *Rising to the Challenge*; Robert Ross, "The Geography of the Peace: East Asia in the Twenty-First Century," *International Security* 23, no. 4 (Spring 1999): 81–118.

16. Peter J. Katzenstein, and Nobuo Okawara, "Japan, Asian-Pacific Security, and the Case for Analytical Eclecticism," *International Security* 26, no. 3 (Winter 2001): 153–85. See also Jack Snyder, "Anarchy and Culture: Insights from the Anthropology of War," *International Organization* 56, no. 1 (Winter 2002): 7–45. Gilbert Rozman notes that "previous efforts to assess regionalism in NEA [Northeast Asia] have been inclined to concentrate on one factor at the expense of others . . ." See Rozman, *Northeast Asia's Stunted Regionalism: Bilateral Distrust in the Shadow of Globalization* (Cambridge: Cambridge University Press, 2004), p. 15.

17. Kenneth Waltz has written that "secondary states, *if they are free to choose*, flock to the weaker side." Waltz, *Theory of International Politics* (Reading, Mass.: Addison-Wesley, 1979), p. 127.

18. Todd Sechser, "Winning Without a Fight: Power, Reputation, and Compellent Threats" (Ph.D. diss., Stanford University, 2006); Andrew Kydd, *Trust and Mistrust in International Relations* (Princeton: Princeton University Press, 2005); Charles Glaser, "Political Consequences of Military Strategy: Expanding and Refining the Spiral and Deterrence Models," *World Politics* 44 (July 1992).

19. Scott Sagan, "The Origins of the Pacific War," *Journal of Interdisciplinary History* 18 (Summer 1988): 893–922.

20. Robert Jervis, "Cooperation under the Security Dilemma," *World Politics* 30, no. 2 (1978): 105.

21. Russia is an East Asian state, but it is focused mostly on Europe and the United States. See William Wohlforth, "Russia's Soft Balancing Act," in Richard Ellings and Aaron Friedberg, with Michael Wills, eds., *Strategic Asia, 2003–4: Fragility and Crisis* (Seattle: National Bureau of Asian Research, 2003).

22. Nobuo Okawara and Peter Katzenstein, "Japan and Asia-Pacific Security: Regionalization, Entrenched Bilateralism, and Incipient Multilateralism," *Pacific Review* 14, no. 2 (2001): 165–94.

23. Robert Ayson, "Regional Stability in the Asia-Pacific: Towards a Conceptual Understanding," *Asian Security* 1, no. 2 (2005): 190–213. See also Katzenstein, *A World of Regions*; Alexander Woodside, "The Asia-Pacific Idea as a Mobilization Myth," in Arif Dirlik, ed., *What's in a Rim? Critical Perspectives on the Pacific Region Idea* (Lanham, Md.: Rowman & Littlefield, 1998), pp. 13–28; Gil Rozman, "Flawed Regionalism: Reconceptualizing Northeast Asia in the 1990s," *Pacific Review* 11, no. 1 (1998): 1–27; Michael Ng-Quinn, "The Internationalization of the Region: The Case of Northeast Asian International Relations," *Review of International Studies* 12, no. 1 (1986): 107–25.

24. Barry Buzan and Ole Weaver, *Regions and Powers: The Structure of International Security* (Cambridge: Cambridge University Press, 2003), pp. 27, 48.

25. Amitav Acharya, "Will Asia's Past Be Its Future?," *International Security* 28, no. 3 (Winter 2004): 148–64.

26. Figures derived from World Bank, "World Development Indicators," http://devdata.worldbank.org/dataonline/.

27. World Bank, Shanghai Poverty Conference, "China's 8-7 Poverty Reduction

Program," http://info.worldbank.org/etools/docs/reducingpoverty/case/33/summary/China-8-7PovertyReduction%20Summary.pdf.

28. Figures from *CIA World Factbook 2006,* http://www.cia.gov/cia/publications/factbook/; and World Bank, "World Development Indicators."

29. Organisation for Economic Co-operation and Development, "Statistic Brief: Purchasing Power Parities: Measurement and Uses," www.oecd.org/dataoecd/32/34/2078177.pdf.

30. Keith Bradsher, "The Two Faces of China: Producer and Consumer," *New York Times,* December 6, 2004, p. C1.

31. Betts, "Wealth, Power, and Instability," pp. 52–53. See also Tom Christensen, "Posing Problems Without Catching Up," *International Security* 25, no. 4 (Spring 2001): 49–88; Steven Greenhouse, "New Tally of World's Economies Catapults China into Third Place," *New York Times,* May 20, 1993, pp. A1, A8.

32. Angus Maddison, *Monitoring the World Economy, 1820–1992* (Paris: Development Centre, Organisation for Economic Co-operation and Development, 1995).

33. J. David Singer, "Reconstructing the Correlates of War Dataset on Material Capabilities of States, 1816–1985," *International Interactions* 14 (1987): 115–32, updated dataset at the Correlates of War project, http://www.correlatesofwar.org/.

34. Quoted by Christine Heath, "Repercussions of China's Economic Boom," United Press International, July 19, 2004. See also Don Lee, "World Scrambles to Feed China's Appetite for Metal," *Los Angeles Times,* March 19, 2006, www.latimes.com/

35. Tom Plate, "The Quiet Evolution of a New Japanese Diplomacy," http://www.asia-media.ucla.edu/. See also Tom Holland, "Between Hype and a Hard Place," *Far Eastern Economic Review,* June 28, 2001, p. 40. See also Louis Uchitelle, "When the Chinese Consumer Is King," *New York Times,* December 14, 2003, p. 5.

36. World Bank, "World Development Indicators."

37. *CIA World Factbook 2004,* http://www.cia.gov/cia/publications/factbook/index.html.

38. The World Bank, "World Development Indicators Online," http://web.worldbank.org/WBSITE/EXTERNAL/DATASTATISTICS/contentMDK:20394802~menuPK:1192714~pagePK:64133150~piPK:64133175~theSitePK:239419,00.html.

39. National Bureau of Asian Research, "Strategic Asia Online," www.nbr.org.

40. All data from the National Bureau of Asian Research, "Strategic Asia Online."

41. See Kurt Radtke, "Sino-Indian Relations: Security Dilemma, Ideological Polarization, or Cooperation Based on 'Comprehensive Security?'," *Perspectives on Global Development & Technology,* 2, no. 3 (2003): 499–520; Jacek Kugler, "The Asian Ascent: Opportunity for Peace or Precondition for War?," *International Studies Perspectives* 7, no. 1 (February 2006): 36–42.

2. POWER, INTERESTS, AND IDENTITY IN EAST ASIAN INTERNATIONAL RELATIONS, 1300 TO 1900

1. James Fearon and Alexander Wendt, "Rationalism v. Constructivism: A Skeptical View," in Walter Carlsnaes, Thomas Risse, and Beth Simmons, eds., *Handbook of International Relations Theory* (London: Sage, 2002), pp. 55, 59.

2. Jeffrey Legro and Andrew Moravsick, "Is Anybody Still a Realist?," *International Security* 24, no. 2 (1999): 5–56.

3. Robert Powell, "Bargaining Theory and International Conflict, *American Review of Political Science* 5 (2002): 17. See also James D. Fearon, "Signaling Foreign Policy Interests: Tying Hands Versus Sinking Costs," *Journal of Conflict Resolution* 41, no. 1 (February 1997): 68–90; Robert Powell, *In the Shadow of Power: States and Strategies in International Politics* (Princeton: Princeton University Press, 1999); James D. Fearon, "Domestic Politics, Foreign Policy, and Theories of International Relations," *Annual Review of Political Science* 1, no. 1 (Fall 1998): 289–314; Bruce Bueno de Mesquita and David Lalman, *War and Reason* (New Haven: Yale University Press, 1992); Stephan Haggard, "The Balance of Power, Globalization, and Democracy in Northeast Asia: Reflections on Long-run Forces," paper presented at conference on Peace, Development, and Regionalization in East Asia, Seoul, Korea, September 2–3, 2003, p. 60.

4. Stephen Walt, *The Origin of Alliances* (Ithaca: Cornell University Press, 1990); Andrew Kydd, *Trust and Mistrust in International Relations* (Princeton: Princeton University Press, 2005); Charles Glaser, "Political Consequences of Military Strategy: Expanding and Refining the Spiral and Deterrence Models," *World Politics* 44 (July 1992); Legro and Moravsick, "Is Anybody Still a Realist?"; Jacek Kugler, "The Asian Ascent: Opportunity for Peace or Precondition for War?," *International Studies Perspectives* 7 (2006): 36–42.

5. James Fearon, "Rationalist Explanations for War," *International Organization* 49, no. 3 (Summer 1995): 379–414, p. 381; Fearon, "Signaling Foreign Policy Interests"; David Austen-Smith and Jeffrey Banks, "Cheap Talk and Burned Money," *Journal of Economic Theory* 91, no. 1 (Winter 2000): 1–16; Alexandra Guisinger and Alastair Smith, "Honest Threats: The Interaction of Reputation and Political Institutions in International Crises," *Journal of Conflict Resolution* 46 (April 2002): 175–200; Robert Powell, "Bargaining Theory and International Conflict," p. 17.

6. Fearon, "Domestic Politics, Foreign Policy, and Theories of International Relations," p. 294.

7. On different types of rising powers, see Glaser, "Political Consequences of Military Strategy."

8. E.g., James Fearon, "Rationalist Explanations for War."

9. Chaim Kaufmann and Robert Pape, "Explaining Costly International Moral Action: Britain's Sixty-Year Campaign Against the Atlantic Slave Trade," *International Organization* 53, no. 4 (1999): 631–68.

10. Alexander Wendt, "Anarchy is What States Make of It: The Social Construction of Power Politics," *International Organization* 46, no. 3 (1992): 391–425; Alexander Wendt, *Social Theory of International Politics* (Cambridge: Cambridge University Press, 1999).

11. James Fearon, "What is Identity (as We Now Use the Word)?" (manuscript, Stanford University, 1999), p. 30; Rawi Abdelal, Yoshiko M. Herrera, Alastair Iain Johnston, and Terry Martin, "Treating Identity as a Variable: Measuring the Content, Intensity, and Contestation of Identity" (manuscript, Harvard University, 2001).

12. Peter Gries, *China's New Nationalism: Pride, Politics, and Diplomacy* (Berkeley: University of California Press, 2004), chapters 2 and 3; Peter Katzenstein, *A World of Regions: Asia and Europe in the American Imperium* (Ithaca: Cornell University Press, 2005), p. 77.

13. Randall Schweller defines a revisionist state as one that "values what they covet more than what they currently possess . . . [and] they will employ military force to change the status quo and to extend their values." A. F. K. Organski and Jacek Kugler emphasize "challengers" to the existing status quo as those who want a "new place for themselves in international society." See Organski and Kugler, *The War Ledger* (Chicago: University of Chicago Press, 1980), pp. 19–23; Robert Gilpin, *War and Change in World Politics* (Cambridge: Cambridge University Press, 1981), p. 34; Randall Schweller, "Bandwagoning for Profit: Bringing the Revisionist State Back In," *International Security* 19, no. 1 (Summer 1994): 72–108; Alastair Iain Johnston, "Is China a Status Quo Power?," *International Security* 27, no. 4 (Spring 2003): 5–56.

14. Robert Powell, "Uncertainty, Shifting Power, and Appeasement," *American Political Science Review* 90, no. 4 (December 1996): 749–64.

15. Jason Lyall, "Ghost in the Machine: Patterns in the Study and Practice of Revisionism" (manuscript, Princeton University, 2005), p. 3.

16. Alastair Iain Johnston, *Social States: China in International Institutions, 1980–2000* (Princeton: Princeton University Press, forthcoming), p. 9.

17. Lyall, Ghost in the Machine," p. 11.

18. Katzenstein, *A World of Regions*, p. 40.

19. Rawi Abdelal, Yoshiko Herrera, Alastair Iain Johnston, and Rose McDermott, "Identity as a Variable," *Perspectives on Politics* 4, no. 4 (December 2006): 695–711.

20. Kenneth Waltz, *Theory of International Politics* (Reading, Mass.: Addison-Wesley, 1979); Walt, *The Origin of Alliances*; John Mearsheimer, *The Tragedy of Great Power Politics* (New York. Norton, 2001).

21. Kenneth N. Waltz, "The Emerging Structure of International Politics," *International Security* 18 (Fall 1993): 44–79.

22. Barry Buzan and Richard Little, *International Systems in World History: Remaking the Study of International Relations* (Oxford and New York: Oxford University Press, 2000); Claudio Cioffi-Revilla, "Origins and Evolution of War and Politics," *International Studies Quarterly* 40 (1996): 1–22; Claudio Cioffi-Revilla and Todd Landman, "Evolution of Maya Politics in the Ancient Mesoamerican System," *International Studies Quarterly* 43 (1999): 559–98; Stuart J. Kaufman, "The Fragmentation and Consolidation of International Systems," *International Organization* 51 (1997): 173–208; David Wilkinson, "The Polarity Structure of the Central World System/Civilization, 1500–700 B.C." (paper prepared for the International Studies Association Annual Meeting, New Orleans, March 23–28, 2002); David Wilkinson, "Unipolarity Without Hegemony," *International Studies Review* 1 (Summer 1999): 141–72.

23. D. Scott Bennett and Allan Stam, *The Behavioral Origins of War* (Ann Arbor: University of Michigan Press, 2003), pp. 191–95.

24. Bennett and Stam, *The Behavioral Origins of War*, p. 174.

25. Jack Snyder and Robert Jervis, eds., *Coping with Complexity in the International System* (Boulder, Colo.: Westview, 1993).

26. Stuart Kaufman, Richard Little, and William Wohlforth, eds., *The Balance of Power in World History* (London: Palgrave, forthcoming).

27. Alastair Iain Johnston notes that "the strategic culture approach challenges the ahistorical, non-cultural neorealist framework for analyzing strategic choices . . . ." Johnston, "Thinking about Strategic Culture," *International Security* 19, no. 4 (Spring 1995): 32–64, 35. See also Johnston, "Social States: China in International Institutions, 1980–2000" (manuscript, Harvard University, 2006), p. 9.

28. See, for example, Stuart Kaufman, 'The Fragmentation and Consolidation of International Systems,'" *International Organization* 51, no. 2 (1997): 173–208; Wilkinson, "Unipolarity Without Hegemony"; Buzan and Little, *International Systems in World History*; Victoria Tin-bor Hui, *War and State Formation in Ancient China and Early Modern Europe* (Cambridge: Cambridge University Press, 2004).

29. John Fairbank, ed., *The Chinese World Order: Traditional China's Foreign Relations* (Cambridge: Harvard University Press, 1968); Alastair Iain Johnston, *Cultural Realism* (Princeton: Princeton University Press, 1994); Victor Cha, "Defining Security in East Asia: History, Hotspots, and Horizon-gazing," in Eunmee Kim, ed., *The Four Asian Tigers: Economic Development and the Global Political Economy* (San Diego: Academic Press, 1998), pp. 33–60.

30. Andre Gunder Frank, *ReOrient: Global Economy in the Asian Age* (Berkeley: University of California Press, 1998); Benedict Anderson, *The Spectre of Comparisons: Nationalism, Southeast Asia, and the World* (London: Verso, 2002).

31. Buzan and Little, *International Systems in World History*, p. 2.

32. Traditional theorists mark the beginning of the "modern era" in international relations from the "Peace of Westphalia," signed in 1648. The "Peace," actually a set of treaties, formalized a number of key principles, among them the sovereign status of states, equality among states, and non-interference into internal matters of states. For discussion and critiques, see Andreas Osiander, "Sovereignty, International Relations, and the Westphalian Myth," *International Organization* 55, no. 2 (2001): 251–301; and Stephen Krasner, *Sovereignty: Organized Hypocrisy* (Princeton: Princeton University Press, 1999).

33. Hui, *War and State Formation*.

34. Lien-sheng Yang, "Historical Notes on the Chinese World Order," in Fairbank, ed., *The Chinese World Order*, p. 21.

35. Key-hiuk Kim, *The Last Phase of the East Asian World Order* (Berkeley: University of California Press, 1980), p. 40; Bruce Cumings, "The Historical Origins of North Korean Foreign Policy" (paper prepared for the Conference on North Korean Foreign Policy in the Post–Cold War Era, 1996), p. 3.

36. Kim, *The Last Phase of the East Asian World Order*, p. 16.

37. Gregory Smits, *Visions of Ryukyu: Identity and Ideology in Early-Modern Thought and Politics* (Honolulu: University of Hawaii Press, 1999).

38. Janet L. Abu-Lughod, *Before European Hegemony: The World System A.D. 1250–1350* (Oxford: Oxford University Press, 1989), p. 303.

39. Jurgis Elisonas, "The Inseparable Trinity: Japan's Relations with China and Korea," in *The Cambridge History of Japan*, vol. 4, *Early Modern Japan*, ed. John Hall (Cambridge: Cambridge University Press, 1988), p. 241.

40. U-bong Ha, "Choson jeongi-ui daeil gwangye (Early Choson's Foreign Policy

Toward Japan)," in Hang-rae Cho, U-bong Ha, and Seung-chol Son, eds., *Kangjwa hanilgwangye-sa (Lectures on Korea-Japan Relations)* (Seoul: Hyonumsa, 1994); Etsuko Kang, *Diplomacy and Ideology in Japanese-Korean Relations: From the Fifteenth to the Eighteenth Century* (New York: St. Martin's, 1997), p. 25.

41. Elisonas, "The Inseparable Trinity," p. 244.
42. Shoji Kawazoe, "Japan and East Asia," in *The Cambridge History of Japan*, vol. 3, *Medieval Japan*, ed. Kozo Yamamura (Cambridge: Cambridge University Press, 1990), p. 430.
43. Duck-gi Min, Seung-chol Son, U-bong Ha, Hun Lee, and Song-il Chung, "Hanilgan Pyoryuminae gwanhan yongu (A Study on the Pyoryummin between Korea and Japan)," in Duck-gi Min et al., eds., *Hanilkwangye-ui sahhakheo (Aspects in the History of Korea-Japan relations)* (Seoul: Gukhakjaryowon, 2000).
44. Elisonas, "The Inseparable Trinity," p. 250, emphasizes that although called "*wako*," many of the pirates were actually Chinese, living along the coasts of China itself.
45. Kang, *Diplomacy and Ideology in Japanese-Korean Relations*, p. 2.
46. Kenneth Robinson, "Centering the King of Choson: Aspects of Korean Maritime Diplomacy, 1392–1592," *Journal of Asian Studies* 59, no. 1 (February 2000): 109–25.
47. Paul Bairoch, "International Industrialization Levels from 1750 to 1980," *Journal of European Economic History* 11, no. 2 (1982): 269–334; Angus Maddison, "A Comparison of the Levels of GDP Per Capita in Developed and Developing Countries, 1700–1980," *Journal of Economic History* 43, no. 1 (1983): 27–42; Paul Kennedy, *The Rise and Fall of the Great Powers: Economic Change and Military Conflict from 1500 to 2000* (New York: Random House, 1987).
48. David Marr, "Sino-Vietnamese Relations," *Australian Journal of Chinese Affairs* 6 (1981): 49.
49. Joseph Buttinger, *The Smaller Dragon: A Political History of Vietnam* (New York: Praeger, 1958).
50. Paul K. Davis, *Encyclopedia of Invasions and Conquests: From Ancient Times to the Present* (Santa Barbara, Calif.: ABC-CLIO, 1996), p. 131; Edmund Capon, *Tang China* (London: Macdonald Orbis, 1989).
51. Kawazoe, "Japan and East Asia," p. 418.
52. Louise Levathes, *When China Ruled the Seas: The Treasure Fleet of the Dragon Throne, 1405–1433* (Oxford: Oxford University Press, 1994).
53. Levathes, *When China Ruled the Seas*, p. 82.
54. Abu-Lughod, *Before European Hegemony*, p. 321.
55. Abu-Lughod, *Before European Hegemony*, p. 317.
56. John Lee, "Trade and Economy in Preindustrial East Asia, c. 1500–1800: East Asia in the Age of Global Integration," *Journal of Asian Studies* 58, no. 1 (1999): 14.
57. Gang Deng, "The Foreign Staple Trade of China in the Pre-Modern Era," *International History Review* 19, no. 2 (1997): 254.
58. Deng, "The Foreign Staple Trade," p. 254. See also C. I. Beckwith, "The Impact of the Horse and Silk Trade on the Economies of T'ang China and the Uighur Empire," *Journal of the Economic and Social History of the Orient* 34 (1992): 183–98.
59. William Atwell, "International Bullion Flows and the Chinese Economy circa 1530–1650," *Past and Present* 95 (1982): 68–90.
60. Kang, *Diplomacy and Ideology in Japanese-Korean Relations*, p. 28.

61. Deng, "The Foreign Staple Trade," p. 283.
62. Stephen K. Sanderson, *Social Transformations: A General Theory of Historical Development* (Oxford: Blackwell, 1995), p. 153.
63. Kawazoe, "Japan and East Asia," p. 408.
64. Frank, *ReOrient*, p. 106; Peter Klein, "The China Seas and the World Economy between the Sixteenth and Nineteenth Centuries: The Changing Structures of Trade," in Carl-Ludwig Holtfrerich, ed., *Interactions in the World Economy: Perspectives from International Economic History* (New York: New York University Press, 1989), p. 76; Christopher Howe, *The Origins of Japanese Trade Supremacy: Development and Technology in Asia from 1540 to the Pacific War* (London: Hurts, 1996), p. 37.
65. Howe, *The Origins of Japanese Trade Supremacy*, p. 40.
66. Richard von Glahn, "Myth and Reality of China's Seventeenth Century Monetary Crisis," *Journal of Economic History* 56, no. 2 (1996): 429–54.
67. Lee, "Trade and Economy in Preindustrial East Asia," p. 7.
68. Yoneo Ishii, *The Junk Trade from Southeast Asia: Translations from the Tosen Fusetsu-gaki, 1674–1723* (Singapore: Institute of Southeast Asian Studies, 1998).
69. Ishii, *The Junk Trade from Southeast Asia*, pp. 6–11; Satoshi Ikeda, "The History of the Capitalist World-System vs. the History of East-Southeast Asia," *Review* 19, no. 1 (1996): 49–78.
70. Klein, "The China Seas and the World Economy," p. 67.
71. Ronald P. Toby, *State and Diplomacy in Early Modern Japan: Asia in the Development of the Tokugawa Bakufu* (Stanford: Stanford University Press, 1991), p. xxviii.
72. Victor Lieberman, "Local Integration and Eurasian Analogies: Structuring Southeast Asian History, c. 1350–c. 1830," *Modern Asian Studies* 27, no. 3 (1993): 475–572.
73. Frank, *ReOrient*, p. 97; Anthony Reid, *Southeast Asia in the Age of Commerce, 1450–1680*, vol. 2, *Expansion and Crisis* (New Haven: Yale University Press, 1993).
74. Sarasin Viraphol, *Tribute and Profit: Sino-Siamese Trade 1652–1853* (Cambridge: Harvard University Press, 1977), p. 20.
75. Quoted in Viraphol, *Tribute and Profit*, p. 54.
76. Jennifer W. Cushman, *Fields from the Sea: Chinese Junk Trade with Siam during the Late Eighteenth and Early Nineteenth Centuries* (Ithaca: Southeast Asia Program, Cornell University, 1993), p. 78.
77. Klein, "The China Seas and the World Economy," p. 76.
78. Quoted in Toby, *State and Diplomacy in Early Modern Japan*, p. 9.
79. Klein, "The China Seas and the World Economy," p. 70.
80. See, e.g., Frank, *ReOrient*, p. 101; J. C. van Leur, *Indonesian Trade and Society: Essays in Asian Social and Economic History* (The Hague and Bandung: W. van Hoeve, 1955), p. 125.
81. Klein, "The China Seas and the World Economy," p. 86.
82. Takeshi Hamashita, "The Tribute Trade System and Modern Asia," in A. J. H. Latham and Heita Kawakatsu, eds., *Japanese Industrialization and the Asian Economy* (London: Routledge, 1994), p. 92.
83. Myung-ki Han, *Imjin Yeoran-gwa Han-jung gwangye (The Imjin Intervention and Sino-Korean Relations)* (Seoul: Yuksa Bipyoungsa, 1999).

84. Seonmin Kim, "Ginseng and Border Trespassing between Qing China and Choson Korea" (paper presented at the annual meetings of the Association for Asian Studies, San Diego, April 6–9, 2006).

85. Kim, "Ginseng and Border Trespassing."

86. Jeremiah Curtin, *The Mongols: A History* (Westport, Conn.: Greenwood, 1972).

87. Kawazoe, "Japan and East Asia," p. 424.

88. Mary Berry, *Hideyoshi* (Cambridge: Harvard University Press, 1982).

89. Johnston, *Cultural Realism*, p. 234; Hans J. Van de Ven, "War and the Making of Modern China," *Modern Asian Studies* 30, no. 4 (1996): 737.

90. Immanuel Shu, *The Rise of Modern China* (Oxford: Oxford University Press, 1995).

91. Luc Kwanten, *Imperial Nomads* (Philadelphia: University of Pennsylvania Press, 1979); Davis, *Encyclopedia of Invasions and Conquests*.

92. Kaufman, "The Fragmentation and Consolidation of International Systems," p. 176.

93. Kawazoe, "Japan and East Asia," p. 437.

94. Gari Ledyard, "Confucianism and War: the Korean Security Crisis of 1598," *The Journal of Korean Studies* 6 (1988–89), pp. 81–119; Adriana Boscaro, *101 Letters of Hideyoshi* (Tokyo: Sophia University, 1975).

95. U-bong Ha, *Choson Hugi Silhakja-ui Ilbon gwan yongu (A Study of Late Choson Silhakja's Views on Japan)* (Seoul: Iljisa, 1989).

96. David Wyatt, *Thailand: A Short History* (New Haven: Yale University Press, 1984), p. 104.

97. Kozo Yamamura, "The Growth of Commerce in Medieval Japan," in *The Cambridge History of Japan*, vol. 3, *Medieval Japan*, ed. Yamamura, p. 358.

98. Kawazoe, "Japan and East Asia," pp. 435–6.

99. Smits, *Visions of Ryukyu*.

100. Seung-chol Son, *Choson sidae hanil gwangywe yonku (Korea-Japan Relations during the Choson Period)* (Seoul: Jisungui Sam, 1994); Seung-chol Son, *Gunsae Choson-ui Hanil gwagye yonku (Korea-Japan Relations during the Pre-Modern Choson Era)* (Seoul: Kukhakjaryowon, 1999).

101. Quoted in Hun-Chang Lee and Peter Temin, "Trade Policies in China under the Tribute System as Bounded Rationality" (manuscript, Korea University, Seoul, 2004), p. 29.

102. Kang, *Diplomacy and Ideology in Japanese-Korean Relations*, pp. 6–9.

103. Gari Ledyard, posting to Korea Web, March 22, 2006.

104. Truong Buu Lam, "Intervention versus Tribute in Sino-Vietnamese Relations," in Fairbank, ed., *The Chinese World Order*, p. 178.

105. Marr, "Sino-Vietnamese Relations," p. 49.

106. Keith Taylor, "The Rise of Dai viet and the Establishment of Thang-Long," in Kenneth Hall and John K. Whitmore, eds., *Explorations in Early Southeast Asian History: The Origins of Southeast Asian Statecraft* (Ann Arbor: University of Michigan Press, 1976), pp. 149–92.

107. *The Cambridge History of China*, vol. 7, *The Ming Dynasty, 1368–1644, Part 1*, ed. Frederick Mote and Denis Twitchett (Cambridge: Cambridge University Press, 1988).

108. Kozo Yamamura, "Introduction," in *The Cambridge History of Japan*, vol. 3,

Medieval Japan, ed. Yamamura, pp. 1–45; John Hall, *Japan: From Prehistory to Modern Times* (New York: Delacorte, 1968).

109. *The Cambridge History of Japan,* vol. 2, *Heian Japan,* ed. Donald Shively and William McCullough (Cambridge: Cambridge University Press, 1999).
110. Ki-baek Lee, *A New History of Korea,* trans. Edward Wagner (Cambridge: Harvard University Press, 1984).
111. David C. Kang, *Crony Capitalism: Corruption and Development in South Korea and the Philippines* (Cambridge: Cambridge University Press, 2002), pp. 78–81.
112. Gari Ledyard, posting to Korea Web, March 16, 2006.
113. Keith Taylor, *The Birth of Vietnam* (Berkeley: University of California Press, 1983); Alexander Woodside, *Vietnam and the Chinese Model: A Comparative Study of the Nguyen and Ch'ing Civil Government in the First Half of the Nineteenth Century* (Cambridge: Harvard University Press, 1971); G. Coedes, *The Making of Southeast Asia,* trans. H. M. Wright (Berkeley: University of California Press, 1969).
114. Tashiro Kazui, "Foreign Relations During the Edo Period: Sakoku Reexamined," *Journal of Japanese Studies* 8, no. 2 (1982): 286.
115. Kawazoe, "Japan and East Asia," p. 425.
116. Kang, *Diplomacy and Ideology in Japanese-Korean Relations,* p. 18.
117. Kazui, "Foreign Relations During the Edo Period," p. 286.
118. Kim, *The Last Phase of the East Asian World Order,* p. 15.
119. Kim, *The Last Phase of the East Asian World Order,* p. 15.
120. Kim, *The Last Phase of the East Asian World Order,* p. 15.
121. Ishii, *The Junk Trade from Southeast Asia,* p. 2.
122. William Wray, "The 17th Century Japanese Diaspora: Questions of Boundary and Policy" (manuscript, University of British Columbia, n.d.), p. 2.
123. Howe, *The Origins of Japanese Trade Supremacy,* p. 40.
124. Kazui, "Foreign Relations During the Edo Period," pp. 283–306.
125. Klein, "The China Seas and the World Economy," p. 69.
126. Wray, "The 17th Century Japanese Diaspora," p. 12.
127. Toby, *State and Diplomacy in Early Modern Japan,* p. xvi.

3. DESCRIBING EAST ASIA: ALIGNMENT STRATEGIES TOWARD CHINA

1. Exceptions are Evelyn Goh, "Meeting the China Challenge: The U.S. in Southeast Asian Regional Security Strategies," *East-West Center Policy Studies* 16 (April 2005); Robert Sutter, *China's Rise in Asia: Promise and Perils* (Lanham, Md.: Rowman, Littlefield, 2005); David Shambaugh, ed., *Power Shift: China and Asia's New Dynamics* (Berkeley: University of California Press, 2005).
2. James F. Hoge, Jr., "A Global Power Shift in the Making: Is the United States ready?," *Foreign Affairs* 83, no. 4 (July/August 2004): 2–7; Fareed Zakaria, "What Bush and Kerry Missed," *Newsweek,* October 25, 2004.
3. Keir Lieber and Gerard Alexander, "Waiting for Balancing: Why the World is Not Pushing Back," *International Security* 30, no. 1 (Summer 2005): 109–39, 119.
4. James D. Morrow, "Arms Versus Allies: Tradeoffs in the Search for Security," *International Organization* 47, no. 2 (Spring 1993): 207–53. The classic statement is

Kenneth Waltz, *Theory of International Politics* (Reading, Mass.: Addison-Wesley, 1979).

5. Stephen Walt, *The Origins of Alliances* (Ithaca: Cornell University Press, 1987); Randall Schweller, "Bandwagoning for Profit: Bringing the Revisionist State Back In," *International Security* 19, no. 1 (Summer 1994): 72–107.

6. T. V. Paul, "Soft Balancing in the Age of U.S. Primacy," *International Security* 30, no. 1 (Summer 2005): 46–71; Robert A. Pape, "Soft Balancing Against the United States," *International Security* 30, no. 1 (Summer 2005): 7–45; T. V. Paul, James J. Wirtz, and Michel Fortmann, eds., *Balance of Power: Theory and Practice in the 21st Century* (Stanford: Stanford University Press, 2004); Randall Schweller, "Unanswered Threats: A Neoclassical Realist Theory of Underbalancing," *International Security* 29, no. 2 (Fall 2004): 159–201. For counterarguments, see Stephen Brooks and William Wohlforth, "Hard Times for Soft Balancing," *International Security* 30, no. 1 (Summer 2005): 72–108; William Wohlforth, "The Stability of a Unipolar World," *International Security* 24, no. 1 (Summer 1999): 5–41; G. John Ikenberry, ed., *America Unrivaled: The Future of the Balance of Power* (Ithaca: Cornell University Press, 2002); Lieber and Alexander, "Waiting for Balancing."

7. Pape, "Soft Balancing Against the United States," p. 10.

8. These definitions come from Waltz, *Theory of International Politics*, p. 118.

9. Goh, "Meeting the China Challenge"; Ja Ian Chong, "Testing Alternative Responses to Power Preponderance: Buffering, Binding, Bonding, and Beleaguering in the Real World," Working Paper 60 (Singapore: IDSS, 2004).

10. Stephen Van Evera, *Causes of War: Power and the Roots of Conflict* (Ithaca: Cornell University Press, 1999).

11. This may also reflect South Korea's decision that theater missile defense (TMD) will not help it in a conventional war with the North. See Victor Cha, "TMD and Nuclear Weapons in Asia," in Muthiah Alagappa, ed., *Asian Security Order* (Stanford: Stanford University Press, 2003).

12. Author's interview, March 17, 2006.

13. *Dong-a Ilbo*, April 19, 2004.

14. Jae-ho Chung, "The 'Rise' of China and Its Impact on South Korea's Strategic Soul-Searching," in James Lister, ed., *The Newly Emerging Asian Order and the Korean Peninsula* (Washington, D.C.: Korea Economic Institute, 2005), pp. 1–12.p. 4.

15. South Korea National Security Council, *Peace, Prosperity, and National Security: National Security Strategy of the Republic of Korea* (Seoul: National Security Council, 2004), http://www.korea.net/.

16. Interview with author, March 17, 2006.

17. For a review, see Cecil B. Currey, "Vietnam: Foreign and Domestic Policies," *Journal of Third World Studies* 16, no. 2 (Fall 1999): 197–98; and Ang Cheng Guan, "Vietnam-China Relations since the End of the Cold War," *Asian Survey* 38, no. 12 (December 1998): 1122–41.

18. Sheldon Simon, "Vietnam's Security: Between China and ASEAN," *Asian Affairs: An American Review* 20, no. 4 (Winter 1994): 187–205, 191.

19. Cheng-guan Ang, "Vietnam: Another Milestone and the Country Plods On," in Daljit Singh and Anthony Smith, eds., *Southeast Asian Affairs 2002* (Singapore: Institute of Southeast Asian Studies, 2003): 345–56.

20. Radio Australia, October 27, 2005, http://www.abc.net.au/ra/news/stories/s1493343.htm.

21. Simon, "Vietnam's Security," p. 193.

22. Alice Ba, "Who's Socializing Whom? Complex Engagement in Sino-ASEAN relations," *Pacific Review* 19, no. 2 (June 2006): 157–79.

23. Michael Vatikiotis, "Catching the Dragon's Tail: China and Southeast Asia in the 21st Century," *Contemporary Southeast Asia* 25, no. 1 (April 2003): 74–75.

24. Quoted in Esther Pan, "New Focus on U.S.–Southeast Asia Military Ties," backgrounder, Council on Foreign Relations, February 2, 2006, http://www.cfr.org/publication/9742/.

25. On Southeast Asia–China relations, see Brantley Womack, "China and Southeast Asia: Asymmetry, Leadership, and Normalcy," *Pacific Affairs* 76, no. 4 (Winter 2003–2004): 526; Henry Kenny, *Shadow of the Dragon: Vietnam's Continuing Struggle with China and the Implications for U.S. Foreign Policy* (Washington, D.C.: Brassey's, 2002); Amitav Acharya, "Containment, Engagement, or Counter-Dominance? Malaysia's Response to China's Rise," in Alastair Iain Johnston and Robert S. Ross, eds., *Engaging China: The Management of an Emerging Power* (London: Routledge, 1999); Michael Leifer, "Indonesia and the Dilemmas of Engagement," in Johnston and Ross, eds., *Engaging China*; Leszek Buszynski, "Realism, Institutionalism, and Philippine Security," *Asian Survey* 42, no. 3 (2002): 483–501.

26. Janadas Devan, "Containing China an American Conceit," *Singapore Straits Times*, October 29, 2005, http://taiwansecurity.org/ST/2005/ST-291005.htm.

27. All figures from Strategic Asia (National Bureau of Asian Research), http://strategicasia.nbr.org/.

28. Figures from the International Institute for Strategic Studies, *The Military Balance, 2003–04* (London: IISS, 2004), p. 337.

29. Sheldon Simon, "Southeast Asia's Defense Needs: Change or Continuity?," in Ashley Tellis and Michael Wills, eds., *Strategic Asia 2005–06: Military Modernization in an Era of Uncertainty* (Seattle: National Bureau of Asian Research, 2005), p. 275.

30. Leifer, "Indonesia and the Dilemmas of Engagement," p. 107.

31. Leifer, "Indonesia and the Dilemmas of Engagement," p. 101. See also Robert Ross, "Beijing as a Conservative Power," *Foreign Affairs* 76, no. 2 (March/April 1997): 33–44.

32. Alan Dupont, "Indonesia Defense Strategy and Security: Time for a Rethink?," *Contemporary Southeast Asia* 18, no. 3 (December 1996): 275–95.

33. Tatik Hafidiz, "The War on Terror and the Future of Indonesian Democracy," Working Paper 46 (Singapore: Institute of Defense and Strategic Studies, 2003), http://www.ntu.edu.sg/.

34. Ministry of Defense, *Indonesia: Defending the Country Entering the 21st Century* (Jakarta: Ministry of Defense, 2003), http://merln.ndu.edu/whitepapers.html. See also Rizal Sukma, "The Evolution of Indonesia's Foreign Policy: An Indonesian View," *Asian Survey* 35, no. 3 (March 1995): 304–15.

35. Leifer, "Indonesia and the Dilemmas of Engagement," p. 101.

36. Mokhzani Zubir, "Should Malaysia Join the U.S. Maritime Domain Awareness Scheme?" (Kuala Lumpur, Maritime Institute of Malaysia, 2005), www.mima.gov.my/mima/htmls/papers/pdf/mokhzani/usmda.pdf.

37. Helen Nesadurai, "Malaysia and the United States: Rejecting Dominance, Embracing Engagement," Working Paper 72 (Singapore: Institute for Defense and Strategic Studies, 2004), p. 23.

38. Amitav Acharya, 1999, p. 146. See also Joseph Chin-Yong Liow, Malaysia-China Relations in the 1990s," *Asian Survey* 40, No. 4 (July/August 2000), pp. 672–92.

39. Quoted in Abdul Razak Baginda, "Malaysian Perceptions of China: From Hostility to Cordiality," in Herbert Yee and Ian Storey, eds., *The China Threat: Perceptions, Myths, and Reality* (London: RoutledgeCurzon, 2002), p. 242.

40. Khong, "Coping with Strategic Uncertainty: The Role of Institutions and Soft Balancing in Southeast Asia's Post–Cold War Strategy," in J. J. Suh, Peter Katzenstein, and Allen Carlson, eds., *Rethinking Security in East Asia: Identity, Power and Efficiency* (Stanford: Stanford University Press, 2004), p. 27.

41. Quoted in Acharya, "Containment, Engagement, or Counter-Dominance?," p. 134.

42. Acharya, "Containment, Engagement, or Counter-Dominance?," p. 135.

43. Ronald Montaperto, "China–Southeast Asia Relations: Find New Friends, Reward Old Ones, But Keep All in Line," *Comparative Connections* 5, no. 3 (October 2004): 82.

44. Simon, "Southeast Asia's Defense Needs," p. 283.

45. "Strident Washington, Compliant Japan and Cautious Australia—Containment and Consequences" (Singapore Institute of International Affairs, South East Asia Peace and Security Net, March 16, 2006), http://www.siiaonline.org/home?wid = 171&func = viewSubmission&sid = 655.

46. Personal interview, January 24, 2006.

47. Jane Perlez, "China's Role Emerges as Major Issue for Southeast Asia," *New York Times,* March 14, 2006, p. A3.

48. Khong, "Coping with Strategic Uncertainty," p. 26.

49. Quoted in Yuen Foong Khong, "Singapore: A Time for Economic and Political Engagement," in Johnston and Ross, eds., *Engaging China,* p. 114.

50. "Lee Calls on West to Help China, Knocks Patten," Reuters News Service, October 13, 1994, quoted in Ian Storey, "Singapore and the Rise of China: Perceptions and Policy," in Yee and Storey, eds., *The China Threat,* p. 217.

51. Quoted in Gaye Christoffersen, "The Role of East Asia in Sino-American Affairs," *Asian Survey* 42, no. 3 (May/June 2002): 369–96, 393.

52. National Security Coordination Center, *The Fight Against Terror: Singapore's National Security Strategy* (Singapore: National Security Coordination Center, 2004).

53. Rita Zahara, "Chinese Defense Minister Visits Changi Naval Base," Channel NewsAsia, April 14, 2006.

54. "Leave Manila alone, Palace Tells US on RP-China ties," *Daily Tribune,* October 29, 2005, www.tribune.net.ph/.

55. Robert Sutter, "China–Southeast Asia Relations: Emphasizing the Positive; Continued Wariness," *Comparative Connections* 7, no. 4 (January 2006): 11.

56. Avelino Cruz, "Turn Over of China Grants to the Philippines," January 23, 2006, http://www.dnd.gov.ph/DNDWEBPAGE_files/speech/sp-jan23-06.htm.

57. "PLA Navy (PLAN) Flotilla Visits U.S., Canada, and Philippines," China Military http://www.chinamil.com.cn/.

58. Sheldon Simon, "Southeast Asia's Defense Needs," p. 273.

59. Aileen San Pablo-Baviera, "Perceptions of a Chinese Threat: A Philippine Perspective," in Yee and Storey, eds., *The China Threat*, p. 258.

60. Sheldon Simon, "Southeast Asia's Defense Needs: Change or Continuity?" in Ashley Tellis and Michael Wills, eds., *Strategic Asia 2005–06: Military Modernization in an Era of Uncertainty* (Seattle, WA: National Bureau of Asian Research, 2005), p. 280.

61. Martin Stuart-Fox, "Southeast Asia and China: The Role of History and Culture in Shaping Future Relations," *Contemporary Southeast Asia* 26, no. 1 (2004): 133.

62. Alice Ba, "China and ASEAN: Renavigating Relations for a 21st-Century Asia," *Asian Survey* 43, no. 4 (July/August 2003): 625.

63. Sukhumbhand Paribatra, "Dictates of Security: Thailand's Relations with the PRC," in Joyce K. Kallgren, Noordin Sopiee, and Soedjati Djiwandono, eds., *ASEAN and China: An Evolving Relationship* (Berkeley: Institute of East Asian Studies, University of California, 1988); Khien Theeravit, "The United States, Thailand, and the Indochinese Conflict," in Hans Indorf, ed., *Thai-American Relations in Contemporary Affairs* (Singapore: Executive Publications, 1982).

64. Goh, "Meeting the China Challenge," p. 17.

65. Interview quoted in Goh, "Meeting the China Challenge," p. 18.

66. Shannon Tow, "Southeast Asia in the Sino-U.S. Strategic Balance," *Contemporary Southeast Asia* 26, no. 3 (December 2004): 450–51.

67. Sutter, "China–Southeast Asia Relations," p. 7.

68. Khong, "Coping with Strategic Uncertainty," p. 29.

69. Storey, "Singapore and the Rise of China," p. 216.

70. Chisake Watanabe, "Japan Calls China a Threat," Associated Press, December 22, 2005.

71. Michael Mastanduno, "Japan: Back to the Future?," in Ashley Tellis and Michael Wills, eds., *Strategic Asia 2006–2007* (Seattle: National Bureau of Asian Research, 2006), p. 29.

72. "The Geography of the Peace: East Asia in the Twenty-First Century," *International Security* 23, no. 4 (Spring 1999): 115.

73. There is much speculation about the goals and motives behind China's military modernization. See John Lewis and Xue Litai, "China's Search for a Modern Air Force," *International Security* 24, no. 1 (Summer 1999): 64–94; Bates Gill and Michael O'Hanlon, "China's Hollow Military," *National Interest* 56 (Summer 1999): 55; Lyle Goldstein and William Murray, "Undersea Dragons: China's Maturing Submarine Force," *International Security* 28, no. 4 (Spring 2004): 161–96; RAND, "A New Direction for China's Defense Industry" (Santa Monica, Calif.: RAND, 2005), http://www.rand.org/pubs/monographs/MG334/.

74. Richard J. Samuels, *Securing Japan* (Ithaca: Cornell University Press, 2007).

75. Samuels, *Securing Japan*, chapter 8.

76. On Japan's foreign policy in the new century, see Nobuo Okawara and Peter Katzenstein, "Japan and Asian-Pacific Security: Regionalization, Entrenched Bilateralism and Incipient Multilateralism," *Pacific Review* 14, no. 2 (2001): 165–94; Christopher Hughes, *Japan's Re-emergence as a "Normal" Military Power,* Adelphi Papers 368–69 (London: International Institute for Strategic Studies, 2005); Inoguchi Takashi, ed., *Japan's Asia Policy: Revival and Response* (London: Palgrave, 2002).

77. Jian Yang, "Sino-Japanese Relations: Implications for Southeast Asia," *Contemporary Southeast Asia* 25, no. 2 (August 2003): 325.

78. Zha, Daojiong Zha, "The Taiwan Problem in Japan-China Relations: An irritant or Destroyer?," *East Asia* 19, no. 1 (Spring–Summer 2001): 218. See also Inoguchi Takashi and Purnendra Jain, eds., *Japanese Foreign Policy Today* (New York: Palgrave, 2000).

79. Michael Armacost, "Japan: Tilting Closer to Washington," in Richard J. Ellings and Aaron L. Friedberg with Michael Wills, eds., *Strategic Asia 2003–04: Fragility and Crisis* (Seattle: National Bureau of Asian Research, 2004).

80. David Ignatius and Thomas Crampton, "A Confident Koizumi Keeps His Sails Set," *International Herald Tribune*, June 20, 2002.

81. Quoted in Lee Hudson Teslik, "Japan and Its Military," Backgrounder, Council on Foreign Relations, April 13, 2006, http://www.cfr.org/publication/10439/japan_ and_its_military.html.

82. Barry Buzan, XYZ, "Conclusion: How and To Whom Does China Matter?" in Barry Buzan and Rosemary Foot, eds., *Does China Matter? A Reassessment, Essays in Memory of Gerald Segal* (London: Routledge, 2004), p. 156.

83. James Przystup, p. 37.

84. Maris Martinsons, "Transforming China," *Communications of the ACM* 48, no. 4 (April 2005): 44–49.

85. Dexter Roberts, Wendy Zellner, and Carol Matlack, "Let the Retail Wars Begin," *Business Week* January 17, 2005, pp. 44–45.

86. Gerald Curtis, "East Asia, Regionalism, and U.S. National Interests," *American Foreign Policy Interests* 26 (2004): 205.

87. U.S. State Department, Bureau of Intelligence and Research, "Asian Views of China," November 16, 2005. Poll results are from face-to-face interview surveys conducted in the summer and fall of 2005 with representative samples of adults in seven East Asian countries. Samples were chosen by multi-stage probability selection techniques.

88. "22-Nation Poll Shows China Viewed Positively by Most Countries Including its Asian Neighbors," BBC World Service Poll, January 5, 2005, www.globescan.com/.

89. David Shambaugh, "Rising Dragon and American Eagle, Part I," *YaleGlobal Online* April 20, 2005, http://yaleglobal.yale.edu/.

90. Phillip Pan, "China's Improving Image Challenges U.S. in Asia," *Washington Post*, November 15, 2003, p. A01.

91. See Amitav Acharya, *Constructing a Security Community in Southeast Asia: ASEAN and the Problem of Regional Order* (London: Routledge, 2001); John Ravenhill, *APEC and the Construction of Pacific Rim Regionalism* (Cambridge: Cambridge University Press, 2001); Gilbert Rozman, *Northeast Asia's Stunted Regionalism: Bilateral Distrust in the Shadow of Globalization* (Cambridge: Cambridge University Press, 2004); Peter J. Katzenstein, *A World of Regions: Asia and Europe in the American Imperium* (Ithaca: Cornell University Press, 2005); Ellis Krauss and T. J. Pempel, eds., *Beyond Bilateralism: U.S.-Japan Relations in the New Asia-Pacific* (Stanford: Stanford University Press, 2004).

92. T. J. Pempel, "Introduction," in Pempel, ed., *Remapping East Asia: The Construction of a Region* (Ithaca: Cornell University Press, 2005), p. 19.

93. Pempel, "Introduction," p. 19.

94. Tsutomu Kikuchi, "East Asian Regionalism: A Look at the 'ASEAN plus Three' Framework," *Japan Review of International Affairs* 16 (Spring 2002): 1–23. See also Paul Bowles, "Asia's Post-Crisis Regionalism: Bringing the State Back In, Keeping the (United) States Out," *Review of International Political Economy* 9, no. 2 (May 2002): 230–56; Christopher Hemmer and Peter J. Katzenstein, "Why is There No NATO in Asia? Collective Identity, Regionalism, and the Origins of Multilateralism," *International Organization* 56, no. 3 (Summer 2002): 575–607; Miles Kahler, "Conclusion: The Causes and Consequences of Legalization," *International Organization* 54, no. 3 (Summer 2000): 661–84.

95. Donald K. Emmerson, "What Do the Blind-Sided See? Reapproaching Regionalism in Southeast Asia," *Pacific Review* 18, no. 1 (March 2005): 1–21.

96. Quoted in Emmerson, "What Do the Blind-Sided See?," p. 9.

97. Chalmers Johnson, *MITI and the Japanese Miracle* (Stanford: Stanford University Press, 1982); Stephan Haggard, *Pathways from the Periphery* (Ithaca: Cornell University Press, 1990); Jung-en Woo, *Race to the Swift* (New York: Columbia University Press, 1990).

98. On multilateral institutions in Asia, see Amitav Acharya, "Regional Institutions and Asian Security Order," in Alagappa, ed., *Asian Security Order*, pp. 210–40; Margaret Pearson, "The Major Multilateral Economic Institutions Engage China," in Johnston and Ross, eds., *Engaging China*, pp. 207–34.

99. Muthiah Alagappa, ed., *Asian Security Practice: Material and Ideational Influences* (Stanford: Stanford University Press, 1998); Acharya, *Constructing a Security Community in Southeast Asia*.

100. Amitav Acharya, "How Ideas Spread: Whose Norms Matter? Norm Localization and Institutional Change in Asian Regionalism," *International Organization* 58 (Spring 2004): 239–75; Desmond Ball, "Strategic Culture in the Asia-Pacific Region," *Security Studies* 3, no. 1 (Winter 1995): 44–74.

101. Personal communication with a senior U.S. policy maker.

102. Alexa Olesen, "China Edging out U.S. for APEC leadership," Associated Press, November 16, 2005.

103. See the papers from the conference "China and the WTO: The World Responds" (Tuck School of Business, Dartmouth College, April 24–25, 2004).

104. Xinbo Wu, "China: Security Practice of a Modernizing and Ascending Power," in Alagappa, ed., *Asian Security Practice*, p. 151.

105. On multilateral institutions in Asia, see Amitav Acharya, "Regional Institutions and Asian Security Order," pp. 210–40; Margaret Pearson, "The Major Multilateral Economic Institutions Engage China," pp. 207–34.

106. Yong Deng and Thomas G. Moore, "China Views Globalization: Toward a New Great-Power Politics?" *Washington Quarterly* 27, no. 3 (Summer 2004): 117–36; Thomas G. Moore, "Chinese Foreign Policy in the Age of Globalization," in Yong Deng and Fei-Ling Wang, eds., *China Rising: Power and Motivation in Chinese Foreign Policy* (Lanham, Md.: Rowman & Littlefield, forthcoming); Pieter Bottelier, "Implications of WTO Membership for China's State-Owned Banks and the Management of Public Finances: Issues and Strategies," *Journal of Contemporary China* 11 (2002): 397–411.

107. China's defense white paper commented that "China holds that the ARF [ASEAN Regional Forum] should continue to focus on confidence-building measures, explore new security concepts and methods, and discuss the question of preventive diplomacy." People's Republic of China, *China's National Defense 2000*, October 2000.

108. Keiichi Tsunekawa, "Why So Many Maps There?," in Pempel, ed., *Remapping East Asia*, p. 110.

109. Rozman, *Northeast Asia's Stunted Regionalism*, p. 188.

110. Lyall Breckon, "SARS and a New Security Initiative from China," *Comparative Connections* 103 (July 2003).

111. Amit Prakash, "Envisioning a Single Asian Currency," Bloomberg, March 28, 2006.

112. Asian Development Bank, "East Asian Local Currency Bond Markets Tripled since 1997," Asian Development Bank, November 22, 2004, http://asianbondsonline.adb.org.

113. Xinbo Wu, "China," p. 115. For extended discussion, see Johnston and Ross, eds., *Engaging China*.

114. Treaty of Amity and Cooperation in Southeast Asia, Chapter 1, Article 2, Section E, http://www.aseansec.org/1217.htm; *Final Report of the East Asia Study Group* (Phnom Penh: ASEAN+3 Summit, 2002), p. 79. See also *Forging Closer ASEAN-China Relations in the Twenty-First Century* (2001), prepared for ASEAN by the ASEAN-China Expert Group on Economic Cooperation, http://aseansec.org.

115. *Declaration on the Conduct of Parties in the South China Sea*, signed at the Eighth ASEAN Summit in Phnom Penh, November 2002 (http://www.aseansec.org). For an assessment of the details of the agreement, see Ang Cheng Guan, "The South China Sea Dispute Revisited" (manuscript, Nanyang Technological University, 2004), p. 6; Nguyen Hong Thao, "The 2002 Declaration on the Conduct of Parties in the South China Sea: A Note," *Ocean Development and International Law* 34 (2003): 279–85; Leszek Buszynski, "ASEAN, the Declaration on Conduct, and the South China Sea," *Contemporary Southeast Asia* 25, no. 3 (2003): 343–62.

116. Walter Hatch and Kozo Yamamura, *East Asia in Japan's Embrace: Building a Regional Production Alliance* (Cambridge: Cambridge University Press, 1996).

117. Evan Osnos, "Asia Rides Wave of Korean Pop Culture Invasion," *Chicago Tribune*, December 23, 2005; David Leheny, "A Narrow Place to Cross Swords: 'Soft Power' and the Politics of Japanese Popular Culture in East Asia," in Peter Katzenstein and Takashi Shiraishi, eds., *Beyond Japan: The Dynamics of East Asian Regionalism* (Ithaca: Cornell University Press, 2006).

118. Etel Solingen, "East Asian Regional Institutions: Characteristics, Sources, Distinctiveness," in Pempel, ed., *Remapping East Asia*, pp. 31–53.

119. There is a vast literature on the political economy of East Asian growth. See for example, Andrew MacIntyre, ed., *Business and Government in Industrialising Asia* (Ithaca: Cornell University Press, 1995). On the role of external threats, see Dan Slater, Richard Doner, and Bryan Ritchie, "Systemic Vulnerability and the Origins of Developmental States: Northeast and Southeast Asia in Comparative Perspective," *International Organization* 59, no. 2 (Spring 2005): 327–61.

120. Amitav Acharya, "Culture, Security, Multilateralism: From the 'ASEAN Way' to the 'Asia-Pacific Way,'" in Keith Krause, ed., *Culture and Security: Multilateralism, Arms Control, and Security* Building (London: Frank Cass, 1999), p. 69.

4. CHINA: IDENTITY, SOVEREIGNTY, AND TAIWAN

1. See Avery Goldstein, *Rising to the Challenge: China's Grand Strategy and International Security* (Stanford: Stanford University Press, 2005); Evan Medeiros, "China Debates Its 'Peaceful Rise' Strategy," *YaleGlobal Online* 22 (June 2004); David Shambaugh; Alastair Iain Johnston; and Robert Ross, "China's Grand Strategy: A Kinder, Gentler Turn," *Strategic Comments* 10, no. 9 (November 2004).

2. R. Karl, *Staging the World: Chinese Nationalism at the Turn of the 20th Century* (Durham: Duke University Press, 2002).

3. Michael Leifer, *The ASEAN Regional Forum*, Adelphi Paper 302 (London: IISS, 1996), p. 54.

4. Andrew Nathan and Robert Ross, *The Great Wall and the Empty Fortress: China's Search for Security* (New York: Norton, 1997), p. 34.

5. Alastair Iain Johnston, *Cultural Realism* (Princeton: Princeton University Press, 1994).

6. Denny Roy, *China's Foreign Relations* (New York: Rowman & Littlefield, 1998).

7. Evan Medeiros and M. Taylor Fravel, "China's New Diplomacy," *Foreign Affairs* 82, no. 6 (November/December 2003): 22–35; Xia Liping, "China: A Responsible Great Power," *Journal of Contemporary China* 10 (2001): 18; Shiping Tang, "The Rise of China as a Security Linchpin," *Asia Times*, June 21, 2003; Michael Chambers, "Dealing with a Truculent Ally: A Comparative Perspective on China's Handling of North Korea," *Journal of East Asian Studies* 5, no. 1 (January 2005): 35–75.

8. Medeiros and Fravel, "China's New Diplomacy," p. 32; Peter H. Gries, "A 'China Threat'? Power and Passion in Chinese 'Face Nationalism,'" *World Affairs* 162, no. 2 (Fall 1999): 63–75. See also Peter Gries, *China's New Nationalism: Pride, Politics, and Diplomacy* (Berkeley: University of California Press, 2004).

9. Wang Jisi, "International Relations Theory and the Study of Chinese Foreign Policy: A Chinese Perspective," in Thomas Robinson and David Shambaugh, eds., *Chinese Foreign Policy: Theory and Practice* (Oxford: Clarendon, 1994), pp. 481–505.

10. Michael Hunt, "Chinese Foreign Relations in Historical Perspective," in Harry Harding, ed., *China's Foreign Relations in the 1980s* (New Haven: Yale University Press, 1984), pp. 1–42.

11. Samuel Kim, "Sovereignty in the Chinese Image of World Order," in Ronald St. J. Macdonald, ed., *Essays in Honor of Wang Tieya* (London: Martinus Mijhoff, 1994), p. 428; Alastair Iain Johnston, "Is China a Status Quo Power?" *International Security* 27, no. 4 (Spring 2003): 5–56.

12. Allen Carlson, "Constructing the Dragon's Scales: China's Approach to Territorial and Border Relations in the 1980s and 1990s," *Journal of Contemporary China* 13, no. 37 (November 2003): 678.

13. Lei Guang, "Realpolitik Nationalism: International Sources of Chinese Nationalism," *Modern China* 31, no. 4 (October 2005): 487–514.

14. Steven Levine, "China in Asia: The PRC as a Regional Power," in Harding, ed., *China's Foreign Relations in the 1980s*, pp. 107–45.

15. Quoted in Guang, "Realpolitik Nationalism," p. 500.

16. Gilbert Rozman, "China's Quest for a Great Power Identity," *Orbis* 43, no. 3 (Summer 1999): 383–403.

17. Goldstein, *Rising to the Challenge*, p. 40.
18. This corresponds to the "reassurance" strategies that formal theorists have identified. See Andrew Kydd, *Trust and Mistrust in International Relations* (Princeton: Princeton University Press, 2005).
19. Wang Xiangwei, "Soviet-Style Rise 'Is Not on Agenda,'" *South China Morning Post*, November 23, 2005, p. 1.
20. Robert Sutter, "China's Good Neighbor Policy and Its Implications for Taiwan," *Journal of Contemporary* China 13, no. 41 (November 2004): 717–31; Denny Roy, *China's Foreign Relations* (Lanham, Md.: Rowman & Littlefield, 1999).
21. Christopher Hughes, "Nationalism and Multilateralism in Chinese Foreign Policy: Implications for Southeast Asia," *Pacific Review* 18, no. 1 (March 2005): 119–35.
22. Quoted in Elizabeth Economy, "China's Rise in Southeast Asia: Implications for the United States," *Journal of Contemporary China* 14, no. 44 (August 2005): 413.
23. Wu Baiyi, "The Chinese Security Concept and Its Historical Evolution," *Journal of Contemporary China* 10 (2001): 281. See also Carl Thayer, "China's 'New Security Concept' and Southeast Asia," in David Lovell, ed., *Asia-Pacific Security: Policy Challenges* (Singapore: Institute of Southeast Asian Studies, 2003); Xia Liping, "China: A Responsible Great Power," p. 18; Shiping Tang, "The Rise of China as a Security Linchpin."
24. Michael Swaine, "China: Exploiting a Strategic Opening," in Ashley Tellis and Michael Wills, eds., *Strategic Asia 2004–2005: Confronting Terrorism in the Pursuit of Power* (Seattle: National Bureau of Asian Research, 2005), pp. 67–102.
25. Goldstein, *Rising to the Challenge*, p. 12.
26. Thomas Christensen, "China," in Richard J. Ellings and Aaron Friedberg, with Michael Wills, eds., *Strategic Asia 2002–03: Asian Aftershocks* (Seattle: National Bureau of Asian Research, 2002), p. 53.
27. Minxin Pei, "The Dark Side of China's Rise," *Foreign Policy* 153 (March/April 2006): 32–42.
28. Thomas Christensen, "Chinese Realpolitik," *Foreign Affairs* 75, no. 4 (September/October 1996): 41.
29. Hongying Wang, "The Asian Financial Crisis and Financial Reforms in China," *Pacific Review* 12, no. 4 (1999): 537–56.
30. Thomas Clarke, "Haemorrhaging Tigers: The Power of International Financial Markets and the Weakness of Asian Modes of Corporate Governance," *Corporate Governance* 8, no. 2 (April 2000): 101–16.
31. Pieter Bottelier, "Implications of WTO Membership for China's State-Owned Banks and the Management of Public Finances: Issues and Strategies," *Journal of Contemporary China* 11 (2002): 397–411.
32. Bottelier, "Implications of WTO Membership," p. 401.
33. Bottelier, "Implications of WTO Membership," p. 402.
34. Hongying Wang, "The Asian Financial Crisis and Financial Reforms in China," p 541.
35. David Bloom et al., "Demographic Change and Economic Growth: Comparing China and India" (manuscript, Harvard School of Public Health, March 2006), p. 30.
36. Yasheng Huang, "Managing Chinese Bureaucrats: An Institutional Economics Perspective," *Political Studies* 50 (2002): 61–79.

37. Barry Naughton, "The New Common Economic Program: China's Eleventh Five Year Plan and What It Means," *China Leadership Monitor* 16 (Fall 2005): 2.

38. Minxin Pei, "China: Can Economic Growth Continue Without Political Reform?" in Ashley Tellis and Michael Wills, eds., *Strategic Asia 2006-07* (Seattle: National Bureau of Asian Research, 2006), p. 8.

39. Quoted in Mike Shuster, "Growing Chinese Military Strength Stirs Debate," *Morning Edition*, National Public Radio, October 17, 2005.

40. Johnston, "Is China a Status Quo Power?"

41. Johnston, "Is China A Status Quo Power?," p. 49.

42. Economy, "China's Rise in Southeast Asia: Implications for the United States," *Journal of Contemporary China* 14, no. 44 (August 2005): 409–25, 410.

43. Levine, "China in Asia."

44. Medeiros and Fravel, "China's New Diplomacy," p. 23.

45. Johnston, "Is China a Status Quo Power?" p. 16.

46. People's Republic of China, *China's National Defense 2000* (Beijing: Information Office, State Council of the People's Republic of China, 2000).

47. People's Republic of China, *China's National Defense* (Beijing: Information Office, State Council of the People's Republic of China, 1998).

48. Kenneth Allen, "China's Foreign Military Relations with Asia-Pacific," *Journal of Contemporary China* 10 (2001): 645–62.

49. Kenneth Allen, "China's Foreign Military Relations with Asia-Pacific," p. 648.

50. Kenneth Allen, "China's Foreign Military Relations with Asia-Pacific," p. 649.

51. Taylor Fravel, "Regime Insecurity and International Cooperation: Explaining China's Compromises in Territorial Disputes," *International Security* 30, no. 2 (Fall 2005): 46–83.

52. Medeiros and Fravel, "China's New Diplomacy," p. 26.

53. David Shambaugh, "China Engages Asia: Reshaping the Regional Order," *International Security* 29, no. 3 (Winter 2004/05): 64–99, 66.

54. Medeiros and Fravel, "China's New Diplomacy," p. 26.

55. See the extensive discussion in Allen Carlson, *Unifying China, Integrating with the World: Securing Chinese Sovereignty in the Reform Era* (Stanford: Stanford University Press, 2005); Jianwei Wang, "Territorial Disputes and Asian Conflict: Sources, Management, and Prospects," in Muthiah Alagappa, ed., *Asian Security Order* (Stanford: Stanford University Press, 2003), pp. 380–423. On the Paris Peace Accords, see S. J. Hood, "Beijing's Cambodia Gamble and the Prospects for Peace in Indochina: The Khmer Rouge or Sihanouk?" *Asian Survey* 30, no. 10 (October 1990): 977–91.

56. Jean-Marc Blanchard, "Maritime Issues in Asia: The Problem of Adolescence," in Alagappa, ed., *Asian Security Order*, pp. 424–57.

57. On the Spratlys, see Michael Gallagher, "China's Illusory Threat to the South China Sea," *International Security* 19, no. 1 (Summer 1994): 169–94; Ian Storey, "Creeping Assertiveness: China, the Philippines, and the South China Sea Dispute," *Contemporary Southeast Asia*, 21, no. 1 (April 1999): 95–118; Mark Valencia, "China and the South China Sea Disputes," *Adelphi Papers*, No. 298 (London: IISS, October 1995).

58. Xinbo Wu, "China: Security Practice of a Modernizing and Ascending Power," in Muthiah Alagappa, ed., *Asian Security Practice: Material and Ideational Influences*

(Stanford: Stanford University Press, 1998), p. 115. For extended discussion, see Alastair Iain Johnston and Robert Ross, eds., *Engaging China: The Management of an Emerging Power* (London: Routledge, 1999).

59. Carl Thayer, "Vietnamese Perceptions of the 'China Threat,' in Herbert Yee and Ian Storey, eds., *The China Threat: Perceptions, Myths, and Reality* (London: RoutledgeCurzon, 2002), p. 267.

60. Gerald Segal, *Defending China* (Oxford: Oxford University Press, 1985), p. 213. See also Sheldon Simon, "China, Vietnam, and Asia," *Asian Survey* 19, no. 12 (December 1979); Bruce Burton, "Contending Explanations of the 1979 Sino-Vietnamese War," *International Journal* 34, no. 4 (Autumn 1979); Douglas Pike, "Communist vs. Communist in Southeast Asia," *International Security* 4, no. 1 (Summer 1979).

61. Segal, *Defending China*, p. 142. See also Melvin Gurtov, *China Under Threat* (Baltimore: Johns Hopkins University Press, 1980); Nevil Maxwell, *India's China War* (London: Penguin, 1972).

62. "China and India Sign Border Accord," CNN, April 11, 2005, www.cnn.com.

63. Fravel, "Regime Insecurity and International Cooperation," p. 56.

64. Medeiros and Fravel, "China's New Diplomacy," p. 26.

65. John Lewis and Xue Litai, "China's Search for a Modern Air Force," *International Security* 24, no. 1 (Summer 1999): 64–94.

66. Bates Gill and Michael O'Hanlon, "China's Hollow Military," *National Interest* 56 (Summer 1999): 55.

67. David Shambaugh, "China Engages Asia," p. 85.

68. Lyle Goldstein and William Murray, "Undersea Dragons: China's Maturing Submarine Force," *International Security* 28, no. 4 (Spring 2004): 161–96.

69. Gill and O'Hanlon, "China's Hollow Military," p. 57.

70. On the controversy over theater and national missile defense, see Kori Urayama, "Chinese Perspectives on Theater Missile Defense: Policy Implications for Japan," *Asian Survey* 40, no. 4 (July/August 2000): 599–621; Thomas Christensen, "Theater Missile Defense and Taiwan's Security," *Orbis* (Winter 2000): 18–32; Gill and O'Hanlon, "China's Hollow Military," pp. 55–62.

71. Author's interview, March 21, 2006.

72. Christopher Hughes, *Taiwan and Chinese Nationalism: National Identity and Status in International Society* (New York: Routledge, 1997); Michael Yahuda, "The International Standing of the Republic of China on Taiwan," *China Quarterly* 148 (December 1996): 1319–39.

73. The two main documents that cover U.S.-China and U.S.-Taiwan relations are the Shanghai Communiqué of 1972 and the Taiwan Relations Act of 1979. The Shanghai Communiqué states, "The United States acknowledges that all Chinese on either side of the Taiwan Strait maintain there is but one China and that Taiwan is a part of China. The United States Government does not challenge that position." The Taiwan Relations Act states, "It is the policy of the United States to make clear that the United States decision to establish diplomatic relations with the People's Republic of China rests upon the expectation that the future of Taiwan will be determined by peaceful means."

74. Quoted in Evan Medeiros, "China Debates Its "Peaceful Rise" Strategy," *YaleGlobal Online* 22 (June 2004).

75. Medeiros, "China Debates Its "Peaceful Rise" Strategy."

76. Christopher Hughes, *Taiwan and Chinese Nationalism: National Identity and Status in International Society* (New York: Routledge, 1997); and Michael Yahuda, "The international standing of the Republic of China on Taiwan," *China Quarterly* 148 (December 1996), pp. 1319–39.

77. Quoted in Susan Lawrence, "Yearning to Lead," *Far Eastern Economic Review*, September 16, 1999, p. 19.

78. Thomas Christensen, "China, the U.S.-Japan Alliance, and the Security Dilemma in East Asia," *International Security* 23, no. 4 (Spring 1999): 49–80.

79. Personal communication, July 11, 2005.

80. For the full text of the law, see the *People's Daily Online*, March 14, 2005, http://english.people.com.cn/200503/14/eng20050314_176746.html.

81. John Copper, *Taiwan: Nation-State or Province?* (Boulder, Colo.: Westview, 1990), p. 21.

82. Jonathan Spence, *The Search for Modern China* (New York: Norton, 1991), p. 50; Copper, *Taiwan: Nation-State or Province?*

83. Michael Oksenberg, "The Issue of Sovereignty in the Asian Historical Context," and Robert Madsen, "The Struggle for Sovereignty Between China and Taiwan," both in Stephen D. Krasner, ed., *Problematic Sovereignty: Contested Rules and Political Possibilities* (New York: Columbia University Press, 2001).

84. Gary Klintworth, *New Taiwan, New China: Taiwan's Changing Role in the Asia-Pacific Region* (New York: St. Martin's, 1995).

85. Even the issue of whether Europe was ever "Westphalian" has been raised. See Andreas Osiander, "Sovereignty, International Relations, and the Westphalian Myth," *International Organization* 55, no. 2 (2001): 251–301; Stephen Krasner, *Sovereignty: Organized Hypocrisy* (Princeton: Princeton University Press, 1999).

86. Brad Glosserman, "Taiwan's New Economic Reality," *PacNet* 48, November 30, 2001, p. 1.

87. There is also considerable unapproved Taiwanese investment, meaning that the actual figures are higher. See Economist Intelligence Unit, *Country Profile 2006: Taiwan* (London: EIU, 2006), p. 32.

88. Martin Walker, "Can Taiwan Rely on the U.S.?" United Press International, February 8, 2006.

89. Kathrin Hill, "China and Taiwan Edge Closer to Tourism Deal," *Financial Times* April 17, 2006; Reuters, "Taiwan Proposes Joint Sea Rescue Drill with China," April 26, 2006; Xinhua, "Direct Shipping Route to Open Between Chinese Mainland and Taiwan," May 31, 2006.

90. David Brown, "A Little Sunshine Through the Clouds," *Comparative Connections* 7, no. 1 (January 2005).

91. Alan Romberg, "Recent Developments in Taiwan: Politics in Command—But at What Cost?" *PacNet* 6, February 14, 2006, p. 1.

92. Ko Shu-ling, "Large Majority Say 'Let Us Decide,'" *Taipei Times*, March 6, 2006, p. 3. See also Atlantic Council, *Taiwan in Search of a Strategic Consensus* (issue brief, Washington, D.C., 2006), http://www.acus.org/docs/0603-Taiwan_Search_Strategic_Consensus.pdf.

93. Li Thian-hok, "Ma Shows True Colors in U.S. Speech," *Taipei Times*, March 27, 2006, p. 8.

94. Charles Snyder, "Ma Sells 'Peace' with China to the U.S.," *Taipei Times*, March 24, 2006, p. 3.

95. U.S. Department of Defense, *Annual Report to Congress: Military Power of the People's Republic of China, 2006*, http://www.defenselink.mil/pubs/china.html.

96. Elizabeth Hsu, "Pan-Blues Block Arms Bill in Legislature 48th Time," *Central News Agency*, March 21, 2006.

97. Economist Intelligence Unit, *Country Profile 2006: Taiwan*, p. 18.

98. Quoted in Chang Yun-ping, "Analysts Worried about a Change in Military Balance," *Taipei Times*, November 18, 2005, page 3.

99. "China Will Win Any Confrontation with Taiwan—SM," *Singapore Straits Times*, September 13, 1997, quoted in Storey, *The China Threat*, p. 223.

100. Gordon Chang, "To the Nuclear Brink: Eisenhower, Dulles, and the Quemoy-Matsu Crisis," *International Security* 12, no. 4 (Spring 1988): 96–123.

101. Author's interview, March 29, 2006.

102. Brett Benson and Emerson Niou. "Comprehending Strategic Ambiguity: U.S. Policy Toward the Taiwan Strait Security Issue" (manuscript, Duke University, 2000).

103. David Brown, "A Little Sunshine Through the Clouds," *Comparative Connections* 7, no. 1 (January 2005).

104. Charles Snyder, "U.S. Republican Warns on NUC Moves," *Taipei Times* Thursday, March 9, 2006, http://www.taipeitimes.com/.

105. ROC Central News Agency, "Taiwan Relations Act Does Not Commit U.S. to Defend Taiwan: Armitage," March 10, 2006, http://www.globalsecurity.org/wmd/library/news/taiwan/2006/taiwan-060310-cna03.htm.

106. Brantley Womack, "China and Southeast Asia: Asymmetry, Leadership, and Normalcy," *Pacific Affairs* 76, no. 4 (Winter 2003/2004): 529–548, 544.

107. Taifa Yu, "Relations between Taiwan and China after the Missile Crisis: Toward Reconciliation?" *Pacific Affairs* 72, no. 1 (Spring 1999): 39–55.

108. Shelley Rigger, "Competing Conceptions of Taiwan's Identity," in Suisheng Zhao, ed., *Across the Taiwan Strait: Mainland China, Taiwan, and the 1995–1996 Crisis* (New York: Routledge, 1997).

109. For more detail on Asian nations' reactions to the Taiwan crisis, see Yoichi Funabashi, *Alliance Adrift* (New York: Council on Foreign Relations, 1999), pp. 423–35; Rigger, "Competing Conceptions of Taiwan's Identity."

110. Taifa Yu, "Relations between Taiwan and China after the Missile Crisis."

111. Council on Foreign Relations, "Taiwan Exercises Over, Now the Challenge is to U.S.-China Ties," March 26, 1996, http://www.fas.org/news/taiwan/1996/960326-taiwan-usia.htm.

112. Doug Bandow and Ted Galen Carpenter, "Risking War for Taiwan?" (Cato Institute, June 1, 2000), http://www.cato.org/pub_display.php?pub_id=4838.

113. Greg Austin, "Unwanted Entanglement? The Philippines' Spratly Policy as a Case Study in Conflict Enhancement," *Security Dialogue* 34, no. 1 (March 2003): 51.

114. Author's interviews, April 2, 2005 and April 21, 2005.

115. "Taiwan Conflict 'Up to Australia': U.S." *The Age*, September 23, 2005, http://www

.theage.com.au/news/National/Taiwan-conflict-up-to-Australia-US/2005/09/23/1
126982220855.html.

116. Australian Broadcast Company, "The World Today: Diplomatic Wrangling over
Taiwan," August 20, 2004, http://www.abc.net.au/worldtoday/content/2004/
s1181525.htm.

117. Daojiong Zha, "The Taiwan Problem in Japan-China Relations: An Irritant or
Destroyer?" *East Asia* 19, no. 1 (Spring–Summer 2001): 205–25.

118. Gregory Noble, "What Can Taiwan (and the United States) Expect from Japan?"
Journal of East Asian Studies 5 (2005): 25.

119. Martin Sieff, "Asia's Allies Won't Back Bush," United Press International, April 26,
2001.

120. Ralph Cossa, editor's note, in Yuki Tatsumi, "U.S.-Japan Security Consultative
Committee: An Assessment," *PacNet* 10, March 10, 2005, p. 2.

5. SOUTH KOREA: EMBRACING INTERDEPENDENCE IN SEARCH OF SECURITY

1. Chung-min Lee, "Between Alliance and Autonomy: Reconceptualizing South
Korea's Strategic Choices and Attendant Consequences," paper presented at the
Conference on Peace, Development and Regionalization in East Asia, Seoul, South
Korea, September 2–3, 2003.

2. Gi-wook Shin, *Ethnic Nationalism in Korea* (Stanford: Stanford University Press,
2006), p. 2.

3. Shin, *Ethnic Nationalism in Korea*, p. 3.

4. Shin, *Ethnic Nationalism in Korea*, p. 185.

5. Yong-hwa Chung, "The Modern Transformation of Korean Identity:
Enlightenment and Orientalism," *Korea Journal* (Spring 2006): 109–38.

6. For a detailed exploration of China-Korea relations, see Jae-ho Chung, *Between
Ally and Partner: Korea-China Relations and the United States* (New York:
Columbia University Press, 2007).

7. Hildi Kang, *Under the Black Umbrella: Stories from Colonial Korea* (Ithaca: Cornell
University Press, 1999).

8. Katharine Moon, "South Korean Movements against Militarized Sexual Labor,"
Asian Survey 39, no. 2 (March/April 1999): 310–27. The song is by Maya, "Dokdo-
nun uri-ddang (Dokdo is our land)."

9. See Katharine Moon, "Anti-Americanism in South Korea" (manuscript, Wellesley
College, 2006).

10. Daniel Snyder, "The Myth of the Golden Age: US-ROK Alliance in Historical
Perspective" (manuscript, Stanford University, 2006).

11. On historical U.S.-ROK ties, see Don Oberdorfer, *The Two Koreas: A
Contemporary History* (Reading, Mass.: Addison-Wesley, 1997); Bruce Cumings,
Korea's Place in the Sun (New York: Norton, 1997); William H. Gleysteen, *Massive
Entanglement, Marginal Influence: Carter and Korea in Crisis* (Washington, D.C.:
Brookings Institution Press, 1999); John Adams Wickham, *Korea on the Brink:
From the "12/12 Incident" to the Kwangju Uprising, 1979–1980* (Washington, D.C.:

National Defense University Press, 1999); Linda Lewis, ed., *Laying Claim to the Memory of May: A Look Back at the 1980 Kwangju Uprising* (Honolulu: University of Hawaii Press, 2002); Joseph C. Goulden, *Korea: The Untold Story of the War* (New York: McGraw-Hill, 1982); Yeonmi Ahn, "Political Economy of Foreign Aid: The Nature of American Aid and Its Impact on the State-Business Relationship in South Korea" (Ph.D. diss., Yale University, 1992).

12. David Kang and Paul Chamberlain, "A History of the U.S.-R.O.K. Alliance," in Derek Mitchell, ed., *US-Korea Relations in a Time of Crisis* (Washington, D.C.: CSIS, 2004).

13. Personal communication, August 15, 2006.

14. Official estimates are that 200 civilians were killed by ROK troops, although informal estimates run as high as ten times that amount. See John Adams Wickham, *Korea on the Brink: From the "12/12 Incident" to the Kwangju Uprising, 1979–1980* (Washington, D.C.: National Defense University Press, 1999); Lewis, ed., *Laying Claim to the Memory of May.*

15. Gi-Wook Shin, "South Korean Anti-Americanism," *Asian Survey* 36 no. 8 (August 1996): 787–804.

16. Thomas Kern, "Anti-Americanism in South Korea: From Structural Cleavages to Protest," *Korea Journal* (Spring 2005): 257–88.

17. Katharine Moon, personal communication, August 17, 2006.

18. Victor Cha notes that historically it was South Korea's fear that the U.S. would not take this threat perception seriously that drove the U.S.-Korea relationship. See Cha, *Alignment Despite Antagonism* (Stanford: Stanford University Press, 1999).

19. Much of this section draws on Victor Cha and David Kang, *Nuclear North Korea: A Debate on Engagement Strategies* (New York: Columbia University Press, 2003).

20. For overviews of the 2002 crisis and its aftermath, see Victor Cha and David Kang, "Can North Korea Be Engaged?," *Survival* 46, no. 2 (Summer 2004): 89–108.

21. P. Parameswaran, "North Korea Flexes Missile Muscle to Grab US Attention," Agence France-Presse, June 13, 2006.

22. U.S. Committee for Refugees and Immigrants, *World Refugee Survey 2004*, http://www.refugees.org/data/wrs/04/pdf/key_statistics.pdf.

23. See, for example, Richard Ellings and Nicholas Eberstadt, eds., *Korea's Future and the Great Powers* (Seattle: University of Washington Press, 2001), especially the chapters by Michael McDevitt, Robert Gallucci, and Gifford Combs.

24. Victor Cha and David Kang, "Think Again: The Korea Crisis," *Foreign Policy* 136 (May/June 2003): 24.

25. Gordon Flake and Scott A. Snyder, eds., *Paved with Good Intentions: The NGO Experience in North Korea* (Westport, Conn.: Praeger, 2003).

26. Ministry of Unification, "Peace and Prosperity: White Paper on Korean Unification 2005" (Seoul: Ministry of Unification, 2005), pp. 106–8. See also Ministry of Unification, "Kaesong Kongdan geonseol silmu jobchuk bodo chamgojaryo" (Seoul: Ministry of Unification, 2002).

27. "Inter-Korean Trade Beats $1 Billion in 2005," *JoongAng Ilbo*, January 23, 2006; Economist Intelligence Unit, *North Korea: Country Report 2003* (London: EIU, 2003), p. 19.

28. "Road Connecting The Two Koreas Opens," *Dong-a Ilbo*, December 1, 2004.

29. "First Products from Inter-Korean Project Due on Sale in South This Week," *Yonhap,* December 13, 2004.

30. Sang-young Rhyu, "North Korea's Economy and East Asia's Regionalism: Opportunities and Challenges," paper prepared for conference, Northeast Asia's Economic and Security Regionalism: Old Constraints and New Prospects, Center for International Studies, University of Southern California, Los Angeles, March 3–4, 2006.

31. Personal communication from a senior U.S. official, August 1, 2006.

32. David Kang, "North Korea's Economy," in Robert Worden, ed., *North Korea: A Country Study* (Washington, D.C.: Federal Research Bureau, 2005).

33. James Brooke, "2 Koreas Sidestep U.S. to Forge Pragmatic Links," *New York Times,* June 26, 2004.

34. Christine Ahn, "Reunification Is on the March," *International Herald Tribune,* February 9, 2006.

35. Ruediger Frank, "Economic Reforms in North Korea (1998–2003): Systemic Restrictions, Quantitative Analysis, Ideological Background," *Journal of the Asia Pacific Economy* 10, no. 3 (2005): 278–311.

36. See, for example, Stephan Haggard and Marcus Noland, *Famine in North Korea: Aid, Markets and Reform* (New York: Columbia University Press, 2006); Bradley Babson, "Implications of a 'Bold Switchover' in Security Policy for Involving the International Financial Institutions in Financing North Korean Development" (report, National Bureau of Asian Research, March 2006); Marcus Noland, "Transition from the Bottom-Up: Institutional Change in North Korea" (manuscript, Institute for International Economics, March 20, 2006).

37. Peter Hayes, "US Misses Mines for Nukes Opportunity," Special Report 06–34A (Nautilus Institute, May 2, 2006), p. 3.

38. Marcus Noland, "How North Korea Funds Its Regime," testimony before the Subcommittee on Federal Financial Management, Government Information, and International Security, Committee on Homeland Security and Governmental Affairs, United States Senate, April 26, 2006. See also Noland, "Transition from the Bottom-Up."

39. In 1987, Roh Tae-woo received 36.5 percent of the popular vote; in 1992, Kim Young-sam received 41.4 percent, and in 1997 Kim Dae-jung received 40.3 percent.

40. *Chosun Ilbo,* January 18, 2003, http://english.chosun.com/.

41. Derek Mitchell, ed., *Strategy and Sentiment: South Korean Views of the United States and the U.S.-ROK Alliance* (Washington, D.C.: Center for Strategic and International Studies, 2004).

42. "Opinion Poll on South Korean Attitudes Toward Japan and Other Nations," *Dong-a Ilbo,* March 4–31, 2005.

43. Ahn, "Reunification Is on the March."

44. Author's interview, August 31, 2003.

45. John Adams Wickham, *Korea on the Brink: From the "12/12 Incident" to the Kwangju Uprising, 1979–1980* (Washington, D.C.: National Defense University Press, 1999); Lewis, ed., *Laying Claim to the Memory of May.*

46. Annie I. Bang, "Bill on inter-Korean Special Zone Proposed" *Korea Herald,* February 14, 2006.

47. Research Plus poll conducted October 11–12, 2006; "South Koreans Blame U.S. for Nuclear Test," *Angus Reid Global Monitor,* http://www.angus-reid.com/polls/index.cfm/fuseaction/viewItem/itemID/13537.

48. "Korean Nuclear Tests Shock, Blockade, Sanctions No Answer, Bishops Say," *Catholic Online,* October 13, 2006, http://www.catholic.org/international/.

49. Personal interviews in Seoul, October 14–18, 2006.

50. Korea International Trade Association, *Bridging the Pacific* 34 (January 2004).

51. Scott Snyder, "The Beginning of the End of the U.S.-ROK Alliance?," *PacNet* 36, August 26, 2004.

52. Moon Ihlwan, "Korea's China Play," *BusinessWeek,* March 29, 2004, p. 32.

53. "Korean Banks Race into China Market," *JoongAng Ilbo,* July 1, 2004.

54. "Nihao Mom? A Mandarin Approach to Child-Rearing Schools for Overseas Chinese Sees More Korean Students than Ever," *JoongAng Ilbo,* March 14, 2006.

55. James Brooke, "China 'Looming Large' in South Korea as Biggest Player, Replacing the U.S.," *New York Times,* January 3, 2003.

56. Jae-ho Chung, "The 'Rise' of China and Its Impact on South Korea's Strategic Soul-Searching," in James Lister, ed., *The Newly Emerging Asian Order and the Korean Peninsula* (Washington, D.C.: Korea Economic Institute, 2005), pp. 1–12.

57. "Opinion Poll on South Korean Attitudes Toward Japan and Other Nations," *Dong-a Ilbo,* April 1–5, 2006, results at www.mansfieldfdn.org/polls/poll-05-2.htm.

58. Peter Gries, "The Koguryo Controversy: National Identity, and Sino-Korean Relations Today," *East Asia* 22, no. 4 (Winter 2005): 3–17.

59. David Scofield, "China Puts Korean Spat on the Map," *Asia Times,* August 19, 2004, http://www.atimes.com/atimes/Korea/FH19Dg01.html.

60. For a detailed study of China's territorial dispute resolution, see Taylor Fravel, "Regime Insecurity and International Cooperation: Explaining China's Com-promises in Territorial Disputes," *International Security* 30, no. 2 (Fall 2005): 46–83.

61. Personal communication from a senior official, South Korean Ministry of Finance and the Economy, June 12, 2006.

62. Chung-min Lee, "Between Alliance and Autonomy," p. 162.

63. Joseph Kahn and Susan Chira, "Chinese Official Challenges U.S. Stance on North Korea," *New York Times,* June 9, 2004.

64. Personal communication, June 8, 2006.

65. Robert Marquand, "North Korea's Border Trade Getting Busier," *Christian Science Monitor,* April 14, 2005, http://www.csmonitor.com/2005/0414/p01s04-woap.html.

66. Li Bin, quoted in the *JoongAng Ilbo,* January 14, 2005.

67. Howard French, "Doubting U.S., China is Wary of Korea Role," *New York Times,* February 19, 2005.

68. David Sanger, "About-Face on North Korea: Allies Helped," *New York Times,* June 24, 2004.

69. Lorien Holland and Chester Dawson, "What if? The Dream of Korean Unification Could Be a Nightmare for the World's Superpowers," *Far Eastern Economic Review* June 29, 2000, p. 61.

70. Jae-Ho Chung, "South Korea Between the Eagle and the Dragon: Perceptual Ambivalence and Strategic Dilemma," *Asian Survey* 41, no. 5 (September–October 2001): 781.

71. Jae-ho Chung, *Between Ally and Partner.*

72. Victor Cha, "Korea: A Peninsula in Crisis and Flux," in Ashley Tellis and Michael Wills, eds., *Strategic Asia 2004–05: Confronting Terrorism in the Pursuit of Power* (Seattle: National Bureau of Asian Research, 2004).

73. Scott Snyder, "The Beginning of the End of the U.S.-ROK Alliance?"

74. Kirk Larson, "An Analysis of the September 2003 *Joongang Ilbo*–CSIS Polls of South Korean Attitudes Toward the U.S.," paper prepared for the CSIS Study Group on South Korean Attitudes toward the United States, December 13, 2003, p. 1.

75. Derek Mitchell, ed., *Strategy and Sentiment: South Korean Views of the United States and the U.S.-ROK Alliance* (Washington, D.C.: Center for Strategic and International Studies, 2004).

76. Korea Economic Institute of America, January 2003 basic data, http://www.keia .org/.

77. Chung-in Moon, "Between Banmi and Sungmi: Changing Images of the United States in South Korea," paper presented at Georgetown University, August 20, 2003.

78. Larson, "An Analysis of the September 2003 *Joongang Ilbo*–CSIS Polls," p. 1.

79. Quoted in Michael Gordon, "U.S. Toughens Terms for North Korea Talks," *New York Times*, July 3, 2001, p. A9.

80. For the State of the Union address, see http://www.whitehouse.gov/news/ releases/2002/01/20020129–11.html. For Bush's March 2001 remarks, see "Remarks by President Bush and President Kim Dae-Jung of South Korea," March 7, 2001, http://www.whitehouse.gov/news/releases/2001/03/20010307–6.html. Also see Bob Woodward, *Bush At War* (New York: Simon & Schuster, 2002), pp. 339–40.

81. Jonathan Salant, "Secretary of State Powell says U.S. Is Willing to Talk with North Korea," Associated Press, December 29, 2002.

82. Nicholas Eberstadt, "Tear Down This Tyranny," *Weekly Standard*, November 29, 2004.

83. Ted Galen Carpenter and Douglas Bandow, *The Korean Conundrum: America's Troubled Relations with North and South Korea* (London: Palgrave Macmillan, 2004).

84. Bruce Gilley, "An Immodest Proposal," *Wall Street Journal*, January 5, 2005.

85. "S. Korean President Warns U.S. against Seeking Collapse of the North," *The News*, January 26, 2006 (http://www.ipcs.org/Jan_06_japan.pdf)

86. Andrew Salmon, "Roh Opposes U.S. on Regime Change Plans for North, Warns of 'Difference of Opinion,'" *Washington Times*, January 26, 2006.

87. Soo-dong O, "Defusing North Korea," press release, Embassy of the Republic of Korea, Washington, D.C., December 1, 2004.

88. Editorial, *Hankyoreh Shinmun*, November 7, 2004.

89. *Dong-a Ilbo*, January 12, 2005.

90. Pew Research Center, "What the World Thinks in 2002," http://people-press.org/ reports/pdf/165.pdf.

91. A larger number, 54.2 percent, supported dispatch of noncombat troops to Iraq; see "ROK Poll Shows Koreans Support Dispatch of Non-Combat Troops to Gulf," *Yonhap*, March 20, 2003.

92. See Cha, "Korea."

6. SOUTHEAST ASIA: ACCOMMODATING CHINA'S RISE

1. Personal communication, March 22, 2004.
2. Personal communication, October 30, 2006.
3. Amitav Acharya, *Constructing a Security Community in Southeast Asia: ASEAN and the Problem of Regional Order* (London: Routledge, 2001); Acharya, "Ideas, Identity, and Institution-Building: From the 'ASEAN Way' to the 'Asia Pacific Way,'" *Pacific Review* 10, no. 2 (1997): 319–46; Mely Caballero-Anthony, *Regional Security in Southeast Asia: Beyond the ASEAN Way* (Singapore: Institute of Southeast Asian Studies, 2005); Jurgen Haacke, *ASEAN's Diplomatic and Security Culture* (London: RoutledgeCurzon, 2003); Alastair Iain Johnston, "Socialization in International Institutions: The ASEAN Way and International Relations Theory," in G. John Ikenberry and Michael Mastanduno, eds., *International Relations Theory and the Asia-Pacific* (New York: Columbia University Press, 2003), pp. 107–62.
4. Acharya, *Constructing a Security Community in Southeast Asia*, p. 64.
5. Martin Stuart-Fox, "Southeast Asia and China: The Role of History and Culture in Shaping Future Relations," *Contemporary Southeast Asia* 26, no. 1 (2004): 116–39.
6. Andrew MacIntyre, ed., *Business and Government in Industrializing Asia* (Ithaca: Cornell University Press, 1994); Benedict R. Anderson, *Java in a Time of Revolution: Occupation and Resistance* (Ithaca: Cornell University Press, 1972); John Sidel, *Capital, Coercion, and Crime: Bossism in the Philippines* (Stanford: Stanford University Press, 1999).
7. Amitav Acharya, *The Quest for Identity: International Relations of Southeast Asia* (Oxford: Oxford University Press, 2000), p. 165.
8. Acharya, *Constructing a Security Community in Southeast Asia*; Dewi Anwar, *Indonesia in ASEAN: Foreign Policy and Regionalism* (New York: St. Martin's, 1994).
9. Rizal Sukma, *Indonesia and China: The Politics of a Troubled Relationship* (London: Routledge, 1999).
10. Thomas Christensen, *Useful Adversaries: Grand Strategy, Domestic Mobilization, and Sino-American Conflict, 1947–1958* (Princeton: Princeton University Press, 1996).
11. Allen S. Whiting, "ASEAN Eyes China: The Security Dimension," *Asian Survey* 37, no. 4 (April 1997): 302–3.
12. Brantley Womack, "China and Southeast Asia: Asymmetry, Leadership, and Normalcy," *Pacific Affairs* 76, no. 4 (Winter 2003–2004): 529–48.
13. Womack, "China and Southeast Asia," p. 536.
14. Alice Ba, "China and ASEAN: Renavigating Relations for a 21st-Century Asia," *Asian Survey* 43, no. 4 (July/August 2003): 633.
15. Womack, "China and Southeast Asia," p. 526. See also Joseph Cheng, "China's Post-Tiananmen Diplomacy," in George Hicks, ed., *The Broken Mirror: China After Tiananmen* (Chicago: St. James, 1990), pp. 401–18.
16. *Final Report of the East Asia Study Group* (Phnom Penh: ASEAN+3 Summit, 2002), p. 79. See also *Forging Closer ASEAN-China Relations in the Twenty-First Century* (2001), prepared for ASEAN by the ASEAN-China Expert Group on Economic Cooperation, http://aseansec.org.

17. Michael Leifer, "Indonesia and the Dilemmas of Engagement," in Alastair Iain Johnston and Robert S. Ross, eds., *Engaging China: The Management of an Emerging Power* (London: Routledge, 1999), p. 104.

18. Michael Richardson, "Japan's Lack of Leadership Pushes ASEAN toward Cooperation with China," *International Herald Tribune*, April 17, 1998, p. 6.

19. Quoted in Alice Ba, "China and ASEAN: Renavigating Relations for a 21st-Century Asia," *Asian Survey* 43, no. 4 (July/August 2003): 637.

20. Treaty of Amity and Cooperation in Southeast Asia, Chapter 1, Article 2, Section e, http://www.aseansec.org/1217.htm.

21. Quoted in Michael Vatikiotis, "A Too-Friendly Embrace," *Far Eastern Economic Review*, June 17, 2004, p. 20.

22. Vatikiotis, "A Too-Friendly Embrace," p. 22.

23. Vatikiotis, "A Too-Friendly Embrace," p. 22.

24. Personal communication, April 28, 2004.

25. Figures from the ASEAN Secretariat, http://www.aseansec.org/13100.htm.

26. Donald Weatherbee, "Strategic Dimensions of Economic Interdependence in Southeast Asia," in Ashley Tellis and Michael Wills, eds., *Strategic Asia 2006–2007* (Seattle: National Bureau of Asian Research, 2006), p. 6.

27. Ronald Montaperto, "Building Integration?," *Comparative Connections* 7, no. 3 (October 2005): 5.

28. Robert Sutter, "China–Southeast Asia Relations: Emphasizing the Positive; Continued Wariness," *Comparative Connections* 7, no. 4 (January 2006): 9.

29. Figures cited by Chan Heng Chee, "China and ASEAN: A Growing Relationship," speech by Ambassador Chan Heng Chee at the Asia Society Texas Annual Ambassadors' Forum and Corporate Conference, Houston, Texas, February 3, 2006.

30. Documents at http://*www.aseansec.org*.

31. Quoted in Alice Ba, "Who's Socializing Whom? Complex Engagement in Sino-ASEAN relations," *Pacific Review* 19, no. 2 (June 2006): 166.

32. Jose T. Almonte, "Ensuring Security the 'ASEAN Way,'" *Survival* 30, no. 4 (Winter 1997–1998): 80–92.

33. Quoted in Gaye Christoffersen, "The Role of East Asia in Sino-American Affairs," *Asian Survey* 43, No. 3 (May/June 2002): 393.

34. "Singapore Leader Warns China on Military Ambitions," Reuter News Service, May 13, 1995. Quoted in Ian Storey, "Singapore and the Rise of China: Perceptions and Policy," in Herbert Yee and Ian Storey, eds., *The China Threat: Perceptions, Myths, and Reality* (London: RoutledgeCurzon, 2002), p. 210.

35. Montaperto, "Building Integration?," p. 6.

36. Jane Perlez, "China's Role Emerges as Major Issue for Southeast Asia," *New York Times*, March 14, 2006, p. A3.

37. Bruce Vaughn and Wayne Morrison, *China–Southeast Asia Relations: Trends, Issues, and Implications for the United States* (Washington, D.C.: Congressional Research Service, 2006), p. 25.

38. Quoted in Christoffersen, "The Role of East Asia in Sino-American Affairs," p. 381.

39. Harry Harding, "The Concept of 'Greater China': Themes, Variations, and Reservations," *China Quarterly* 136 (December 1993): 660–86; Murray Weiden-

baum and Samuel Hughes, *The Bamboo Network: How Expatriate Chinese Entrepreneurs Are Creating a New Economic Superpower in Asia* (New York: Free Press, 1996); Barry Naughton, *The China Circle: Economics and Technology in the PRC, Taiwan, and Hong Kong* (Washington, D.C.: Brookings Institution Press, 1997); Aihwa Ong and Donald Nonini, eds., *Ungrounded Empires: The Cultural Politics of Modern Chinese Transnationalism* (New York: Routledge, 1997); Dajin Peng, "Invisible Linkages: A Regional Perspective of East Asian Political Economy," *International Studies Quarterly* 46, no. 3 (September 2002): 423–48.

40. Gerald Curtis, "East Asia, Regionalism, and U.S. National Interests," *American Foreign Policy Interests* 26 (2004): 205.

41. Dajin Peng, "Invisible Linkages," p. 431; Nicole Biggart and Gary Hamilton, "On the Limits of a Firm-Based Theory to Explain Business Networks: The Western Bias of Neoclassical Economics," in Michael Orru, Nicole Biggart, and Gary Hamilton, eds., *The Economic Organization of East Asian Capitalism* (London: Sage, 1997), pp. 33–54.

42. Natasha Hamilton-Hart, *Asian States, Asian Bankers: Central Banking in Southeast Asia* (Ithaca: Cornell University Press, 2002).

43. T. J. Pempel, "Introduction: Emerging Webs of Regional Connectedness," in T. J. Pempel, ed., *Remapping East Asia: The Construction of a Region* (Ithaca: Cornell University Press, 2005), p. 22.

44. Hongying Wang, *Weak State, Strong Networks: The Institutional Dynamics of Foreign Direct Investment in China* (New York: Oxford University Press, 2001).

45. Dajin Peng, "Invisible Linkages," pp. 432, 442.

46. Andrew MacIntyre and Barry Naughton, "The Decline of the Japan-Led Model of the East Asian Economy," in Pempel, ed., *Remapping East Asia*, p. 88.

47. Mitchell Bernard and John Ravenhill, "Beyond Product Cycles and Flying Geese: Regionalization, Hierarchy, and the Industrialization of East Asia," *World Politics* 47, no. 2 (April 1995): 187.

48. Tyler Marshall, "China Poised to Dominate Influence in Asia," *Boston Globe*, August 13, 2006.

49. Michael Vatikiotis, "Catching the Dragon's Tail: China and Southeast Asia in the 21st Century," *Contemporary Southeast Asia* 25, no. 1 (April 2003): 71.

50. David Shambaugh, "China Engages Asia," *International Security* 29, no. 3 (Winter 2004/5): 78.

51. Perlez, "China's Role Emerges as Major Issue," p. A3.

52. Chan Heng Chee, "China and ASEAN: A Growing Relationship."

53. See, for example, Denny Roy, "The China-Threat Issue: Major Arguments," *Asian Survey* 36, no. 8 (1996): 758–71; Gary Klintworth, "Greater China and Regional Security," *Australian Journal of International Affairs* 48, no. 2 (1994): 211–28.

54. Walden Bello, "South China Sea Incident Was an Event Waiting to Happen," *Business World* (Manila), April 23, 2001, cited in Alice Ba, "China and ASEAN," p. 628. See also Michael Gallagher, "China's Illusory Threat to the South China Sea," *International Security* 19, no. 1 (Summer 1994): 169–94.

55. Robert Ross, "The Geography of the Peace: East Asia in the Twenty-First Century," *International Security* 23, no. 4 (Spring 1999): 81–118.

56. Leszek Buszynski, "Realism, Institutionalism, and Philippine Security," *Asian Survey* 42, no. 3 (2002): 483–501.

57. Greg Austin, "Unwanted Entanglement? The Philippines' Spratly Policy as a Case Study in Conflict Enhancement?," *Security Dialogue* 34, no. 1 (March 2003): 41–54.

58. *Declaration on the Conduct of Parties in the South China Sea*, signed at the Eighth ASEAN Summit in Phnom Penh, November 2002, http://www.aseansec.org. For an assessment of the agreement, see Nguyen Hong Thao, "The 2002 Declaration on the Conduct of Parties in the South China Sea: A Note," *Ocean Development and International Law* 34 (2003): 279–85; Leszek Buszynski, "ASEAN, the Declaration on Conduct, and the South China Sea," *Contemporary Southeast Asia* 25, no. 3 (2003): 343–62.

59. Personal communication, March 22, 2004.

60. Department of Defense, *A Strategic Framework for the Asian Pacific Rim: Looking Towards the 21st Century* (Washington: DOD, 1995, 1998).

61. Ang Cheng Guan, "Vietnam-China Relations Since the End of the Cold War," *Asian Survey* 38, no. 12 (December 1998): 1140.

62. "China, ASEAN Agree to Jointly Safeguard Peace of South China Seas," *Xinhua News*, February 9, 2006.

63. Montaperto, "Building Integration?," p. 2.

64. Sheldon Simon, "Southeast Asia's Defense Needs: Change or Continuity?," in Ashley Tellis and Michael Wills, eds., *Strategic Asia 2005–06: Military Modernization in an Era of Uncertainty* (Seattle: National Bureau of Asian Research, 2005), p. 278.

65. Philippine Embassy in Beijing, "Philippine-China Trade Hits $17.6B in 2005," *Philippines-China Chronicle* 6, no. 4 (October–December 2005), http://www.philembassy-china.org/chronicle_issues/2005.4.pdf.

66. U.S.-Philippine trade data from the U.S. Census Bureau, *Foreign Trade Statistics*, http://www.census.gov/foreign-trade/balance/c5650.html#2006.

67. Marshall, "China Poised to Dominate Influence in Asia."

68. Christoffersen, "The Role of East Asia in Sino-American Affairs," p. 381.

69. "Bases Primer Part 2," *Philippine Daily Inquirer*, September 19, 1990, p. 49. Quoted in Renato Cruz De Castro, "The Revitalized Philippine-U.S. Security Relations: A Ghost from the Cold War or an Alliance for the 21st Century?," *Asian Survey* 43, no. 6 (November/December 2003): 974.

70. Aileen San Pablo-Baviera, "Perceptions of a Chinese Threat: A Philippine Perspective," in Yee and Storey, eds., *The China Threat*, pp. 248–49.

71. I should point out that Khong is not himself a realist, but rather is conveying the standard explanation. Yuen Foong Khong, "Coping with Strategic Uncertainty: The Role of Institutions and Soft Balancing in Southeast Asia's Post–Cold War Strategy," to appear in J. J. Suh, Peter Katzenstein, and Allen Carlson, eds., *Rethinking Security in East Asia: Identity, Power and Efficiency* (Stanford: Stanford University Press, 2004).

72. Barton Brown, "The Philippine–United States Bases Debate: Why the Twain Never Met," *Asian Affairs: An American Review* 20, no. 3 (Fall 1993): 162–79.

73. Sheldon Simon, "U.S.–Southeast Asia Relations: Philippines Withdraws from Iraq and JI Strikes Again," *Comparative Connections* 6, no. 3 (October 2004): 68.

74. Renato Cruz de Castro, "The Revitalized Philippine-U.S. Security Relations," pp. 982–87; Sheldon Simon, "Theater Security Cooperation in the U.S. Pacific Command: An Assessment and Projection," *NBR Analysis* 14, no. 2 (August 2003): 33–40.

75. Buszynski, "Realism, Institutionalism, and Philippine Security," p. 498.

76. Jane Perez, "Manila Is Still Uneasy Over American Troops," *International Herald Tribune*, January 28, 2002, p. 3; Jim Garamone, "U.S. Forces to Help Philippines Fight Terrorists," American Forces Press Service, January 16, 2002, p. 1.

77. San Pablo-Baviera, "Perceptions of a Chinese Threat: A Philippine Perspective," pp. 248–9.

78. Poll cited in Carijane C. Dayag-Laylo, Pedro Laylo, Jr., and Vladymir Joseph Licudine, "Filipino Public Opinion, Presidential Leadership, and the US-Led War in Iraq," *International Journal of Public Opinion Research*, 16, no. 3 (2004): 344–59.

79. Goldstein, "Balance of Power Politics," in *Asian Security Order*.

80. Interview with a senior Singaporean diplomat, March 22, 2004.

81. Henry Kenny, *Shadow of the Dragon: Vietnam's Continuing Struggle with China and the Implications for U.S. Foreign Policy* (Washington, D.C.: Brassey's, 2002), p. 125.

82. Kim Ninh, "Vietnam: Struggle and Cooperation," in Muthiah Alagappa, ed., *Asian Security Practice: Material and Ideational Influences* (Stanford: Stanford University Press, 1998), p. 447.

83. Nayan Chanda, *Brother Enemy: The War after the War* (New York: Collier, 1986).

84. Ang Cheng Guan, "Vietnam-China Relations Since the End of the Cold War," p. 1141.

85. See Michael Leifer, "Vietnam's Foreign Policy in the Post-Soviet Era: Coping with Vulnerability," in Robert Ross, ed., *East Asia in Transition: Toward a New Regional Order* (Armonk, N.Y.: M. E. Sharpe, 1995).

86. Carl Thayer, "Vietnamese Perceptions of the 'China Threat,'" in Yee and Storey, eds., *The China Threat*, p. 268.

87. Nayan Chanda, "Friend or Foe?," *Far Eastern Economic Review*, June 22, 2000, p. 22, quoted in Kenny, *Shadow of the Dragon*, p. 100.

88. Quoted in Ang Cheng Guan, "The South China Sea Dispute Revisited" (manuscript, Nanyang Technological University, 2004), p. 6.

89. Martin Stuart-Fox, "Southeast Asia and China: The Role of History and Culture in Shaping Future Relations," *Contemporary Southeast Asia* 26, no. 1 (2004): 133.

90. Cheng-guan Ang, "Vietnam: Another Milestone and the Country Plods On," in Daljit Singh and Anthony Smith, eds., *Southeast Asian Affairs 2002* (Singapore: Institute of Southeast Asian Studies, 2003): 345–56.

91. See, for example, the interview with Chinese Vice Minister of Foreign Affairs Wang Yi on the entry into force of the China-Vietnam Agreements on Delimitation of Border and Fishery Cooperation in Beibu Bay, http://www.fmprc.gov.cn/eng/zxxx/t142010.htm; and Stein Tonnesen, "Sino-Vietnamese Rapprochement and the South China Sea Irritant," *Security Dialogue* 34, no. 1 (March 2003): 55–70.

92. Sheldon Simon, "Southeast Asia's Defense Needs: Change or Continuity?," p. 274.

93. Thayer, "Vietnamese Perceptions of the 'China Threat,'" p. 282.

94. Kim Ninh, "Vietnam: Struggle and Cooperation," p. 462.

95. Singaporean foreign ministry official, interview, March 21, 2004.

96. Kenny, *Shadow of the Dragon*, p. 80.

97. Carlyle Thayer, "Vietnam: Coping with China," *Southeast Asian Affairs 1994* (Singapore: Institute of Southeast Asian Studies, 1994): 351-67, 353.

98. Kenny, *Shadow of the Dragon*, p. 81.

99. Gu Xiaosong and Brantly Womack, "Border Cooperation between China and Vietnam in the 1990s," *Asian Survey* 40, no. 6 (November/December 2000): 1045.

100. Tuyet Minh, "The Chinese Are Coming," *Vietnam Economic News* 33 (December 2000): 24.

101. *Business Vietnam* 12, no. 6 (June 2000): 4.

102. Quoted in Kenny, *Shadow of the Dragon*, p. 81.

103. Carl Thayer, "China Consolidates Its Long-term Bilateral Relations with Southeast Asia," *Comparative Connections*, 2nd quarter, 2000, p. 8, quoted in Kenny, *Shadow of the Dragon*, p. 105.

104. Quoted in Kenny, *Shadow of the Dragon*, p. 155.

105. Kenny, *Shadow of the Dragon*, p. 103.

106. Shambaugh, "China Engages Asia," p. 80.

107. Robert Templer, Agence France-Presse correspondent in Hanoi, quoted in Carlyle Thayer, "Vietnam," p. 359.

108. "Vietnam Seeks Stronger Bonds with China," *Xinhua News,* February 9, 2006.

109. Guan, "Vietnam-China Relations Since the End of the Cold War," p. 1129.

110. Personal communication, March 23, 2004.

111. Allen E. Goodman, "Vietnam and ASEAN: Who Would Have Thought It Possible?," *Asian Survey* 36, no. 6 (June 1996): 592–600.

112. "China and Vietnam Join Hands in Developing Oil and Natural Gas in Tonkin Gulf," *Wenweipo News*, November 1, 2005.

113. David Wurfel, "Between China and ASEAN: The Dialectics of Recent Vietnamese Foreign Policy," in Carlyle A. Thayer and Ramses Amer, eds., *Vietnamese Foreign Policy in Transition* (Singapore: Institute of Southeast Asia Studies, 1999), p. 156.

114. "Vietnam Seeks Stronger Bonds with China."

115. Morton Abramowitz and Stephen Bosworth, "Rethinking Southeast Asia," Century Foundation, April 21, 2005, http://www.tcf.org/list.asp?Type = NC ??PUBID?? = 955.

116. Muthiah Alagappa, *U.S.-ASEAN Security Co-operation: Limits and Possibilities* (Kuala Lumpur: Institute of Strategic and International Studies, 1986); Tan Loong-Hoe and Narongchai Akrasanee, eds., *ASEAN-U.S. Economic Relations: Changes in the Economic Environment and Opportunities* (San Francisco: Asia Foundation, and Singapore: Institute of Southeast Asian Studies, 1988).

117. Nayan Chanda, "The External Environment for Southeast Asian Foreign Policy," in David Wurfel and Bruce Burton, eds., *The Political Economy of Foreign Policy in Southeast Asia* (London: Macmillan, 1990), p. 68, quoted in Alice Ba, "China and ASEAN," p. 629.

118. MacIntyre and Naughton, "The Decline of the Japan-Led Model of the East Asian Economy," p. 85.

119. Yoichi Funabashi, "The Asianization of Asia," *Foreign Affairs* 72, no. 5 (November/ December 1993): 75–85.

120. Saori Katada, "Japan and Asian Monetary Regionalization: Cultivating a New Regional Leadership after the Asian Financial Crisis," *Geopolitics* 7, no. 1 (Summer 2002): 85–112; Eric Altbach, "The Asian Monetary Fund Proposal: A Case Study of Japanese Regional Leadership," *Japan Economic Institute Report*, no. 47A, December 19, 1997; Christopher Hughes, "Japanese Policy and the East Asian Currency Crisis: Abject Defeat or Quiet Victory?," *Review of International Political Economy* 7, no. 2 (Summer 2000): 219–53.

121. Shambaugh, "China Engages Asia," p. 69.

122. Rodney Hall, "The Discursive Demolition of the Asian Development Model," *International Studies Quarterly* 47, no. 1 (March 2003): 71–99.

123. Robert Wade, "The Asian Debt-and-Development Crisis of 1997–? Causes and consequences," *World Development* 26, no. 8 (August 1998): 1535–53; Jeffrey Winters, "The Determinants of Financial Crisis in Asia," in T. J. Pempel, ed., *The Politics of the Asian Economic Crisis* (Ithaca: Cornell University Press, 1999).

124. Michael Vatikiotis, "Pacific Divide: Southeast Asians Are Smouldering over What They See as America's Cool Response to Their Economic Woes," *Far Eastern Economic Review,* November 6, 1997, p. 14.

125. Donald K. Emmerson, "What Do the Blind-Sided See? Reapproaching Re-gionalism in Southeast Asia," *Pacific Review* 18, no. 1 (March 2005): 1–21.

126. Marcus Noland, quoted on *Marketplace,* May 5, 2006, http://www.marketplace. org.

127. Vatikiotis, "Pacific Divide," p. 14.

128. Jagdish Bhagwati, "The Capital Myth: The Difference Between Trade in Widgets and Dollars," *Foreign Affairs* 77, no. 3 (May/June 1998): 7–12. See also Robert Wade and Frank Veneroso, "The Asian Crisis: The High Debt Model vs. the Wall Street-Treasury-IMF Complex," *New Left Review* 228 (March/April 1998): 3–23.

129. Vatikiotis, "Pacific Divide"; David P. Rapkin, "The United States, Japan, and the Power to Block: The APEC and the AMF Cases," *Pacific Review* 14, no. 3 (2001): 373–410.

130. Quoted in Vatikiotis, "Pacific Divide."

131. Alexa Olesen, "China Edging Out U.S. for APEC Leadership," Associated Press, November 16, 2005.

132. Chan Heng Chee, "China and ASEAN: A Growing Relationship."

133. Quoted in Esther Pan, "New Focus on U.S.–Southeast Asia Military Ties," (Council on Foreign Relations, February 2, 2006).

134. Chan Heng Chee, "China and ASEAN: A Growing Relationship."

135. Mokhzani Zubir and Mohd Nizam Basiron, "The Straits of Malacca: The Rise of China, America's Intentions and the Dilemma of the Littoral States" (Maritime Institute of Malaysia, Kuala Lumpur, April 2005), pp. 4–5.

136. Donald Weatherbee, "Strategic Dimensions of Economic Interdependence in Southeast Asia," p. 2.

137. Tatik Hafidiz, "The War on Terror and the Future of Indonesian Democracy," Working Paper 46 (Institute of Defense and Strategic Studies, Singapore, March 2003).

138. Andi Widjajanto, "Transnational Challenges to RI's Security," *Korea Herald,* January 7, 2003, p. 8.

139. Helen Nesadurai, "Malaysia and the United States: Rejecting Dominance, Embracing Engagement," Working Paper 72 (Institute of Defense and Strategic Studies, Singapore, December 2004), p. 18. See also Satu Limaye, "Minding the Gaps: The Bush Administration and US–Southeast Asia Relations," *Contemporary Southeast Asia* 26, no. 1 (2004): 73–93.

140. Pew Research Center, *Views of a Changing World 2003*, June 3, 2003, http://people-press.org/reports/display.php3?ReportID=185.

141. "Mahatir Blasts U.S. and Britain," *International Herald Tribune*, June 20, 2003, p. 1; N. Ganesan, "Malaysia in 2003: Leadership Transition with a Tall Shadow," *Asian Survey* 44, no. 1 (January/February 2004): 70–77.

142. Quoted in Marshall, "China Poised to Dominate Influence in Asia."

143. Pacific Forum CSIS, "Countering the Spread of Weapons of Mass Destruction: The Role of the Proliferation Security Initiative," *Issues and Insights* 4, no. 5 (July 2004).

144. Mark Valencia, "Bring the Proliferation Security Initiative into the UN," Policy Forum Online 05–101A, Nautilus Institute, December 20, 2005, http://www.nautilus.org/fora/security/0510lValencia.html.

145. Barry Wain, "Strait Talk: A U.S. Admiral's Remarks Could Hinder Moves Against Piracy and Terrorism in Southeast Asia," *Far Eastern Economic Review*, April 22, 2004, p. 17.

146. Testimony of Admiral Thomas B. Fargo, USN Commander, U.S. Pacific Command, Before the House Armed Service Committee, United States House of Representatives, Q&A Session, March 31, 2004, http://www.pacom.mil/speeches/sst2004/040331hasc-qa.shtml.

147. Nesadurai, "Malaysia and the United States," p. 19.

148. Rungrawee Pinnyorat, "Bangkok backs US in Straits Initiative," *The Nation* (Bangkok), June 25, 2004, http://www.nationmultimedia.com/search/page.arcview.php?clid = 4&id = 101302&usrsess.

149. Ca-Mie De Souza, "China to Work with Singapore and Region to Fight Terror and Sea Piracy," *Channelnewsasia*, October 25, 2005, http://www.channelnewsasia.com/stories/singaporelocalnews/view/175279/1/.html.

150. Ministry of Defense, Singapore, "Launch of Trilateral Coordinated Patrols: MALSINDO Malacca Straits Coordinated Patrol," July 20, 2004, http://www.mindef.gov.sg/imindef/news_and_events/nr/2004/jul/20jul04_nr.html.

151. "China, Korea Keen to Preserve Security in Malacca Strait," Malaysian National News Agency (Bernama), March 22, 2006, (http://www.bernama.com/bernama/v3/news.php?id = 187404.

152. ReCAAP Information Sharing Centre, http://www.recaap.org/.

153. Madeleine Coorey, "Australia May Grow Closer to China: Ex-Defense Chief," Agence France-Presse, January 31, 2006.

154. "Rice Says Iraq Transition Will Take Time," Associated Press, March 16, 2006.

155. Richard Baker, "The Tsunami and U.S.-Muslim Relations," *PacNet* 2, January 12, 2005, http://www.csis.org/media/csis/pubs/pac0502.pdf.

156. Murray Hiebert and Barry Wain, "Same Planet, Different World," *Far Eastern Economic Review*, June 17, 2004, p. 26.

157. Chua Chin Hon, "China's Rise 'the Single Biggest Event of Our Age,'" *Singapore Straits Times*, October 26, 2005, http://taiwansecurity.org/ST/2005/ST-261005.htm.

7. JAPAN: A NORMAL IDENTITY

1. Chalmers Johnson, "Japan in Search of a "Normal" Role," *Daedalus* 121 (Fall 1992): 1–33; Christopher Hughes, *Japan's Re-Emergence as a "Normal" Military Power,* Adelphi Papers 368–69 (London: IISS, 2005); Michael Mastanduno, "Japan: Back to Normal?," in Ashley Tellis and Michael Wills, eds., *Strategic Asia 2006–2007* (Seattle: National Bureau of Asian Research, 2006); Kent Calder, "Japanese Foreign Economic Policy Formation: Explaining the 'Reactive' State," *World Politics* 40 (1988): 517–41; Masaru Tamamoto, "Japan's Search for a World Role," *World Policy Journal* 7 (1990): 493–520; Hugo Dobson, "Rethinking Japan's 'Lost Decade,'" *Global Society* 19, no. 2 (April 2005): 212.

2. Richard J. Samuels, *Securing Japan* (Ithaca: Cornell University Press, 2007), p. 3.

3. John J. Mearsheimer, *The Tragedy of Great Power Politics* (New York: Norton, 2001), p. 382; Eric Heginbotham and Richard J. Samuels, "Mercantile Realism and Japanese Foreign Policy," *International Security* 22, no. 4 (Spring 1998): 171–203; Michael Green, *Japan's Reluctant Realism: Foreign Policy Challenges in an Era of Uncertain Power* (New York: Palgrave, 2001); Thomas U. Berger, "From Sword to Chrysanthemum: Japan's Culture of Anti-Militarism," *International Security* 17, no. 4 (Spring 1993): 119–50.

4. Richard J. Samuels and Eric Heginbotham, "Japan's Dual Hedge," *Foreign Affairs* 81 (September/October 2002): 110–21.

5. G. John Ikenberry, "Japan and the Burden of History," *America Abroad,* August 18, 2006, www.tpmcafe.com/blog/americaabroad/2006/aug/18/Japan_and_the_burden_of_history.

6. Robert Ross, "The Geography of the Peace: East Asia in the Twenty-First Century," *International Security* 23, no. 4 (Spring 1999): 81–118.

7. Samuels, *Securing Japan,* ms. p. 9. On Japanese bandwagoning, see Eamonn Fingleton, "The Sun and the Dragon: The Fantasy of Sino-Japanese Enmity," *American Conservative,* August 2, 2004, p. 9.

8. Nobuo Okawara and Peter Katzenstein, "Japan and Asian-Pacific Security: Regionalization, Entrenched Bilateralism and Incipient Multilateralism," *Pacific Review* 14, no. 2 (2001): 165–94; Takashi Inoguchi, ed., *Japan's Asia Policy: Revival and Response* (London: Palgrave, 2002).

9. Thanks to Dave Leheny for this point.

10. Peter Katzenstein and Nobuo Okawara, *Japan's National Security: Structures, Norms, and Policy Responses in a Changing World* (Ithaca: Cornell University Press, 1993), p. 92.

11. John Dower, "Peace and Democracy in Two Systems," in Andrew Gordon, ed., *Postwar Japan as History* (Berkeley: University of California Press, 1993); and Eric Heginbotham and Richard J. Samuels, "Mercantile Realism and Japanese Foreign Policy," *International Security* 22, no. 4 (Spring 1998): 171–203.

12. Haruhiro Fukui, "The Liberal Democratic Party Revisited," *Journal of Japanese Studies* 10 (Summer 1984): 384–435.

13. See, for example, Peter Katzenstein, *Cultural Norms and National Security: Police and Military in Postwar Japan* (Ithaca: Cornell University Press, 1996); Berger, "From Sword to Chrysanthemum"; Yoshihide Soeya, "Japan: Normative

Constraints versus Structural Imperatives," in Muthiah Alagappa, ed., *Asian Security Practice: Material and Ideational Influences* (Stanford: Stanford University Press, 1998), pp. 198–233; Heginbotham and Samuels, "Mercantile Realism and Japanese Foreign Policy."

14. The classic remains Chalmers Johnson, *MITI and the Japanese Miracle* (Stanford: Stanford University Press, 1982).

15. On Chinese development, see Yasheng Huang, *Selling China: Foreign Direct Investment During the Reform Era* (New York: Cambridge University Press, 2003); Alvin So, ed., *China's Developmental Miracle: Origins, Transformations, and Challenges* (Armonk, N.Y.: M. E. Sharpe, 2003).

16. Andrew MacIntyre and Barry Naughton, "The Decline of the Japan-Led Model of the East Asian Economy," in T. J. Pempel, ed., *Remapping East Asia: The Construction of a Region* (Ithaca: Cornell University Press, 2005), pp. 77–100; Mitchell Bernard and John Ravenhill, "Beyond Product Cycles and Flying Geese: Regionalization, Hierarchy, and the Industrialization of East Asia," *World Politics* 47, no. 2 (April 1995): 171–209; Walter Hatch and Kozo Yamamura, *East Asia in Japan's Embrace: Building a Regional Production Alliance* (Cambridge: Cambridge University Press, 1996).

17. Personal communication, October 30, 2006.

18. Charles Kindleberger, *The World In Depression 1929–1939* (Berkeley: University of California Press, 1986), p. 289; Herman Schwartz, "Hegemony, International Debt, and International Economic Instability," in Chronis Polychroniu, ed., *Current Perspectives and Issues in International Political Economy* (New York: Praeger, 1992).

19. See, for example, R. Taggart Murphy, *The Weight of the Yen: How Denial Imperils America's Future and Ruins an Alliance* (New York: Norton, 1996); David Arase, *Buying Power: The Political Economy of Japan's Foreign Aid* (Boulder, Colo.: Lynne Rienner, 1995); Hatch and Yamamura, *East Asia in Japan's Embrace*.

20. Peter Katzenstein, *A World of Regions: Asia and Europe in the American Imperium* (Ithaca: Cornell University Press, 2005), p. 33.

21. Murphy, *The Weight of the Yen*.

22. Leonard Schoppa, *Bargaining with Japan: What American Pressure Can and Cannot Do* (New York: Columbia University Press, 1997).

23. Michael Mastanduno, "Japan: Back to Normal?" p. 20.

24. Richard Samuels, *Rich Nation, Strong Army* (Ithaca: Cornell University Press, 1995).

25. Yum-Chul Park and Won-Am Park, "Changing Japanese Trade Patterns and the East Asian NICs," in Paul Krugman, ed., *Trade with Japan: Has the Door Opened Wider?* (Chicago: University of Chicago Press, 1991), pp. 85–120.

26. Dajin Peng, "Invisible Linkages: A Regional Perspective of East Asian Political Economy," *International Studies Quarterly* 46 (2002): 423–47.

27. Hatch and Yamamura, *East Asia in Japan's Embrace*.

28. Dajin Peng, "Invisible Linkages," p. 429.

29. Richard Doner, "Japan in East Asia," in Peter Katzenstein and Takashi Shiraishi, eds., *Network Power: Japan and Asia* (Ithaca: Cornell University Press, 1997), pp. 228–29.

30. Bernard and Ravenhill, "Beyond Product Cycles," pp. 190–91.

31. David Kang and Jiyoung Lee, "Korea-Japan Relations: The Big Chill," *Comparative Connections* 7, no. 4 (January 2006): 14.

32. Dajin Peng, "Invisible Linkages," p. 441.

33. MacIntyre and Naughton, "The Decline of the Japan-Led Model of the East Asian Economy," p. 89.

34. MacIntyre and Naughton, "The Decline of the Japan-led Model of the East Asian Economy," p. 86.

35. People's Daily Online, "Investment Into China Records 8% Rise," March 14, 2006, http://english.people.com.cn/200603/14/eng20060314_250433.html.

36. Green, *Japan's Reluctant Realism*, p. 213.

37. Sharon Noguchi, "Hard Work, Furtive Living: Illegal Immigrants in Japan," *Yale Global Online*, March 2, 2006, http://yaleglobal.yale.edu/display.article?id = 7067.

38. Study cited in Eugene Matthews, "Japan's New Nationalism," *Foreign Affairs* 82, no. 6 (November/December 2003): 85.

39. Quoted in Matthews, "Japan's New Nationalism," p. 85.

40. Mastanduno, "Japan: Back to Normal?" p. 17.

41. Dobson, "Rethinking Japan's 'Lost Decade,'" p. 213.

42. "Japan Adopts New Defense Policy Guidelines," *Mainichi Shimbun*, December 8, 2004, http://mdn.mainichi.co.jp/.

43. Japanese Security Council, "National Defense Program Guideline for FY 2005 and After," December 10, 2004, http://www.mod.go.jp/e/defense_policy/japans_defense_policy/4/ndpgf2005/1.pdf.

44. Japanese Security Council, "National Defense Program Guideline for FY 2005 and After," pp. 5–6.

45. Howard French, "Top Bush Aide Urges Japan to Form In-Depth Ties with the U.S.," *New York Times*, May 8, 2001, p. A10. See also "The Best Response to the U.S. on Missile Defense Is a Flat 'No,'" *Asahi Shimbun*, May 11, 2001, www.asahi.co.jp.

46. Poll quoted in Mochizuki, "Between Alliance and Autonomy: Japan," in Ashley Tellis and Michael Wills, eds., *Strategic Asia 2004–2005: Confronting Terrorism in the Pursuit of Power* (Seattle: National Bureau of Asian Research, 2004), p. 111.

47. *Nikkei Shimbun* poll, "April 2005 regular telephone poll," downloaded from the Mansfield Foundation., www.mansfieldfdn.org/polls/poll-0508.htm.

48. Tamamoto, "How Japan Imagines China and Sees Itself," Commentary, Japan Institute of International Affairs, May 31, 2006, www2.jiia.or.jp/en_commentary/200605/31-MasaruTamamoto.html.

49. Mochizuki, "Between Alliance and Autonomy," p. 113.

50. Samuels, *Securing Japan*.

51. See the extended discussion in Hughes, *Japan's Re-Emergence as a "Normal" Military Power*, pp. 51–57.

52. Nobuhiro Hiwatari, "Japan in 2005: Koizumi's Finest Hour," *Asian Survey* 46, no. 1 (January/February 2006): 22–36.

53. Takeshi Hamashita, "The Intra-regional System in East Asia in Modern Times," in Katzenstein and Shiraishi, eds., *Network Power*, pp. 113–35; Yoshihide Soeya, *Nihon no* [midoru pawā] gaikō (Japan as a Middle Power) (Tokyo: Chikuma Shobo, 2005); Soeya, "Japan: Normative Constraints versus Structural Imperatives," in

Alagappa, ed., *Asian Security Practice*; Akiko Fukushima, *Japanese Foreign Policy: The Emerging Logic of Multilateralism* (Basingstoke, U.K.: Macmillan, 1999).

54. Personal interview, March 28, 2006.

55. Personal interview, March 2, 2006.

56. Richard J. Samuels, *Machiavelli's Children: Leaders and Their Legacies in Italy and Japan* (Ithaca: Cornell University Press, 2003), Chapter 12.

57. Samuels, *Securing Japan*, chapter 6.

58. Hughes, *Japan's Re-Emergence as a "Normal" Military Power*.

59. "Ishihara Says U.S. Can't Win War against China, Calls U.S. Troops 'Incompetent,'" *Kyodo*, November 5, 2005, http://www.howardwfrench.com/archives/2005/11/.

60. Prime Minister's Task Force, "Basic Strategies for Japan's Foreign Policy in the 21st Century: New Era, New Vision, New Diplomacy," November 2002, p. 1; http://www.kantei.go.jp/foreign/policy/2002/1128tf_e.html. See also Reinhard Drifte, *Japan's Security Relations with China since 1989: From Balancing to Bandwagoning?* (London: RoutledgeCurzon, 2003), pp. 180–82.

61. Prime Minister's Commission on Japan's Goals in the 21st Century, "The Frontier Within: Individual Empowerment and Better Governance in the New Millennium," January 2000, http://www.kantei.go.jp/jp/21century/report/htmls/1preface.html#preface.

62. However, Japanese interests over North Korea are not identical to those of the United States.

63. Brad Glosserman, "Changing Asia Needs the U.S.-Japan Alliance," *PacNet* 47, October 21, 2004.

64. Quoted by Eugene Matthews, "Japan's New Nationalism," *Foreign Affairs* 82, no. 6 (November/December 2003): 75.

65. Personal communication, February 12, 2005.

66. Samuels, *Securing Japan*, chapter 8.

67. Brad Glosserman, "U.S.-Japan Relations: Be Careful What You Wish For," *Comparative Connections* October 1, 2005, p. 2.

68. *The National Security Strategy of the United States of America*, September 2002, p. 26, www.whitehouse.gov/nsc/nss.pdf.

69. Tamamoto, "How Japan Imagines China and Sees Itself."

70. G. John Ikenberry, "Japan and the Burden of History."

71. Wu Xinbo, "The End of the Silver Lining: A Chinese View of the U.S.-Japan Alliance," *Washington Quarterly* 29, no. 1 (Winter 2005–06): p. 119.

72. Author's interview, October 4, 2005.

73. Matthews, "Japan's New Nationalism," p. 76.

74. Quoted in Mochizuki, "Between Alliance and Autonomy," p. 113.

75. Samuels, *Securing Japan*, chapter 8.

76. Mochizuki, "Between Alliance and Autonomy," p. 113.

77. Leonard Schoppa, remarks at Seminar 31, Airlie, Va., April 29, 2006.

78. Matthews, "Japan's New Nationalism," p. 87.

79. For good overviews, see Saburo Ienaga, "The Glorification of War in Japanese Education," *International Security* 18, no. 3 (Winter 1993/1994): 113–33; Yoshimi Yoshiaki, *Comfort Women: Sexual Slavery in the Japanese Military During World War II* (New York: Columbia University Press, 2002); Katharine H. S. Moon,

"South Korean Movements Against Militarized Sexual Labor," *Asian Survey* 39, no. 2 (March/April 1999): 310–27; Eric Heginbotham and Richard Samuels, "Japan's Dual Hedge," *Foreign Affairs* 81, no. 5 (2002): 110–21; Sung-jae Choi, "The Politics of the Dokdo Issue," *Journal of East Asian Affairs* 5, no. 3 (September 2005): 465–94; and Erica Strecker Downs and Phillip Saunders, "Legitimacy and the Limits of Nationalism: China and the Diaoyu Islands," *International Security* 23, no. 3 (Winter 1998/1999): 114–46.

80. Matthews, "Japan's New Nationalism," p. 77.

81. Wu Xinbo, "The End of the Silver Lining," pp. 119–30.

82. Gilbert Rozman, *Northeast Asia's Stunted Regionalism: Bilateral Distrust in the Shadow of Globalization* (Cambridge: Cambridge University Press, 2004), p. 358.

83. Tamamoto, "How Japan Imagines China and Sees Itself."

84. Quoted in David Kang and Jiyoung Lee, "Japan- Korea Relations: *Seirei Keinetsu (Cold Politics, Warm Economics)*," *Comparative Connections,* April 1, 2006, p. 5.

85. Ming Wan, "Tensions in Recent Sino-Japanese Relations," *Asian Survey* 43, no. 5 (September–October 2003): 826–44.

86. Interview with a senior ROK foreign ministry official, December 8, 2005.

87. "South Korea's Roh Tells Japan to Win Trust from Asian Neighbors," *Yahoo News,* March 1, 2006, http://sg.news.yahoo.com/060301/1/3z1wn.html.

88. Joseph Ferguson, "Fishing Wars: Japan-Russia Relations Continue Downward spiral," *PacNet* 41, August 22, 2006, p. 1.

89. Ralph Cossa, "Northern Territories: Searching for a Solution," *PacNet* 41A, August 23, 2006, p. 1.

90. Ferguson, "Fishing Wars," p. 1.

91. Editorial, "Japan's History Lesson," *Boston Globe,* February 9, 2006.

92. Hugo Restall, "Opposing the Sun: Japan Alienates Asia," *Far Eastern Economic Review* 168 (April 2005): 8–13.

93. Michiyo Ishida, "Japan Should Draw Line under War Past and Meet China, S Korea: MM Lee," Channel News Asia, May 26, 2006, http://www.channelnewsasia.com/stories/eastasia/view/210514/1/.html.

94. Keiichi Tsunekawa, "Why So Many Maps There? Japan and Regional Cooperation," in T. J. Pempel, ed., *Remapping East Asia*, p. 106.

95. Quoted in Shane Green, "New Hawks Bloom under Korea Threat," *The Age,* April 5, 2003.

96. Ryutaro Hashimoto, remarks at Stanford University, January 26, 2006.

97. *Mainichi Shimbun,* December 15, 2005.

98. Quoted by David Ibison, "Japanese Investment into China Hits Record High," *Financial Times,* April 3, 2006.

99. Vivian Wu, "Entrepreneurs Fight Sino-Japan Freeze," *South China Morning Post,* April 26, 2006.

100. Figures quoted in Wonhyuk Lim, "KORUS FTA: A Strategic and Pragmatic View," Policy Forum Online 06–46A (Nautilus Institute, June 13, 2006), p. 6.

101. Hiwatari, "Japan in 2005," pp. 22–36.

102. Andy Xie, Morgan-Stanley Global Economic Forum, April 10, 2006, http://www.morganstanley.com/.

103. Tamamoto, "How Japan Imagines China and Sees Itself."

104. As one American Japanologist told me, "if I have to go to another diplomatic meeting in Tokyo where a Chinese diplomat uses the term 'win-win' ten times, I will scream." Personal communication, September 26, 2005.

105. Saadia Pekkanen, "Japan's FTA Frenzy" (manuscript, University of Washington, 2004), p. 2.

106. Pekkanen, "Japan's FTA Frenzy," p. 2.

107. "China Again Tops Japan Trade," *Japan Times*, January 27, 2006.

108. Japanese Ministry of Internal Affairs and Communications, *Statistical Handbook of Japan, 2005*, http://www.stat.go.jp/English/data/handbook/c11cont.htm#cha11_1.

109. Eric Heginbotham and Richard J. Samuels, "Japan," in Richard J. Ellings and Aaron L. Friedberg with Michael Wills, eds., *Strategic Asia 2002–03: Asian Aftershocks* (Seattle: National Bureau of Asian Research, 2003), p. 112.

110. Figures from the *Statistical Handbook of Japan, 2005*, pp. 124–29.

111. Japan Ministry of Foreign Affairs, "Recent Developments in China and Japan-China Relations," briefing, January 16, 1999.

112. David Arase, "Public-Private Sector Interest Coordination in Japan's ODA," *Pacific Affairs* 67, no. 2 (Summer 1994): 171–200.

113. Clay Chandler, "China's Rivals Slow to Grasp Export Might: Beijing Building Trade Powerhouse," *Washington Post*, May 25, 2002.

114. Fingleton, "The Sun and the Dragon," p. 9.

115. Pekkanen, "Japan's FTA Frenzy," p. 17.

116. Howard French and Norimitsu Onishi, "Economic Ties Binding Japan to Rival China," *New York Times*, October 31, 2005.

117. Sebastian Moffett, "Japan Hopes China Ties Will Ease Friction," *Wall Street Journal*, May 1, 2006, p. 4.

118. Heginbotham and Samuels, "Japan," p. 115.

119. David Kang and Ji-young Lee, "No Major Changes," *Comparative Connections* 7, no. 3 (July–September 2005), http://www.csis.org/media/csis/pubs/0503q.pdf.

120. David Kang and Ji-young Lee, "Missiles and Prime Ministers May Mark a Turning Point," *Comparative Connections* 8, no. 3 (July–September 2006), http://www.csis.org/media/csis/pubs/0603q.pdf.

121. Pekkanen, "Japan's FTA Frenzy," p. 1.

122. Heginbotham and Samuels, "Japan," p. 109.

123. Pekkanen, "Japan's FTA Frenzy," p. 6.

124. Fingleton, "The Sun and the Dragon," p. 8.

125. Michael Armacost, *Friends or Rivals? The Insider's Account of U.S.-Japan Relations* (New York: Columbia University Press, 1996), p. 191.

126. Quoted in Joseph Y. S. Cheng, "Sino-Japanese Relations in the Twenty-First Century," *Journal of Contemporary Asia* 33, no. 2 (2003): 252.

127. Michael Armacost, "Japan: Tilting Closer to Washington," in Richard J. Ellings and Aaron L. Friedberg with Michael Wills, eds., *Strategic Asia 2003–04: Fragility and Crisis* (Seattle: National Bureau of Asian Research, 2004), p. 96.

128. Okawara and Katzenstein, "Japan and Asia-Pacific Security," pp. 165–94.

129. Lam Peng-Er, "Japan-Taiwan Relations: Between Affinity and Reality," *Asian Affairs: An American Review* 30, no. 4 (Winter 2004): 249–68.

130. Armacost, "Japan: Tilting Closer to Washington," pp. 95–96.

131. Jian Yang, "Sino-Japanese Relations: Implications for Southeast Asia," *Contemporary Southeast Asia* 25, no. 2 (August 2003): 306.

132. Cited in Gregory Noble, "What Can Taiwan (and the United States) Expect from Japan?," *Journal of East Asian Studies* 5 (2005): 1–34.

133. Both polls cited in Noble, "What Can Taiwan (and the United States) Expect from Japan?"

134. *Asahi Shimbun*, "Special Research on Japanese Attitudes toward China and Other Nations," April 26, 2005, http://www.mansfieldfdn.org/polls/poll-05-4.htm.

135. *Asahi Shimbun*, "Special Research on Japanese Attitudes toward China and Other Nations."

136. Tamamoto, "How Japan Imagines China and Sees Itself."

137. Michael Wills, "Japan," in Tellis and Wills, eds., *Confronting Terrorism in the Pursuit of Power*, p. 123.

138. *National Defense Program Guideline, FY 2005-*, approved by the Japanese Security Council and Cabinet, December 10, 2004.

139. "Joint Statement of the U.S.-Japan Security Consultative Committee," February 19, 2005, http://www.state.gov/r/pa/prs/ps/2005/42490.htm.

140. Ralph Cossa, editor's note, in "U.S.-Japan Security Consultative Committee: An Assessment," *PacNet* 10, March 10, 2005, p. 2.

141. Noble, "What Can Taiwan (and the United States) Expect from Japan?," p. 26.

142. As Richard Samuels notes, Japan is seeking a "Goldilocks consensus" that will allow it to "exist securely without being too dependent on the United States or too vulnerable to China." Samuels, *Securing Japan*, ms. p. 14.

8. THE ROLE OF THE UNITED STATES IN EAST ASIA

1. Barry Buzan, "A Framework for Regional Security Analysis," in Barry Buzan and Gowher Rizvi, eds., *South Asian Insecurity and the Great Powers* (New York: St. Martin's, 1986), pp. 3–8.

2. Tom Christensen, "China, the U.S.-Japan Alliance, and the Security Dilemma in East Asia," *International Security* 23, no. 4 (Spring 1999): 50; Christopher Layne, "From Preponderance to Offshore Balancing," *International Security* 22, no. 1 (Summer 1997): 86–125. See also the detailed discussion on the United States as a global, not regional, actor, in Barry Buzan and Ole Weaver, *Regions and Powers: The Structure of International Security* (Cambridge: Cambridge University Press, 2003), esp. pp. 93–184.

3. Ronald Takaki, *Strangers From a Different Shore: A History of Asian Americans* (Boston: Little, Brown, 1989); William A. Clark, "Immigration and the Hispanic Middle Class," Center for Immigration Studies, April 2001, http://www.cis.org/articles/2001/hispanicmc/toc.html.

4. Tony Horwitz, "Immigration and the Curse of the Black Legend," *New York Times*, July 9, 2006, Section 4, p. 13.

5. See, for example, Stuart Banner, *Anglo-American Securities Regulation: Cultural and Political Roots, 1690–1860* (Cambridge: Cambridge University Press, 2002).

6. U.S. Census Bureau, "Table 1. Population by Sex and Age, for Asian Alone and White Alone, Not Hispanic: March 2004," http://www.census.gov/population/socdemo/race/api/ppl-184/tab1.html.

7. See, for example, Patrick Buchanan, *A Republic, Not an Empire* (Washington, D.C.: Regnery, 1999).

8. "Fallon, U.S. Commander, Pushes China to Modernize Its Military," Bloomberg, May 18, 2006, http://www.bloomberg.com/apps/news?pid=10000080&sid=a8Wqk11umook&refer=asia.

9. Victor Cha, *Alignment Despite Antagonism* (Stanford: Stanford University Press, 2005).

10. Brantley Womack, "China Between Region and World" (manuscript, University of Virginia, 2006), p. 7.

11. Stephen Brooks and William Wohlforth, "American Primacy in Perspective," *Foreign Affairs* 81, no. 4 (July/August 2002): 20–33.

12. Gerald Curtis, "Rethinking U.S. East Asia Policy," "Jidai o yomu" column, *Tokyo Shimbun*, January 11, 2004, http://www.rieti.go.jp/en/papers/contribution/curtis/03.html.

13. Dennis Blair and John Hanley, "From Wheels to Webs: Reconstructing Asia-Pacific Security Arrangements," *Washington Quarterly* 24, no. 1 (Winter 2001): 7–17.

14. Thomas J. Christensen, "Fostering Stability or Creating a Monster? The Rise of China and U.S. Policy Toward East Asia," *International Security* 31, no. 1 (Summer 2006): 81–126, 108.

15. Michael O'Hanlon, "United States: U.S. Military Modernization: Implications for U.S. Policy in Asia," in Ashley Tellis and Michael Wills, eds., *Strategic Asia 2005–06: Military Modernization in an Era of Uncertainty* (Seattle: National Bureau of Asian Research, 2005), p. 40.

16. Stephen Cohen, "The Super-power as Super-debtor: Implications of Economic Disequilibria for U.S.-Asian Relations," in Ashley Tellis and Michael Wills, eds., *Strategic Asia 2006–2007* (Seattle: National Bureau of Asian Research, 2006).

17. Figures quoted from Cohen, "The Super-power as Super-debtor."

18. Niall Ferguson, "Hu and the Dog That Didn't Bark," *Los Angeles Times*, April 24, 2006.

19. Ferguson, "Hu and the Dog That Didn't Bark."

20. Bates Gill and Michael Green, "Sino-American Relations Need Actions Not Words," *Financial Times*, April 23, 2006.

21. Roger Cohen, "U.S. and China Joined at the Hip on Stability," *International Herald Tribune*, April 22, 2006.

22. Jason Dean and Jay Solomon, "Business Gives Hu a Thumbs-Up, But Washington is More Muted," *Wall Street Journal*, April 22, 2006, p. 1.

23. "Locke: U.S.-China Ties Stronger than Ever Before," Xinhua, April 18, 2006, http://www.chinadaily.com.cn/china/2006–04/18/content_570487.htm.

24. U.S. Department of Defense, *Quadrennial Defense Review 2006*, http://www.comw.org/qdr/qdr2006.pdf, pp. 29–30.

25. U.S. Department of Defense, *Quadrennial Defense Review 2006*, p. 47.

26. John Tkacik, Jr., "Panda Hedging: Pentagon Report Urges New Strategy for China," Heritage Foundation, http://www.heritage.org/research/asiaandthe

pacific/wm1093.cfm. See also Dan Blumenthal, "Get Serious About China's Rising Military," *Washington Post*, May 25, 2006, p. A29.

27. *National Security Strategy of the United States, 2002* (Washington, D.C. September 2002), chapter 8.

28. "India, U.S. Agree Chinese Navy Needs to Be Engaged," *Indian Express*, May 24, 2006.

29. "Fallon, U.S. Commander, Pushes China to Modernize Its Military."

30. "Fallon, U.S. Commander, Pushes China to Modernize Its Military."

31. "U.S. Invites China to Military Exercise," Associated Press, May 15, 2006 http://www.breitbart.com/news/2006/05/15/D8HK09FG1.html.

32. "U.S. Planning Joint Naval Drills with China," NHK, May 11, 2006, http://www.nhk.or.jp/daily/english/index2.html.

33. *National Security Strategy of the United States of America, 2006*, http://www.whitehouse.gov/nsc/nss/2006/nss2006.pdf, p. 42.

34. U.S. Department of State, "Deputy Secretary Zoellick Statement on Conclusion of the Second U.S.-China Senior Dialogue," December 8, 2005, http://www.state.gov/r/pa/prs/ps/2005/57822.htm.

35. "It's Unfair to Make China a Scapegoat: Zoellick," Reuters, April 18, 2006, www.chinadaily.com.cn/china/2006-04/18/content_570468.htm.

36. Alastair Iain Johnston, *Social States: China in International Institutions, 1980–2000* (Princeton: Princeton University Press, 2006), p. 13.

37. William Perry, "U.S. Strategy: Engage China, Not Contain It," *Defense Issues* 10, no. 109 (October 30, 1995), http://www.defenselink.mil/speeches/1995/s19951030-kaminski.html.

38. Robert Ross, "The Geography of the Peace: East Asia in the Twenty-First Century," *International Security* 23, no. 4 (Spring 1999): 96.

39. Michael Mastanduno, "Incomplete Hegemony: The United States and Security Order in Asia," in Muthiah Alagappa, ed., *Asian Security Order* (Stanford: Stanford University Press, 2003); Thomas Christensen, "China, the U.S.-Japan Alliance, and the Security Dilemma in East Asia," *International Security* 23, no. 4 (Spring 1999): 49–80; G. John Ikenberry, "American Hegemony and East Asian Order," *Australian Journal of International Affairs* 58, no. 3 (September 2004).

40. Richard K. Betts, "Wealth, Power, and Instability: East Asia and the United States after the Cold War," *International Security* 18, no. 3 (Winter 1993): 56.

41. Aaron Friedberg, "Ripe for Rivalry," *International Security* 18, no. 3 (Winter 1993/94): 25.

42. Sheldon Simon, "Southeast Asia's Defense Needs: Change or Continuity?," in Tellis and Wills, eds., *Strategic Asia 2005–06*, p. 272.

43. Paul Chambers, "U.S.-Thai Relations After 9/11: A New Era of Cooperation?," *Contemporary Southeast Asia* 26, no. 3 (December 2004): 465–66.

44. Pamela Sodhy, "U.S.-Malaysia Relations During the Bush Administration: The Political, Economic, and Security Aspects," *Contemporary Southeast Asia* 25, no. 3 (December 2003): 378–81.

45. Cited in Robert Sutter, "United States: Leadership Maintained Amid Continuing Challenges," in Ashley Tellis and Michael Wills, eds., *Strategic Asia 2004–2005: Confronting Terrorism in the Pursuit of Power* (Seattle: National Bureau of Asian Research, 2004), p. 45.

46. Council on Foreign Relations, "Taiwan Exercises Over, Now the Challenge Is to US-China Ties," http://www.fas.org/news/taiwan/1996/960326-taiwan-usia.htm.

47. Council on Foreign Relations, "Taiwan Exercises Over, Now the Challenge is to US-China Ties."

48. Quoted in Amitav Acharya, "Containment, Engagement, or Counter-Dominance? Malaysia's Response to China's Rise," in Alastair Iain Johnston and Robert S. Ross, eds., *Engaging China: The Management of an Emerging Power* (London: Routledge, 1999), p. 140.

49. Michael Vatikiotis, "Catching the Dragon's Tail: China and Southeast Asia in the 21st Century," *Contemporary Southeast Asia* 25, no. 1 (April 2003): 65–80.

50. Nikolas Busse, "Constructivism and Southeast Asian Security," *Pacific Review* 12, no. 1 (1999): 39–60.

51. Ikenberry, "American Hegemony and East Asian Order," pp. 353–67.

9. CONCLUSIONS AND IMPLICATIONS

1. Jeffrey Frieden and David Lake, "International Relations as a Social Science: Rigor and Relevance," *Annals of the American Academy of Political and Social Science* 600, no. 1 (July 2005): 136–56.

2. Robert Ross, "The Geography of the Peace: East Asia in the Twenty-First Century," *International Security* 23, no. 4 (Spring 1999): 81–118.

3. Thomas J. Christensen, "Fostering Stability or Creating a Monster? The Rise of China and U.S. Policy Toward East Asia," *International Security* 31, no. 1 (Summer 2006): 81–126, 83.

4. Chan Heng Chee, "China and ASEAN: A Growing Relationship," speech by Ambassador Chan Heng Chee at the Asia Society Texas Annual Ambassadors' Forum and Corporate Conference, Houston, Texas, February 3, 2006.

5. Martin Stuart-Fox, "Southeast Asia and China: The Role of History and Culture in Shaping Future Relations," *Contemporary Southeast Asia* 26, no. 1 (2004): 136.

6. James Fearon, "Rationalist Explanations for War," *International Organization* 49, no. 3 (Summer 1995): 379–414.

7. Avery Goldstein, *Rising to the Challenge: China's Grand Strategy and International Security* (Stanford: Stanford University Press, 2005), p. 39.

8. Robert Jervis, "The Future of World Politics: Will It Resemble the Past?," *International Security* 16, no. 3 (Winter 1991/92): 39–46.

9. Amitav Acharya, "How Ideas Spread: Whose Norms Matter? Norm Localization and Institutional Change in Asian Regionalism," *International Organization* 58, no. 2 (Spring 2004): 239–75.

10. Stephan Haggard, "Institutions and Growth in East Asia," *Studies in Comparative International Development* 38, no. 4 (Winter 2004): 53–81.

SELECTED BIBLIOGRAPHY

THEORY AND EAST ASIAN INTERNATIONAL RELATIONS

Acharya, Amitav. *The Quest for Identity: International Relations of Southeast Asia.* Oxford: Oxford University Press, 2000.

Alagappa, Muthiah, ed. *Asian Security Order.* Stanford: Stanford University Press, 2003.

———, ed. *Asian Security Practice: Material and Ideational Influences.* Stanford: Stanford University Press, 1998.

Ball, Desmond. "Strategic Culture in the Asia-Pacific Region." *Security Studies* 3, no. 1 (Winter 1995): 44–74.

Bennett, D. Scott, and Allan Stam. *The Behavioral Origins of War.* Ann Arbor: University of Michigan Press, 2003.

Brooks, Stephen, and William Wohlforth. "Hard Times for Soft Balancing." *International Security* 30, no. 1 (Summer 2005): 72–108.

Brzezinski, Zbigniew and John Mearsheimer. "Clash of the Titans." *Foreign Policy* 146 (January/February 2005): 47.

Buzan, Barry, and Richard Little. *International Systems in World History: Remaking the Study of International Relations.* New York: Oxford University Press, 2000.

Christensen, Thomas. "China, the U.S.-Japan Alliance, and the Security Dilemma in East Asia." *International Security* 23, no. 4 (Spring 1999): 49–80.

———. "Posing Problems without Catching Up: China's Rise and Challenges for U.S. Security Policy." *International Security* 25, no. 4 (Spring 2001): 5–40.

Curtis, Gerald. "East Asia, Regionalism, and U.S. National Interests." *American Foreign Policy Interests* 26 (2004): 199–208.

Fearon, James, and Alexander Wendt. "Rationalism v. Constructivism: A Skeptical View." In Walter Carlsnaes, Thomas Risse, and Beth Simmons, eds., *Handbook of International Relations Theory.* London: Sage, 2002.

Fearon, James. "Rationalist Explanations for War." *International Organization* 49, no. 3 (Summer 1995): 374–414.

Friedberg, Aaron. "Ripe for Rivalry." *International Security* 18, no. 3 (Winter 1993/94): 5–33.

Glaser, Charles. "Political Consequences of Military Strategy: Expanding and Refining the Spiral and Deterrence Models." *World Politics* 44, no. 2 (July 1992).

Ikenberry, G. John, and Michael Mastanduno, eds. *International Relations Theory and the Asia-Pacific.* New York: Columbia University Press 2003.

Kang, David C. "Getting Asia Wrong: The Need for New Analytic Frameworks." *International Security* 27, no. 4 (Spring 2003): 57–85.

Katzenstein, Peter J. *A World of Regions: Asia and Europe in the American Imperium.* Ithaca: Cornell University Press. 2005.

Katzenstein, Peter, and Nobuo Okawara. "Japan, Asian-Pacific Security, and the Case for Analytical Eclecticism." *International Security* 26, no. 3 (Winter 2001): 153–85.

Katzenstein, Peter, and Takashi Shiraishi, eds. *Beyond Japan: The Dynamics of East Asian Regionalism.* Ithaca: Cornell University Press, 2006.

Kaufman, Stuart J., Richard Little, and William Wohlforth, eds. *The Balance of Power in World History.* London: Palgrave, 2007.

Kydd, Andrew. *Trust and Mistrust in International Relations.* Princeton: Princeton University Press, 2005.

Legro, Jeffrey, and Andrew Moravsick. "Is Anybody Still a Realist?" *International Security* 24, no. 2 (1999): 5–56.

Lieber, Keir, and Gerard Alexander. "Waiting for Balancing: Why the World Is Not Pushing Back." *International Security* 30, no. 1 (Summer 2005): 109–39.

Mearsheimer, John. *The Tragedy of Great Power Politics.* New York: Norton, 2001.

Pape, Robert A. "Soft Balancing Against the United States." *International Security* 30, no. 1 (Summer 2005): 7–45.

Paul, T. V. "Soft Balancing in the Age of U.S. Primacy." *International Security* 30, no. 1 (Summer 2005): 46–71.

Pempel, T. J., ed. *The Politics of the Asian Economic Crisis.* Ithaca: Cornell University Press, 1999.

———, ed. *Remapping East Asia: The Construction of a Region.* Ithaca: Cornell University Press, 2005.

Powell, Robert. "Bargaining Theory and International Conflict." *American Review of Political Science* 5 (2002): 1–30.

———. *In the Shadow of Power: States and Strategies in International Politics.* Princeton: Princeton University Press. 1999.

Ross, Robert. "The Geography of the Peace: East Asia in the Twenty-First Century." *International Security* 23, no. 4 (Spring 1999): 81–118.

Rozman, Gilbert. *Northeast Asia's Stunted Regionalism: Bilateral Distrust in the Shadow of Globalization.* Cambridge: Cambridge University Press, 2004.

Schweller, Randall. "Unanswered Threats: A Neoclassical Realist Theory of Underbalancing." *International Security* 29, no. 2 (Fall 2004): 159–201.

Shambaugh, David. "China Engages Asia: Reshaping the Regional Order." *International Security* 29, no. 3 (Winter 2004/05): 64–99.

Tellis, Ashley and Michael Wills, eds. *Strategic Asia 2005–06: Military Modernization in an Era of Uncertainty.* Seattle: National Bureau of Asian Research, 2005.

Waltz, Kenneth N. "The Emerging Structure of International Politics." *International Security* 18 (Fall 1993): 44–79.

Wendt, Alexander. "Collective Identity Formation and the International State." *American Political Science Review* 88, no. 2 (June 1994): 384–96.

Wohlforth, William. "The Stability of a Unipolar World." *International Security* 24, no. 1 (Summer 1999): 5–41.

Abu-Lughod, Janet L. *Before European Hegemony: The World System A.D. 1250–1350.* Oxford: Oxford University Press, 1989.

Atwell. William. "International Bullion Flows and the Chinese Economy circa 1530–1650". *Past and Present* 95 (1982): 68–90.

Berry, Mary. *Hideyoshi.* Cambridge: Harvard University Press, 1982.

Coedes, G. *The Making of Southeast Asia.* Trans. H. M. Wright. Berkeley: University of California Press, 1969.

Cushman. Jennifer W. *Fields from the Sea: Chinese Junk Trade with Siam during the Late Eighteenth and Early Nineteenth Centuries.* Ithaca: Southeast Asia Program, 1993.

Deng, Gang. "The Foreign Staple Trade of China in the Pre-Modern Era." *International History Review* 19, no. 2 (1997): 253–85.

Elisonas, Jurgis. "The Inseparable Trinity: Japan's Relations with China and Korea." In *The Cambridge History of Japan. Vol. 4, Early Modern Japan,* ed. John Hall. Cambridge: Cambridge University Press, 1988.

Fairbank, John, ed. *The Chinese World Order.* Cambridge: Harvard University Press, 1968.

Frank, Andre Gunder. *ReOrient: Global Economy in the Asian Age.* Berkeley: University of California Press, 1998.

Hall, John. *Japan: From Prehistory to Modern Times.* New York: Delacorte, 1968.

Hamashita, Takeshia. "The Tribute Trade System and Modern Asia." In A. J. H. Latham and Heita Kawakatsu, eds., *Japanese Industrialization and the Asian Economy.* London: Routledge, 1994.

Howe, Christopher. *The Origins of Japanese Trade Supremacy: Development and Technology in Asia from 1540 to the Pacific War.* London: Hurts, 1996.

Hui, Victoria Tin-bor. *War and State Formation in Ancient China and Early Modern Europe.* Cambridge: Cambridge University Press, 2004.

Ishii, Yoneo. *The Junk Trade from Southeast Asia: Translations from the Tosen Fusetsu-gaki, 1674–1723.* Singapore: Institute of Southeast Asian Studies, 1998.

Kang, Etsuko. *Diplomacy and Ideology in Japanese-Korean Relations: From the Fifteenth to the Eighteenth Century.* New York: St. Martin's, 1997.

Kawazoe, Shoji. "Japan and East Asia." In *The Cambridge History of Japan. Vol. 3, Medieval Japan,* ed. Kozo Yamamura. Cambridge: Cambridge University Press, 1990.

Kazui, Tashiro. "Foreign Relations During the Edo Period: Sakoku Reexamined." *Journal of Japanese Studies* 8, no. 2 (1982): 283–306.

Kim, Key-hiuk. *The Last Phase of the East Asian World Order.* Berkeley: University of Californa Press, 1980.

Klein, Peter. "The China Seas and the World Economy between the Sixteenth and Nineteenth Centuries: The Changing Structures of Trade." In Carl-Ludwig Holtfrerich, ed., *Interactions in the World Economy: Perspectives from International Economic History.* New York: New York University Press, 1989.

Kwanten, Luc. *Imperial Nomads.* Philadelphia: University of Pennsylvania Press, 1979.

Ledyard, Gari. "Confucianism and War: The Korean Security Crisis of 1598." *Journal of Korean Studies* 6 (1988–1989): 81–119.

Lee, John. "Trade and Economy in Preindustrial East Asia, c. 1500–1800: East Asia in the Age of Global Integration." *Journal of Asian Studies* 58, no. 1 (1999): 2–26.

Levathes, Louise. *When China Ruled the Seas: The Treasure Fleet of the Dragon Throne, 1405–1433*. Oxford: Oxford University Press, 1994.

Maddison, Angus. "A Comparison of the Levels of GDP Per Capita in Developed and Developing Countries, 1700–1980." *Journal of Economic History* 43, no. 1 (1983): 27–42.

Marr, David. "Sino-Vietnamese Relations." *Australian Journal of Chinese Affairs* 10, no. 6 (1981): 45–64.

Mote, Frederick, ed. *The Cambridge History of China. Vol. 7, The Ming Dynasty, 1368–1644. Part 1*. Cambridge: Cambridge University Press, 1988.

Reid, Anthony. *Southeast Asia in the Age of Commerce, 1450–1680. Vol. 2, Expansion and Crisis*. New Haven: Yale University Press, 1993.

Shively, Donald, et al., ed. *The Cambridge History of Japan. Vol. 2, Heian Japan*. Cambridge: Cambridge University Press, 1999.

Shu, Immanuel. *The Rise of Modern China*. Oxford: Oxford University Press, 1995.

Smits, Gregory. *Visions of Ryukyu: Identity and Ideology in Early-Modern Thought and Politics*. Honolulu: University of Hawaii Press, 1999.

Taylor, Keith. *The Birth of Vietnam*. Berkeley: University of California Press, 1983.

———. "The Rise of Dai viet and the Establishment of Thang-Long." In Kenneth Hall and John K. Whitmore, eds., *Explorations in Early Southeast Asian History: The Origins of Southeast Asian Statecraft*. Ann Arbor: University of Michigan Press, 1976.

Toby, Ronald P. *State and Diplomacy in Early Modern Japan: Asia in the Development of the Tokugawa Bakufu*. Stanford: Stanford University Press, 1991.

Van de Ven, Hans J. "War and the Making of Modern China." *Modern Asian Studies* 30, no. 4 (1996): 737–56.

van Leur, J. C. *Indonesian Trade and Society: Essays in Asian Social and Economic History*. The Hague and Bandung: W. van Hoeve, 1955.

Viraphol, Sarasin. *Tribute and Profit: Sino-Siamese Trade 1652–1853*. Cambridge: Harvard University Press, 1977.

von Glahn, Richard. "Myth and Reality of China's Seventeenth Century Monetary Crisis." *Journal of Economic History* 56, no. 2 (1996): 429–54.

Yamamura, Kozo, ed. *The Cambridge History of Japan. Vol. 3, Medieval Japan*. Cambridge: Cambridge University Press, 1990.

SOUTHEAST ASIA

Acharya, Amitav. *Constructing a Security Community in Southeast Asia: ASEAN and the Problem of Regional Order*. London: Routledge, 2001.

———. "How Ideas Spread: Whose Norms Matter? Norm Localization and Institutional Change in Asian Regionalism." *International Organization* 58 (Spring 2004): 239–75.

Almonte, Jose T. "Ensuring Security the 'ASEAN Way.'" *Survival* 30, no. 4 (Winter 1997–1998): 80–92.

Austin, Greg. "Unwanted Entanglement? The Philippines' Spratly Policy as a Case Study in Conflict Enhancement." *Security Dialogue* 34, no. 1 (March 2003): 41–54.

Ba, Alice. "China and ASEAN: Renavigating Relations for a 21st-Century Asia." *Asian Survey* 43, no. 4 (July/August 2003): 622–47.

———. "Who's Socializing Whom? Complex Engagement in Sino-ASEAN Relations." *Pacific Review* 19, no. 2 (June 2006): 157–79.

Buszynski, Leszek. "ASEAN, the Declaration on Conduct, and the South China Sea." *Contemporary Southeast Asia* 25, no. 3 (2003): 343–62.

———. "Realism, Institutionalism, and Philippine Security." *Asian Survey* 42, no. 3 (2002): 483–501.

Emmerson, Donald K. "What Do the Blind-Sided See? Reapproaching Regionalism in Southeast Asia." *Pacific Review* 18, no. 1 (March 2005): 1–21.

Gallagher, Michael. "China's Illusory Threat to the South China Sea." *International Security* 19, no. 1 (Summer 1994): 169–94.

Goh, Evelyn. "Meeting the China Challenge: The U.S. in Southeast Asian Regional Security Strategies." *East-West Center Policy Studies* 16 (2005).

Guan, Ang Cheng. "Vietnam-China Relations Since the End of the Cold War." *Asian Survey* 38, no. 12 (December 1998): 1122–41.

Kenny, Henry. *Shadow of the Dragon: Vietnam's Continuing Struggle with China and the Implications for U.S. Foreign Policy.* Washington, D.C.: Brassey's, 2002.

Klintworth, Gary. "Greater China and Regional Security." *Australian Journal of International Affairs* 48, no. 2 (1994): 211–28.

Naughton, Barry. *The China Circle: Economic and Technology in the PRC, Taiwan, and Hong Kong.* Washington, D.C.: Brookings Institution Press, 1997.

Nesadurai, Helen. "Malaysia and the United States: Rejecting Dominance, Embracing Engagement." Working Paper 72. Singapore: Institute for Defense and Strategic Studies, 2004.

Nguyen, Hong Thao. "The 2002 Declaration on the Conduct of Parties in the South China Sea: A Note." *Ocean Development and International Law* 34 (2003): 279–85.

Ong, Aihwa, and Donald Nonini, eds. *Ungrounded Empires: The Cultural Politics of Modern Chinese Transnationalism.* New York: Routledge, 1997.

Peng, Dajin. "Invisible Linkages: A Regional Perspective of East Asian Political Economy." *International Studies Quarterly* 46, no. 3 (September 2002): 423–48.

Ravenhill, John. *APEC and the Construction of Pacific Rim Regionalism.* Cambridge: Cambridge Univeresity Press, 2001.

Storey, Ian. "Creeping Assertiveness: China, the Philippines, and the South China Sea Dispute." *Contemporary Southeast Asia.* 21, no. 1 (April 1999): 95–118.

Stuart-Fox, Martin. "Southeast Asia and China: The Role of History and Culture in Shaping Future Relations." *Contemporary Southeast Asia* 26, no. 1 (2004): 116–39.

Sukma, Rizal. *Indonesia and China: The Politics of a Troubled Relationship.* London: Routledge, 1999.

Thayer, Carl. "Vietnam: Coping with China." In *Southeast Asian Affairs 1994.* Singapore: Institute of Southeast Asian Studies, 1995.

———. "Vietnamese Perceptions of the 'China Threat.'" In Herbert Yee and Ian Storey, eds., *The China Threat: Perceptions, Myths, and Reality.* London: RoutledgeCurzon, 2002.

Tow, Shannon. "Southeast Asia in the Sino-U.S. Strategic Balance." *Contemporary Southeast Asia* 26, no. 3 (December 2004): 450–51.

Vatikiotis, Michael. "Catching the Dragon's Tail: China and Southeast Asia in the 21st Century." *Contemporary Southeast Asia* 25, no. 1 (April 2003): 65–80.

Wang, Hongying. *Weak State, Strong Networks: The Institutional Dynamics of Foreign Direct Investment in China.* New York: Oxford University Press. 2001.

Weatherbee, Donald. "Strategic Dimensions of Economic Interdependence in Southeast Asia." In Ashley Tellis and Michael Wills, eds., *Strategic Asia 2006-2007.* Seattle: National Bureau of Asian Research, 2006.

Weidenbaum, Murray, and Samuel Hughes. *The Bamboo Network: How Expatriate Chinese Entrepreneurs are Creating a New Economic Superpower in Asia.* New York: Free Press, 1996.

Womack, Brantley. "China and Southeast Asia: Asymmetry, Leadership, and Normalcy." *Pacific Affairs* 76, no. 4 (Winter 2003–2004): 529–48.

Yee, Herbert, and Ian Storey, eds. *The China Threat: Perceptions, Myths, and Reality.* London: RoutledgeCurzon, 2002.

Zubir, Mokhzani. "Should Malaysia Join the U.S. Maritime Domain Awareness Scheme?" Kuala Lumpur: Maritime Institute of Malaysia, 2005.

Zubir, Mokhzani, and Mohd Nizam Basiron. "The Straits of Malacca: the Rise of China, America's Intentions, and the Dilemma of the Littoral States." Kuala Lumpur: Maritime Institute of Malaysia, 2005.

CHINA

Allen, Kenneth. "China's Foreign Military Relations with Asia-Pacific." *Journal of Contemporary China* 10 (2001): 645–62.

Carlson, Allen. *Unifying China, Integrating with the World: Security Chinese Sovereignty in the Reform Era.* Stanford: Stanford University Press, 2005.

Christensen, Thomas. "Chinese Realpolitik." *Foreign Affairs* 75.4 (September/October 1996). p. 41.

Economy, Elizabeth. "China's Rise in Southeast Asia: Implications for the United States." *Journal of Contemporary China* 14, no. 4 (August 2005): 409–25.

Fravel, Taylor. "Regime Insecurity and International Cooperation: Explaining China's Compromises in Territorial Disputes." *International Security* 30, no. 2 (Fall 2005): 46–83.

Gill, Bates, and Michael O'Hanlon. "China's Hollow Military." *National Interest* 56 (Summer 1999): 55–62.

Goldstein, Avery. *Rising to the Challenge: China's Grand Strategy and International Security.* Stanford: Stanford University Press, 2005.

Goldstein, Lyle, and William Murray. "Undersea Dragons: China's Maturing Submarine Force." *International Security* 28, no. 4 (Spring 2004): 161–96.

Gries, Peter. *China's New Nationalism: Pride, Politics, and Diplomacy.* Berkeley: University of California Press, 2004.

Huang, Yasheng. *Selling China: Foreign Direct Investment During the Reform Era.* New York: Cambridge University Press, 2003.

Hughes, Christopher. *Taiwan and Chinese Nationalism: National Identity and Status in International Society*. New York: Routledge, 1997.

Johnston, Alastair Iain. "Is China a Status Quo Power?" *International Security* 27, no. 4 (Spring 2003): 5–56.

———. *Social States: China in International Institutions, 1980–2000*. Princeton: Princeton University Press, 2007.

Johnston, Alastair Iain, and Robert Ross, eds. *Engaging China: The Management of an Emerging Power*. London: Routledge, 1999.

Lewis, John, and Xue Litai. "China's Search for a Modern Air Force." *International Security* 24, no. 1 (Summer 1999): 64–94.

Medeiros, Evan, and M. Taylor Fravel. "China's New Diplomacy." *Foreign Affairs* 82, no. 6 (November/December 2003): 22–35.

Oksenberg, Michael. "The Issue of Sovereignty in the Asian Historical Context." In Stephen D. Krasner, ed., *Problematic Sovereignty: Contested Rules and Political Possibilities*. New York: Columbia University Press, 2001.

Pei, Minxin. "The Dark Side of China's Rise." *Foreign Policy* 153 (March/April 2006): 32–42.

Rigger, Shelley. "Competing Conceptions of Taiwan's Identity." In Suisheng Zhao, ed., *Across the Taiwan Strait: Mainland China, Taiwan, and the 1995–1996 Crisis*. New York: Routledge, 1997.

Robinson, Thomas, and David Shambaugh, eds. *Chinese Foreign Policy: Theory and Practice*. Oxford: Clarendon Press, 1994.

Roy, Denny. *China's Foreign Relations*. New York: Rowman & Littlefield, 1998.

Segal, Gerald. *Defending China*. Oxford: Oxford University Press, 1985.

Shambaugh, David. "China Engages Asia: Reshaping the Regional Order." *International Security* 29, no. 3 (Winter 2004/05): 64–99.

So, Alvin. ed. *China's Developmental Miracle: Origins, Transformations, and Challenges*. Armonk, N.Y.: M. E. Sharpe, 2003.

Thayer, Carl. "China's 'New Security Concept' and Southeast Asia." In David Lovell, ed., *Asia-Pacific Security: Policy Challenges*. Singapore: Institute of Southeast Asian Studies, 2003.

JAPAN

Bernard, Mitchell, and John Ravenhill. "Beyond Product Cycles and Flying Geese: Regionalization, Hierarchy, and the Industrialization of East Asia." *World Politics* 47, no. 2 (April 1995): 171–209.

Calder, Kent. "Japanese Foreign Economic Policy Formation: Explaining the 'Reactive' State." *World Politics* 40 (1988): 517–41.

Cheng, Joseph Y. S. "Sino-Japanese Relations in the Twenty-First Century." *Journal of Contemporary Asia* 33, no. 2 (2003): 251–73.

Dower, John. "Peace and Democracy in Two Systems." In Andrew Gordon, ed., *Postwar Japan as History*. Berkeley: University of California Press, 1993.

Drifte, Reinhard. *Japan's Security Relations with China since 1989: From Balancing to Bandwagoning?* London: RoutledgeCurzon, 2003.

Fingleton, Eamonn. "The Sun and the Dragon: The Fantasy of Sino-Japanese Enmity." *American Conservative*, August 2, 2004.

Fukushima, Akiko. Japanese Foreign Policy: *The Emerging Logic of Multilateralism*. Basingstoke: Macmillan, 1999.

Green, Michael. *Japan's Reluctant Realism: Foreign Policy Challenges in an Era of Uncertain Power*. New York: Palgrave, 2001.

Hatch, Walter, and Kozo Yamamura. *East Asia in Japan's Embrace: Building a Regional Production Alliance*. Cambridge: Cambridge University Press, 1996.

Heginbotham, Eric, and Richard J. Samuels. "Mercantile Realism and Japanese Foreign Policy." *International Security* 22, no. 4 (Spring 1998): 171–203.

Hughes, Christopher. *Japan's Re-emergence as a "Normal" Military Power*. Oxford: Oxford University Press, 2005.

Inoguchi, Takashi, ed. *Japan's Asia Policy: Revival and Response*. London: Palgrave, 2002.

Johnson, Chalmers. "Japan in Search of a 'Normal' Role." *Daedalus* 121 (Fall 1992): 1–33.

Katzenstein, Peter. *Cultural Norms and National Security: Police and Military in Postwar Japan*. Ithaca: Cornell University Press, 1996.

———, ed. *Network Power: Japan and Asia*. Ithaca: Cornell University Press, 1997.

Kikuchi, Tsutomu. "East Asian Regionalism: A Look at the 'ASEAN plus Three' Framework." *Japan Review of International Affairs* 16 (Spring 2002): 1–23.

MacIntyre, Andrew, and Barry Naughton. "The Decline of the Japan-Led Model of the East Asian Economy." In T. J. Pempel, ed., *Remapping East Asia: The Construction of a Region*. Ithaca: Cornell University Press, 2005.

Mastanduno, Michael. "Japan: Back to Normal?" In Ashley Tellis and Michael Wills, eds., *Strategic Asia 2006–2007*. Seattle: National Bureau of Asian Research, 2006.

Mochizuki, Michael. "Between Alliance and Autonomy: Japan." In Ashley Tellis and Michael Wills, eds., *Strategic Asia 2004–2005: Confronting Terrorism in the Pursuit of Power*. Seattle: National Bureau of Asian Research, 2004.

Murphy, R. Taggart. *The Weight of the Yen: How DenialImperils America's Future and Ruins an Alliance*. New York: Norton, 1996.

Noble, Gregory. "What Can Taiwan (and the United States) Expect from Japan?" *Journal of East Asian Studies* 5 (2005): 1–34.

Pekkanen, Saadia. "Japan's FTA Frenzy." Manuscript, University of Washington, 2004.

Restall, Hugo. "Opposing the Sun: Japan Alienates Asia." *Far Eastern Economic Review* 168 (April 2005): 8–13.

Samuels, Richard J. *Rich Nation, Strong Army: National Security and the Technological Transformation of Japan*. Ithaca: Cornell University Press, 1995.

———. *Securing Japan*. Ithaca: Cornell University Press, 2007.

Schoppa, Leonard. *Bargaining with Japan: What American Pressure Can and Cannot Do*. New York: Columbia University Press, 1997.

Tamamoto, Masaru. "How Japan Imagines China and Sees Itself." *Commentary*, Japan Institute of International Affairs, May 31, 2006.

Wan, Ming. "Tensions in Recent Sino-Japanese Relations." *Asian Survey* 43, no. 5 (September–October 2003): 826–44.

Wu, Xinbo. "The End of the Silver Lining: A Chinese View of the U.S.-Japan Alliance." *Washington Quarterly* 29, no. 1 (Winter 2005–2006): 119–30.

Yang, Jian. "Sino-Japanese Relations: Implications for Southeast Asia." *Contemporary Southeast Asia* 25, no. 2 (August 2003). 306.

KOREA

Cha, Victor. *Alignment Despite Antagonism:The U.S.-Korea-Japan Security Triangle.* Stanford: Stanford University Press, 1999.

Cha, Victor, and David Kang. *Nuclear North Korea: A Debate on Engagement Strategies.* New York: Columbia University Press, 2003.

Chung, Jae-ho. *Between Ally and Partner: Korea-China Relations and the United States.* New York: Columbia University Press, 2007.

Cumings, Bruce. *Korea's Place in the Sun.* New York: Norton, 1997.

Flake, L. Gordon, and Scott A. Snyder, eds. *Paved with Good Intentions: The NGO Experience in North Korea.* Westport, Conn.: Praeger, 2003.

Frank, Ruediger. "Economic Reforms in North Korea (1998–2003): Systemic Restrictions, Quantitative Analysis, Ideological Background." *Journal of the Asia Pacific Economy* 10, no. 3 (2005): 278–311.

Gleysteen, William H. *Massive Entanglement, Marginal Influence: Carter and Korea in Crisis.* Washington, D.C.: Brookings Institution Press, 1999.

Haggard, Stephan, and Marcus Noland. *Famine in North Korea: Aid, Markets, and Reform.* New York: Columbia University Press, 2006.

Kang, David C. "International Relations Theory and the Second Korean War." *International Studies Quarterly* 47, no. 3 (September 2003): 301–24

Kang, Hildi. *Under the Black Umbrella: Stories from Colonial Korea.* Ithaca: Cornell University Press, 1999.

Lewis, Linda, ed. *Laying Claim to the Memory of May : A Look Back at the 1980 Kwangju Uprising.* Honolulu: University of Hawaii Press, 2002.

Mitchell, Derek, ed. *Strategy and Sentiment: South Korean Views of the United States and the U.S.-ROK Alliance.* Washington, D.C.: Center for Strategic and International Studies, 2004.

Moon, Katharine. "South Korean Movements against Militarized Sexual Labor." *Asian Survey* 39, no. 2 (March/April 1999): 310–27.

Oberdorfer, Don. *The Two Koreas: A Contemporary History.* New York: Basic Books, 2002.

Shin, Gi-wook. *Ethnic Nationalism in Korea.* Stanford: Stanford University Press, 2006.

Snyder, Scott. "The Beginning of the End of the U.S.-ROK Alliance?" *PacNet* 36, August 26, 2004.

Wickham, John Adams. *Korea on the Brink: From the "12/12 incident" to the Kwangju Uprising, 1979–1980.* Washington, D.C.: National Defense University Press, 1999.

UNITED STATES

Armacost, Michael. *Friends or Rivals? The Insider's Account of U.S.-Japan Relations.* New York: Columbia University Press, 1996.

Betts, Richard K. "Wealth, Power, and Instability: East Asia and the United States after the Cold War." *International Security* 18, no. 3 (Winter 1993): 34–77.

Blair, Dennis, and John Hanley. "From Wheels to Webs: Reconstructing Asia-Pacific Security Arrangements." *Washington Quarterly* 24, no. 1 (Winter 2001): 7–17.

Brooks, Stephen, and William Wohlforth. "American Primacy in Perspective." *Foreign Affairs* 81, no. 4 (July/August 2002): 20–33.

Chambers, Paul. "U.S.-Thai Relations After 9/11: A New Era of Cooperation?" *Contemporary Southeast Asia* 26, no. 3 (December 2004): 465–66.

Christensen, Thomas. "China, the U.S.-Japan Alliance, and the Security Dilemma in East Asia." *International Security* 23, no. 4 (Spring 1999): 49–80.

——. "Fostering Stability or Creating a Monster? The Rise of China and U.S. Policy toward East Asia. *International Security* 31, no. 1 (Summer 2006): 81–126.

Ikenberry, G. John. "American Hegemony and East Asian Order." *Australian Journal of International Affairs* 58, no. 3 (September 2004): 353–67.

Krauss, Ellis, and T. J. Pempel, eds. *Beyond Bilateralism: U.S.-Japan Relations in the New Asia-Pacific.* Stanford: Stanford University Press, 2004.

Mastanduno, Michael. "Incomplete Hegemony: The United States and Security Order in Asia." In Muthiah Alagappa, ed., *Asian Security Order.* Stanford: Stanford University Press, 2003.

O'Hanlon, Michael. "United States: U.S. Military Modernization: Implications for U.S. Policy in Asia." In Ashley Tellis and Michael Wills, eds., *Strategic Asia 2005–06: Military Modernization in an Era of Uncertainty.* Seattle: National Bureau of Asian Research, 2005.

Samuels, Richard J., and Eric Heginbotham. "Japan's Dual Hedge." *Foreign Affairs* 81 (September/October 2002): 110–21.

Sodhy, Pamela. "U.S.-Malaysia Relations During the Bush Administration: The Political, Economic, and Security Aspects." *Contemporary Southeast Asia* 25, no. 3 (December 2003): 378–81.

Sutter, Robert. *China's Rise in Asia: Promises and Perils.* Lanham, Md.: Rowman & Littlefield, 2005.

——. "United States: Leadership Maintained Amid Continuing Challenges." In Ashley Tellis and Michael Wills, eds., *Strategic Asia 2004–2005: Confronting Terrorism in the Pursuit of Power.* Seattle: National Bureau of Asian Research, 2004.

INDEX

peaceful rise strategy, 5, 80, 83–85, 224*n*18; and regional integration, 72, 84, 88, 89, 130, 222*n*107; and Southeast Asia, 90, 129–132, 141; and territorial disputes, 82, 89–90, 91–92, 130. *See also* Taiwanese independence issue

Chinese military capabilities, 59, 64, 65, 92–93, 95, 97–98, 190

Chinese national identity, 79–83; East Asian perceptions of, 4–5, 198; future of, 11, 102–103, 201–202; and U.S. alignment strategy toward China, 191–192

Chinese power/influence, 3, 12–16; and great power status, 13, 197–198; historical, 27, 29–30, 41–42, 45–46; and Japanese-Chinese relations, 175; and North Korea, 118–120

Christensen, Thomas, 85, 187, 189

Christofferson, Gaye, 134

Chun Doo-hwan, 108, 114

Chung, Jae-ho, 56, 120

Clinton, Bill, 191

Cohen, Stephen, 189

Cold War: and Chinese foreign policy, 90–91, 129; and Japan, 154, 156, 165, 170; and regional integration, 71, 129; and Thailand, 62; and U.S.–East Asian relations, 62, 154, 170, 185–186, 188

colonialism, 107, 128, 141, 172

comfort women, 107, 169

"commitment problem," 201

Committee on Security and Cooperation in the Asia Pacific (CSCAP), 72, 89

conflicts: and alignment strategies, 53–54; and Chinese foreign policy, 90–92; decrease in, 198; historical patterns, 37, 38–40. *See also* Taiwanese independence issue; territorial disputes

constructivism, 18–19, 49

Container Security Initiative, 194

Correlates of War project, 13, 14

Cossa, Ralph, 102, 180

Cruz, Avelino, 62

CSCAP (Committee on Security and Cooperation in the Asia Pacific), 72, 89

Cultural Revolution, 81, 87

culture: and bamboo network, 136; and Filipino-Chinese relations, 138; historical Chinese influence, 45, 46; and regional integration, 74; and South Korean–Chinese relations, 116

Curtis, Gerald, 66, 135

Cushman, Jennifer, 35

daguo xintai (great power mentality), 81

Declaration on the Conduct of Parties in the South China Sea, 73, 137

Democratic Party of Japan (DPJ), 163

Deng, Gang, 31–32

Deng Xiaoping, 178

Devan, Janadas, 59

developmental state model, 71–72

Diaoyu (Senkaku) Islands dispute, 90

Dokdo (Takeshima) Islands dispute (Japan–South Korea), 90, 107, 118, 171, 172

domestic politics: and Chinese foreign policy, 85–87; Japan, 65, 153, 156, 160–165; and regional integration, 74; and South Korean national identity, 108–109; and South Korean–North Korean relations, 113–114, 231*n*39; and Taiwanese independence issue, 98; and U.S.-Filipino relations, 139, 237*n*71

Doner, Richard, 159

Downer, Alexander, 61, 69, 101, 151

DPJ (Democratic Party of Japan), 163

DuPont, Alan, 60

East Asian region, defined, 11–12, 207*n*21

East Asian stability, 3; and Chinese national identity, 83; historical, 24–25, 42, 49; and regional integration, 198–199; Southeast Asia, 128; and Taiwanese independence issue, 99; and U.S. alignment strategy toward China, 201

East Asia Summit, 12, 54, 72

Eberstadt, Nicholas, 123

economic balancing, 52

economic relations. *See* regional economic relations

Emmerson, Donald, 71, 147
Estrada, Joseph, 140
European experience: conflict, 37, 38–40; political actors, 41; sovereignty, 82, 95, 96; as theoretical norm, 18, 22, 23, 25, 82, 197, 202; and U.S. national identity, 187; Westphalian norms, 96, 211*n*32, 227*n*85
export-oriented development, 71–72, 74
extra-regional states, 11–12. *See also* U.S.–East Asian relations

Fallon, James, 187
Fallon, William, 191
Fargo, Thomas, 150
fear, absence of. *See* absence of fear
Fearon, James, 19, 20
Ferguson, Joseph, 172
Ferguson, Niall, 190
financial crisis (1997). *See* Asian financial crisis (1997)
Five Principles of Peaceful Coexistence (China), 85, 130
flying geese model, 73, 157
formal theory, 19, 20, 201, 224*n*18
Frank, Andre Gunder, 35
Fravel, Taylor, 81–82, 88, 89, 92
Friedberg, Aaron, 193
Frieden, Jeffrey, 197
Fukushima, Akiko, 164
future possibilities, 10–11, 69, 70, 102–103, 201–202

game theory, 19
Geary, Roy, 13
Genghis Khan, 40
Gill, Bates, 92, 190
Gilley, Bruce, 123
Goh, Evelyn, 63
Goh Chok Tong, 61, 133–134
Goldstein, Avery, 84, 85, 201–202
Goodman, Allen, 145
Great Leap Forward, 87
Green, Michael, 161, 190
Gries, Peter, 8, 81, 82
Guang, Lei, 82
GWOT. *See* U.S. global war on terror

Hale, David, 13
hallyu, 74
Hamashita, Takeshi, 36, 164
Hanley, John, 189
Hashimoto, Ryutaro, 173
Hatch, Walter, 158–159
Hayes, Peter, 112–113
Heginbotham, Eric, 177, 178
hedging strategies: defined, 53; Japan, 54, 166, 180, 181–182, 199, 248*n*142; United States, 190; Vietnam, 141–142
Hideyoshi (Japanese general), 40, 42, 47
hiding strategies, 53
Hill, Christopher, 167
historical East Asian system, 23–49; actors in, 27–29, 41; behavioral patterns, 36–41; breakup of, 36, 37, 49; Chinese power/influence in, 27, 29–30, 41–42, 45–46; formal hierarchy, 43–45, 49; geographical scope, 25–27; importance of, 23–24; Japanese role in, 26, 28, 30, 46–48, 155; and Korean national identity, 106–107; military capabilities, 29–30; peacefulness of, 37, 38–40; political systems, 26; regional economic relations, 27, 30–36, 42–43, 48; stability of, 24–25, 42, 49; strategic culture approach, 211*n*27; and Taiwanese independence issue, 95; and Vietnamese-Chinese relations, 30, 141, 142, 145. *See also* historical narratives
historical narratives, 117, 169–174. *See also* territorial disputes
Hiwatari, Nobuhiro, 174
Ho Chi Minh, 141–142
Hokkaido Declaration (2006), 177
Hong Kong, 74, 96
Hongwu (Emperor of China), 28, 40
Horwitz, Tony, 187
Hosokawa, Morihiro, 179
Howard, John, 101
Hsu Wen-lung, 97
Huang Taiji (Emperor of China), 37
Hughes, Christopher, 164–165
Hu Jintao, 62, 131, 142, 145, 190
Hunt, Michael, 82

ideas, importance of, 8–9, 18–19, 128, 198. *See also* national identity

Ieyasu (shogun), 33

Ikenberry, John, 8, 154, 167

IMF (International Monetary Fund), 72, 147–148

India: Chinese relations with, 90, 91–92; economic growth, 15–16; as extra-regional state, 11, 12; and regional integration, 12, 73; and Southeast Asia, 133

Indonesia: Chinese relations with, 59–60, 134; territorial disputes, 90; and U.S. relations with, 60, 149, 194

Injo (Choson King), 37

interests, 4, 9, 19–20; and Chinese national identity, 79–80; and U.S.-Chinese relations, 199; and U.S.–East Asian relations, 186, 187–188, 195–196

International Monetary Fund (IMF), 72, 147–148

international relations theory: on alignment strategies, 51–54; on balancing, 7–8, 10, 22–23, 24, 52; and Chinese national identity, 81; and historical East Asian system, 24, 49; on Japanese foreign policy, 153; and national identity, 18–19, 21. *See also* balancing, East Asian absence of; European experience

investiture, 41–42, 43–44

Iraq War: and Australia, 194; and Japan, 162, 166–167, 168; and Southeast Asia, 140, 149–150; and South Korea, 121, 124, 233*n*91. *See also* U.S. global war on terror

Ishiba, Shigeru, 166

Ishihara, Shintaro, 161, 165

Ishii, Yoneo, 33

Japan, 153–182; cultural influence of, 74; domestic politics, 65, 153, 156, 160–165; economic growth, 12, 13, 14, 15, 156–159, 160–161; and historical East Asian system, 26, 28, 30, 46–48, 155; historical trade, 32, 33, 34, 42–43, 48; military capabilities, 64–65, 180; national identity, 6–7, 154–155, 168–169, 170, 181;

and North Korea, 166, 174, 179–180; piracy, 28–29, 212*n*44; and regional economic relations, 156–159, 174, 177–178; and regional integration, 72–73, 177–178; Russian relations with, 90, 172; Southeast Asian relations with, 133, 158, 173; and Taiwanese independence issue, 100, 101–102, 179. *See also* Japanese-Chinese relations; Japanese–South Korean relations; U.S.-Japanese relations

Japanese-Chinese relations, 174–182; economic, 174–178; hedging strategies, 54, 180, 181–182, 199, 248*n*142; and historical narratives, 170–171, 173; Japanese alignment strategy toward China, 54, 55, 63–66, 155, 161, 162; Japanese attitudes toward China, 67, 179–180; political, 178–181, 247*n*104; territorial disputes, 90; and U.S.-Japanese relations, 154

Japanese–South Korean relations: economic, 159; and historical narratives, 171, 173–174; and Japanese-Chinese relations, 177; strain in, 5, 6, 104; territorial disputes, 90, 107, 118, 171, 172

Java, 26

Jiang Zemin, 142, 179

Johnston, Alastair Iain, 8, 21, 88, 191, 211*n*27

Joint Vietnam-China Statement for Comprehensive Cooperation, 142–143

Jung Yak-yong, 42

Kaesong Industrial Park, 111–112, 114, 115

Kaneyoshi (Prince of Japan), 46–47

Kang, Etsuko, 32

Katzenstein, Peter, 8, 9, 21, 156, 157

Kaufman, Stuart, 22–23

Kawazoe, Shoji, 28, 42–43

Kazui, Tashiro, 46, 47

Kelly, James, 167

Kenny, Henry, 141

Kern, Thomas, 108

Khamis, Salem Hanna, 13

Khong, Yuen Foong, 60, 61, 63, 139, 237*n*71

Khrushchev, Nikita, 141–142
Kikuchi, Tstutomu, 71
Kim, Key-huik, 47–48
Kim, Samuel, 82
Kim, Seonmin, 37
Kim, Stephen, 124
Kim Dae-jung, 110, 231n39
Kim Jong-il, 110, 112, 119, 123
Kim Kyung-won, 114
Kim Young-sam, 110, 231n39
Kindleberger, Charles, 157
King, Blair, 59, 148
Klein, Peter, 33, 36, 48
Koguryo dispute, 117–118
Koizumi, Junichiro: on alignment strat-
    egy toward China, 65; and domestic
    politics, 163, 164; and Japanese-
    Chinese relations, 176, 177; and South
    Korea, 171–172, 173; and U.S.-Japanese
    relations, 166–167, 181
Korea: and historical East Asian system,
    26, 27, 32, 33, 106–107, 155; unification,
    6, 105, 106, 109–110. See also Korean
    War; North Korea; South Korea
Korean War, 91, 104, 107, 108, 110, 111
kowtow, 43–44
Koxingga, 95
Kugler, Jacek, 19, 210n13
Kuril Islands dispute (Japan-Russia),
    172
Kwangju massacre (South Korea), 108,
    230n14
Kydd, Andrew, 19

Lake, David, 197
Lam, Truong Buu, 44
language. See culture
Laos, 57, 142
Larson, Eric, 122
Larson, Kirk, 121
Layne, Christopher, 187
LDP (Liberal Democratic Party) (Japan),
    162, 163
Le Duan, 142
Ledyard, Gari, 44
Lee, Chung-min, 105, 118
Lee, John, 31, 33

Lee Hoi-chang, 113
Lee Hsien Loon, 152
Lee Kwan Yew, 61, 98, 173
Lee Teng-hui, 100, 179
Leifer, Michael, 60, 81
Le Kha Phieu, 142, 144
Levine, Stephen, 82–83
Li Bin, 119
Li Junru, 84
Li Peng, 60–61, 130
Liberal Democratic Party (LDP) (Japan),
    162, 163
liberalism, 49
Lieber, Keir, 52
Little, Richard, 22–23, 24
Locke, Gary, 190
Lu, Xiaobo, 190
Lyall, James, 21

Macapagal-Arroyo, Gloria, 62, 139, 140
MacIntyre, Andrew, 146, 159
Maddison, Angus, 13
Mahatir, Mohammed, 60, 131, 146, 149,
    195
Malaya, 26. See also Malaysia
Malaysia: alignment strategy toward
    China, 55, 60; military capabilities, 59;
    territorial disputes, 90, 130, 136, 137;
    and U.S. global war on terror, 149; U.S.
    military presence, 194
Manchu invasion, 40–41
Mao Zedong, 80
Marr, David, 30, 44–45
Mastanduno, Michael, 63, 158, 161
material theories, 19, 198. See also inter-
    national relations theory; realism
Matthews, Eugene, 167–168
Ma Ying-jeou, 97
McKinley, William, 183
Mearsheimer, John, 8
Medeiros, Evan, 81–82, 88, 92, 94
military capabilities: China, 59, 64, 65,
    92–93, 95, 97–98, 190; historical East
    Asian system, 29–30; Japan, 64–65,
    180; North Korea, 113; Philippines, 59,
    62; Southeast Asia, 57, 59–60; South
    Korea, 55–56

military cooperation: and Chinese foreign policy, 88–89; Southeast Asia-China, 60, 61, 62; South Korea-China, 56; U.S.-China, 191; Vietnam-China, 56, 57, 58, 143. *See also* U.S. military presence

military exchanges. *See* military cooperation

military modernization. *See* military capabilities

Mochizuki, Michael, 162–163, 168

Mongolia, 89

Mongol invasions, 40

Moon, Katharine, 108–109

Mulally, Alan, 190

multilateralism. *See* regional integration

Murayama, Tomiichi, 163

Mussomeli, Joseph, 140

Nakatani, Gen, 177–178

Nakayama, Taro, 72

Nanjing massacre (1937), 169

Naresuan (King of Siam), 42

Nathan, Andrew, 81

national identity, 4–5; defined, 9, 20–21; and future possibilities, 11; and historical narratives, 169–174; and historical trade, 35; and international relations theory, 18–19, 21; Japan, 6–7, 154–155, 168–169, 170, 181; and Korean unification, 6, 105, 106; measurement of, 21–22; South Korea, 6, 105, 106–109, 113, 171–172; and status quo vs. revisionist states, 21, 80, 210n13; and Taiwanese independence issue, 5, 80, 93–94, 96, 98–99; United States, 186–189. *See also* Chinese national identity; sovereignty

nationalism, 81, 82. *See also* national identity

Naughton, Barry, 87, 146, 159

Nepal, 89

Nesadurai, Helen, 149

Nguyen Dy Nien, 57, 142

Ninh, Kim, 141, 143

Noble, Gregory, 101–102, 180–181

Noland, Marcus, 113, 147

Nong Duc Manh, 145

Northern Territories dispute (Japan-Russia), 90

North Korea: alignment strategy toward China, 54, 55; Chinese relations with, 89, 119; Japanese policy toward, 166, 174, 179–180; and South Korean–Chinese relations, 118–120; South Korean relations with, 5, 6, 105, 106, 109–115, 123, 171, 231n39. *See also* U.S. policy toward North Korea

nuclear crises. *See* North Korea

Obuchi, Keizo, 179

OECD (Organisation for Economic Cooperation and Development), 12–13

O'Hanlon, Michael, 92, 189

Ohira, Masayoshi, 178

Okawara, Nobuo, 9, 156

Olesen, Alexa, 72

Organisation for Economic Co-operation and Development (OECD), 12–13

Organski, A. F. K., 210n13

Osborne, Milton, 61

overseas Chinese. *See* bamboo network

Ozawa, Ichiro, 164

Pape, Robert, 52

Park Chung-hee, 114

peaceful rise strategy (China), 5, 80, 83–85, 224n18

Peace of Westphalia, 211n32. *See also* European experience

Pei, Minxin, 87

Pekkanen, Saadia, 175, 178

Pempel, T. J., 71, 135

Peng, Dajin, 135, 158

Perry, William, 191

Pham Van Tra, 57

Philippines, 138–140; alignment strategy toward China, 54, 55, 62; attitudes toward China, 67; attitudes toward the United States, 67, 69; and historical East Asian system, 26, 32; military capabilities, 59, 62; and Taiwanese independence issue, 100; territorial disputes, 130, 136, 137; and